EXPORTING GLOBAL JIHAD

EXPORTING GLOBAL JIHAD

Critical Perspectives from Africa and Europe

Edited by
Tom Smith and Hussein Solomon

I.B. TAURIS
LONDON • NEW YORK • OXFORD • NEW DELHI • SYDNEY

I.B. TAURIS
Bloomsbury Publishing Plc
50 Bedford Square, London, WC1B 3DP, UK
1385 Broadway, New York, NY 10018, USA

BLOOMSBURY, I.B. TAURIS and the I.B. Tauris logo are trademarks of
Bloomsbury Publishing Plc

First published in Great Britain 2020

Copyright © Tom Smith and Hussein Solomon, 2020

Tom Smith and Hussein Solomon have asserted their right under the Copyright,
Designs and Patents Act, 1988, to be identified as Authors of this work.

Cover design by Adriana Brioso
Cover image © Lauren Frayer

All rights reserved. No part of this publication may be reproduced or transmitted in any form or by any means, electronic or mechanical, including photocopying, recording, or any information storage or retrieval system, without prior permission in writing from the publishers.

Bloomsbury Publishing Plc does not have any control over, or responsibility for, any third-party websites referred to or in this book. All internet addresses given in this book were correct at the time of going to press. The authors and publisher regret any inconvenience caused if addresses have changed or sites have ceased to exist, but can accept no responsibility for any such changes.

A catalogue record for this book is available from the British Library.

A catalog record for this book is available from the Library of Congress.

ISBN: HB: 978-1-7883-1330-8
PB: 978-1-8386-0470-7
ePDF: 978-1-8386-0755-5
eBook: 978-1-8386-0754-8

Typeset by Deanta Global Publishing Services, Chennai, India

To find out more about our authors and books visit www.bloomsbury.com and sign up for our newsletters.

CONTENTS

About the Editors	vii
Contributor Bios	viii

INTRODUCTION: EXAMINING THE GLOBAL LINKAGES OF AFRICAN AND EUROPEAN JIHADISTS
   Tom Smith and Hussein Solomon — 1

'GLOCALIZED' JIHAD, POLITICAL CONFLICT, AND CONSPIRACY THEORIZATION ACROSS A FRAGMENTED SOMALIA
   Peter Chonka — 13

GLOBAL OR LOCAL? EXPLORING THE EMERGENCE AND OPERATION OF A VIOLENT ISLAMIST NETWORK IN KENYA
   Ngala Chome — 37

REFLECTIONS ON ISLAMIST MILITANCY IN THE SAHEL
   Hussein Solomon — 55

JIHAD IN MALI: REGIONAL CONDITIONS, REGIONAL GOALS, GLOBAL IMPORTANCE
   Stephen A. Harmon — 73

NIGERIA: THE RISE AND 'FALL' OF BOKO HARAM
   Caroline Varin — 95

LIBYAN JIHADISM: FROM GADHAFI AND TRIBALISM TO THE ARAB SPRING AND TRIBALISM
   Anneli Botha — 113

JIHAD AND THE UNITED KINGDOM
   Paul Gill, Zoe Marchment, Bettina Rottweiler and Sanaz Zolghadriha — 139

CONFRONTING ORIENTALISM, COLONIALISM AND DETERMINISM: DE-CONSTRUCTING CONTEMPORARY FRENCH JIHADISM
   Joseph Downing — 157

EXPORTING JIHAD FROM THE STREET-LEVEL GROUPS IN THE LOW COUNTRIES
   Marion van San — 175

SCANDINAVIAN JIHAD
   Marco Nilsson — 187

THE EVOLUTION OF THE JIHAD IN GERMANY
  Jan Raudszus   205

AL-ANDALUS: THE CALIPHATE OF CORDOBA REIMAGINED
  Maria do Céu Pinto Arena   223

Index   247

ABOUT THE EDITORS

Tom Smith is a Principal Lecturer in International Relations at the University of Portsmouth. He is based at the Royal Air Force College Cranwell where he works as the Assistant Academic Director for the University of Portsmouth team at RAF College Cranwell delivering professional military education to over 500 students a year on courses relating to international security. His research focuses on security in Southeast Asia with specific focus on terrorism and the conflict in the Philippines and Thailand. Tom has monitored the Abu Sayyaf Group for over a decade, which has involved periods of fieldwork and a position as Visiting Lecturer at De La Salle University in Manila. Tom has had his research published in both the major terrorism academic journals, *Terrorism and Political Violence* and *Studies in Conflict and Terrorism*. Tom is a regular media commentator on Asian security and Filipino political issues and a prominent critic of President Duterte's regime. He writes regularly for outlets such as the Guardian, the Independent, the Diplomat and the Conversation, and has given testimony on the human rights abuses of the Duterte regime to the UK Parliament.

Hussein Solomon is Senior Professor in the Department of Political Studies and Governance at the University of the Free State, Republic of South Africa. He is also a visiting professor at the Osaka School for International Public Policy and a Senior Research Associate for the Jerusalem-based think tank Research on Islam and Muslims in Africa (RIMA). His research interests straddle Political Islam, International Relations theory and security in Africa. His most recent books include *Islamism, Crisis and Democratization: Implications of the World Values Survey for the Muslim World* (with Arno Tausch, 2020), *African Security in the Twenty-First Century: Challenges and Opportunities* (with Stephen Emerson, 2018), *Understanding Boko Haram and Insurgency in Africa* (with Jim Hentz, 2017), *Islamic State and the Coming Global Confrontation* (2016), *Terrorism and Counter-Terrorism in Africa: Fighting Insurgency from Al Shabaab, Ansar Dine and Boko Haram* (2015) and *Jihad: A South African Perspective* (2013).

CONTRIBUTOR BIOS

Anneli Botha is a senior lecturer at the Department Political Studies and Governance at the University of the Free State in Bloemfontein, South Africa. She also serves as an independent consultant on radicalization, deradicalization, reintegration and terrorism in Africa. During the period from 2003 to 2016 she worked as a senior researcher on terrorism at the Institute for Security Studies (ISS) in Pretoria, South Africa. Anneli has travelled extensively throughout Africa where she conducted research on terrorism and delivered specialized training on various aspects of the threat of terrorism, extremism, radicalization and counterterrorism to law enforcement and criminal justice officials on the continent. Prior to her position at the ISS, she served in the South African Police Service (SAPS) for 10 years. Anneli holds a Magister Artium degree from Rand Afrikaans University in Political Studies (1998) and Philosophiae Doctor from the Department of Political Studies and Governance at the University of the Free State (2014). Her PhD thesis was titled Radicalisation to Commit Terrorism from a Political Socialisation Perspective in Kenya and Uganda.

Maria do Céu Pinto Arena is Associate Professor with Agregação in the School of Economics and Management/EEG, University of Minho (Braga), Portugal. She has a PhD from the Centre of Middle Eastern and Islamic Studies, Faculty of Social Sciences, University of Durham, UK. Maria's areas of expertise are Middle Eastern and Islamic Studies and International Organizations, with a focus on the United Nations and peacekeeping activities in general, including that of the UN and other regional organizations. Maria is the Portuguese expert within the international research group Providing for Peacekeeping Project, a project of the International Peace Institute (IPI) in collaboration with George Washington and Griffith universities. Her current research projects are centred on the new Portuguese jihadi phenomenon, the reinterpretation and hybridization of the contemporary jihadi ideological thinking, and small states and peace missions. Her work has been published in various academic journals including *International Peacekeeping*, *The Journal of Policing, Intelligence and Counter Terrorism* and *Intelligence and Counter Terrorism*.

Ngala Chome is a doctoral candidate in African History and Politics at Durham University. His research investigates militant jihad in East Africa, the Kenya Coast and contemporary politics in the Indian Ocean region, with a particular focus on the 'Swahili' (East African) Coast. His work has been published in peer-reviewed journals, edited volumes, and policy reports, and his opinion and commentary pieces have appeared in a number of online and print-based magazines.

Peter Chonka is a Lecturer in Global Digital Cultures at King's College London's Department of Digital Humanities. His research looks at relationships between media technologies, conflict, political/cultural identity and state (re)construction, with a regional focus on the Horn of Africa. He holds a PhD in African Studies from the University of Edinburgh, and his research has been published in academic journals such as *African Affairs, New Media & Society, Political Geography* and the *Journal of Eastern African Studies*. He previously worked as an interpreter for the Somalia Delegation of the International Committee of the Red Cross, and for the University of Hargeisa in Somaliland.

Joseph Downing was a Marie-Curie Fellow at the CNRS Aix-Marseille Université and the School of Oriental and African Studies, London and Guest Lecturer, European Institute, London School of Economics and Political Science. He has undertaken two major fully funded research projects that focus on the position of Muslims in French society. The first was a comparative analysis of urban policies in Paris, Lyon and Marseille to analyse the variance in their rioting behaviour in 2005. The second is ongoing and is an analysis of social media and how new forms of communication platforms could offer an avenue to 'desecuritize' Muslims in both France and the UK. Joseph has taught widely on subjects relevant to this book, including Muslims in Europe, nationalism, international security, radicalization and Middle East politics.

Paul Gill is a professor of Security and Crime Science at University College London. He has over 70 publications on the topic of terrorist behaviour. He has conducted research funded by the Office for Naval Research, the Department of Homeland Security, DSTL, the European Union, the National Institute of Justice, CREST, Public Safety Canada and MINERVA. He currently manages the European Research Council Starter Grant project entitled GRIEVANCE. Collectively these grants have been worth over 9 million euro. These projects focused upon various aspects of terrorist behaviour including the IED development, creativity, terrorist network structures, risk assessment and management, and lone-actor terrorism. His doctoral research focused on the individual and organizational motivations underlying suicide bombing. This piece of research won the Jean Blondel Prize for the best PhD thesis in Political Science in Europe for 2010. He has published in leading psychology, criminology and political science journals.

Stephen A. Harmon is a professor of African and Middle Eastern history at Pittsburg State University in Kansas (USA). He completed his PhD in West African Islamic history at the University of California at Los Angeles. He is a two-time Fulbright scholar and has done extensive field research in Senegal and Mali, most recently in 2012 and again in 2015–2016. His current research focuses on the Sahara-Sahel region of Northwest Africa, especially the role of Islamic radicalism there. His book, *Terrorism and Insurgency in the Sahara-Sahel Region: Corruption, Contraband, Jihad and the Mali War of 2012–2013*, appeared in 2014. He is working on a second book with the working title of *Beyond Jihad: Sectarian*

Violence and Ethnic Rivalry along the Mali-Libya Axis. Harmon has been consulted as a regional expert by numerous domestic and international news agencies. His work has been published in a variety of peer-reviewed journals and anthologies. He is a frequent presenter at national and international conferences, notably a UN-sponsored workshop on terrorism in Turin, Italy, in 2008, and in 2015 in Washington, DC, as the principal presenter at a US Defense Department conference on the Mali War.

Zoe Marchment is a postdoctoral research associate for the European Research Council-funded GRIEVANCE Project, in the Department of Security and Crime Science, University College London. Her doctoral research examined the spatial decision-making of terrorist target selection, with a focus on lone actors and violent dissident Republican activity. Zoe has worked on projects for the UK Defence Science and Technology Laboratory; Centre for Research and Evidence on Security Threats (CREST); FP7 Preventing, Interdicting and Mitigating Extremism (PRIME) and the VOX-Pol Network of Excellence.

Marco Nilsson is an associate professor of Political Science at Jönköping University, Sweden. He received his PhD from the University of Gothenburg, Sweden, in 2010. His research has dealt with various aspects of violent conflicts in international politics, but it has mainly focused on terrorism and jihadism. Using quantitative methods, he has studied the effectiveness and logic of various terror tactics. With the help of qualitative methods, interviewing both active and former Swedish jihadis, he has studied generational variation in jihadism and changing motivations from the early stages of radicalization to fighting as part of a jihadi group and finally leaving jihad. He has argued that jihadism can be analysed as a discursive journey of 'jihadiship' including ideas, problems and solutions that change with new circumstances.

Jan Raudszus leads the intelligence analysis unit of the National Security Division of the State Bureau of Investigations, Bremen (Germany). In addition, He is an adjunct lecturer at the University of Applied Science in Public Administration (HföV), Bremen, where he teaches classes on extremism and terrorism to police cadets. Previously, he was an investigative reporter working for, among others, the public broadcasting agency *Westdeutscher Rundfunk* and the regional newspaper *Weser-Kurier*. He has published, among others, in the CTC Sentinel, Jane's Intelligence Review, *DIE ZEIT* and for several formats of the International Institute for Strategic Studies (IISS).

Bettina Rottweiler is a PhD candidate at the Security and Crime Science department at University College London. She also works as a research assistant on the ERC-funded GRIEVANCE project. Her PhD project analyses risk and protective factors for violent extremism. Previously, she worked as a research assistant on a research project analysing election campaigning funded by the Economic and Social Research Council (ESRC) at Brunel.

Hussein Solomon is Senior Professor in the Department of Political Studies and Governance at the University of the Free State, Republic of South Africa. He is also a visiting professor at the Osaka School for International Public Policy and a Senior Research Associate for the Jerusalem-based think tank Research on Islam and Muslims in Africa (RIMA). His research interests straddle Political Islam, International Relations theory and security in Africa. His most recent books include *Islamism, Crisis and Democratization: Implications of the World Values Survey for the Muslim World* (with Arno Tausch, 2020), *African Security in the Twenty-First Century: Challenges and Opportunities* (with Stephen Emerson, 2018), *Understanding Boko Haram and Insurgency in Africa* (with Jim Hentz, 2017), *Islamic State and the Coming Global Confrontation* (2016), *Terrorism and Counter-Terrorism in Africa: Fighting Insurgency from Al Shabaab, Ansar Dine and Boko Haram* (2015) and *Jihad: A South African Perspective* (2013).

Marion van San studied sociology and criminology at the Free University of Brussels. In 1998 she graduated from the University of Amsterdam with a dissertation on violent crime. She works as Senior Researcher at the Rotterdam Institute for Social Policy Research, Erasmus University, Rotterdam. She has been involved with metropolitan issues such as (youth) crime, irregular immigrants, prostitution, and ethnicity and crime. She is the author of numerous publications on these subjects. Since 2009 her research has focused on radicalism and extremism from a pedagogical perspective. She conducted research into the family circumstances of youths with extreme ideals and the family circumstances of youths who have joined the armed struggle in Syria.

Sanaz Zolghadriha is a lecturer of Crime Science at University College London, where her teaching focus lies in organised crime. Currently, her research lies in terrorism risk assessment, where she applies experimental methods to the testing of risk assessment tools. Sanaz has a background in clinical and forensic psychology, and an interest in research on offending behaviour and law enforcement investigative practices.

Caroline Varin is senior lecturer in International Relations at Regent's University London and Fellow of the Higher Education Academy (HEA). She is also a co-founder of the non-profit Professors Without Borders and Associate at LSEIDEAS at the London School of Economics. Caroline is a member of the Geneva Consultation for Security Policy and has previous experience working in Intelligence Analysis, the Swiss armed forces and the UNHCR. Her academic interests lie in African security and the networks and strategies of violent non-state actors. She has published four books and numerous articles and presented her research on Boko Haram and Nigerian security to the UK government.

INTRODUCTION

EXAMINING THE GLOBAL LINKAGES OF AFRICAN AND EUROPEAN JIHADISTS

Tom Smith and Hussein Solomon

On Christmas Day 2009 Umar Farouk Abdulmutallab boarded Detroit-bound Northwest Airlines 253 at Amsterdam's Schiphol Airport. During the flight, he attempted to detonate explosives hidden in his underwear, as a result of which he would come to be known as the 'underwear bomber'. Even though his plan was thwarted by alert passengers and the explosives did not go off as planned, it raised troubling questions as to the nature of the terrorist threat confronted. The 'global' nature of the terrorist threat confronted was encapsulated by the fact that Abdulmutallab was a Nigerian national studying at University College London, who was recruited by the American-born Muslim preacher of Yemeni extraction, Anwar al-Awlaki, and that he had travelled to the Netherlands to board a US-bound airplane.[1] Abdulmutallab's case heightened the sense of a global jihad where jihad is not confined to its historical *centres* of Afghanistan and the Middle East and is increasingly being exported to the *periphery*. Islamist attacks that have taken place in Europe and Africa and the involvement of European and African jihadis elsewhere suggest a jihad unbounded by human and physical geography.

Problematizing the periphery in the scholarship on jihad

Exporting the global jihad: Critical perspectives from the 'periphery' creates a purpose-built platform for the ongoing battle to better understand the dynamics of the global reality of jihad. By providing tools to assess just how global jihad has become (or was) from a breadth of international viewpoints, this collection of works asks a series of critical questions about research and reporting on jihad in the 'exotic' lands far from Afghanistan, Iraq or Syria, questions that include the following: How connected are remote militant groups to ISIS and Al Qaeda? And what is the nature of these 'linkages'? In doing so the book looks to assist in shifting the traditional research focus from the Middle East and ideological radicalization by prominent groups like Al Qaeda and ISIS towards the jihadis in lesser discussed *peripheries*. Critically examining the global reach of jihad in these *peripheries* has the potential to tell us much about both local mobilization and rejection of a grander centrally themed and administered jihad. By examining the various claims made by jihadis and experts of connections between the remote Islamist insurgencies of the 'periphery' and the global jihad this book challenges portrayals of a pervasive global network of an exotic and cosmopolitan cadre of like-minded and similarly motivated jihadis in global union.

As the two volumes of this book evidence, *the global jihad* is somewhat cosmopolitan and diverse but the limits and variations to this vary greatly depending on the nature of that union and the geographies under analysis. As such the works included here have been authored with the premise that exoticizing jihad is a dangerous tendency and the default to globalize rather than localize our understanding of these conflicts, groups and individuals undermines true analysis of the mixed local and global dynamics of jihad. This *glocalism* requires attention if we are to better understand the appeal of jihadism and so evidence-based analysis on the linkages throughout the global jihad is required at regular intervals with specific geographic concentration, and expertise above and beyond that of the general terrorism analyst.

Exporting the Global Jihad is a direct response to two leading publications – Olivier Roy's now seminal 2004 work *Globalised Islam* and Faisal Devji's much under-appreciated 2005 work *Landscapes of the Jihad* – that began to scrutinize the global nature of jihad and the relationships among its wide variety of participants. Roy was quite adamant that a conscious decision was made by Al Qaeda to prioritize exploiting opportunities as far as the Muslim world stretched:

> The decision to wage a peripheral jihad was reached because the locations of such jihads seem like 'virgin lands' that have relatively poor organised resistance movements. Thus foreign volunteers can hope to influence not only their local comrades in arms but also society as whole. This is certainly not the case in areas like Israel/Palestine or other Middle Eastern countries, where nobody is likely to accept a lecture from a western Muslim. The periphery is more receptive to the jihadis' millenarianist dream. But in Bosnia as in Afghanistan many local fighters, specifically Sufis, were antagonised by Salafi and Wahhabi propaganda. Ultimately no foreign jihadis have been able to impose their religious agenda on any Muslim society, though it would be fair to concede that they have played significant military roles in conflicts in Chechnya, Bosnia and Kashmir.[2]

Exporting Global Jihad is an attempt to answer how successful that attempt to exploit the 'virgin lands' of the periphery has been and test Roy's assertion. Has the periphery been receptive to an *exported* jihad from the *centre* as Roy suggested? Or does the locally *rooted cosmopolitanism* of the jihad in the periphery suggest a more complex *glocal* relationship? Portrayals of jihadis from across the globe joining ISIS in Syria and Iraq seem to support Devji's observance that 'the jihad, instead of being exported from the centre to the periphery, will be imported from the periphery to the centre.'[3]

As *Exporting Global Jihad* was being written, ISIS was losing its base in Syria and Iraq and many commentators wondered how ISIS and the global jihad more broadly will rebrand. Will a new centre emerge and reassert its claims to the periphery or will the next centre for jihad be in the periphery? In *Exporting Global Jihad*, we are presented with some interesting patterns as well as unique characteristics. The jihad, and its participants, are concurrently 'exoticized' by connecting them with remote and exotic insurgencies in the periphery, yet also normalized into the everyday with constant coverage of conflicts, groups and individuals around the world within a single dominant global narrative.[4] The global nature of jihad is too often taken for granted; yet the extent of the glocal connections deserves continued and focused investigation. Without such inquiry we risk a reductive understanding of the global jihad fostering Orientalist and Eurocentric attitudes towards local conflicts and remote violence in the periphery. *Exporting Global Jihad* draws attention to those who overlook and undermine the distinct and rich particularities of the global jihad: 'The fact that the jihad today happens to be based for the most part outside the Middle East among populations that have barely an inkling of Salafi or Wahhabi traditions, seems to have escaped the notice of scholarly genealogies.'[5]

In bringing together experts from these periphery locations where 'jihadi insurgencies' or perhaps more accurately – where acts of violence labelled as jihadi – proliferate and are said to be part of a global phenomenon, this volume provides a unique reference to the reader to scrutinize the global nature of jihad. This scrutiny can be confidently based on the fact that the authors understand these geographies intimately and the debates on the complexities of their violence. Each chapter explores the extent of connections to the global jihad and the relationship between 'the centre' and the 'periphery'. In doing so, the volume challenges the reductive import/export notion of a global jihad and notions of a *centre* and *periphery* as they relate to *jihad*. Scepticism about the portrayals of global jihad is strongest where the claims of these connections stretch the furthest and so this collection is born out of the community of regional experts, who have invested themselves in understanding the peripheries' relationship to *the global jihad*. This volume attempts to turn that scepticism and disenchantment into an intellectual resistance against clichéd expressions of a global jihad often advocated by hollow connections to exotic Asian and African landscapes.

While *the global jihad* may be notably cosmopolitan with a rich and diverse, ethnic and cultural community, *just how global is this jihad?* And what is the extent of these connections outside the traditionally viewed centre of the Middle East? This is a volume that understands its heritage in the literature and the ideas that have laid the ground to allow us to ask and answer such pertinent and impertinent questions. From Richard W. Bulliet's *Islam: The View from the Edge*[6] published in 1994, this book proposes to develop that 'peripheral vision' often lacking in discussion of global jihad: focusing solely on the relationship with the periphery. This allows us to ask how *rooted* the global jihad is in the periphery, and whether Roy's 'jihadi jet set' was ever realized? If so, where, why and how?

> This new breed was above all largely uprooted and more westernised than its predecessors, had few links (if any) to any particular Muslim country, and

moved around the world, travelling from jihad to jihad. The flying jihadi was born, the jihadi jet set.[7]

Devji recognized the importance of Roy's claim, if not necessarily the accuracy of it. 'According to Roy, the global jihad has to be distinguished from local struggles not simply by its geographical sweep, but also because it has become an individual duty for which these causes have been reduced to abstractions. He even suggests that such local struggles exist for it only as stereotypes.'[8] This volume goes to that next stage and examines the validity of the peripheries' 'local struggles' connections to the global jihad. This examination is built on an appreciation of the rich history of Muslim kinship and on crucially understanding that when it comes to jihad, as Fred Halliday noted, such unity only goes so far:

> The world today contains more than fifty Muslim-majority countries, in which strong nationalist and patriotic sentiments flourish – often directed against fellow Muslim peoples (Iranians / Iraqis, Sudanese / Egyptians, Uzbeks / Tajiks, to name a few). This adherence to national as opposed to Islamic identities is reflected in the way that middle-eastern Muslim states (except Saudi Arabia) invoke elements of the pre-Islamic past as a form of legitimation; this, even though Islam formally denounces the pre-Islamic period as one of jahiliya (ignorance). Thus Egypt celebrates the Pharaohs, Tunisia the Phoenicians, Iran the ancient Persian empires, Yemen the kingdoms of Saba and Himyar. These considerations are relevant to Osama bin Laden's transnational project; research on jihadi documents, and interviews with former or imprisoned members, reveal strong inter-ethnic tensions within the movement.[9]

For Halliday, the inherent danger in much of the material written on *the global jihad*, and the policies enacted off the back of that material, was that it rarely took account of the concurrent unifying and divisionary competing dynamics. Muslim kinship in the global jihad only goes so far – but how far? These dynamics and limits are acknowledged by only a few, and recognized as important for understanding the global nature of *the jihad* by fewer still. Yet from very early on, with reference to Al Qaeda, Jason Burke also found that 'national and ethnic divisions re-asserted themselves among the volunteers. bin Laden's group was formed with the aim of rousing Muslims, through active campaigning or "propaganda by deed", to create an "international army" that would unite the umma or world Islamic community against oppression.'[10] This disjuncture between aim and reality needs continual vigilance and exposure, and this book seeks to do this across the landscape of the 'periphery'. The vicissitudes in the Al Qaeda franchise model were the first and most striking point of confusion, for it 'led, not to the formation of a huge and disciplined group "with tentacles everywhere"… But imagining that all these groups were all created or run by bin Laden is to denigrate the particular local factors that led to their emergence.'[11] A critical perspective is vital therefore to be able to identify the stereotyped jungle jihadi, and to avoid any such denigration in the particular. It is also critically important for policy. As Burke recognized when trying to decipher the supposed networked capabilities of Al Qaeda back in 2003, the flaws in understanding the reach and reality of *the global jihad* have adverse consequences:

> Little that had previously been published helped. It was clear to me that profound misconceptions were widespread. Foremost among them was the idea that bin Laden led a cohesive and structured terrorist organisation called 'Al Qaeda'. Every piece of evidence I came across in my own work contradicted this notion of Al Qaeda as an 'Evil Empire' with an omnipotent mastermind at its head ... but it was clearly deeply flawed. As a result, the debate over the prosecution of the on-going 'war on terror' had been skewed.[12]

In many of the peripheries, particularly those with intensive large-scale insurgencies, there is extensive, often international, military alliance and cooperation. The Bush doctrine to 'fight them over there, so we don't have to fight them over here' certainly looks to be alive and well in places like the Philippines, Nigeria, Mali and Somalia. Crucially we must regularly and repeatedly ask: Is such reasoning sound? Further, is action in the peripheries under the guise of combating global jihad overlooking the local jihad and threatening to increase the threat where it was otherwise contained? Diagnoses of nations or regions as 'afflicted'[13] by a global jihad that has 'shifted from the Middle East to the Asia-Pacific region'[14] and elsewhere as this volume demonstrates, often come with warnings that these remote locations become 'ideal as substitute targets for anti-American aggression'.[15] The spectre of choosing sides in a *battle of civilizations* looms over an increasing number of nations and regions, many reliant on good Western relations. Then there are the Western nations themselves whose own citizens present various challenges to our understanding of how the global connections often revolve around individual motivations and behaviour without wider group involvement.

ISIS, Al Qaeda and Islamist violence more broadly – particularly where it is claimed in the remotest regions of the periphery – has at times become a 'cottage industry'[16] for those claiming a global menace by reciting the same propaganda of cohesive connections as the jihadis themselves. bin Laden regularly invoked *local struggles*, perhaps never more pointedly than in his most famous address five years before 9/11:

> It should not be hidden from you that the people of Islam had suffered from aggression, iniquity and injustice imposed on them by the Zionist-Crusaders alliance and their collaborators; to the extent that the Muslims blood became the cheapest and their wealth *as loot in the hands of the enemies. Their blood was spilled in Palestine and Iraq. The horrifying pictures of the massacre of Qana, in Lebanon, are still fresh in our memory. Massacres in Tajikistan, Burma, Cashmere, Assam, Philippine, Fatani [sic], Ogadin, Somalia, Eritrea, Chechnia [sic] and in Bosnia-Herzegovina took place, massacres that send shivers in the body and shake the conscience. All of this and the world watch and hear, and not only didn't respond to these atrocities, but also with a clear conspiracy between*

the USA and its allies and under the cover of the iniquitous United Nations, the dispossessed people were even prevented from obtaining arms to defend themselves.[17]

Fawaz Gerges astutely noted how 'the shift to globalism masked an inverted orientation and propensity toward localism. We should not be fooled by the rhetoric of global jihad because lying just under the surface is a powerful drive to capture the state at home'.[18] Yet, sadly, many commentators – especially those relating to the periphery – have been 'fooled' by the jihadi propaganda. The scepticism we have needed thus far must remain. Critical analysis of the propaganda itself can tell us a great deal about the ambition of the global jihad and likewise its reception in the periphery. Similarly, the value of fieldwork in the periphery, speaking to local communities about the claims of jihadi connections, is especially important when gossip is often the basis of many claims. This analysis is built on an understanding that the global jihad, as Halliday explained, has 'fissures' that need to be better understood and reconciled:

> The Muslim world is not, nor has ever been, defined wholly or mainly in terms of the umma or transnational linkages and identities. To be sure, forms of solidarity over the Muslim-related political conflicts and issues such as Palestine, Kashmir and now Iraq do exert a hold on many people, and inspire radical activism. But just as the international communist movement after 1917 masked sharp internal differences of culture, politics and interest, so today's global jihadi movement contains such fissures. The umma may not be as stateless, fluid or international as it appears.[19]

Without critical scrutiny of propaganda and gossip when claimed as evidence of the global jihad's reach into the periphery, those looking from afar, and often designing policy affecting the periphery, can be misled. Yet, Devji offered an alternative to understanding the peripheries in more locally nuanced terms: 'The jihad is not a collective movement of the traditional kind, nor one that seduces alienated and vulnerable young men, but, like other global movements, attracts diverse volunteers for equally diverse reasons.'[20] Rather than a network where 'malignant "radicalisers" prey upon 'vulnerable' individuals'[21] we are likely to find more solid evidence of the global nature of *the jihad* in the periphery if we can attest to what Scott Atran describes as 'moral commitment'[22] and if this extends beyond the locale.

Unpacking the jihad in the periphery

Understanding the futility of pursuing 'the truth' and recognizing the importance of debates that highlight different facets of the truth, the volume brings together a diversity of scholars who represent both the global north and the global south, thereby highlighting the truism that one's perspective is determined by one's position. Moreover, the different authors in this volume utilize a plethora of approaches in attempting to examine the complex relationship between centre and periphery. Peter Chonka examines conspiracy theorization in attempting to unpack political discourses in Somalia, while Ngala Chome adopts an empirical and descriptive approach based on fieldwork conducted in Kenya. While Anneli Botha examines the manifestation of jihad in Libya through a historical lens, Hussein Solomon's and Joseph Downing's approaches to the Sahel and France, respectively, rely on a critical terrorism studies perspective. The authors of the chapter on the United Kingdom, meanwhile, attempt to create their own theoretical framework as they try to connect the individual, organizational and societal dimensions of jihad in the country. The very eclecticism of this volume allows for a plurality of perspectives on the myriad manifestations of jihad in the periphery.

Focusing on Al Shabaab, Peter Chonka argues that in Somalia, where the early Al Qaeda had bases of operations, the jihad can only be understood through understanding the varying local political fault lines that arose from processes of state-making and state collapse stretching back to the immediate postcolonial era. While not disregarding the global dimensions of jihadism, the presence of foreign fighters and the saliency of various brands of internationally oriented political Islam, Chonka stresses the primacy of local historical context and the various local political formations vying for political authority. The chapter on Kenya by Ngala Chome, meanwhile, examines the evolution of the Islamist network in Kenya. While the Islamist networks between 1993 and 2002 were inspired by the call for a global jihad by Al Qaeda, the subsequent Islamist networks were largely driven by local Muslim grievances even though this was expressed through a language of global jihad. Chome's chapter highlights the danger of static understandings of global and local factors and why an understanding of local dynamics is imperative if researchers and policy makers seek to understand and end the violence.

Examining developments in the Sahel, Hussein Solomon argues that Islamist extremism originates in the form of sub-state terrorist groups as a result of local grievances. Western support for often-corrupt and oppressive regimes in the region – through counterterrorism initiatives – then compels these groupings to find external sources of financial and military support. Local insurgencies then morph into regional franchises for international terror networks like Al Qaeda and ISIS. Despite this, these groupings remain locally grounded, like the Macina Liberation Front which remains an ethnic Fulani movement despite its global Islamist rhetoric. In a similar vein, Stephen Harrison persuasively argues that youth unemployment, regional droughts, the democracy deficit, predatory behaviour by political elites and Tuareg marginalization are just some of the local factors driving *the jihad* in Mali. Despite ideological support and branding from Al Qaeda Central, these Islamist movements remain nationally and regionally focused as opposed to being international in dimension.

Tracking the development of Boko Haram from an isolated community of ultra-Salafists to its insurgent campaign against Abuja and its forays into neighbouring Niger, Chad and Cameroon, Caroline Varin presents an incisive chapter on Nigeria's Islamists. While cognizant of Boko Haram's international dimensions – its cooperation with Al Qaeda in the Islamic Maghreb and Al Shabaab and its oath of allegiance to ISIS – Varin argues that the movement is still anchored in domestic priorities and that its alliances with international groupings has more to do with opportunism. Stressing the point, she points to the fact that Boko Haram's inability to attract foreign fighters from outside its immediate region indicates the narrowness of its agenda. Anneli Botha, meanwhile, traces the evolution of *the jihad* in Libya from acting as a state sponsor of terrorism to a target of acts of terrorism to serving as a regional hub of terrorist groups following the fall of the Gaddafi regime in 2011. Islamism, Botha reminds us, is not a new phenomenon. Gaddafi himself, was the target of the ire of Islamists following his perceived move away from shari'a. *The jihad* in Libya was the product of a closed political system, geographic and ethnic divisions and environmental conditions like desertification. ISIS has made use of these local conditions to advance its agenda in Libya.

Turning to the United Kingdom, Gill, Marchment, Rottweiler and Zolghadriha disaggregate the import and export of jihadi narratives and their impact on the individual terrorist, the terrorist organization and the broader community. In creating a holistic framework for all three units of analysis, the authors examine the differing roles of various foreign-born figures of epistemic authority, and the community support for jihadi narratives and goals, and finally assess their impact within the United Kingdom. What emerges is a highly sophisticated centre-periphery debate on the jihad. Related to this, by adopting a deconstructive approach, Joseph Downing casts doubt on analysis of French jihadism, which is rooted in grand theories and a traditional focus on 'problem-solving'. In an incisive chapter he stresses the tremendous diversity of those recruited into jihadi ranks. This, he notes, is hardly surprising given the remarkably diverse nature of French Muslims – socio-culturally and doctrinally. Distancing his chapter from other scholarship that serves to essentialize and homogenize such diversity, he appeals for an individual approach in explaining how French Muslims are recruited into jihadi movements.

A total of 693 young men and women have, since 2012, left the Low Countries (Netherlands, Belgium and Luxembourg) to join ISIS in Iraq and Syria. In attempting to understand their recruitment into militant ranks, Marion van San argues that while the global Islamist narratives are appealing, these are mediated by local conditions. In particular, these local conditions affect group formation and even the form radicalization takes. In the process, greater insights into a process of 'bottom-up radicalization' are gained. Examining the global and local peculiarities of the jihad in Scandinavia, Marco Nilsson notes that local context and experiences are manipulated to recruit individuals into jihadi ranks. More specifically, the targets' local experiences are re-framed so that they are connected to international events affecting the global ummah. The terrorist threat confronted by Denmark, Norway and Sweden is also impacted by domestic circumstances. Following the publication of the caricatures of Prophet Muhammad in Jyllands-Posten in 2005, most of the domestic terror plots targeted that newspaper.

The relationship between core and periphery in the case of Germany has been a dynamic one, changing over time. Tracing the development of the manifestation of jihad, Jan Raudszus argues that Germany has been a source of volunteers for global jihad and a logistical base since at least the 2000s. In its initial phases, ideas and conflict dynamics were largely *exported* from the Islamic core into Germany. But this changed over time, with the jihadi discourse developing its own local dynamics adapting to local concerns and integrating itself into Germany's social landscape. In the case of Iberia, Maria do Céu Pinto Arena identifies similar dynamics at play. Both Al Qaeda and ISIS, she argues, have tapped into the alienation and disenchantment of Muslims in Spain and Portugal as a result of the failed integration. This is not a new phenomenon and stretches back to the 1990s when Muslims from the Iberian Peninsula were recruited for the jihad in Bosnia, Chechnya and Afghanistan. The contested nature of core and periphery is especially evident in Spain, due to its proximity to the Maghreb and on account of it historically being part of the House of Islam (Dar al Islam) when it was Al-Andalus. An interesting aspect of the Portuguese experience is that many of the Portuguese jihadis were recent converts who were radicalized while living abroad in European metropolitan and suburban areas with large concentrations of Muslim populations.

Conclusion

In attempting to understand the relationship between core and periphery, the chapters in this volume highlight that these phenomena are never static and evolve over time. In Europe the meaning of exporting or importing the jihad has arguably become reversed: instead of *the jihad* being imported from the Middle East, it is imported from the periphery to the centre with the passage of foreign fighters. As such, all our contributors highlight the problems with deterministic analysis which does not allow for local peculiarities. In the United Kingdom, and to some extent France, we note that their being former colonial powers, which experienced successive immigration flows from their former colonies, comparison must be nuanced. In a similar vein, the peculiar status of Spain in Muslim history sets it apart from other European countries. These factors have to be considered and often further dissolve any of the distinction between a centre and periphery. On the contemporary question of how global *the jihad is*, history still matters, more in some geographies than in others, but it explains the nature of some of the connections in the European and African periphery.

While there is always an interplay between global and local, even without a strong colonial history, the road to jihadism is extremely diverse as seen at the individual level across Europe. Within the African context, the local context often takes precedence over the global, despite the international jihadi rhetoric emanating from local militants. Group participation dominates as our analysis demonstrates and those groups bind individuals – at least originally – to local causes. Groups like Al Shabaab, Boko Haram or the Macina Liberation Front all remain deeply rooted in local and, at best, regional considerations. Chapters across the continent remind us that violence is not only the result of militant Islamist groups but also the result of the violence emanating from the state itself. The use of militias by some of the Sahel's states has seen atrocious human rights abuses committed on hapless citizens who cannot distinguish between the violence perpetrated on them by jihadis and that committed by the security services of the state and its proxies. Understanding these blurred lines is essential for an informed critical analysis of the *glocality* of the jihadism in the region and is strongly advocated throughout.

This is made worse by the predatory behaviour of political elites as outlined by Stephen Harrison in his chapter on Mali. The local factors driving jihad – unemployment and the concomitant impoverishment, ethnic chauvinism, the dearth of democratic governance and accountability measures, as Ngala Chome reminds us in the chapter on Kenya, are often deliberately obscured by local governments as they seek classical rent-seeking behaviour to solicit international aid to combat the menace of 'global jihadism'. In seeking to end this carnage there is an urgent need to problematize the African state and for the international community to use its leverage over states to open up the democratic space and compel it to practise better inclusive governance. As Stephen Harrison notes, not France and its allies, none of the regional states and no United Nations peacekeeping force can halt the ongoing jihadi attacks with military force alone. Instead, other tools should be utilized to mitigate the underlying factors at the roots of jihadi rage. These tools include diplomatic, educational and developmental initiatives and all rely on a local understanding of the problem.

None of this implies that there is no international dimension to *the jihad* taking place across several African states. It is a fact that local jihadis have got material and ideological support from Al Qaeda and ISIS. But local militants' affiliation to international jihadi groups, as Carline Varin argues, is at best opportunistic. Their insurgencies against incumbent regimes are motivated by local grievances and therefore solutions lie primarily in that local context. Distraction from this and intervention and aid that focuses on inoculating the 'global menace' and not the local one, is not just flawed, but also likely to be inflammatory.

Notes

1 Scott Shane, 'Inside Al Qaeda's plot to blow up an American Airliner', *The New York Times*, 22 February 2017. Internet: https://www/nytimes/com/2017/02/22/us/politics/anwar-awlaki-underwear-bomber/abdulmuttalab.html (accessed 30 June 2018).
2 Olivier Roy, *Globalised Islam: The Search for a New Ummah* (London: Hurst and Company, 2004), p. 313.
3 Faisal Devji, *Landscapes of the Jihad: Militancy, Morality and Modernity* (London: Hurst and Company, 2005), p. 63.
4 Tom Smith, 'Stop portraying Islamic State as a band of exotic globetrotters', *The Conversation*, 2017. https://theconversation.com/stop-portraying-islamic-state-as-a-band-of-exotic-globetrotters-87402.

5   Devji, *Landscapes of the Jihad: Militancy, Morality and Modernity*, p. 21.
6   Richard W. Bulliet, *Islam: The View from the Edge* (New York: Columbia University Press, 1995).
7   Roy, *Globalised Islam: The Search for a New Ummah*, p. 215.
8   Devji, *Landscapes of the Jihad: Militancy, Morality and Modernity*, p. 4.
9   Fred Halliday, 'A transnational umma: Reality or myth?'. Available at http://www.opendemocracy.net/globalization/umma 2904.jsp (Accessed 25 May 2013).
10 Jason Burke, 'What is al-Qaeda?', *The Guardian*, 2003.
11 Ibid.
12 Ibid.
13 Bilveer Singh, *The Talibanization of Southeast Asia: Losing the War on Terror to Islamist Extremists* (New Delhi: Praeger Security International, 2007), p. ix.
14 Andrew Tan and Kumar Ramakrishna, *The New Terrorism: Anatomy, Trends, and Counter-Strategies* (Singapore: Times Academic Press, 2002), p. 10.
15 Peter Chalk, 'Al Qaeda and its links to terrorist groups in Asia', in *The New Terrorism Anatomy, Trends and Counter-Strategies*, ed. Andrew Tan and Kumar Ramakrishna (Singapore: Times Academic Press, 2002), pp. 107–28 (p. 118).
16 Thitinan Phongsutthirak, 'Review of conflict and terrorism in Southern Thailand', *Contemporary Southeast Asia: A Journal of International and Strategic Affairs*, xxviii, no. 1 (2006): 160–3 (p. 160).
17 'Declaration of War against the Americans Occupying the Land of the Two Holy Places', Osama bin Laden, 1996. PBS, 'Bin Laden's Fatwa, Aug. 23, 1996'. Available at http://www.pbs.org/newshour/updates/military/july-dec96/fatwa_1996.html (Accessed 31 October 2013).
18 Fawaz A. Gerges, *The Far Enemy: Why Jihad Went Global* (Cambridge: Cambridge University Press, 2009), p. 273.
19 Halliday, 'A transnational umma: Reality or myth?'
20 Devji, *Landscapes of the Jihad: Militancy, Morality and Modernity*, p. 20.
21 Andrew Hoskins, Akil Awan and Ben O'Loughlin, *Radicalisation and Media: Connectivity and Terrorism in the New Media Ecology* (Abingdon: Routledge, 2011), p. 10.
22 Scott Atran, *Talking to the Enemy: Faith, Brotherhood, and the (un)Making of Terrorists* (New York: Routledge, 2011), p. 298.

'GLOCALIZED' JIHAD, POLITICAL CONFLICT, AND CONSPIRACY THEORIZATION ACROSS A FRAGMENTED SOMALIA

Peter Chonka

Introduction

Despite the presence of foreign fighters, transnational connections and discursive linkages to international militant Islamist causes, narratives of 'global jihad' in Somalia need also to be understood, this chapter argues, within a local historical context of state collapse and current contestations over ongoing reconstructions of political authority.[1] Harakaat Al Shabaab Al Mujahidiin's campaign against the internationally recognized Federal Government of Somalia (FGS) represents one (albeit distinct) dynamic of conflict affecting the Somali territories. It simultaneously overlaps and interplays with other struggles for political power, such as those ongoing among and between the Mogadishu-based FGS and various regional administrations of different levels of consolidation and autonomy. Al Shabaab's militancy against the FGS and its international backers continues in a wider arena where various brands of internationally oriented political Islam have historically been on the ascendency, and where popular expressions of Sunni religious piety take more orthodox forms to past practices of 'traditional' or 'Somali' Islam. Focusing primarily on the 2012–2017 FGS of President Xasan Sheekh Maxamuud,[2] this chapter surveys some of the multiple ways in which the concept of politico-religious 'radicalism' (*xagjirnimo*) has been understood and used in recent history by local political actors or commentators active in these arenas of conflict and state reconstruction.

Conspiracy theorization is an important mode of political discourse within a highly fragmented yet dynamic and transnational 'public sphere' of Somali debate.[3] On one hand, Al Shabaab frames its militancy in opposition to tropes of 'Western' conspiracy and foreign cultural agendas. At the same time, it may itself be understood by local commentators and political actors as a conspiratorial force entwined and active in the power struggles ongoing between different clan, regional or quasi-state administrations that make up the patchwork of authority that characterizes a still divided Somalia. Regardless of the truth behind these narratives, Al Shabaab has been discursively 'spectralized' as a problem affecting the broader 'Somali Ummah', and has been seen as an important clandestine actor in the contestation between regional authorities. This demonstrates the need to understand 'global jihad' in this part of the Horn of Africa with consideration to local political fault lines whose legacies stretch back to the processes of Somali state-making and state-breaking in the postcolonial era.

Conspiracy is understood here in Wolfe's formulation as 'less a particular narrative than a particular way of assembling narratives that performs the function of not only supplying a moral map to the political landscape but, more profoundly, of rescuing truth by rediscovering it in a particular discursive technique.'[4] The chapter highlights this process to reflect on the ways in which the modern Somali public sphere facilitates such complex and transnational assemblage of narratives. This approach builds on an increasing appreciation in the political science and media/cultural studies literature of the role of conspiracy theorization,[5] particularly within the de-centred 'new' media environment, and considering the broader importance of so-called post-truth politics.[6] My discussion of various conspiracy theories in the chapter does not amount to the endorsement of any of their truth-claims. Nonetheless, I argue that these narratives deserve critical attention because, as my analysis demonstrates, they have been periodically (re)articulated by 'official' political actors, and they relate closely to the complex and opaque theatre of military operations in which multiple local and international forces are engaged.

Although the chapter recognizes the instrumentalist manipulation of a conspiracy-laden public sphere by elite political actors, it nonetheless argues that 'radical' ideologies in this communicative context themselves also require scrutiny. Crone argues that many contemporary analyses of 'radicalization' in the West often overemphasize abstract religious ideology as a motivating factor at the expense of adequate conceptualizations of politicization, or an understanding of the role of bodily techniques and the influence of prior experience of violence.[7] While the distinction between 'ideology' and 'politicization' in that particular account arguably requires more precise definition, this chapter echoes that sensitivity to the political rationales behind militancy. It also speculates that the notion of 'violent habitus'[8] is relevant for a context such as Somalia, where regional fragmentation and endemic (if sporadic) armed conflict has been a powerful feature of political life for many parts of the territory for the last quarter century of statelessness.

Conventional policy or security studies narratives that attribute Al Shabaab violence to the brainwashing of uneducated youths and foreign-inspired 'harsh' applications of *Sharia* against a 'moderate' or 'Sufi-oriented' Somali public, often overlook the complex interplay of religious orthodoxy and factional political interests within a wider context of Somali state reconstruction. Problematic definitions and conceptualizations of cognitive or behavioural 'radicalism' have plagued wider political science and security studies analyses of militant-religious mobilization and violence.[9] With regard to Islam in particular, critical explorations of the politics of naming doctrines, sects or movements have highlighted the difficulties of employing terminology not used by particular groups themselves – for instance, labels such as *Salafi* or *Wahhabi*. There is also an issue here with analysts' uncritical reproduction of descriptors of militant agency (like *jihad/jihadi*) that such groups do employ, but which are rejected by a Muslim mainstream that decries the use of such terminology to justify political violence.[10] A politics of naming is also relevant for the regional case study addressed in this chapter – Somalia. Although 'clan' divisions are important in Somali society, and Somalia remains a politically fractured nation state, virtually the entire population identify as practising Sunni Muslims, and speak dialects of Somali. Language is important here and this chapter pays particular attention to the ways in which different labels are used in local political debates.

Conversely, the 'internationalization' of Al Shabaab is frequently emphasized by security-focused accounts.[11] Al Shabaab formally affiliated itself with Al Qaeda in 2012 and has undoubtedly benefited from the manpower and technical expertise of foreign fighters. There is also no doubt that it has significantly broadened its scope of networks and operations into the broader East Africa region and it maintains tangible links with other affiliated groups such as Al Qaeda in the Arabian Peninsula, primarily through arms trade routes from Yemen across the Gulf of Aden. Debates between 'internationalist' and (Somali) 'nationalist' factions within the group have played out since its inception and have led to significant and violent internal divisions, themselves overlapping with power struggles between high-ranking members. This was particularly apparent under the leadership of 'Emir' Axmed Cabdi Godane (nom de guerre Mukhtar Abu Zubeyr), who was killed by a US drone strike in 2014, shortly after executing a widespread purge against former internal allies.[12] His successor, Axmed Diriiye 'Abu Cubeyda', was a close confidant of Godane. Despite his low profile he has (perhaps surprisingly) managed to maintain a fairly firm grip on the organizational structure of the group in the wake of these earlier ruptures. Although the legacy of Godane's rule and succession has, arguably, been the entrenchment of the most 'radical' and 'internationalist' orientations of the group – and overt tensions between foreign and local fighters have apparently diminished – Al Shabaab in its rank and file and top leadership remains a largely 'Somali' organization. This account does not ignore Al Shabaab's evolution as a regional security threat, but nevertheless argues that its future prospects are closely tied to its territorial position and revenue-generating capacity inside Somalia itself. Al Shabaab's financial and administrative networks have remained remarkably resilient inside Somalia despite its progressive and significant loss of urban territory since 2011.[13] As such, and international operations or links notwithstanding, its activities on the ground in Somalia remain highly contingent on local regional, clan and resource-based power struggles in a context of continued (national) political fragmentation.

This analysis focuses on various Somali political understandings of what Al Shabaab 'is' and 'does'. In doing so, the chapter foregrounds the importance of a 'glocal' Somali-language public sphere of media production, which engages producers and consumers on the ground in Somalia *and* in the global diaspora. Although particular networks of news media production have built up around emergent regional or secessionist administrations, there also exists a wider discursive arena in which Somali statehoods are articulated and contested.[14] This wider public sphere is structured by the pan-Somali broadcasting of externally based Somali-language news media networks, which range from the BBC's Somali service and private satellite television networks, to the myriad 'news' websites that characterize Somali cyberspace and social media. The chapter uses various Somali-language texts (online and print editorials, audio/visual propaganda broadcasts) to illustrate the discursive tenor of many of the contemporary debates concerning religious and political contestation. The texts introduced here are taken from a wider sample of media production gathered during my PhD fieldwork in Mogadishu (national capital and base of the FGS), Hargeysa (capital of the independent but unrecognized Republic of Somaliland) and Garowe (administrative capital of the non-secessionist but autonomous Puntland State). This comparative discursive approach cannot hope to adequately cover the full range of political argumentation but does demonstrate the fact that while the parameters and technologies of these debates may be 'global', the content often features explicitly 'Somali' themes of political, religious or national identity.

The chapter begins with a brief historical contextualization of Islamist mobilization in Somalia and recent trajectories of state reconstruction and conflict. Focusing primarily on the Government of President Xasan Sheekh Maxamuud (2012–17), it goes on to discuss ideological influences on state reconstruction in Mogadishu, before introducing Al Shabaab's oppositional conflict narrative. Looking at the political projects of Somaliland and Puntland, as well as the highly contested Lower Shabelle region, the chapter surveys aspects of the wider political fragmentation of Somalia and discusses certain ways in which Al Shabaab is understood (or presented) by different actors. The dynamic and persistent security challenges faced by the current FGS and President Maxamed Cabdilaahi 'Farmaajo' are addressed here. These relate to the apparent resilience of Al Shabaab, the ongoing emergence and evolution of a local ISIS affiliate, and the prospect of African Union troop withdrawal.

Islamist mobilization and sociocultural religious change

Al Shabaab has emerged as a modern manifestation of militancy from a much longer historical lineage of political Islamist mobilization and activism in Somalia. Increased economic migration of Somalis to the Gulf during the 1970s oil boom precipitated a sociocultural change in religious practice as returnees brought with them ideas of doctrinal orthodoxy and reformist visions for 'Somali' Islam, hitherto heavily influenced by Sufi traditions and *tariqa* brotherhoods.[15] What might be termed an increased 'Arabization' of Somali Islam coincided with efforts by Siyaad Barre's secular, 'scientific-socialist' military regime to 'modernize' legal codes and societal attitudes towards gender relations and religious conduct. A portentous juncture was reached in 1975 with the execution of prominent religious scholars who publicly opposed the regime's imposition of a new family law granting equal inheritance rights to women.[16] From this point onwards, elements of anti-regime activism took on a distinctly 'Islamist' character, and organizations such as Al Itixaad Al Islaam began to increasingly mobilize underground networks to infiltrate and oppose a corrupt state which, for all its anti-'tribalist' rhetoric, had been seen to centralize power around certain Daarood sub-clans of Barre and his close associates.[17]

The 1980s saw the emergence of regional and clan-based armed *jabhad* (guerrilla or 'freedom fighter') resistance movements in the north against Barre's state.[18] These included the Isaaq clan-family-dominated Somali National Movement (SNM) in the north-west (what would later become the secessionist Republic of Somaliland) and the Daarood/Majeerteen-dominated Somali Salvation Democratic Front in the north-east (what would become the non-secessionist but autonomous state of Puntland). Both campaigns drew counter-insurgency responses from the military regime, and the communities from which the resistance movements drew support (or were perceived to have drawn support) suffered greatly from the indiscriminate violence of Barre's forces.[19] Ultimately, it would be the Hawiye clan-family-dominated United Somali Congress (USC) sweeping down upon Mogadishu from central regions that would oust Barre from power in 1991. A failure to reach a comprehensive political settlement between the aforementioned insurgent forces (and various other resistance groups) set the scene for the ensuing civil war: fierce contestation over Mogadishu, clan 'cleansing' and land grabbing in the capital and through the southern regions, the breakaway of the north-west into a self-declared independent Somaliland, and the foreign intervention of UN and US forces.

The descent into clan-based civil war and regional/clan fragmentation in this period brought tremendous humanitarian suffering for huge swathes of the Somali population. It remains highly contested history in both academic and popular analyses,[20] and still constitutes a pivotal temporal point of reference for many competing narratives and arguments today. There is a complex political fluidity to genealogical (clan) affiliations in the Somali context, which cannot be adequately explored or problematized here, particularly in regard to highly contestable notions of 'primordial' identity, or changing associations with territorial claims.[21] With such debates in mind, this account attempts to highlight intersections in modern public sphere discourse between religiously articulated agency or argumentation, and popular vocabularies of clan and regional political identities.

Although Islamist mobilization remained an undercurrent of political struggle in the pre- and post-1991 periods, groups such as Al Itixaad failed to live up to their stated potential to unite competing clan interests under a banner of Islamist authority. Indeed, such organizations were themselves undermined by clan/regional factional intrigue which, in part, explains an episode such as the expulsion of Al Itixaad from a stronghold in the north-east (the port city of Bosaaso, in what would become Puntland) and its subsequent reorganization in the southern hinterlands.[22] Nevertheless, such networks – often overlapping and intersecting in the stateless economy with *salafi*-oriented business fraternities – would re-emerge in the context of later political experimentation.

In the two decades that followed 1991, 'national' political reconciliation or reconstruction of a unitary state was not achieved, despite multiple peace conferences and abortive attempts at consolidating a stable government in Mogadishu. Experiments such as the Union of Islamic Courts – alliances in Mogadishu and south-central Somalia between Islamist activists often linked to long-standing networks such as Al Itixaad, local religious-judicial authorities and certain business clan groupings – were enacted largely in reaction to the perceived failures of the political class. They still remain an understudied phenomenon[23] and are often (mis)understood by many outside observers as being merely the precursor to Al Shabaab's later militancy.

Ethiopia's US-backed invasion of Somalia in 2006 to oust the Courts' administration is another important historical juncture, very much alive in the political imagination of current actors and commentators. Ultimately, it served to empower the most 'radical' offshoot of the broader experiment – Al Shabaab. The group gained both power and a veneer of nationalist legitimacy in the resistance it put up against the historical 'Christian' foe, whose invasion is often remembered primarily for the high number of civilian casualties it caused.[24] The Ethiopian-backed Transitional Federal Government (TFG) of Cabdullahi Yuusuf Axmed established itself in Mogadishu from 2007, achieving control over only parts of the capital and kept afloat almost solely by the presence of African Union 'peacekeepers'. Power was subsequently handed to an administration led by Shariif Sheekh Axmed, a one-time leader of the Courts' administration and representative of the 'moderate' Islamist faction the Alliance for the Re-liberation of Somalia, which participated in Djibouti-held talks in 2008. The withdrawal of Ethiopian forces negotiated at this conference primarily benefited Al Shabaab, as opposed to the beleaguered and Mogadishu-confined TFG, and between 2009 and 2010 the militants rapidly expanded their structures of administrative governance across a huge swathe of south-central Somalia.[25]

In 2011, African Union Mission for Somalia (AMISOM) forces, alongside TFG-aligned troops, expelled Al Shabaab from the parts of Mogadishu it controlled, setting the scene for the selection of what would become an internationally recognized Somali Federal Government under President Xasan Sheekh Maxamuud in 2012. Although his tenure was characterized by economic optimism generated by improving security conditions in the capital (and an influx of diaspora investment), this was frequently punctuated by Al Shabaab attacks on civilian and 'apostate' government targets.[26] Genuine development of state capacity in Mogadishu and the gradual and painful emergence of a new federal framework for regional governance coincided with political turbulence in the capital and an ongoing counter-insurgency campaign in the hinterlands.[27] In this period, Al Shabaab was displaced from most of its former urban centres of power but was not comprehensively defeated. It continues to hold large swathes of territory in the south-central hinterlands, taxes populations under its control, and retains the capacity to engage AMISOM/FGS-aligned forces in direct and asymmetric operations.

Islamism and modern state reconstruction in Mogadishu

In the context of state reconstruction in Mogadishu, secularism – as a political discourse – has been practically non-existent. In the absence of recognizable political parties, contestation in the Xasan Sheekh period was often characterized in terms of factional Islamism, underpinned by commercial interests and a semi-institutionalized clan-arithmetic of appointments and perceived allegiances. With security conditions preventing the holding of one-person-one-vote elections, Parliamentary selections and Cabinet appointments in Mogadishu have been made on the basis of the controversial '4.5' system. This divides representation between the four predominant clan families (Daarood, Dir, Hawiye, and Digil & Mirifle) with a half share for various so-called minorities, for instance, Jareer/'Bantu' groups who fall outside of the main Somali lineages. This system has operated alongside internationally connected networks of primarily Islamist-oriented politicians. For instance, the Dam Jadiid ('new blood') clique was popularly perceived to have dominated the 2012–2017 presidency, and had itself emerged as a splinter group of the Muslim Brotherhood-oriented Al Islaax movement. Figures associated with Dam Jadiid were in receipt of financial support from Qatar, which enabled Xasan Sheekh Maxamuud to prevail in the 2012 Presidential selection process undertaken by the Somali Parliament.[28]

The FGS, beholden to multiple sources of foreign patronage, was obligated to defer to some of the normative preferences of the 'international community' in terms of support for the 'federalization' agenda, while receiving significant military and intelligence support from both AMISOM and individual states such as the United States. At the same time, the increasing role of newly assertive and (financially) persuasive players from the Islamic world – sensitive, like the West, to Somalia's evolving geopolitical importance in the Horn – set an ideological context that further established various strands of Islamist political thought, increased Sunni orthodoxy and a continued shift in popular cultural orientation towards the Arab/Islamic world. Somalia has been courted by important regional players, notably Saudi Arabia and Turkey in the context of competition for influence vis-á-vis the broader Horn of Africa. Both governments, espousing different brands of political Islam, have invested heavily in the FGS. Turkey is a highly visible humanitarian, diplomatic and economic actor in Mogadishu while Saudi Arabia pledged $50 million in aid in 2016 in return for the FGS's severing of diplomatic ties with Iran.[29]

The geopolitical pressure on Xasan Sheekh Maxamuud's successor, President Maxamed Cabdulaahi 'Farmaajo', intensified early in his tenure with the escalation of Gulf tensions and the Saudi/United Arab Emirates-led blockade on Qatar. Somalia has become an important arena in which these struggles play out. States like the United Arab Emirates are increasing their footprint in the Horn through direct engagement with 'regional' political authorities such as Somaliland and Puntland in fields such as port development. This apparent bypassing of the FGS in Mogadishu has itself created tensions and influenced the Farmaajo government's controversial position of neutrality on the dispute, in contrast to the Saudi-leanings of the political leaders of the new federal regions.[30] These geopolitical wranglings also have direct security implications related to the funding and training provided by external actors to various federal and regional forces, as well as other armed proxy agents. For instance, Qatar has recently found itself in the ostensibly contradictory position of offering significant support to the FGS in Mogadishu, while also being accused of using Al Shabaab-linked proxies against UAE interests elsewhere in Somalia.[31]

Back at the level of domestic politics, the lack of a popularly recognizable or institutionalized party system has provided fertile ground for narratives in the public sphere highlighting various shadowy clan- or religious clique-based political groupings. In the Xasan Sheekh era, popular resentment against groups such as Dam Jadiid did not centre around their ill-defined political Islamist ideology, but rather the nefarious influence of unaccountable networks on the office of the Presidency and perceived corruption.[32] Although the state has insisted (particularly to its Western backers) that it has been waging an 'ideological' battle against Al Shabaab,[33] there remains no clear secular/Islamist divide in political discourse; Somalia is being reconstructed as an Islamic state whose current power holders condemn Al Shabaab violence as an affront to the Somali nation and as running contrary to Islam.

In this environment, a terminology of 'radicalism' (*xagjirnimo*) has developed in political discourse, deployed primarily by those broadly opposed to Al Shabaab's stated jihad, and in support of FGS attempts to re-establish power in Mogadishu and beyond. The pastoral etymology of *xagjir* relates to the she-camel who will not act as a surrogate milk-provider to another's offspring. In political usage, it refers to a lack of neutrality or excessive bias towards one side. Popular reference to religious terrorism (*argagixiso*) using this terminology is largely a post-9/11 phenomenon, and political 'radicalism' in public sphere discourse can take many forms, such as in critiques of those beholden to clan or tribalist 'ideologies'.[34]

Through multimedia, widely reproduced, and slick propaganda,[35] Al Shabaab's conflict narrative defines the FGS as an 'apostate stooge' to the 'black infidels' of the African Union and, by extension, their 'Western' puppet masters.[36] This axis of foreign interests is presented as inherently hostile to Islam and configured to perpetuate the division of Somalia into tribal fiefdoms beholden to its oldest and closest enemy – Ethiopia. Although elements of this discourse (particularly around the allegedly nefarious role of Addis Ababa) have found expression in the wider public sphere of southern Somali popular political commentary, Al Shabaab advocates the *takfiri* (declaration of apostasy) excommunication of any state-affiliated individuals, legitimizing their frequent attacks on both clearly governmental and ostensibly civilian targets. Pro-Al Shabaab propagandists present binary images of a religiously homogeneous Somali Ummah (*Ummadda Soomaaliyeed*) contrasted with the infidelity of the state associated with foreign interests. Both explicitly pro-Al Shabaab propaganda sources and 'mainstream' sites of debate may problematize the idea of radicalism (*xagjir*) in that it (like the concept of the so-called moderate Muslim) makes little sense in the wider socio-religious context where the vast majority of the population identify with Islam as a totalizing and coherent system of belief and bodily practice.[37]

In its mainstream and social media propaganda, the FGS in Mogadishu has presented Al Shabaab violence as a problem for the wider *Ummadda Soomaaliyeed* – a religiously inflected expression of the global community of Somalis. It has attempted to de-legitimize Al Shabaab's eponymous appeal to the youth by promoting an alternative acronym label: UGUS (*Ururka Gumaadka Ummadda Soomaaliyeed* [Organization for the slaughter of the Somali Ummah]), which it directed private media networks to use. Its 2015 announcement of a 'campaign of inoculation' against UGUS (*'Ololaha Tallaalka Ka Hortaga UGUS'*) epitomized physical portrayals of the imagined body politic beset by external (un-Somali) influences.[38] Predictably, the media-savvy militants hit back with their own 'UGUS' acronym for the FGS: *'Ururka Gumeeya Ummadda Soomaaliyeed'* – Organization for the (colonial) humiliation of the Somali Ummah.

The war of words between the state and the armed insurgency has been no mere sideshow to the conventional military operations or counter-insurgency that has been waged alongside it. Instead, it cuts to the heart of linguistic and cultural contestation over the identity of the re-emerging (southern) Somali state. Here the politics of Somali-usage versus and alongside Arabic has echoed debates in the early 1970s (when the Somali orthography was formalized[39]) and has illustrated the fluid linguistic context with which emerging state structures engage. However, political claims to authentic 'Somali' cultural preservation are multiple and even the ostensibly internationalist *jihadis* may cast their governance and militancy in these terms. Al Shabaab's narratives of economic ethno-nationalism have portrayed a 'traditional' Somali rural idyll and propaganda around their dealings with clan representatives demonstrates a sensitivity to *Xeer* (customary law)-based norms of inter-clan reconciliation, as well as strict adherence to Sharia.[40]

This, of course, stands in direct contrast to their critics who often brand Al Shabaab militancy, social and political Salafi-ism or growing doctrinal Sunni orthodoxy as a foreign import – quintessentially 'un-Somali' in their restrictive and intolerant attitudes to cultural and religious (Islamic) expression. An older generation of commentators has frequently lamented the young people from the diaspora who join Al Shabaab's jihad in Somalia or, for example, that of groups such as ISIS in Syria and Iraq. They may also, in less explicitly political terms, advocate a nostalgic imagining of a pre-state-collapse cultural idyll based on 'traditional' Somali Islam, pastoral customs and literature.[41] It is important to note, however, that such discourses rarely entertain – in public, at least – a nostalgia for the secular state itself or its social liberalism. This is a function of the notion of the failure of 'Somali/scientific socialism' as a political experiment for the 'Somali Ummah', and sensitivity to increased popular orientations towards increased public piety and doctrinal orthodoxy.

Political fragmentation and conspiracy

Under the Xasan Sheekh presidency an internationally sponsored roadmap for the federal reconfiguration of Somalia was implemented, the most notable achievement of which was the formalization of the boundaries and administrations of the south-central Federal States of Jubbaland, the South-West, Galmudug and HirShabelle. These in turn facilitated the clan elder and electoral delegate selection of MPs to the new Parliament by the end of 2016, which then went on to select

President Farmaajo soon after. In one sense, the federal model simply reflects the post-1991 trajectory of intense and prolonged power fragmentation and the polarization of clan politics that accompanied and followed the civil war.[42] At the same time, the process has drawn hostile popular reactions from some parts of a population that emphasize the sense of (relative) cultural, linguistic and religious homogeneity inherent in the historical 'Greater Somalia' ideal. This was novel in comparison with the historical experience of most other sub-Saharan African states, which have had to deal with far higher levels of ethno-linguistic diversity. Such criticisms have decried the alleged formalization of clan-based fiefdoms and the capacity of foreign powers to manipulate the system to keep Somalia weak and divided. Of course, fragmentation predates the much more recent establishment of the aforementioned south-central states, and can be traced back to Somaliland's unilateral declaration of independence in 1991, and the formation of the autonomous (but non-secessionist) state of Puntland in 1998. Starting with Somaliland, the following section explores different interpretations of Al Shabaab's Islamist militancy across and between these regions, and the ways these intertwine with understandings of the broader dynamics of regional contestation.

Since 1991, the Republic of Somaliland has emerged as a polity that passes what Bryden called the 'banana test' of sovereignty[43] – if it looks, tastes and smells like a state, then it probably is one. Political development in the north-western territory has produced distinctive institutional frameworks for governance and relatively democratic and peaceful transitions of executive power.[44] The functioning of democratic elections is a key facet of the unrecognized Republic's narrative of legitimacy: not only do elections allocate power within Somaliland but they also play a role in defining the polity vis-á-vis the 'other Somalia', which remains mired in ongoing conflict. Al Shabaab rejects the secession of Somaliland from what it conceives of as the 'Greater Somalia' – territories that include the ethnically Somali parts of neighbouring Kenya, Ethiopia and Djibouti. Ostensibly for this reason, the Somaliland state has been targeted by the group, though not recently: the last significant attacks occurred in 2008 in Hargeysa against the Presidential Compound, the Ethiopian consulate and the United Nations Development Programme's headquarters in the city. Fearing the impact of destabilization on its nationalist narrative of peaceful independent state development, Somaliland authorities have cooperated closely with Western intelligence agencies (particularly the British[45]) and have developed institutions such as the Police Force's paramilitary Rapid Response Unit to monitor and act on suspicions of extremist activity.

There exists in Somaliland a popular discursive environment that rejects Al Shabaab's militancy, either as a threat to the Republic's independence claims, or as a spectre of 'southern' instability. Nonetheless, the sociocultural influence of reformist Islamism is also visible in the context of Somaliland's relative political stability, partisan competition and functioning democratic system. Somaliland's governmental and judicial structures incorporate elements of Islamic law and all politicians identify as Muslims (as does virtually the entire population). Although certain politicians may have a reputation for a more hard-line 'Islamist' stance, partisan conventions prevent explicit religiously oriented campaigning. Although

Al Shabaab is seen from Hargeysa as a problem facing 'Somalia' (and indicative of insecurity and political mismanagement there), narratives around Islam, Somali 'culture' and foreign influence engineered or exploited by these militants are not absent from Somaliland's own public sphere. Here, while political discourse often revolves around the party system and electoral politics, similar dynamics of socio-religious change, increased expression of public piety[46] and critiques of foreign, 'un-Islamic' influences are frequently visible. High-profile preachers can influence public sentiment around moral controversies, and suspicions of foreign agendas periodically manifest themselves in local debates. Humanitarian agencies have come under scrutiny (or have had staff deported) for alleged Christian proselytizing,[47] while political interventions from *Beesha Caalamka* (the 'International Community') may be interpreted as being culturally or religiously motivated.

During my fieldwork in Hargeysa in 2015, local newspapers were full of heated commentary on the European Union's response to Somaliland's apparent reinstatement of the death penalty after an unofficial moratorium. Commentators were universally opposed to the EU's rebuke, which was seen as an affront to both Islam and the 'national' integrity of Somaliland. At its most extreme, the rhetoric from the Hargeysa mosques stretched to accusations of Western conspiracy: foreign exhortations against the application of Sharia interpreted as a plot to promote insecurity in Somaliland, fomenting violence among the *Ummah*, who would kill each other or become refugees, going to live in camps from which Western agencies or states benefit.[48] Although such conspiracy narratives (which echo the Al Shabaab discourse on Western humanitarian agencies) cannot be said to be directly representative of wider public opinion on the streets of Hargeysa, that they are expressed at all in public is significant, particularly in a context where sensitivities towards religious fidelity are of great popular concern.

Although Al Shabaab exists as one of multiple military-political actors operating in the arena of state contestation in Somalia, it nevertheless occupies a distinctive position within the Somali political imaginary. In popular media discourse beyond Somaliland, Al Shabaab is often seen as sitting at once outside state institutions, while simultaneously also playing an alleged clandestine role within the strategic manoeuvres of these various 'state' power holders. The relative lack of violent Al Shabaab activity in Somaliland, combined with the fact that several high-profile Al Shabaab leaders (including its late Emir, Axmed Cabdi Godane) hailed from the north-west, has fuelled conspiracy theories in Mogadishu, and periodic official allegations from Puntland, that the administration in Hargeysa (or Somaliland-linked business networks) either support or provide safe haven to Al Shabaab operatives. The theory goes that this has been in order for pro-Somaliland elements to destabilize southern or north-eastern Somalia, in pursuit of their own separatist agenda. An apparently bogus account of the 'nexus between Somaliland and Al Shabaab' appeared in February 2016 on the Kenyamedia.net news blog (since taken down). This account by the (fictional) 'Swedish investigative journalists Peter Wolfson & Greta Backstrom' was both reproduced and debunked across Somali cyberspace, and is indicative of the lengths to which parties will go to influence the narrative around Somaliland's relationship with Al Shabaab and, by extension, the wider Somali territories.[49]

Such 'fake news' aside, Puntland officials have in the past directly accused Somaliland of supporting Al Shabaab's operations against its forces in the context of the two autonomous administrations' dispute over their mutual border in Sool and Sanaag regions, though little more than circumstantial evidence was produced to back this up.[50] Turning away from Somaliland to look south, the Puntland Minister of Security, Cabdi Xirsi Qarjab, in 2016, also accused the FGS in Mogadishu of facilitating an Al Shabaab troop movement along the coast north into Puntland-controlled Mudug as a move designed to destabilize his territory.[51] This, he alleged, was due to Puntland's opposition to the '4.5' system of clan representation (being used for MP selection) advocated by the Mogadishu-based government.[52]

A prevalent conspiracy narrative in the Puntland public sphere held that Xasan Sheekh-era FGS authorities in Mogadishu manipulated or even directed Al Shabaab violence for clan-related political objectives. The assassination of Daarood Members of Parliament (discursively associated in these narratives with their 'home territory' of Puntland) in drive-by shootings or high-profile attacks on hotels were cited as evidence for a 'Hawiye' conspiracy against Puntland's interests vis-á-vis the reconstruction of a Federal Government. A piece such as '*Muuqdisho*' on Dunida Online (a Puntland-focused news website), played on the name of the city in question as an 'image of killing', and used various other forms of wordplay to portray a collusion between Al Shabaab ('Al Habaab/the lost') and the Dam Jadiid faction (here 'Dulmi Jadiid' or the 'new oppression') to advance the political agenda of the President.[53] While this polemic was high on emotive rhetoric and low on evidence to substantiate the claims made, it highlighted discursive distinctions between clan 'home' territory (*deegaan*) and the allegedly hostile arena of Mogadishu.[54]

Territorial considerations around security and theories of hidden conspiracy have proliferated among a wider public with a heightened sense of where they may or may not feel safe in Somalia. An outcome of the civil war and the lack of a national political settlement or reconciliation, these personal considerations were noted to me by many different informants across the territories. These were often recounted in relation to people's expectations or experiences when travelling, usually in a professional capacity or 'returning' from the diaspora. While Al Shabaab retains its own distinctive narrative of the wider Somali conflict, these examples illustrate how it has in itself been frequently invoked, spectral-like, by various state political actors to illustrate issues of insecurity (which can be blamed on competing administrations) or outlines of broader political conspiracy. When not engaging domestic political actors, the popular rumour mill also accuses external forces of taking advantage of the Al Shabaab threat: in Mogadishu it has not been uncommon to hear speculation that AMISOM forces are content to allow the conflict with Al Shabaab to continue in order to prolong their deployment and lucrative internationally financed salaries. These narratives have been aided by the apparent pervasiveness of Al Shabaab agents and informants within the Somali state or security apparatuses,[55] fuelling rumours of ulterior motives or hidden agendas vis-á-vis foreign actors who may not know exactly who they are dealing with.[56]

The footprint of the 'Global War on Terror' has expanded in Somalia over recent years, culminating in the Trump administration's 2017 designation of south-central Somalia as a 'theatre of active hostilities'.[57] Although the number of US drone strikes and Special Forces raids against high-value Al Shabaab targets has increased significantly since 2014, this re-categorization of the Somali theatre gave more discretion to military commanders and increased the likelihood of further intensifications of the campaign.[58] These kinetic foreign operations may closely intersect with the agendas or manoeuvres of regional actors across the fragmented Somali political space. For example, in September 2016, a US airstrike targeted a group of fighters in Galmudug region, close to the town of Gaalkacyo. In communication with Puntland authorities across the border (with whom US intelligence maintains links), the targets were initially identified as Al Shabaab fighters and were engaged accordingly. In fact, the 22 men killed in the strike were militia of the Galmudug federal region administration, who subsequently accused Puntland of deliberately misdirecting the US airstrike.[59] Galmudug and Puntland share a disputed border, on which sits the divided town of Gaalkacyo. This city and the borderlands are a frequent flashpoint of conflict over clan-linked disputes around access to pastoral resources such as water points, and a wider political debate over control of the Mudug region, which is currently split (along clan lines) between Puntland and the new Galmudug state.

Another highly contested area where international forces have been highly active is Lower Shabelle. This coastal region is rich in agricultural land and is adjacent to, and runs south from, Mogadishu. Al Shabaab were expelled from the region's primary port towns of Marka and Baraawe in 2012 and 2014, respectively, by advances of AMISOM and FGS troops. However, the group retained a significant presence in the region as well as the ability to move back into urban centres when allied military assets are redeployed elsewhere. Conflict in Lower Shabelle has long been characterized by contestation over land and the influx (and political dominance) of clan groups from outside the region. The expansion of the influence of the Habar Gedir sub-clans of the Hawiye into the region can be traced back to the pursuit of the remnants of the Barre dictatorship southwards from Mogadishu in the early 1990s.[60] Up until the present day, conflict continues between the Habar Gedir and several of the groups who consider themselves indigenous to the region, such as the Biyomaal of the wider Dir clan-family.

The clan dynamics of the region overlap messily with the alignment of 'official' forces active in the area, and the distinctions between 'clan militia' and Somali National Army (SNA) personnel are often blurred. On one side, Al Shabaab has attempted to appeal to so-called minority groups by presenting itself as a neutral governing force that rules by the impartial application of Sharia law.[61] This is emphasized in the group's propaganda, and also demonstrated (to an extent) by cross-clan representation at the highest levels of the organization,[62] and its reported past practice of appointing governors who hail from clans from outside the region and not considered to be implicated in local disputes.[63] On the other side, the expansion of FGS power into Lower Shabelle during the previous government's tenure was largely undertaken by SNA units heavily dominated by the Habar Gedir and enjoying close political links with the capital.

Regardless of these broad dynamics, a clear alignment of forces along clan lines has been difficult to pin down. Patterns of support are highly fluid and often based on short-term calculations of political advantage as opposed to ideology. Al Shabaab leverages the ongoing intercommunal conflict by playing different roles (mediator, instigator, combatant) towards different actors and groups. Furthermore, in this murky security arena, the objectives of Somali National Army personnel or units (ostensibly fighting alongside AMISOM forces, against Al Shabaab) may be unclear. Reports have emerged of soldiers 'moonlighting' as Al Shabaab operatives for opportunistic financial gain, and clan-motivated attacks on civilians by combined forces including SNA, clan-militia *and* Al Shabaab fighters.[64] What is evident is that a complex conflict economy of checkpoint taxation/extortion exists along important trade routes, and that this engages Al Shabaab, SNA and clan militias. A general shift of Biyomaal affiliation towards AMISOM forces had occurred, as suggested by reports from 2017, in an attempt to counterbalance the increasing dominance of Habar Gedir networks that operate through links with both the SNA and Al Shabaab.[65]

It is in this opaque and conspiracy-laden security context that US forces have been intensifying kinetic operations, either unilaterally and directly through drone strikes and special forces raids, or indirectly through operational 'training' of national Somali elite forces and leading SNA units on the ground. In this theatre it is unsurprising that identifying a clearly aligned enemy (Al Shabaab) has been difficult, leading to incidents such as the raid carried out on the village of Bariire in August 2017. This led to the deaths of ten Habar Gedir civilian farmers. Investigative reporting from the *Daily Beast* alleged that Biyomaal-affiliated actors had manipulated intelligence to direct the US-supported operation in this direction.[66]

The international military footprint has clearly further complicated an already potentially bewildering alignment of security actors and political/economic motivations on the ground in different parts of Somalia. Al Shabaab remains, and will continue to remain for the foreseeable future, a significant player across these different fault lines of regional conflict. The group has suffered a number of high- profile defections to the FGS, though the impact of this will likely be limited given the background of some of these figures (such as Mukhtar Roobow who had long been estranged from the top leadership) and the fact that the group has consistently maintained operational capacity in the wake of the targeted killings of earlier commanders. Perhaps most importantly, Al Shabaab revenues appear to have picked up following pressures caused in 2014/2015 by its loss of coastal territory. Al Shabaab collects 'zakat' from individuals and businesses in the hinterland areas it controls. As noted earlier, it also charges levies on trucking across these territories – reportedly in a more consistent and predictable fashion than SNA troops or nominally aligned militias.[67] Even in Mogadishu, Al Shabaab has continued to run a business taxation (or extortion) system in parallel with the FGS, and its violence in the city may, in part, be directed to enforce and maintain this racket.[68] Furthermore, the inability or unwillingness of regional authorities such as the Jubbaland administration in Kismaayo (or Kenyan Forces in the region and on the border) to prevent charcoal exports in accordance with international sanctions has continued to generate revenue for Al Shabaab and those ostensibly anti-Al Shabaab actors themselves.[69]

Al Shabaab's international alignment was tested by the rise of the global 'islamic state' brand, and the group faced internal and external pressure for it to switch its allegiance away from Al Qaeda. This was resisted and a splinter Somali ISIS affiliate emerged in 2015, centred on a Puntland-based ideologue, Cabdulqaadir Muumin. From a kernel of 20 fighters, the group has reportedly expanded in size and attracted recruits from the south, further diversifying its clan makeup.[70] This apparent diversification is, however, only relative to the structures of the wider Somali clan 'system'. Some local reports – based on interviews with defectors – suggest that many of those joining the ISIS-affiliate from the south are leaving an Al Shabaab whose leadership has become increasingly dominated by figures from Hawiye sub-clans.[71] Indeed, the top figures of ISIS in Puntland continue to hail primarily from (a now wider range of) Daarood sub-clans, and not just Muumin's Majeerteen/Cali Saleebaan lineage group.[72]

ISIS's most dramatic operation in the north-east was the taking of the coastal town of Qandala in October 2016. It withdrew from this position prior to a Puntland/US forces ground and sea recapture mission in December of that year. ISIS has maintained its presence in the mountainous Puntland hinterlands and has increased its frequency of asymmetrical attacks on Puntland forces and attempted assassinations in Bosaaso, Puntland's commercial port hub. ISIS's increased activity in Puntland may have also prompted the competitive reassertion of Al Shabaab's activities in the region. In June 2017, the latter launched its most deadly conventional assault on a fixed Puntland military position at Af-Urur, killing around 60 *Daraawiish* soldiers.

The Somali ISIS affiliate's tangible operational connections with the group's global network have yet to be proven, and local political dynamics would appear to be determining factors in its ongoing evolution. The organization has received regular arms shipments from Yemen, and may have had an intermediary based there who is linked to ISIS figures in Syria/Iraq.[73] Nonetheless, the continuing and lucrative weapons trade across the Gulf of Aden has long been a feature of the wider Somali conflict, and multiple groups such as Al Shabaab and other local militias have benefited from this smuggling. ISIS-affiliated operatives have increased their activities in Southern Somalia since 2016, with an intensification in 2018 of pistol assassinations of security service-linked personnel, and IED attacks in Mogadishu and Afgooye. Nonetheless, ISIS has remained a much smaller player than Al Shabaab in the south, and operational links between its cells and ISIS in Puntland remain unclear and potentially tenuous.[74]

The ambiguous spectre of ISIS aside, of greater overall significance to the wider security picture in Somalia is the planned process of withdrawal of African Union Forces from southern and central regions. If the current timetable is not revised, this could mean the continued drawing down of the the 21,000-strong

AMISOM contingent after the next scheduled (s)election process for a new Somali Government in 2020/2021. At the time of writing, serious questions still remain as to the potential for regional and national security forces to effectively fill the inevitable security vacuum. The Somali National Army is compromised by a lack of operational capacity and sufficient equipment, and unit divisions along clan lines remain prevalent. This current disorder is evidenced in the previous discussion of conflicts in Lower Shabelle. A high-level multilateral London conference held in May 2017 focused on security sector reform and the need for the integration of federal and regional forces. A 'National Security Architecture' funded with an extra £21 million of UK support was formulated, although evidence has yet to emerge that significant progress has been made in this area of force integration.[75]

Conclusion

In Somalia's complex security environment, and in an era of fragmented news and 'post-truth' narratives of conflict, it can be difficult to pin down exactly what Al Shabaab 'is' in relation to both state contestation in the region and the so-called global jihad. With this in mind, the chapter has attempted to do two things: First, it has problematized straightforward notions of 'radicalization' in the complex and contentious sociocultural environment of a fragmented Somalia. Second, it has highlighted multiple *political* understandings of global jihad that can be read into the conflict against and between the different authorities that struggle for influence across the territory. Underwriting these politics, a dense conflict economy has emerged in which Al Shabaab engages as one actor among many. Nevertheless, Al Shabaab's penchant for spectacular terrorist violence, the maintenance of its clandestine cross-clan and cross-regional networks, and its international reputation in the Global War on Terror, all make the organization distinct in the wider Somali political environment. These characteristics contribute to its spectralization in the commentary of many local actors, and its militancy (while transnational in scope) has engaged contentious ideological debates around the cultural-religious identity of new governance structures across the Somali territories.

Amid the material realpolitik that characterizes the ongoing federal or secessionist reconfiguration of the Somali state (or states), it can be easy to dismiss these cultural and ideological elements of the conflict. This chapter has emphasized the complex intertwining of political and ideological influences, which structure the agency and world views of actors in an arena of extreme fragmentation. A purely instrumentalist account of Al Shabaab ideologues manipulating and brainwashing a generation of uneducated and marginalized youth into suicide operations for a religiously misguided jihad is inadequate in that it overlooks the potentially elite backgrounds of some of those fighters who themselves willingly give up their lives in military or terrorist attacks, and the risks faced by an insurgent leadership in taking on US power in the Horn of Africa.[76] Such recognition is not intended to romanticize Al Shabaab's campaign but, rather, forces us to think more deeply about the agency and motivations of 'radical' ideologues, military planners and would-be Islamist governors who operate under the constant threat of death by *Reaper* drones and *Hellfire* missiles.

Conceptualizing radicalization in Somalia as constituting a kind of counter-public to a coherent, consolidated secular state is unhelpful, as such conditions (whether imagined in a European or post-Arab Spring context) simply do not exist. State authority has been fractured and contested across these territories for at least the last quarter of a century and even today there is no sovereign power that enjoys (even nominal) control over the entirety of Somalia. Skirting around the wider socio-religious and political context of 'radicalization', external studies on 'Countering Violent Extremism' may make such explanatory statements as the following: 'It is significant that all the interviewees [demobilized Al Shabaab recruits] grew up in areas where Muslims were in the majority and that they had a very negative perception of religious diversity and acceptance of other religions.'[77] This prompts the question as to where in Somalia this is *not* the case? Where in Somalia (or Somaliland) does religious diversity (particularly in terms of other faiths) actually exist? It may be unfair to highlight this particular comment in isolation; however, I would argue that it reflects many similar 'CVE' analyses, which tend to dichotomize 'radical' and 'legitimate' political agency. This comes at the expense of more accurate presentations of discursive and socio-religious complexity on the ground, and a blurring of these problematically pejorative categorizations.

These types of studies are not without merit and often accurately identify many of the key and interlinked factors involved in Al Shabaab youth recruitment: economic motivations, lack of alternative educational or employment prospects, prior exposure to violence, and religio-nationalist sentiment directed against malignant foreign influence. This chapter has not attempted to replicate this type of explanatory account for 'radicalization' but has, instead, argued that 'radical' narratives can be usefully understood in terms of conspiracy theorization within the context of a wider and decentred public sphere of political communication. This discussion of religious practice and culture in modern Somalia has not conflated religious militancy with political Islam or broader socio-religious change. It has, instead, attempted to present a more nuanced and comparative account of how terminologies of the 'global jihad' are popularly understood in different Somali contexts characterized by ongoing processes of state-reconfiguration, continued fragmentation and perceived foreign interference. This account demonstrates how the very vocabularies of the War on Terror – and the spectres of religious violence themselves – become political symbols and practical tools actively utilized in state-contestation processes in the post-9/11 world. As such, they demand critical attention not simply for generating understandings of radical violence, but also in terms of their impact on the potential for state-building in other political arenas affected by prolonged conflict.

Notes

1 I am grateful to Mahad Wasuge of Somali Public Agenda for his comments on a draft of this chapter.

2. This chapter uses standard Somali orthography and spelling for Somali names (e.g., Xasan, as opposed to Hassan).
3. Jurgen Habermas, *The Structural Transformation of the Public Sphere: An Inquiry into a Category of Bourgeois Society* (Cambridge: The MIT Press, 1991).
4. Thomas C. Wolfe, 'The most invisible hand: Russian journalism and media-context', in G. Marcus (ed.), *Cultural Producers In Perilous States: Editing Events, Documenting Change Volume* 4 (Chicago: University of Chicago Press, 1997), p. 70.
5. Mark Fenster, *Conspiracy Theories: Secrecy and Power in American Culture* (Minneapolis: University of Minnesota Press, 2008).
6. Ilya Yablokov, 'Conspiracy theories as a Russian public diplomacy tool: The case of Russia today', *Politics*, 35, nos. 3–4 (2015): 301–15; David Patrikarakos, *War in 140 Characters: How Social Media Is Reshaping Conflict in the Twenty-First Century* (New York: Basic Books, 2017).
7. Manni Crone, 'Radicalization revisited: Violence, politics and the skills of the body', *International Affairs*, 92, no. 3 (2016): 587–604.
8. Ibid., p. 600.
9. Randy Borum, 'Radicalization into violent extremism I: A review of social science theories', *Journal of Strategic Security*, 4, no. 4 (2011): 7–36; Peter Neumann, 'The trouble with radicalization', *International Affairs*, 89, no. 4 (2013): 873–93.
10. Quintan Wiktorowicz, 'Anatomy of the Salafi movement', *Studies in Conflict & Terrorism*, 29, no. 3 (2006): 207–39; Thomas Hegghammer, 'Jihadi-Salafis or revolutionaries? On religion and politics in the study of militant Islamism', in R. Meijer (ed.), *Global Salafism: Islam's New Religious Movement* (London: Hurst, 2008), pp. 244–66.
11. Intergovernmental Authority on Development (IGAD) report, 'Al Shabaab as a transnational security threat', March 2016. Available at https://igadssp.org/index.php/documentation/4-igad-report-al-shabaab-as-a-transnational-security-threat.
12. Matt Bryden, 'The reinvention of Al Shabaab', Centre for Strategic and International Studies report, February 2014. Available at https://www.csis.org/analysis/reinvention-al-shabaab.
13. Hiraal Institute Report, 'The Al Shabaab finance system', Mogadishu, July 2018. Available at https://hiraalinstitute.org/wp-content/uploads/2018/07/AS-Finance-System.pdf.
14. Peter Chonka, 'News media and political contestation in the Somali territories: Defining the parameters of a transnational digital public', *Journal of Eastern African Studies*, 13, no. 1 (2019): 140–57.
15. Hussein M. Adam, 'Political Islam in Somali history', in M. Hoehne and V. Luling (eds), *Milk and Peace, Drought and War: Somali Culture, Society and Politics* (London: Hurst, 2010), pp. 119–35.
16. Abdurahman M. Abdullahi, 'Women, Islamists and the military regime in Somalia: The new family law and its implications', in M. Hoehne and V. Luling (eds), *Milk and Peace, Drought and War: Somali Culture, Society and Politics* (London: Hurst, 2010), pp. 137–60.
17. Abdi I. Samatar, 'Destruction of state and society in Somalia: Beyond the tribal convention', *The Journal of Modern African Studies*, 30, no. 4 (1992): 625–41; Cabdishakur Mire Aadam, *Kobocii Islaamiyiinta Soomaaliya* [Rise of the Islamists in Somalia] (Nairobi: Horyaal Printing, 2013).
18. Daniel Compagnon, 'Somali armed movements', in Christopher Clapham (ed.), *African Guerillas* (Oxford: James Currey, 1998), pp. 73–90.

19 Mark Bradbury, *Becoming Somaliland* (Bloomington: James Currey, 2008); Lidwien Kapteijns, *Clan Cleansing in Somalia: The Ruinous Legacy of 1991* (Philadelphia: University of Pennsylvania Press, 2012).
20 Catherine Besteman, 'Primordialist blinders: A reply to IM Lewis', *Cultural Anthropology*, 13, no. 1 (1998): 109–20; Ioan Lewis, 'Doing violence to ethnography: A response to Catherine Besteman's "representing violence and 'othering' Somalia"', *Cultural Anthropology*, 13, no. 1 (1998): 100–8.
21 Cedric Barnes, 'The Somali Youth League, Ethiopian Somalis and the Greater Somalia idea, C. 1946–48', *Journal of Eastern African Studies*, 1, no. 2 (2007): 277–91; Lee Cassanelli, 'Hosts and guests: A historical interpretation of land conflicts in Southern and Central Somalia', *RVI Research Paper: Rift Valley Institute* (Nairobi: Rift Valley Institute, 2015). Available at http://www.riftvalley.net/publication/hosts-and-guests#.Vdm91peYGJI; Virginia Luling, 'Genealogy as theory, genealogy as tool: Aspects of Somali "clanship"', *Social Identities*, 12, no. 4 (2008): 471–85.
22 Alex DeWaal, *Islamism and Its Enemies in the Horn of Africa* (London: Hurst, 2004).
23 Exceptions here being: Cedric Barnes and Harun Hassan, 'The rise and fall of Mogadishu's Islamic courts', *Journal of Eastern African Studies*, 1, no. 2 (2007): 151–60; Oskar G. Mwangi, 'The Union of Islamic Courts and security governance in Somalia', *African Security Review*, 19, no. 1 (2010): 88–94; Aisha Ahmad, 'The security bazaar: Business interests and Islamist power in civil war Somalia', *International Security*, 39, no. 3 (2015): 89–117.
24 Human Rights Watch, 'So much to fear: War crimes and the devastation of Somalia', 8 December 2008. Available at https://www.hrw.org/report/2008/12/08/so-much-fear/war-crimes-and-devastation-somalia (accessed 1 August 2019).
25 Stig J. Hansen, *Al-Shabaab in Somalia: The History and Ideology of a Militant Islamist Group, 2005-2012* (London: Hurst, 2013).
26 Peter Chonka, 'New media, performative violence, and state reconstruction in Mogadishu', *African Affairs*, 117, no. 468 (2018): 392–414.
27 Jason Mosley, 'Somalia's federal future: Layered agendas, risks and opportunities', Horn of Africa Project Report, Chatham House, London, 2015. Available at https://www.chathamhouse.org/publication/somalias-federal-future-layered-agendas-risks-and-opportunities.
28 Rasnah Warah, *War Crimes: How Warlords, Politicians, Foreign Governments and Aid Agencies Conspired to Create a Failed State in Somalia* (Bloomington: Author House, 2014), p. 11.
29 Alex DeWaal, 'Africa's $700 billion problem waiting to happen', *Foreign Policy*, 17 March 2016. Available at http://foreignpolicy.com/2016/03/17/africas-700-billion-problem-waiting-to-happen-ethiopia-horn-of-africa/ (accessed 19 March 2016).
30 Muhyadin Ahmed Roble, '"Neutral" Somalia finds itself engulfed in Saudi Arabia-Qatar dispute', *African Arguments*, 16 August 2017. Available at http://africanarguments.org/2017/08/16/neutral-somalia-finds-itself-engulfed-in-saudi-arabia-qatar-dispute/ (accessed 16 August 2017).
31 Ronen Bergman and David D. Kirkpatrick, 'With guns, cash and terrorism, Gulf states vie for power in Somalia', *New York Times,* 22 July 2019. Available at https://www.nytimes.com/2019/07/22/world/africa/somalia-qatar-uae.html (accessed 23 July 2019).
32 See Xaqiiqa Times newspaper editorial, Mogadishu, 10–23 March 2015, *'Dam Jadiid ma ihi'* ['I'm not Dam Jadiid']. The writer gives an overview of the various Islamist cliques jockeying for position in Mogadishu and decries the lack of clear partisan competition.
33 Somali Federal Government, Deputy Prime Minister Maxamed Cumar Carte, Chatham House, London, 16 March 2016 (event held 'on the record').

34 For example of this usage see: Keydmedia, 'Prof Togane yiri Soomaali waxaa baabiiay Darood' ['Prof. Togane says The Soomaali were destroyed by the Daarood'], December 2014. Available at http://www.keydmedia.net/news/article/prof._togane_yiri_soomaali_waxaa_baabiiyay_daarood_-_cakaara_action_gr/ (accessed 27 May 2015). Here the writer alleges a 'Daarood' conspiracy against the FGS by a group of 'extremists who believe in clan ideology'.

35 Peter Chonka, 'Spies, stonework and the suuq: Somali nationalism and the narrative politics of Harakat Al Shabaab Al Mujaahidiin's online propaganda', *Journal of Eastern African Studies*, 10, no. 2 (2016): 247–65; Alexander Meleagrou-Hitchens, Shiraz Maher and J. Sheehan, 'Lights, camera, jihad: Al-Shabaab's western media strategy', International Centre for the Study of Radicalisation and Political Violence Report, 2012. Available at http://icsr.info/2012/11/icsr-report-lights-camera-jihad-al-shabaabs-western-media-strategy/; Christopher Anzalone, 'Al-Shabab's tactical and media strategies in the wake of its battlefield setbacks', *Combating Terrorism Centre Sentinel*, West Point (2013). Available at https://www.ctc.usma.edu/posts/al-shababs-tactical-and-media-strategies-in-the-wake-of-its-battlefield-setbacks.

36 AS Spokesman Sheekh Cali 'Dheere' gives press statement detailing their 'operation against the Xalane camp and the large scale damage caused' *('Dhageyso:Hoggaanka Xarakada Al Shabaab oo faah faahiyay howlgalkii xerada Xalane ee khasaaraha badan dhaliyay.')* 25 December 2014. Available at http://somalimemo.net/articles/1794/DhageysoHoggaanka-Xarakada-Al-Shabaab-Oo-Faah-Faahiyay-Howlgalkii-Xerada-Xalane-Ee-Khasaaraha-Badan-Dhaliyay (accessed 27 December 2014).

37 Mohamed Musa Shiikh Noor, *'Waa kuma xag-jirku!?'* ['Who is the radical!?'], published first on Laashin.com, 15 January 2015. Available at http://laashin.com/?p=1013 and then reproduced on pro-Jihadi Voice of Somalia platform on 2 February 2015. Available at https://voiceofsomalia.net/2015/02/02/maqaal-waa-kuma-xag-jirku/ (accessed 4 June 2014).

38 I am grateful to journalist Liban Ahmed for drawing my attention to this type of language. See Radio Mogadishu, *'Ololaha talaalka ka hortaga UGUS oo galabta furmay'* ['Campaign for inoculation against UGUS commenced this afternoon'] 18 May 2015. Available at http://www.radioMogadishu.net/ololaha-talaalka-ka-hortaga-ugus-oo-galabta-furmay/ (accessed 29 May 2015).

39 David Laitin, *Politics, Language, and Thought: The Somali Experience* (Chicago: University of Chicago Press, 1977).

40 Chonka, 'Spies'.

41 For an example of this type of commentary see Xaashi Yassiin Cismaan, *'Waa wareeeey!!'* ['A call for help'] 23 December 2013. Available at http://www.raxanreeb.com/2013/12/waa-wareeeeeeey-wq-xaashi-yaasiin-cismaan (accessed 22 May 2015).

42 Markus Hoehne, 'The rupture of territoriality and the diminishing relevance of cross-cutting ties in Somalia after 1990', *Development and Change*, 47, no. 6 (2016): 1379–1411.

43 Matt Bryden, '"The banana test": Is Somaliland ready for recognition?' *Annales d'Ethiopie*, 19, no. 1 (2003), Editions de la Table Ronde.

44 Marleen Renders, *Consider Somaliland: State-Building with Traditional Leaders and Institutions* (Leiden: Brill, 2012).

45 United Kingdom Parliamentary records, 'Gifting of equipment (Somaliland)', 19 November 2013. Available at http://www.publications.parliament.uk/pa/cm201314/cmhansrd/cm131119/wmstext/131119m0001.htm.

46 Marja Tiilikainen, 'Spirits in the human world in Northern Somalia', in M. Hoehne and V. Luling (eds), *Milk and Peace, Drought and War: Somali Culture, Society and Politics* (London: Hurst, 2010), pp. 163–84.

47 Somaliland Live.com, *'Sheekh Aden Sunne oo sheegay in ay Hargeisa joogaan rag faafinaya Diinta Kiristanka'* [Sheekh Aden Sunne says that there is a man in Hargeysa promoting Christianity], 16 March 2013. Available at http://somalilandlive.com/articles/3586/Sheekh-Aden-Sunne-Oo-Sheegay-in-ay-Hargeisa-Joogaan-Ragg-Faafinay a-Diinta-Kiristanka (accessed 20 March 2013). This particular preacher has waged a campaign against alleged Christian missionary activity in Hargeysa and has succeeded in lobbying the Somaliland government to deport this particular individual (a doctor) as well as a Norwegian humanitarian organization (NNM) in 2014. Sheekh Sunne's provocative preaching (and ambiguous support for a Somali Jihad) has attracted the attention of Somaliland security forces wary of 'extremist' rhetoric and he has been detained on several occasions.

48 The Imam of the Daarul Quraan Mosque in Xawaadle neighbourhood, Hargeysa, quoted in *Saxansaxo* newspaper Hargeysa, 18 April 2015.

49 Sola, *'Wada shaqeynta Somaliland iyo Al Shabaab ee la yiri waxaa soo qoray wariyaal Swedish ah maxaa ka jira? SOLA investigates'* ['Cooperation between Somaliland and Al Shabaab said to be written by Swedish journalists – what's it all about?' SOLA investigates], 17 February 2016. Available at http://solaportal.com/Archive/2016/2/56s olaportal (accessed 24 March 2016).

50 *Xog-doon* newspaper, Mogadishu, *'Puntland oo ku eedeysay Somaliland inay taageerto xoogaga Al-Shabaab ee Galgala'* ['Puntland accuses Somaliland of supporting Al Shabaab in Galgala'], 31 January 2014.

51 *Horn Cable TV, 'Puntland oo Xukuumada Somaliya ku eedaysay galitaanka Alshabab gudaha Puntland'* ['Puntland accuses the Government of Somalia over the Al Shabaab incursion inside Puntland'], 15 March 2016. Available at https://www.youtube.com/watch?v=f1fpzutR2Ew (accessed 20 March 2016).

52 An agreement forged between Mogadishu and states that the 2016/2017 process would be the last time that the '4.5' mechanism would be used, paving the way for future one-person-one-vote elections. Some political actors (e.g., in Puntland or Jubaland) oppose the '4.5' system in that it is felt to disadvantage the Daarood who are geographically the most widespread of the main clan families across the Somali Horn (a fact they would argue is not reflected in their share of the '4.5' representation).

53 Ahmed Yusuf Ahmed, 'Muuq-disho', *Dunida Online*, 29 March 2015. Available at http://dunidaonline.com/index.php?id=14345 (accessed 1 June 2015).

54 Muuse Xaji Abees, *'Digniin culus ku socota xildhibaanada daarood'* ['Strong warning to Daarood MPs'], *Dunida Online*, 20 July 2014. Available at http://www.dunidaonline.com/index.php?id=12999 (accessed 8 June 2015).

55 Hills (2016) presents anecdotal evidence of FGS soldiers in Mogadishu 'sympathetic' to Al Shabaab. Stories of defections and infiltration are a common feature of news, propaganda and rumours in the city. Alice Hills, 'Making Mogadishu safe', *RUSI Journal*, 161, no. 6 (2016): 10–16 (p. 15).

56 *The Africa Report*, 'Ugandan officers in Somalia trained Al Shabaab fighters', 16 April 2014. Available at http://www.theafricareport.com/East-Horn-Africa/ugandan-army-officers-in-somalia-trained-al-shabab-fighters.html (accessed 3 December 2015).

57 *New York Times*, 'Trump eases combat rules in Somalia intended to protect civilians', 30 March 2017. Available at https://www.nytimes.com/2017/03/30/world/africa/trump-is-said-to-ease-combat-rules-in-somalia-designed-to-protect-civilians.html (accessed 1 April 2017).

58 Jason Burke, 'Somali citizens count cost surge of US airstrikes under Trump', *The Guardian*, 23 January 2018. Available at https://www.theguardian.com/world/2018/j

an/23/somali-citizens-count-cost-of-surge-in-us-airstrikes-under-trump (accessed 23 January 2018).
59 Abdi Sheikh, 'US accused of killing 22 in misdirected Somalia airstrike', *Reuters*, 28 September 2016. Available at https://www.reuters.com/article/us-somalia-security/u-s-accused-of-killing-22-in-misdirected-somalia-air-strike-idUSKCN11Y0UC (accessed 1 October 2016).
60 Catherine Besteman and Lee Cassanelli, eds, *The Struggle for Land in Southern Somalia; The War Behind the War* (Washington: Westview, 2000); Alex DeWaal, 'Class and power in a stateless Somalia', *Social Science Research Council* 20 (2007). Available at http://hornofafrica.ssrc.org/dewaal/.
61 At one point a majority of AS's rank and file were believed to hail from Digil & Mirifle (A.K.A. Raxanweyne) sub-clans, recruited in large numbers in part because of the historical grievances of these primarily agro-pastoralist clans in the inter-riverine areas of south-central Somalia against the predations of dominant pastoral clans, particularly in the post-1991 civil war period (see Hussein Solomon, 'Somalia's Al Shabaab: Clans vs. Islamist nationalism', *South African Journal of International Affairs*, 21, no. 3 (2016): 351–66 (p. 352)). This balance likely shifted somewhat after 2010's failed Ramadan offensive on the FGS/AMISOM in Mogadishu (where the majority of frontline casualties were suffered by these groups) and the subsequent defection of charismatic AS commander Mukhtar Roobow along with a significant contingent of his clansmen. There is currently little verifiable data about the current makeup of AS rank and file and while the Digil & Mirifle may represent a significant proportion of the group's fighters in the Bay and Bakool regions, this is not necessarily reflected in the clan makeup of senior AS leadership. See Hiraal Institute Report, 'Taming the clans: Al Shabaab's clan politics', Mogadishu, 31 May 2018, pp. 2–3.
62 A 'most wanted' list of high-level AS figures published in 2015 by the FGS included clan affiliations and illustrated this diversity of backgrounds across the major Somali 'clan-families'. See *Halgan.net*, 'Dowladda Federaalka Soomaaliya oo lacag dul dhigtay 11 hogaamiye oo ka tirsan Al-shabaab' ['The Federal Government puts money on the head of 11 Al Shabaab leaders'] 9 April 2015. Available at http://halgan.net/2015/04/dowladda-federaalka-soomaaliya-oo-lacag-dul-dhigtay-11-hogaamiye-oo-ka-tirsan-al-shabaab/ (accessed 1 May 2015).
63 Hansen, *Al Shabaab*, p. 80.
64 United Nations Monitoring Group on Somalia and Eritrea, report S/2016/919 (October 2016), Annex 7.5. p. 161.
65 United Nations Monitoring Group on Somalia and Eritrea, report S/2017/924 (November 2017), p. 17.
66 Christina Goldbaum, 'Strong evidence that U.S. special operations forces massacred civilians in Somalia', *The Daily Beast*, 29 November 2017. Available at https://www.thedailybeast.com/strong-evidence-that-us-special-operations-forces-massacred-civilians-in-somalia (accessed 29 November 2017).
67 United Nations Monitoring Group on Somalia and Eritrea, report S/2017/924 (November 2017) p. 40.
68 Evidence of the link between the payment (or non-payment) of 'protection money' and AS's targeting of certain hotels is difficult to prove. However, the FGS recognizes the problem of Al Shabaab's parallel 'taxation' system and has warned businesses that they will be subject to prosecution if they pay (Security Minister Maxamed Abuukar Ducaale, statement to local press, 22 July 2017).

69 United Nations Monitoring Group on Somalia and Eritrea, report S/2017/924 (November 2017), p. 46.
70 Ibid., p. 15.
71 Hiraal Institute Report, 'Taming the clans', p. 5.
72 United Nations Monitoring Group on Somalia and Eritrea, report S/2017/924 (November 2017), p. 68.
73 Ibid., p. 65.
74 Caleb Weiss, 'Analysis: Islamic State ramps up attack claims in Somalia', *Long War Journal*, 9 May 2018. Available at https://www.longwarjournal.org/archives/2018/05/analysis-islamic-state-ramps-up-attack-claims-in-somalia.php (accessed 12 May 2018).
75 London Somalia Conference, 'Security pact', 11 May 2017. Available at https://www.gov.uk/government/publications/london-somalia-conference-2017-security-pact.
76 *The Star Newspaper*, 'Garissa campus terrorist was a law graduate', 4 June 2015. http://www.the-star.co.ke/news/2015/04/06/garissa-campus-terrorist-was-a-law-graduate_c1113802 (accessed 5 June 2015); see also the case of Somaliland opposition party leader Faysal Cali, 'Waraabe's son joining "Islamic State" in Syria: BBC Somali Service', *Faysal: Wiilku waa wiilkeyga* [Faysal: 'The boy is mine'] 6 August 2014. Available at http://www.bbc.com/somali/maqal_iyo_muuqaal/2014/08/140806_warabe (accessed 7 August 2014).
77 Anneli Botha and Mahdi Abdile, 'Radicalisation and al-Shabaab recruitment in Somalia', *Institute for Security Studies Papers*, 266, no. 20 (2014): 6.

GLOBAL OR LOCAL? EXPLORING THE EMERGENCE AND OPERATION OF A VIOLENT ISLAMIST NETWORK IN KENYA

Ngala Chome

Introduction

On 2 April 2015, four Al Shabaab militants stormed Garissa University College – a campus located in Garissa town near the Kenya-Somalia border in Kenya's north-east region – and killed 148 people, injuring seventy-nine others.[1] The attack came after another by Al Shabaab militants at a prestigious shopping mall in Nairobi on 21 September 2013, when the gunmen laid siege to the mall for hours and killed sixty-seven people, wounding 175.[2] In addition to a series of brutal and protracted killings on the mainland of Lamu County on Kenya's northern coastal region in June–July of 2014, Kenya had suffered 133 attacks attributed to Al Shabaab since the Kenya Defence Forces, or KDF, ventured into Southern Somalia in late 2011 – ostensibly to root out Al Shabaab from its key bases.[3] Following these attacks, former US president, Barrack Obama made a stop in Kenya during his 2015 tour of Africa, where counterterrorism was key among the agenda. During the visit, Kenya's current president Uhuru Kenyatta stated – in a joint news conference with Obama – that 'the battle that we're fighting is not a Kenyan war … Kenya just happens to be the frontier of it, being a neighbor to [Somalia] a country that for a long time has not had any kind of formal government'.[4] Following Kenyatta's remark, and continuing a close relationship between US finance and Kenya's counterterrorism programme, Obama pledged (unspecified) additional funding to Kenya's counterterrorism activities.[5] Several months later, the Kenyan government announced plans to close refugee camps at Dadaab (which borders Somalia in Kenya's north-east region) within a year, citing 'pressing national security concerns'.[6] Confirming critics' assertions that the announcement was a ploy to garner more international assistance for hosting refugees, the government announced a softening of the plans to close the camps after the USA pledged millions to support refugee operations in Kenya.[7]

Kenya's decision to send its military to Somalia had in itself been part of a long-established alliance between the interests of Kenyan elites and those of Western governments in countering the threat of 'global terrorism'.[8] In this relationship, Kenyan elites have been adept at exploiting Western concerns regarding the spread of Islamist violence from the Middle East and South Asia to other parts of the world, presenting it as essentially a non-Kenyan issue, and as a result, ignoring local sources of Islamist violence.[9] This narrative, which ascribes the origins of Islamist violence in Kenya to foreign or 'global' sources, is routinely entwined with common perceptions that regard Kenya's minority Muslim population, of Somalis, Arabs and Swahilis, as foreign.[10] As illustrated earlier, this narrative continues to exist, despite evidence that suggests that Kenyan nationals are planning, fundraising for, and executing most of the attacks attributed to Al Shabaab within Kenya's borders.[11]

Taking a different perspective, this chapter adopts an empirical and descriptive approach to examine the emergence and operation of a Kenyan Islamist network. While the chapter submits that the emergence of an early Islamist network in Kenya (active between 1993 and 2002) was directly inspired by the global objectives of Al Qaeda, the network of Kenyan Islamists that emerged from 2006 is largely driven by a 'glocal' strategy, where local Muslim grievances are increasingly being expressed through a language of 'global Jihad'. In this way, the chapter traces the emergence of an Islamist network in Kenya from 1993 to 2002, when a number of Kenyan nationals made contact with Al Qaeda operatives, and its continued operation since 2006, when Al Shabaab emerged in Somalia. Using this empirical and descriptive approach, the chapter concludes that the simple, yet powerful 'glocal' strategy adopted by this network is based on an Islamist ideology that borrows ideas from Islamic reform movements (especially Wahhabism), which seek a restoration of classical Islamic traditions, in particular, the adoption of Sharia Law as a 'cure for all' solution to what some may regard as improper religious practice and contemporary Muslim marginality.[12] In this way, while Kenyan Islamists might be driven, at least discursively, by the need to reform Islamic practice, that is, rejecting Islamic innovation, or practices regarded as *bi'da*, they, unlike most Islamic reformers, also seek to capture political power – mostly through violent means – through which a redressing of Muslim grievances and a return to classical Islamic traditions can be realized.[13]

The empirical foundations of the chapter include a synthesis of field research that was conducted between February 2015 and August 2016, which was part of related research projects supported separately by the United States Institute of Peace and International Alert. The interviews and Focused Group Discussions involved conversations with religious leaders and clerics, village elders, women and youth activists, administration officials, officials of county governments, local politicians and academics drawn from select neighbourhoods of Mombasa, Nairobi and North-east Kenya. This data was triangulated with secondary literature, including existing academic literature, and newspaper, government and non-governmental reports.

The next section of the chapter examines the literature on Islamist violence in Kenya and East Africa more widely, followed by a discussion of the 'externalizing discourse' of Islamist violence within Kenya, especially how this has been entwined with common perceptions regarding Kenya's minority Muslim population.[14] The fourth section describes the emergence of an early network of violent Islamists in Kenya, while the fifth section examines the operation of a distinctively Kenyan network of Islamists since late 2006. The chapter ends with a few concluding remarks.

Understanding Islamist violence in Kenya and beyond.

The common tendency among analysts and academics studying the origins of Islamist violence in Kenya has been to locate them either in local or external (global) factors, presenting these as separate and distinct. For instance, a number of studies published between 9/11, the day of the Al Qaeda attacks in the United States, and 2011, the year Al Shabaab was implicated in over one-quarter of all recorded violent incidents in Kenya dedicated their analyses to examining the possibility of the Horn of Africa becoming a new springboard for Islamist politics directed from elsewhere.[15] Influenced perhaps by a dominant view that the Horn of Africa merely constituted what Alex de Waal referred to as 'a laboratory for political Islam',[16] this perspective aligned with Roy Olivier's idea of 'exporting jihad' from a centre/core (the Middle East and South Asia) to a periphery (areas outside the centre).[17] The general conclusion was that Al Qaeda (the most influential Islamist organization at the time) had achieved minimal success in attracting the largely Sufi-oriented Muslim community of the region to its Islamist agenda.[18] The 'cause for concern', the authors cautioned, was the region's porous borders, pervasive corruption and low policing capacities that may allow 'international terrorists' to find a safe haven and establish logistical hubs.[19] With the notable exception of Jeffrey Haynes, these analysts made little reference to the political role of Islam in the region, and the debates around participation and citizenship, in which Muslim communities had engaged among themselves and with the region's states since the early 1920s.[20]

A more nuanced, and recently published body of work has nonetheless placed undue emphasis on local factors, in particular, physical state responses to Islamist violence on one level, and the role of a narrative of Muslim marginalization in driving Islamist violence on another.[21] The limitations of this literature, given the fact that many who are affected by marginalization do not, in fact, resort to violence, and that it is often unclear that those among them who do are motivated primarily by these conditions, have been noted by those who examine, instead, the role played by an interplay of socioeconomic conditions and psychosocial factors.[22] In this way, the argument is that socioeconomic conditions, such as the exclusion of Muslim interests, may provide substantial explanations for support for Islamist violence in any given location, but that there is also a very strong case that they can only poorly explain behaviours that contribute to such violence.[23]

These criticisms are common with arguments postulated by Jonathan Githens-Mazer and Robert Lambert, who contend that studies that are specifically focused on the concept of 'Islamist radicalization' are 'plagued by assumption and intuition, [and] are unhappily dominated by "conventional wisdom" rather than systematic scientific and empirically based research'.[24] Adding their voice to the debate, James Khalil and Martine Zuethen – on the same lines as those suggested by Githens-

Mazer and Lambert – have argued that understanding the particular context in which the Islamist violence in question has occurred is key, and that accounts that posit universal explanations for such violence should be treated with scepticism.[25]

Following this precedent, a number of studies have found that the reasons for joining Islamist movements are diverse and varied, and that ideology alone might not offer substantial explanations for involvement in Islamist violence.[26] Despite this observation, it is important to note that Islamist movements invest heavily in presenting themselves as driven primarily by the conventions of an Islamist ideology, and that this is crucial to their recruitment strategies. For instance, Roland Marchal, who examined Al Shabaab recruitment strategies in Somalia, suggested that their success was based on their ability to play religious emotions and engage a smart process of de-socialization or re-socialization. Marchal argued that Al Shabaab membership offers more than just a salary and a weapon, but a way for one to live his or her faith within a community that shares the same values.[27] Stig Jarle Hansen implicitly agrees, and notes that while motives for joining Al Shabaab are highly varied, these usually include a quest for justice through Sharia legislation, and an idea of 'defensive or offensive jihad'.[28] This way of understanding the world is itself empowering. Membership can be compared to a conversion process, which can be considered a central benefit – more than access to material resources – of participating in 'jihad movements'.[29]

Stressing the significance of ideology in Islamist violence, Muhsin Hassan suggests that 'to convince a Muslim that paradise is waiting, Al Shabaab must justify that one's struggle is indeed valid jihad'.[30] Hassan then explains that most of his informants (former Al Shabaab members) admitted to not being well versed in Islam, and as such, the task of recruitment was not particularly challenging.[31] Despite this, the 'conversion' process one undergoes ensures that previous 'social outcasts' within mainstream society become 'heroes' in an alternative world offered by membership in Al Shabaab.[32] This chapter will also illustrate how Kenya's violent Islamist network self-legitimizes, similar to Al Shabaab tactics in Somalia, on the basis of an Islamist ideology, through which local Muslim concerns are increasingly being expressed using a language of 'global Jihad'.[33] It is this 'glocalization' strategy that provides a powerful narrative through which a section of Kenya's minority Muslim population have been drawn into the ranks of a distinctively Kenyan Islamist network.

Externalizing the sources of Islamist violence in Kenya

On 8 August 1998, and again on 28 November 2002, Kenya became a victim of 'terrorist' attacks claimed by Al Qaeda in East Africa (AQEA), the now defunct East African cell of Al Qaeda. Two-hundred and thirteen people died in the truck bombing targeting the American embassy in Nairobi, injuring hundreds of others, while fifteen died in the second attack targeting an Israeli-owned hotel north of Mombasa, which injured tens of more people. Prior to these attacks, Kenya, a predominantly Christian country – and where a publicized narrative of 'peace' had constantly been deployed by the state since the country gained its independence from Britain in 1963 – had no previous history of violence with religious overtones.

Following the attacks, a public and dominant narrative externalizing the causes of Islamist violence in Kenya ensued, despite evidence, which emerged from the investigations of the two attacks, that an East African cell of Al Qaeda had been active in Kenya since 1993.[34] While the cast of men involved in the first attack was largely non-Kenyan, those involved in the second, including the suicide bombers, Haruni Bamusa and Fumo Mohamed, were Kenyan.[35] A few days after the first attack in August 1998, the then president, Daniel Arap Moi, was videoed stating that the 'perpetrators of the blast could not have done the deed if they were Christians'.[36] In the aftermath of the second attack, John Sawe, who was then Kenya's ambassador to Israel, said, 'There is no doubt in my mind that Al Qaeda is behind this attack, because we have no domestic problems, no terrorism in our country, and we have no problem with our neighbours, no problem whatsoever.'[37]

This framing of common perceptions regarding Kenya's minority Muslim population within a wider narrative that externalizes the origins of Islamist violence in Kenya found resonance with Western perspectives on the global manifestations of Islamist politics as well. For Kenya, the proposals of a US Military Academy's Combating Terrorism Center (CTC) report that summed up the American perspective were instructive: Kenya's lax security, open borders and proximity to Somalia, were all considered as factors that made Kenya particularly attractive for Al Qaeda.[38] In addition, the report singled out Kenya's Somali and Arab/Swahili minorities concentrated on the Kenya coast and North-east Kenya as the primary players, due to their closer ties outside Kenya: in Somalia and the Middle East.[39]

These assumptions would soon be translated into physical state responses to Islamist violence within Kenya. The responses, as a result, provided evidence for the state's hostility towards the minority Muslim population – a hostility that may have been informed by the attempts of a section of Kenyan Muslims to either secede, or seek autonomy from the rest of Kenya, on the eve of Kenyan independence from British colonial rule in the early 1960s.[40] For instance, in September 2003, after the second attack, Kenyan police arrested 800 individuals in the historically Muslim-dominated coastal city of Mombasa, which was part of a wider campaign in which an estimated 1,200 individuals, mostly Arabs, Swahilis and foreigners, were arrested in an effort to identify terrorism suspects.[41] This began a trend, where the Kenyan police, acting through the Anti-terrorist Police Unit (ATPU) that was established in 2003, would embark on a programme of not only arbitrary arrests, detention and interrogation of young Swahili, Somali and Arab men, but also rendition of suspects to foreign countries.[42] In 2007, when a new wave of Somali refugees to Kenya followed the US-backed military intervention by Ethiopian proxy forces against the Islamic Courts Union (ICU) in Mogadishu, the Kenyan government responded by shutting the border, citing security reasons.[43] In addition, refugee registration services were suspended, leaving thousands stranded and hundreds of asylum seekers forcibly returned by Kenyan authorities.[44]

The sum of these policy actions – all of which were aimed at salvaging Kenya's international image by presenting the problem of Islamist violence as distinctively non-Kenyan and therefore, of manageable proportions – came when Kenya decided to intervene militarily in Southern Somalia in late 2011.[45] While the operation, code-named *Linda Nchi* (Protect the Nation), came after a series of kidnappings of foreign tourists and aid workers in parts of the Kenya coast and North-east Kenya, it was later revealed that such a plan was already in existence by 2009, and was meant to create an autonomous administration in Southern Somalia that would act as a buffer region between Kenya and Al Shabaab-controlled territory.[46] The then Kenyan Minister of Internal Security, George Saitoti, echoed these sentiments when he said, 'Kenya has been and remains an island of peace and we shall not allow criminals from Somalia, which has been fighting for over two decades, to destabilise our peace.'[47] In addition to shutting the border again, and stopping registration of new refugee arrivals, the Kenyan government launched security crackdowns in predominantly Somali and Muslim neighbourhoods in Nairobi and Mombasa ostensibly to flush out illegal immigrants and Al Shabaab members.[48] During one such operation, which was conducted in the predominantly Somali neighbourhood of Eastleigh in Nairobi in April 2014, the then Assistant Minister for Internal security, Orwa Ojode, was quoted as saying '[terrorism] is a big animal with its head in Eastleigh, and its tail in Somalia'.[49]

Despite this externalization, the dominant Muslim perspective within Kenya of the responses to Islamist violence was that they presented the latest example of state hostility towards Muslim activism.[50] State suspicions towards Muslim politics in Kenya are as old as the postcolonial state itself. During the 1950s to the early 1960s, a series of district-based political organizations emerged on the Muslim-dominated Kenyan coast to demand the full autonomy of the Protectorate of Kenya, which was a narrow strip of the East African coast that stretched from Lamu to the Tanzanian border.[51] Britain had administered the protectorate, but per an 1895 treaty with the Sultan of Zanzibar, the Sultan had retained nominal sovereignty.[52] Muslims on the coast were of the opinion that postcolonial domination by a government dominated by Christian up-country elites would be disastrous for their future.[53] In addition, a proposal for the predominantly Muslim, Somali-dominated north-eastern region to join, not an independent Kenya, but a 'Greater Somalia' republic had been popular among the Somali population of what was in colonial Kenya referred to as the Northern Frontier District.[54] Both proposals – coastal autonomy and Greater Somalia – were rejected by an emerging class of Christian political elites from Western Kenya, the central highlands and the coast. The debates these proposals elicited were accusatory and recriminatory, with Christian political elites asking Somalis to vacate Kenya without an inch of Kenyan territory, and castigating Arabs and Swahilis as 'foreigners' who were – through their previous colonial status as 'non-natives' – deemed to have acquired significant privilege at the expense of a majority of 'black' Kenyans.[55] In sum, these proposals by the Muslims of Kenya revealed, quite early enough, Muslim anxieties in joining a postcolonial state largely thought to be secular only in its nominal sense, where Christian imagery was to come and provide the dominant language of power.[56]

As a result, the political voice of Kenyan Muslims would largely be muted for close to three decades after Kenyan independence. This changed with a wider ushering of political liberalization in the 1990s, especially after the repeal of Section 2A of Kenya's former constitution which allowed for the return to multiparty elections in 1992. The result of these political changes was that Muslim concerns would re-enter Kenya's public discourse.[57] This was symbolized by debates – pitying the state and a significant section of Kenya's population of Muslims – on the registration of a proposed Islamic Party of Kenya (IPK) that the government refused to register.[58] While the IPK sought to mobilize the voice of a religious social group, the list of grievances it presented was distinctively secular: Muslim discrimination in education and in state employment, frustrations faced by Muslims when applying for identity papers, perceptions that regarded Muslims as foreigners.[59] While supporters of the party staged mass protests on the streets of Mombasa for the first few years of the 1990s, the unregistered party was decisively defeated by 1997, when the passport of its de facto leader, Khalid Balala, was withdrawn while he was on a trip abroad, complicating his return to Kenya; and IPK counter-protests, most of which were violent, were staged in Mombasa by a militia suspected to have been sponsored by state agents. In a nutshell, the response from the state to the proposal to form and register the IPK revealed that suspicions towards Muslim activism had not changed since the early 1960s. Another consequence of the IPK debate was a deepening of divisions within the Muslim leadership of Kenya, regarding, especially, what needed to be done to address the Muslim condition.[60] It is from these divisions that an Islamist ideology (and later network), found local expression in Kenya, especially when many began drawing parallels between the Kenyan Muslim condition and global events affecting the international community of Muslims, or the *Ummah*.

The emergence of an early Islamist network in Kenya, 1993–2002

The AQEA attacks in Kenya in 1998 and 2002, both of which came on the heels of IPK activism, presented a critical juncture in the history of Muslim politics in Kenya. Initially, the emergence of an Islamist ideology had emanated from an increased invocation of Islam to civic debate, not just by religious leaders, scholars and clerics, but also by a wider Muslim public, and resulting from this, an increased contestation of religious and political authority: processes that were occasioned by the political liberalization of the 1990s.[61] After the IPK debates, protests and riots on the Kenya coast came to a halt, a strand of Muslim opinion emerged that rejected the preferred method of the majority of Kenyan Muslims – which encourages participation in the formal political process as a way of addressing Muslim grievances – and began drawing parallels between the grievances of Kenyan Muslims and those of Muslims elsewhere in the world.[62] In other words, the refusal to register the IPK had shown some Muslims that it would be difficult for Muslims in Kenya to attain a formal political platform for the representation of their concerns, and as a result, select Kenyan mosques established themselves as alterative centres for the mobilization of the Muslim voice.[63]

In these spaces, speakers became explicitly radical and increasingly anti-American, expressing – sometimes at great length – their opinion on events that affected Muslims all over the world.[64] New media – films, photographs and tapes of recorded speeches – appeared on the streets of major urban centres in Kenya, encouraging Kenyan Muslims to see themselves as part of a global struggle.[65] The increased use of the internet coincided with the arrival of preachers from elsewhere in the Muslim world, especially the Middle East, Somalia and Tanzania, and an increased labour migration of Kenyans into the Gulf States. While these trends encouraged empathy with the concerns and ideas of the global community of Muslims, they also created the ideological and institutional infrastructure for a later emergence of a violent Islamist network in Kenya that would combine local Muslim concerns – such as those that were articulated by IPK leaders – and events affecting Muslims globally.

Important to this chapter's thesis is the fact that the first Islamist network in Kenya had direct connections with Al Qaeda, which had transformed itself from an Islamist rebel force fighting Soviet troops at the close of the anti-Soviet Jihad in Afghanistan in the late 1980s, to a transnational 'Jihadist' organization with global ambitions.[66] It was the investigations that followed the two suicide bomb attacks in Kenya (in 1998 and 2002) that suggested that an Al Qaeda cell, or AQEA, had been active in Kenya since 1993.[67] The cell received direct orders from Osama bin Laden, the leader of Al Qaeda, for a considerable period of time and would interchangeably be led by Fazul Abdullah Mohamed, a Comorian national who later acquired Kenyan citizenship through marriage; Saleh Nabhan Saleh, a Kenyan born and raised in the Majengo neighbourhood of Mombasa; and Abu Talha al-Sudani of Sudan, an explosives trainer who led Al Qaeda operations in Somalia in the early 1990s.[68] Born in different parts of the Muslim world – across the Indian Ocean littoral and in Sudan – these men had participated in the anti-Soviet Jihad in Afghanistan as members of Al Qaeda.[69]

Their activities, after each of them left Afghanistan, announced Al Qaeda to the world, where the group presented a vision of apocalyptic inter-civilizational conflict that was not influenced primarily by local or national Muslim activist agendas.[70] Arriving in Kenya in 1993, Fazul Mohamed, who spoke fluent English and Swahili (Kenya's official languages) integrated with the coastal Swahili community, where he posed as a local Islamic preacher, using different aliases.[71] By the mid-1990s, bin Laden was ordering surveillance of American installations in East Africa, including the US embassies in Kenya and Tanzania.[72] Mohamed, who was a skilled bomb expert, used his East African networks and connections to Al Qaeda's leadership to not only raise money and import bomb-making materials, but to also bring to Kenya a team of dedicated Al Qaeda fighters, Wadih El-Hage, a Lebanese-American, and Mohamed Odeh, a Palestinian.[73] These individuals, who arrived in Kenya from 1994 onwards, were all, at one time or another, associated with Kenyan-based non-governmental organizations, ostensibly created for the purposes of humanitarian relief and aid work.[74] They had also set up other businesses, particularly commercial fishing and clothing companies on the Kenyan coast, through which they both created employment for locals and presented themselves as individuals leading ordinary lives.[75] While these men were instrumental in the US embassy bombings in Nairobi and Dar-es-salaam in August 1998, one of the two suicide bombers was a Sudanese national and the other, an Egyptian.[76]

In December 2001, surveillance of Israeli targets began, led by Fazul Mohamed, but this time working in close partnership with Saleh Nabhan and other Kenyan nationals. The targets, an Israeli-owned hotel situated north of Mombasa called Paradise Hotel and an Israeli passenger airliner that was departing from the international airport in Mombasa, had been identified by April 2002.[77] While Mohamed supervised the assembling of explosive devices that were used to attack the Paradise Hotel, Saleh Nabhan and another Kenyan, Issa Osman, attempted to shoot down the Israeli airliner (which was at the time departing from Mombasa) with a surface-to-air missile but they missed their target.[78] Consequent investigations (and American pressure) led to a dispersal of the cell, and Mohamed and Nabhan fled to Somalia, where they would, in the following years, become instrumental in bringing to Somalia's inchoate Islamist insurgence, Al Qaeda-like tactics – suicide bombs, roadside bombs and a pipeline of foreign fighters.[79]

Despite Kenya's growing counter-terrorist programme, International Crisis Group reports reveal that after the departure of the AQEA cell in Kenya in 2002, and before the emergence of Al Shabaab in Somalia in late 2006, individuals with links to Fazul Mohamed and Saleh Nabhan, including Kenyan Somali recruits of the Somalia-based Islamist organization Al-Itihad, Al-Islamiyah, were travelling with relative ease, between Kenya, Somalia and Tanzania. In the process (but without launching any new attacks in Kenya), they built an infrastructure of recruitment, fundraising and communication.[80] It was these networks that were activated during the brief rule of the Islamic Courts Union in Somalia in 2006, with the subsequent rise of Al Shabaab, which rapidly emerged as Somalia's most powerful Islamist organization.[81] Using these networks, a number of Kenyans began travelling to Somalia in large numbers in 2006–07 following the Ethiopian invasion and the Courts' overthrow in Mogadishu so as to join the military insurrection against the Transitional Federal Government (TFG) of Somalia.[82] It was from this group that a distinctively Kenyan Islamist network, driven by the local concerns of Kenyan Muslims, would emerge, especially after Kenya sent its troops to Somalia in late 2011.

The operation of a violent Islamist network in Kenya since 2006

Aboud Rogo Mohamed, a leading IPK activist in the 1990s, who was arrested, charged and acquitted in connection with the 28 November 2002 suicide attack north of Mombasa after his phone number was found in Fazul Mohamed's phone, quickly emerged as the ideological leader of the Kenyan Islamist network after

2006.[83] Another leading figure in this network was Mohamed Kunow Dulydeyn, alias 'Gamadhere', from Garissa district in Northern Kenya. While Rogo, like Saleh Nabhan, was widely believed to have been a close associate of Fazul Mohamed, Gamadhere had, instead, worked for the Al-Haramain Foundation, a Saudi-funded charity that was closed in connection with the US embassy bombing of 1998.[84] As a teacher and principal at Madrasa Najah in Garissa district of Kenya between 1997 and 2000, Gamadhere was largely influenced by a conservative Hanbali-Wahhabism promoted by Saudi-Arabian-funded charitable work in the 1990s in North-east Kenya, and by political developments in Somalia.[85] Many in North-east Kenya followed Gamadhere's trajectory, becoming motivated by the ideology of the Courts Union, and as the latter collapsed, joined Al Shabaab.[86] Al Shabaab recruitment activities led by Gamadhere in North-east Kenya combined with those of a host of other Kenyans, notably those of the Muslim Youth Centre (MYC) based at the Pumwani Riyadha Mosque in Nairobi.[87]

These networks received their ideological inspiration from a group of radical preachers who had emerged in Kenya and took over mosque platforms where they openly declared their support for Al Shabaab.[88] The most visible of these preachers was Aboud Rogo, who, by 2007, was commonly being referred to as Sheikh Aboud Rogo, and Samir Khan, who, like Rogo, preached in Mombasa. The others were Sheikh Hassaan Hussein Adam, who preached in the Eastleigh neighbourhood of Nairobi, and Sheikh Ahmed Iman Ali (Rogo's protégé), who preached at the Pumwani Riyadha Mosque neighbouring Eastleigh.[89] While Sheikh Hassan's activism stood beyond the usual dynamic, where he dedicated most of his attention to Somali politics, preachers such as Rogo, Iman Ali and Samir Khan, and activists such as Abubakar Sharif, alias *Makaburi* (Swahili for cemetery) continued to compare Kenyan Muslim grievances to global trends affecting the Islamic *Umma*. Their speeches, recorded on tapes and DVDs, and some posted on YouTube, received faster and wider circulation.[90]

Using resources gained from the relatively wealthy Pumwani Riyadha Mosque, where Ahmed Iman Ali had initiated a forceful takeover of the management committee in January 2007, these preachers funded their trips to mosques in Nairobi, far-off on the coast, and further up-country, and were able to recruit many Kenyans from predominantly Christian ethnic communities. They spoke of key tenets of the Wahhabist doctrine, such as monotheism (*tawhid*) and loyalty to Islam and Muslims, and disavowal of non-Muslims (*al-wala' wal-bara'*).[91] Newsletters, such as the defunct Pumwani Muslim Youth Centre's newsletter, the 'Al-Misbah', including the centre's blog and Twitter account, re-published the works of Islamist ideologues such as Anwar Awlaki, a Yemeni-born American jihadi. The Youth Centre's branded T-shirts were printed with the words, 'Jihaad is our religion', next to an Al Shabaab flag.[92] This revealed the violent outlook of the network, the result of a violent preaching that took the place of esoteric and theological debate, particularly by people who had previously felt excluded from theological debates that were often settled by reciting the *Hadith* in Arabic. During 'training' lectures given to youth who responded favourably to mosque sermons, material evoking images of the global Muslim condition of oppression –

the conflict in Iraq, Afghanistan, Palestine and Yemen – was provided, including profiles of radical clerics and their ideologies.[93]

As a result, by the time Kenya sent its troops to Somalia in late 2011, this network of Kenyan Islamists (known in Kenyan intelligence circles as 'Al-Hijra') had managed to send to Somalia at least 1000 Kenyans from a diversity of ethnic and racial backgrounds, some of whom were recent Christian converts to Islam.[94] Reports indicated that most of these recruits (mostly close family members, or childhood friends) were responsible for the initial blowback (predominantly low-profile grenade and rifle attacks) that Kenya suffered, ostensibly for retaliation to its mission in Somalia between 2011 and 2012.[95] Rogo's many speeches, especially after 2006, consisted of a veritable clutter of political commentary, of both local and global politics, history and Islam.[96] Citing the example of the prophet (*Sunna*), Rogo encouraged Kenyan Muslims to join what he referred to as an international Jihad, as Muslims, according to him, were constantly being victimized at home and abroad.[97] Rogo was gunned down on a highway in Mombasa on 27 August 2012, his murder sparking violent riots in Mombasa for days. Indeed, between 2012 and 2014, a number of Kenyan clerics that openly supported Islamist violence were assassinated by unknown individuals.[98] Perhaps related to the latter, a major break in the operation of the network came in mid-2013, when its performance failed to match the expectations of the ambitious, former slain leader of Al Shabaab, the late Axmed Godane.[99]

Since 2010, Godane had instituted plans to turn Al Shabaab into a transnational, violent Islamist organization imbued with a strong *takfir* ethos, and as a result, he began offering modest logistical and financial support to Kenya's violent Islamists.[100] After declaring a partnership with Al Qaeda in 2010, and commandeering a violent purge of key rivals within the leadership council of Al Shabaab (the *Shura*) on 20 June 2013, Godane moved with speed to reorganize Al Shabaab.[101] According to Matt Bryden, Al Shabaab became even more committed to 'the cause of international jihad and the restoration of an Islamic caliphate' after the purge of June 2013.[102] In this reorganization, Kenyan members of Al Shabaab who are (at the time of writing) still active in Southern Somalia currently dominate the membership of a new military outfit called 'Jaysh Ayman' (the battalion of faith), which has concentrated most of its activities inside the vast Boni forest on Kenya's northern coast and Southern Somalia.[103] Al-Hijra's leading figures who are still active in Somalia, notably Ahmed Iman Ali, Juma Otit, Erick Ogada, Suleiman Irungo Mwangi, Ramadhan Kufungwa and Abdifatar Abubakar have joined forces with the unit and have continued their radicalisation and recruitment efforts through dispersed and atomized cells within Kenya.[104] As part of the June 2013 reorganization, 'Gamadhere', who, by 2013, had risen to become the Al Shabaab commander in Lower and Middle Juba regions, was asked to expand his operations into Garissa and Wajir counties, as his counterpart in the Gedo region, Adan Garar, targeted Mandera County, all in North-east Kenya.[105] Generally, most of Al Shabaab's deadly attacks within Kenya, the majority of which were executed by Kenyan nationals, were conducted as a result of this new strategy. These include the Westgate shopping mall attack on 21 September 2013, a series of attacks on the coastal town of Mpeketoni and its environs in June–July 2014, and the Garissa university attack on 2 April 2015.

It is important to note that this latest (and continuing) Al Shabaab offensive in Kenya is driven by local as much as global narratives of grievance. For instance, video footage (currently deleted) of the June–July 2014 Mpeketoni attacks by 'Jaysh Ayman' fighters indicates that the attackers targeted Christians only, suggesting that the unit doesn't strictly adhere to the *takfiri* ethos espoused by Al Shabaab's current core leadership.[106] This variation forms a common thread within Muslim politics in Kenya, where local activists have historically applied foreign ideas within local contexts, a factor of the specific Kenyan circumstance of a Muslim-minority state.[107] In this way, it is in the interests of Kenya's violent Islamists to create a larger community of support among Kenyan Muslims by exploiting local Muslim grievances, and as such, the strict adoption of *takfiri* (violence targeted at fellow Muslims) remains limited. For instance, an attempt to carefully package coastal and Somali grievances against the Kenyan state as evidence of a systematic alienation of Muslim interests in Kenya was made in the video of the Mpeketoni attacks.[108] In particular, reference was made to state responses to an insurgency in North-east Kenya in the 1960s commonly known as *Shifta*; the perceived loss of coastal (described in the video as Muslim) land to Christian 'outsiders'; the alleged state 'massacres' of Kenyan Somalis in the North-east region in the 1980s; the arrests, torture and unresolved murders of Muslim clerics; and a 2014 security operation in the Nairobi neighbourhood of Eastleigh dominated by Somalis that was reportedly marked by serious human rights violations.[109] In sum, and as Hansen makes note of the rank and file of Al Shabaab in its early days in Mogadishu, the current membership of 'Jaysh Ayman' consists of Kenyan youth with 'nebulous ideas about the global oppression of Islam', but perhaps with more important and largely correct ideas about the exclusion of Muslim interests within Kenya.[110]

Conclusion

The chapter has illustrated a dominant externalization discourse that ascribes the origins of Islamist violence in Kenya to foreign, or global sources. This narrative, as was explained, is entwined with popular perceptions that regard the minority Muslim population of Kenya as foreign. While this discourse influences physical state responses to the threat posed by Islamist violence, it also serves to de-emphasize the local roots of Islamism. The chapter has also examined the academic literature on Islamist violence in Kenya, and in East Africa more widely, and finds that the common tendency to locate the origins of Islamist violence either in local or global factors fails to account for the 'glocalization' strategy that has been adopted by Kenya's violent Islamist network. In its adoption of an empirical and descriptive approach – to describe an early Islamist network in Kenya, followed by the operation of a network of Kenyan Islamists since 2006 – the analysis found that Kenyan Islamists express local Muslim concerns using a language of 'global

Jihad'. This 'glocal' strategy, the chapter concludes, is based on an Islamist ideology that seeks a return, using violent and political means, to classical Islamic traditions as a way of redressing contemporary Muslim marginalization and to get rid of practices that some regard as non-Islamic.

Notes

1. Agree Mutambo, Abdimalik Hajir and Agencies, '147 killed as Garissa University College attacked by gunmen', *The East African*, 2 April 2015. Available at http://www.theeastafrican.co.ke/news/70-killed-as-Garissa-University-College-attacked-by-gunmen/-/2558/2674310/-/gcoefgz/-/index.html (accessed 15 February 2018).
2. Tristan McConnell, 'Close your eyes and pretend to be dead', *Foreign Policy*, 21 September 2015. Available at http://foreignpolicy.com/2015/09/20/nairobi-kenya-westgate-mall-attack-al-shabab/ (accessed 15 February 2018).
3. David Anderson and Jacob McKnight, 'Kenya at war: Al-Shabaab and its enemies in Eastern Africa', *African Affairs*, 114, no. 454 (2014): 1–27.
4. Office of the Press Secretary, 'Remarks by President Obama and President Kenyatta of Kenya in a press conference', *The White House: President Barack Obama*, 25 July 2015. Available at https://www.whitehouse.gov/the-press-office/2015/07/25/remarks-president-obama-and-president-kenyatta-kenya-press-conference (accessed 15 February 2018).
5. Juliet Eilperin and Kevin Sieff, 'Obama commits US to intensified fight against terrorists in East Africa', *The Washington Post*, 25 July 2015. Available at https://www.washingtonpost.com/politics/us-to-expand-support-in-kenya-somalia-for-counterterrorism-operations/2015/07/25/b6f386f0-3210-11e5-97ae-30a30cca95d7_story.html?utm_term=.6b9ab7c83f3c (accessed 15 February 2018).
6. Murithi Mutiga and Emma Graham-Harrison, 'Kenya says it will shut world's biggest refugee camp at Dadaab', *The Guardian*, 11 May 2016. Available at https://www.theguardian.com/world/2016/may/11/kenya-close-worlds-biggest-refugee-camp-dadaab (accessed 15 February 2018).
7. Jeremy Lind, Patrick Mutahi and Marjoke Oosterom, 'Killing a mosquito with a hammer: Al-Shabaab violence and state security responses in Kenya', *Peacebuilding*, 5, no. 2 (2017): 118–35.
8. Jeremy Prestholdt, 'Kenya, the United States, and counterterrorism', *Africa Today*, 57, no. 4 (2011): 3–27; Peter Kagwanja, 'Counter-terrorism in the Horn of Africa: New security frontiers, old strategies', *African Security Review*, 15, no. 3 (2006): 72–86; International Crisis Group, 'The Kenyan military intervention in Somalia' (*ICG*, Brussels, 15 February 2012).
9. Lind, Mutahi and Oosterom, 'Killing a mosquito'.
10. Ibid.
11. See for example, Intergovernmental Authority on Development, 'Al-Shabaab as a transnational security threat' (*IGAD*, Addis Ababa, March 2016); United Nations Security Council, 'Al Shabaab as a regional security threat', in *Letter Dated 18 July 2011 from the Chairman of the Security Council Committee Pursuant to Resolutions 751 (1992) and 1907 (2009) Concerning Somalia and Eritrea Addressed to the President of the Security Council* (UN, New York, U.S., 2011), pp. 135–79.

12　Ngala Chome, 'From Islamic reform to Muslim activism: The evolution of an Islamist ideology in Kenya', *African Affairs*, 118-472 (2019): 531-52.
13　Ibid.
14　See for example, Prestholdt, 'Kenya, the United States, and counterterrorism', p. 10.
15　Rudiger Seesemann, 'East Africa Muslims after 9/11', *Bayreuth African Studies, Working Papers*, 3 (2005): 1-17; William Rosenau, 'Al-Qaeda recruitment trends in Kenya and Tanzania', *Studies in Conflict and Terrorism*, 28, no. 1 (2005): 1-10; David Shinn, 'Al-Qaeda in East Africa and the Horn', *Third World Quarterly*, 26, no. 8 (2005): 1321-39; Jeffrey Haynes, 'Islam and democracy in East Africa', *Democratization*, 13, no. 3 (2006): 490-507; Isaac Kfir, 'Islamic radicalism in East Africa: Is there a cause for concern?' *Studies in Conflict and Terrorism*, 31 (2008): 829-55.
16　Alex de Waal, ed., *Islamism and Its Enemies in the Horn of Africa* (London: Hurst, 2004).
17　Roy Olivier, *Globalised Islam: The Search for a New Ummah* (London: Hurst, 2004).
18　Seesemann, 'East Africa Muslims', p. 5.
19　Kfir, 'Islamic radicalism'.
20　See for example, Kai Kresse, 'Muslim politics in post-colonial Kenya: Negotiating knowledge on the double periphery', *Journal of the Royal Anthropological Institute*, 15 (2009): 76-94.
21　Kagwanja, 'Counter-terrorism in the Horn of Africa'; David Anderson and Jacob McKnight, 'Understanding Al-Shabaab: Clan, Islam and insurgency in Kenya', *Journal of Eastern African Studies*, 9, no. 3 (2015): 536-57; Lind, Mutahi and Oosterom, 'Killing a mosquito'; Anderson and McKnight, 'Kenya at war'; Prestholdt, 'Kenya, the United States, and counterterrorism'.
22　Guilain Denoeux and Lynn Carter, *Guide to Drivers of Violent Extremism* (Washington DC: United States Agency for International Development, February 2009); Anneli Botha, 'Political socialization and terrorist radicalization among individuals who joined Al-Shabaab in Kenya', *Studies in Conflict and Terrorism*, 37, no. 11 (2014): 895-919; Anneli Botha, *Terrorism in Kenya and Uganda; Radicalization from a Political Socialization Perspective* (London: Lexington, 2017).
23　James Khalil, 'Radical beliefs and violent actions are not synonymous: How to place the key disjuncture between attitudes and behaviours at the heart of our research into political violence', *Studies in Conflict and Terrorism*, 37, no. 2 (2014): 204-6.
24　Jonathan Githens-Mazer and Robert Lambert, 'Why conventional wisdom on radicalization fails', *International Affairs*, 86, no. 4 (2010): 889.
25　James Khalil and Martine Zuethen, 'Countering violent extremism and risk reduction: A guide to program design and evaluation' (RUSI Whitehall Report, Royal United Services Institute, London, 2016), p. 1.
26　Ibid.
27　Roland Marchal, 'The rise of a Jihadi movement in a country at war: Harakat Al-Shabaab, Al-Mujahiddin in Somalia' (Independent Report, March 2011), p. 6.
28　Stig Jarle Hansen, *Al-Shabaab in Somalia: The History and Ideology of a Militant Islamist Group* (London: Hurst, 2013), p. 45.
29　Marchal, 'The rise of a Jihadi movement'.
30　Muhsin Hassan, 'Understanding the drivers of violent extremism: The case of Al-Shabaab and Somali youth', *CTC Sentinel*, 5, no. 8 (2012): 18-23.
31　Ibid.
32　Ibid.
33　Ibid.

34 *Daily Nation*, 'Al-Qaeda terror groups active on Kenya coast', 29 November 2002, p. 9; *Daily Nation*, 'Foreigners marry Kenyans to cover their intentions', 22 August 2003, p. 12; *PBS Frontline*, 'Executive summary of status and findings of the FBI investigation into the embassy bombings as of November 18, 1998', 18 November 1998. Available at http://www.pbs.org/wgbh/pages/frontline/shows/binladen/bombings/summary.html (accessed 1 March 2018).
35 Anneli Botha, 'Assessing the vulnerability of Kenyan youths to radicalization and extremism' (Report, Institute for Security Studies, Pretoria, 2013).
36 See, *Daily Nation*, 'Islam is defended', 15 August 1998, p. 32.
37 Botha, 'Assessing', p. 3.
38 Prestholdt, 'Kenya, the United States, and counterterrorism', p. 10.
39 Ibid.
40 James Brennan, 'Lowering the Sultan's flag: Sovereignty and decolonization in coastal Kenya', *Comparative Studies in Society and History*, 50, no. 4 (2008): 831–61; Hannah Whittaker, *Insurgency and Counterinsurgency in Kenya: A Social History of the Shifta Conflict, 1963-1968* (Leiden: Brill, 2015).
41 Botha, 'Assessing', p. 6.
42 Open Society Foundation and Muslims for Human Rights, *We're Tired of Taking You to the Court: Human Rights Abuses by Kenya's Anti-Terrorism Police Unit* (New York: Open Society Foundations, 2013).
43 Lind, Mutahi and Oosterom, 'Killing a mosquito', p. 121.
44 Ibid.
45 International Crisis Group, 'The Kenyan Military Intervention in Somalia' (Africa Report, *ICG*, February, 2012).
46 Ibid.
47 *The Star*, 'Security alert at Kenya's border points, says Saitoti', 10 October 2011.
48 Independent Policing Oversight Authority, *Monitoring Report on Operation Sanitization Eastleigh Publically Known as "Usalama Watch"* (Nairobi: Republic of Kenya, Government Printer, 2014).
49 Lind, Mutahi and Oosterom, 'Killing a mosquito', p. 121.
50 FGD, 10 participants from the neighbourhood of Majengo, Mombasa, Kenya, 30 June 2016; FGD, 10 participants from the neighbourhood of Pumwani, Nairobi, Kenya, 23 June 2016; FGD, 10 participants from the neighbourhood of Likoni, Mombasa, Kenya, 29 June 2016.
51 Brennan, 'Lowering the Sultan's flag'.
52 Jeremy Prestholdt, 'Politics of the soil: Separatism, autochthony, and decolonization at the Kenyan coast', *The Journal of African History*, 55, no. 2 (2014): 249–70.
53 Ibid.
54 Whittaker, *Insurgency and Counterinsurgency in Kenya*.
55 Prestholdt, 'Politics of the soil'.
56 Kresse, 'Muslim politics in post-colonial Kenya'.
57 Hassan Mwakimako and Justin Willis, *Islam, Politics and Violence on the Kenya Coast* (Bourdieu: Observatoire des Enjeux Politiques et Securitaires das la Corne de l'Afrique, 2014).
58 Arye Oded, *Islam and Politics in Kenya* (London: Lynne Rienner Publishers, 2000).
59 Arye Oded, 'Islamic extremism in Kenya: The rise and fall of Sheikh Khalid Balala', *Journal of Religion in Africa*, 26, no. 4 (1996): 406–15.
60 Chome, 'From reform to violence'.
61 Ibid.

62 Mwakimako and Willis, *Islam, Politics and Violence*, p. 12.
63 Ibid.
64 Danna Harman, 'Why radicals find fertile ground in moderate Kenya; President Bush met with President Moi to discuss security issues', *The Christian Science Monitor*, 6 December 2002. Available at https://www.questia.com/newspaper/1P2-32599687/why-radicals-find-fertile-ground-in-moderate-kenya (accessed 16 February 2016).
65 Mwakimako and Willis, *Islam, Politics, and Violence*, p. 13.
66 Vahid Brown, *Cracks in the Foundation: Leadership Schisms in Al-Qa'ida from 1989-2006* (New York: Harmony Project, Combating Terrorism Centre, 2007).
67 *Daily Nation*, 'Al-Qaeda terror groups active on Kenya coast', 29 November 2002, p. 9; *Daily Nation*, 'Foreigners marry Kenyans to cover their intentions', 22 August 2003, p. 12; *PBS Frontline*, 'Executive summary of status and findings of the FBI investigation into the embassy bombings as of November 18, 1998', 18 November 1998. Available at http://www.pbs.org/wgbh/pages/frontline/shows/binladen/bombings/summary.html (accessed 1 March 2018).
68 Shinn, 'Al-Qaeda', p. 59.
69 *CBS News*, 'Elusive Al-Qaeda operative was real deal', 10 January 2007. Available at https://www.cbsnews.com/news/elusive-al-qaeda-operative-was-real-deal/ (accessed 15 March 2018); Bill Rogio, 'Al-Qaeda's East Africa chief Fazul Mohamed killed in Somalia', *FDD's Long War Journal*, 11 June 2011. Available at https://www.longwarjournal.org/archives/2011/06/al_qaedas_east_afric_1.php (accessed 15 February 2018).
70 Brown, *Cracks in the Foundation*, pp. 3–5.
71 *BBC News*, 'Profile: Fazul Abdullah Mohamed', 11 June 2011. Available at http://www.bbc.com/news/world-africa-13738393 (accessed 15 March 2018).
72 *CBS News*, 'Elusive Al-Qaeda operative was real deal'.
73 Ibid.
74 *PBS Frontline*, 'Executive summary of status and findings'.
75 Ibid.
76 Botha, 'Assessing', p. 4.
77 Ibid., p. 5.
78 Ibid.
79 Hansen, *Al-Shabaab in Somalia*.
80 Crisis Group, 'Kenyan Somali', p. 7; Hansen, *Al-Shabaab in Somalia*, pp. 25–9.
81 Crisis Group, 'Kenyan Somali', p. 7.
82 IGAD, 'Al-Shabaab as a transnational', p. 22.
83 Kadara Swaleh, 'The radicalization of Sheikh Aboud Rogo and the formation of a jihadist ideology in coastal Kenya', Paper presented at the conference on 'Pirates and Preachers', Roskilde University, May 2014; Hassan Ndzovu, 'The prospects of Islamism in Kenya as epitomized by Shaykh Aboud Rogo's sermons', *The Annual Review of Islam in Africa*, 12, no. 2 (2013): 7–12.
84 Ngala Chome, 'Violent extremism and clan dynamics in Kenya' (Peaceworks, United States Institute of Peace, September 2016).
85 Ibid.
86 Ibid.
87 UN Security Council, 'Al Shabaab as a regional'.
88 Anderson and McKnight, 'Understanding Al-Shabaab', pp. 544–5.
89 UN Security Council, 'Al Shabaab as a regional', p. 143.
90 Interview, Wajir county government official, 19 April 2016.

91 See for example, Fanah Abu Zinnirah, 'Jihaad katika misingi ya Quran na Sunnah', 20 October 2009. Available at https://archive.org/details/JihaadKatikaMisingiYaQuraanNaSunnah (accessed 13 March 2017).
92 UN Security Council, 'Al Shabaab as a regional', pp. 159–60.
93 Ibid., p. 143.
94 Anderson and McKnight, 'Understanding Al-Shabaab', p. 545; 'Author Reference', 'Portrait of an insurgent, *New African*, April 2016, pp. 48–50.
95 Fred Mukinda, 'Five Kenyans wanted over Al-Shabaab link', *Daily Nation*, 20 October 2015. Available at http://www.nation.co.ke/news/-Five-Kenyans-wanted-over-Al-Shabaab-link/1056-2921698-vu0t0wz/index.html (accessed 13 March 2017); *Hiraan Online*, 'IG unveils Kenya's faces of terror', 18 August 2015. Available at http://www.hiiraan.com/news4/2015/Aug/101169/ig_unveils_kenya_s_faces_of_terror.aspx (accessed 13 March 2017).
96 See for example, Ideal Muslim, 'Mawaidha-Sheikh Aboud Rogo', *You Tube*, 29 September 2012. Available at https://www.youtube.com/watch?v=i1UPnkYRn7E (accessed 4 August 2017).
97 See for example, Al-Wahyein Alikhbaar, 'Eid-Khutba 2006: Sheikh Aboud Rogo', *YouTube*, 2 February 2013. Available at https://www.youtube.com/watch?v=-cSFEu6T_jM (accessed 4 August 2017).
98 Open Society Foundation and Muslims for Human Rights, *We're Tired of Taking You to the Court*.
99 Interview, two security analysts, Nairobi, Kenya, 25 April 2016.
100 IGAD, 'Al-Shabaab as a transnational', p. 20; Matt Bryden, 'The decline and fall of Al-Shabaab? Think again' (Sahan, April 2015), p. 10.
101 Matt Bryden, 'The reinvention of Al-Shabaab: A strategy of choice or necessity?' (Center for Strategic and International Studies, February 2014).
102 Ibid., p. 2.
103 IGAD, 'Al-Shabaab as a transnational', p. 20.
104 See for example, Fred Mukinda, 'Ex-Kenyan footballer Anwar Mwok, among Shabaab fighters killed in Kulbiywo', *Daily Nation*, 14 February 2017. Available at http://www.nation.co.ke/news/Footballer-among-fighters-killed-in-Kulbiyow/1056-3812070-8phuhe/index.html (accessed 14 March 2017); Interview, two security analysts, Nairobi, Kenya, 25 April 2016.
105 IGAD, 'Al-Shabaab as a transnational', p. 20.
106 *Harar 24 News*, 'Mpeketoni: Al-Shabaab releases a chilling new video on attacks', 3 March 2015. Available at http://harar24.com/?p=14699; David Anderson, 'Why Mpeketoni matters: Al-Shabaab and violence in Kenya' (Policy Brief, Norwegian Peacebuilding Resource Center, 2014).
107 Mwakimako and Willis, 'Islam and democracy', p. 22.
108 See also, Anderson, 'Why Mpeketoni matters', pp. 2–3.
109 See for example, 'Author Reference', 'Countering Al-Shabaab's narrative in Kenya's fight against extremism', *All Africa Blog*, 14 April 2015. Available at http://allafrica.com/stories/201504160257.html (accessed 15 March 2017).
110 Hansen, *Al-Shabaab in Somalia*, p. 45.

REFLECTIONS ON ISLAMIST MILITANCY IN THE SAHEL

Hussein Solomon

Introduction

The Sahel is a vast semi-arid region comprising the northernmost parts of sub-Saharan Africa stretching from the coast of the Atlantic Ocean to the Red Sea.[1] Some scholars such as Jeremy Keenan have argued for a narrower definition and maintained that in geopolitical terms, the Sahel comprises Mauritania, Mali, Niger and Chad.[2] Stephen Harrison, however, argues for a wider concept of the Sahel noting the strong historic, cultural, political, religious and economic ties across the entire north-west African region.[3] Following Harrison, this chapter will also make use of the Sahel constituting the north-west African region.

While the geographical scope from the Atlantic Ocean to the Red Sea is too wide an area, and Keenan's geopolitical demarcation too narrow, the added benefit of viewing the Sahel as contiguous with north-west Africa is the fact that the region constitutes an integrated regional conflict system, where sources of insecurity are intertwined and mutually reinforcing. Nigeria's Boko Haram, for instance, constitutes a threat to the entire region. Moreover, the Tuareg and later Islamist insurgency that began in northern Mali in January 2012 was exacerbated with the toppling of Muammar Gaddafi in Libya. With the dissolution of Gaddafi's armed forces, many of its Malian Tuaregs looted the former regime's arsenal and returned home in October 2011. Given the broken promises of previous peace agreements between Mali's Tuaregs and the Bamako government they formed the Tuareg Azawad National Liberation Movement (MNLA). Indeed, Mohammed Ag Najim, the leader of the MNLA, was an officer in Gaddafi's armed forces and the majority of the MNLA were Tuaregs who had served in Gaddafi's army.[4]

Scholarship on terrorism in the region is generally divided into two camps. The first camp portrays terrorism as a relatively new phenomenon and as the latest front of global jihad.[5] The area constitutes a vast ungoverned or poorly governed area where local franchises of Global Jihad, Inc have set up shop. At face value the various militant Islamist groupings occupying the arid region – Al Qaeda in the Islamic Maghreb (AQIM), Boko Haram, Ansaru, Ansar Dine, Ansar al-Sharia, the Movement for Oneness and Jihad in West Africa (MUJAO), Al Mourabitoun, the Macina Liberation Front (MLF) – seem to prove such an assertion correct. The entry of ISIS into the region, specifically with the affiliation of Boko Haram to ISIS, has also added credence to such a perspective. The second camp views terrorism in the region as a product of local conditions, that it has a long history and that far from constituting a new front for global jihad, terrorism is localized or, at best, sub-national in nature.[6] This chapter will explore the arguments of each camp. It will also explore the policy implications of adopting each camp's position with a view to manage the terrorist threat in the region.

The case for local franchises acting as surrogates for global jihadi networks

The dominant narrative is appealing in its simplicity. There have been over 27,000 terrorist attacks globally since 9/11 linked to radical Islam. To put it differently, this is more than five per day.[7] What we are witnessing in the Sahel is yet another front in the global fight against Islamist terrorism.[8] There is certainly evidence to support such a narrative that makes it all the more compelling. This connection between the local and the international is perhaps best summarized in the life of the notorious Algerian jihadi, Mohtar Belmokhtar. He journeyed to Afghanistan to fight the pro-Soviet government following Moscow's withdrawal. There he met leading jihadis who fought alongside the Afghan mujahedeen. These included many who were to form a new, deadlier force: Al Qaeda. He later returned to Algeria, fighting with the Armed Islamic Group during his country's civil war. He then went on to become a commander in Al Qaeda in the Islamic Maghreb (AQIM).[9]

The names of the various terror organizations in the region constitute another such proof. There is Al Qaeda in the Islamic Maghreb that operates in north-west Africa and ISIS in the Greater Sahara, which is active in Tunisia, Libya and Egypt. Moreover, in 2015 Nigeria's Boko Haram rebranded itself as ISIS in West Africa Province clearly seeing itself as part of ISIS's global caliphate.[10] In his testimony to the United States (US) Congress in December 2017, Nathan Sales, the US coordinator for counterterrorism warned that with the fall of their de facto capital in Raqqa, ISIS fighters have flocked to north and west Africa.[11] In the process, Nathan Sales reinforced this dominant narrative of the intimate ties between global and local jihadis.

By affiliating with global terror networks like that of Al Qaeda, Hezbollah or ISIS, local franchises benefit in terms of trained fighters who are battle-hardened veterans from Afghanistan, Chechnya and Iraq. Local beneficiaries also receive the necessary financial assistance and technical know-how, from improvised explosive devices to staging multiple Mumbai-style attacks simultaneously on a target. The training that Boko Haram recruits received at AQIM camps from veterans from other Islamist insurgencies accounts for the growing sophistication of Boko Haram attacks. While initial Boko Haram attacks made use of knives, machetes, bows, arrows and petrol bombs, later attacks saw the use of suicide car bombings and improvised explosive devices, which have been used with such dramatic effect in Afghanistan, Iraq and Syria, and synchronized assaults as we witnessed in Mumbai in November 2008. The quality of the explosives used also demonstrates Boko Haram's increasing sophistication. Increasingly powerful explosives like pentaerythritol tetranitrate (PETN) and the triacetone triperoxide (TATP) are used in shaped charges designed to magnify the impact of the blast.[12]

From 2015 the Sahel region has witnessed an increase in terror attacks. Beginning in 2015, the conflict between Boko Haram and Chadian forces intensified in the Lake Chad Basin resulting in the loss of hundreds of innocent lives, a further 100,000 displaced, and serious damage to the Lake Chad economy. The terror waged by Boko Haram soon spread beyond the Lake Chad Basin, engulfing other Chadian villages, including two suicide bombings on the capital, N'Djamena.[13] The Nigerian militants' attacks on a neighbouring country also give credence to the notion of a Global Jihad Inc with local franchises, which show scant regard for Westphalian borders of supposedly sovereign nation-states. After all, the Islamist perception of a global *ummah* (body of believers) only divides the world between a *Dar al Harb* (a Place of War, wherein non-believers hold sway) and a *Dar al Islam* (a Place of Peace, wherein Muslims hold sway).[14] These two realms are in constant conflict and could provide the Nigerian Boko Haram the supposed legitimacy to attack Chad's territory and people.

Boko Haram also continued its attacks on its home soil. On 16 March 2016 Boko Haram attacked a mosque in its traditional stomping ground of Maiduguri in Nigeria, killing twenty-two people and injuring scores of others.[15] Burkina Faso also found itself in the crosshairs of the jihadis. On 15 January 2017, thirty people were murdered at a hotel in the Burkinabe capital of Ouagadougou. A month later armed Islamists attacked two northern towns in Burkina Faso – Tongomayel and Baraboule – where they attacked police stations, the city hall and homes of local officials.[16] On 13 August 2017 a further eighteen people were killed at a restaurant in Ouagadougou. The frequency of these attacks in Burkina Faso correlated with the emergence of a new militant group in the country, Ansarul Islam (Defenders of Islam).[17] Meanwhile, the Macina Liberation Front also staged multiple attacks on Mauritania and the Ivory Coast during 2016.[18] What both Ansarul Islam and the Macina Liberation Front have in common is that they have used Mali as the staging areas for attacks into neighbouring states and both have a relationship with Mali's Ansar Dine.[19]

Mali, too, has not been spared from this increase in terrorist activities. A suicide truck bomber in Gao drove his explosive-laden vehicle into a group of pro-government Tuareg militias and detonated it. This resulted in the deaths of seventy-seven people and over a hundred were wounded. Al Qaeda in the Islamic Maghreb (AQIM) claimed responsibility for the deadly blast, stating that these Tuaregs were being punished for having signed a peace treaty with the Malian government.[20] UN peacekeepers in Mali, too, were not spared. On 14 August 2017, a terror attack on the United Nations Multidimensional Integrated Stabilization Mission in Mali resulted in seven UN personnel being killed. Indeed, since the mission began in 2013 the increasing attacks on its personnel have made this the deadliest UN mission in the world.[21] To put it differently, although the UN's mission to Mali constitutes less than 15 per cent of all its peacekeepers, it comprises 90 per cent of all UN peacekeeper deaths – a situation that has been constant for the past three years.[22]

Not only is the frequency of these terror attacks increasing, but it would also appear that the terrorist groupings in the Sahel are displaying greater coordination and mounting cross-border attacks, seemingly at will. Consider, for instance, the case of Ansar ul Islam headed by Ibrahim Malam Dicko. While it is headquartered in Mali, it has been staging terror attacks in neighbouring Burkina Faso.[23] In a similar vein, the al Mourabitoun Group of Moktar Belmoktar and the Macina Liberation Front of Amadoun Kouffa – both affiliated to Al Qaeda – staged spectacular attacks on Burkina Faso throughout 2016.[24] It subsequently emerged that Amadoun Kouffa's mentor is Iyad ag Ghali, leader of Mali's militant group, *Ansar Dine* (Defender of the Faith). Belmoktar, in turn, was a key ally of Iyad ag Ghali and Mali's militants played a key role in supplying weapons to the Macina Liberation Front.[25] In March 2017, cooperation between Islamist groupings in the region paved the way for unification. Ansar Dine under Iyad ag Ghali, Belmokhtar's Al Mourabitoun, Amoudoun Kouffa's Macina Liberation Front and AQIM's Sahara Branch, also called the Emirate of the Saharan region, joined forces to form the Group to Defend Islam and Muslims, which was to be led by Iyad ag Ghali.[26] Pointedly, the leaders of the new organization all took an oath of allegiance to Ayman al-Zawahiri, the leader of Al Qaeda.[27] In similar fashion, there seems to be some evidence that ISIS-affiliated networks in the Maghreb and the Sahel are engaging in closer cooperation. Consider for instance, the growing relationships being forged between Nigeria's Boko Haram and a number of north Africa's ISIS franchises including Soldiers of the Caliphate in Algeria, ISIS in Libya (Darnah) and the Jund al-Khilafah in Tunisia.[28]

The dominant narrative would argue that given the fact that militants in the Sahel serve local franchises of global jihadi networks, it would make sense for them not to compete with each other and their connection to the global Al Qaeda would facilitate such cooperation and integration. A similar dynamic is at play among ISIS local franchises. January 2018 witnessed the establishment of ISIS in the Greater Sahara – bringing together local ISIS franchises in Tunisia, Libya and Egypt.[29]

Responding to terrorism in the Sahel in a realist manner

The mounting terrorist attacks in the Sahel region have resulted in growing concern among the international community. On 25 October 2010, the terrorist threat in the Sahel region topped the agenda at a meeting of the European Union (EU) Foreign Council's meeting in Luxembourg. Of particular concern to the EU Foreign Ministers were negative developments in Mauritania, Mali and Niger.[30] In January 2018, the United Nations (UN) Security Council expressed its deep concern relating to escalating terrorist incidents and growing violent extremism in the Sahel region.[31]

To be frank, these concerns were not merely shaped by altruistic reasons, the loss of innocent African lives and damage to critical infrastructure in a developing world context. Washington, for instance, imports 35 per cent of its oil from Africa.[32] Given the growing volatility in the Middle East, Africa's oil has increased in strategic importance. France, meanwhile, has been motivated to get involved in the region given its own national interest considerations. Nearly 75 per cent of France's electricity is produced by nuclear power plants. AREVA is a French parastatal which is 80 per cent state-owned. AREVA's twin mining operations at Arlit and Agadez in Niger are AREVA's second largest source of uranium. The need to protect French energy interests was highlighted in a terrorist attack in May 2013 on the Arlit and Agadez's uranium mines.[33] French President Emmanuel Macron also made clear that the need to stabilize the region was essential if Europe intends to curb the influx of migrants.[34] Beijing, too, has become involved in the Sahel, notably with its troop contribution to the UN mission in Mali. President Macron was also in discussion with Chinese President Xi to expand the Chinese presence in the region. For the Chinese, the increased presence also makes sense given the need to protect the massive investments they have been making in the region's infrastructure.[35]

While realist motivations of narrow national self-interest motivated Western powers, realism also coloured the response to the perceived threat. In October 2017, ISIS lost its de facto capital in Raqqa, Syria, as a result of the direct deployment of overwhelming force.[36] In 2001, Al Qaeda was dislodged by US and coalition forces from its base in Afghanistan. If force worked with the 'mother bodies' then logically, the deployment of such military force on local franchises of these global terror networks will also serve to neutralize the likes of AQIM. Former US National Security Advisor, General James (Jim) Jones envisaged a string of long-term military bases across the African continent that could house 3,000 to 5,000 troops with an airfield nearby. General Jones also envisaged forward operating bases which would be lightly equipped bases where Special Forces marines as well as an infantry rifle platoon could build up quickly in preparation for a mission.[37] By December 2017, Washington had deployed more than 6,000 troops across Africa.[38] Specifically, the US involvement in the Sahel was also seen in military terms. In June 2005, for instance, the United States launched the Trans-Sahara Counterterrorism Initiative (TSCTI) with a budget of US$ 100 million. It specifically involved providing training to the region's armed forces in live fire exercises, rifle marksmanship, border control and airborne operations.[39] With the launch of the United States African Command (AFRICOM) in 2007, this has expanded further. By October 2017, there were 800 military personnel in Niger and at least 1,500 in the wider African region.[40] The American presence soon advanced beyond training and arming local forces when search and destroy missions were undertaken.[41]

Washington, of course, is not alone in its militaristic response. France launched Operation Serval in January 2013 to dislodge the Islamists in northern Mali. However, this soon became a bigger problem as they crossed the borders into neighbouring states and became a regional problem.[42] Paris launched Operation Barkhane on 1 August 2014 to secure the region with 4,000 troops in the Sahel equipped with 200 armoured vehicles, 20 transport and attack helicopters, six jet fighters, three large unarmed aerial vehicles (drones) as well as two twin-engine C-160 air transport planes to move troops quickly across the region. North Atlantic

Treaty Organization (NATO) allies, specifically Britain and the United States, using long-range transport like C-17s supplied the French force.[43] Given the vast nature of the area to be covered, its topography and limited resources, the French realized that they needed the support of other countries. Germany has moved a thousand troops to the region and provided four NH 90 transport helicopters and four Tiger gunships to be deployed against the Sahel's Islamist insurgents.[44] Italian Prime Minister, Paolo Gentiloni, also announced that 470 soldiers from his country would be deployed in the Sahel to fight the Islamist threat.[45] London has also undertaken to support the French forces on the ground with aircraft and helicopters to provide them with intelligence, surveillance, target acquisition and reconnaissance.[46]

This militaristic response to the threat posed was confined not only to international actors but also included regional ones. Burkina Faso, Chad, Mali, Mauritania and Niger formed the G-5 Sahel in July 2017, a 5,000 strong joint force to robustly engage with militant Islamists in the region. These five countries have agreed to facilitate the movement of French Operation Barkhane troops through their respective countries and share intelligence. France and Germany, meanwhile, have agreed to provide training and infrastructure as well as to supply the force with weapons, ammunition and military vehicles.[47] Funding for the G-5 Sahel has been sourced from the European Union (50 million euros), Saudi Arabia (100 million euros), the United Arab Emirates (30 million euros), and the United States (60 million euros), and a further 10 million euros from each of the five G-5 Sahel states themselves.[48] Some analysts such as Daphne Benoit are of the opinion that the size of the force is much too small given the vastness of the territory covered. The G5 countries are essentially a desert the size of Europe.[49] Also emphasizing the same point, Ralph Peters notes that Niger alone is twice the size of California.[50]

Individual states in the region also responded militarily to the threat posed. In response to various terror attacks, Chad imposed a state of emergency in the Lake Chad region as well as militarily intervened in neighbouring states given the fact that attacks on Chad were often planned over the borders – specifically in Nigeria. Local defence militias were also organized to act as a force multiplier for Chad's overstretched armed forces.[51]

What is clear is that this current strategy is simply not working. As alluded to earlier, in spite of the billions spent on counterterrorism operations in the Sahel region, the threat posed has actually intensified. Malik Ibrahim refers to the US military-centred approach as 'America's Self-Defeating Sahel Strategy'.[52] Concurring with Ibrahim, Stephen Harrison argues, 'These securitization initiatives have not worked, I argue, because they do not address the root causes of terrorism, which are not military but social and economic.'[53] Harrison's argument sees the emergence of Islamist militants in the Sahel as the result of local conditions and holds that terrorist groups have their own separate identities and are not mere local franchises of global terror networks. This debate has divided policymakers and academics. The US Pentagon, for instance, views local Islamist groups as yet another front of the likes of Al Qaeda and ISIS, while the US State Department's position is far closer to the position of Harrison.[54] Academics are similarly divided. To understand the complexity of which position is correct in the context of the Sahel, we need to engage in some of these academic debates.

Critical terrorism studies and its insights into the Sahel

Very simply, critical terrorism studies is critical of the existing terrorism literature, it is critical of the discourse on terrorism produced by academics and policymakers and it is critical of the institutional structures that produce and interact with this discourse.[55] While there is a diversity of views among critical terrorism scholars, all reject the state-centric perspective of traditional terrorism discourses. More to the point, Stump and Dixit[56] cogently argue that 'those utilizing the critical terrorism studies perspective argue that conventional terrorism scholarship takes for granted the object of study (terrorism), is non-reflexive about the effects of portraying particular groups of people as 'terrorist', ignores the role of the state as a producer of violence, and is uncommitted to social emancipation'. Indeed, much of terrorism scholarship is confined to that of non-state actors.[57] In this discourse, the state's role as a producer of insecurity is never analysed or critiqued. Yet, historically, states have employed terrorism to control dissidents within its own borders as well as a foreign policy tool. Richard Jackson, Eamon Murphy and Scott Poynting[58] remind us that 'during the twentieth century, modern states were responsible for the deaths of 170 million to 200 million people outside of war, a great many of them murdered during notorious campaigns of state terrorism such as Stalin's great terror, Mao's Great Leap Forward, and Kampuchea's return to Year Zero, and the rule of various dictatorial regimes…'. This is especially true in the Sahel where the human rights records of regimes are atrocious. In November 2017, for instance, Aboubakar Siddiki, a prominent Cameroonian opposition leader was jailed for twenty-five years by a military court for 'hostility against the homeland and contempt of the president'. The human rights group, Amnesty International, rightly condemned the verdict as part of a concerted campaign on the part of government to stifle all criticism.[59] Since the launch of the US-led Global War on Terrorism in 2003, Mauritania's former president 'Ould Sid' Ahmed Taya would make use of counter-terror legislation to suppress legitimate civil dissent against his autocratic rule.[60] The current president of Mauritania is Ould Abel Aziz who initially came to power in a military coup and was subsequently 'elected' president. Following Taya's example, he has cracked down on legitimate dissent ostensibly on the basis of fighting extremism while strengthening his security apparatus with the support of Washington and Paris. His reign, however, has only served to galvanize support for AQIM in the country as hapless residents seek an alternative to the draconian rule of Aziz.[61]

During 2007–9, in Niger, former president Tandja conducted a policy of systemic human rights abuses against ethnic Tuaregs. According to Jeremy Keenan this negatively affected two million ethnic Tuaregs in varying ways and degrees.[62] Niger's current president, Mahammadou Issoufou, is no democrat. He was re-elected president in February 2016 after his main opponent was imprisoned and then forced to flee the country to exile. Other opposition leaders boycotted the polls.[63] Ali Idrissa, a Nigerien journalist, notes that the president and his regime enjoy no legitimacy and that the people feel alienated from the political class. As a result, the government routinely uses repressive means to stay in power. Issoufou and his government see cooperation with Western powers in the fight against terrorism as a means to extend their reign. While providing the United States with bases from which to launch drones against terrorists, Issoufou's regime receives financial assistance from Washington as well as training and arming of his already repressive security apparatus. This financial assistance hardly reaches the ordinary citizen. As Ali Idrissa bluntly states, 'We have a super-rich political class and a mass of people who have been abandoned'.[64] At the same time, political resentment breeds insurgency. Given the fact that 94 per cent of Nigeriens are Muslims, this insurgency takes on an Islamic flavour. The government then labels this 'terrorist' and gets Western countries to help suppress an often-legitimate opposition. The discourse of terrorism together with a repressive state security apparatus, armed and trained by Western governments, then becomes a self-fulfilling prophecy as moderate Sufi Islam is then replaced by a more radical Salafi Islam.

A similar dynamic occurs in Nigeria as they attempt to eradicate Boko Haram. Here, violent counterterrorism measures not only failed to stop jihadi terrorism but also served to increase recruits into terrorist organizations. In 2009, Boko Haram's founder Muhammad Yusuf was captured by the police and was summarily executed. His death, however, did not lead to the demise of the organization he led. Incensed by the extrajudicial execution of their leader, which was captured on cell phone footage that went viral on the internet, his successor, Abubaker Shekau led the organization along a far more violent trajectory.[65] This is hardly surprising and has been confirmed by a recent UN survey, which found that 'government action' was the tipping point when an individual joined an extremist organization. Among those interviewed, 71 per cent said that the death or incarceration of a family member or friend prompted them to join.[66] Indeed, state violence in the form of counterterrorism has been indistinguishable from Boko Haram terrorism for the hapless residents of Borno state in northern Nigeria. Here members of the Joint Military Task Force (JTF) have resorted to unlawful killings, dragnet arrests, and extortion and intimidation of residents in their fight against Boko Haram. In one incident, the JTF cordoned off areas, conducted house to house searches, at times shooting young men in these homes for no apparent reason.[67]

Critical terrorism scholars such as Richard Jackson have employed the methodology of critical discourse analysis to the post-9/11 terminology such as 'war on terror' and have pointed that it is not value-neutral but deliberately constructed to make war appear 'reasonable, responsible and inherently good'.[68] This, of course, contributed to the Manichean framework of good versus evil that was so apparent in the Bush administration. In the process, the action of the good is hardly scrutinized. Bush's Global War on Terror resulted after all in the invasion of sovereign-state, internment camps in Guantanamo Bay, extraordinary rendition and other extrajudicial mechanisms, which witnessed the erosion of civil liberties.[69]

In the Sahel region, the counterterrorism tactics and instruments employed by states have served to undermine human security, harden the region's ethnic, racial and religious fault lines and have thus made reconciliation almost impossible. The Malian armed forces have made use of Songhai ethnic militias in northern Mali as a force multiplier. These Ganda Koy (Masters of the Land) and Ganda Iso (Sons of the Land) militias, however, engaged in human rights atrocities, which further incensed Tuareg and Arab populations in the north, preventing the emergence of a truly inclusive Malian state.[70] To illustrate the point, one Ganda Iso recruit, spoke of what he had learned at his training camp:[71]

> Lets' face it! Tuareg do not want to share a country with us. They feel that we are inferior. Before the 2012 crisis, we did not understand that this is our land that they want. Before they invented Azawad [Tuareg desire for an independent homeland called Azawad], this was the Songhai Empire, the Ghana Empire, and the Mali Empire. They would have to understand that we Black sedentary people, we are the owners of the land. The time when we are divided and controlled by enslavers [reference to Tuaregs historically enslaving Africans] is over. Before, we did not realize this. This is what I have learned here, as well as making good friends. And we are ready to die to defend our land against these narco-terrorists.

A similar dynamic is at play in the Lake Chad Basin. Concerned about the infiltration of Boko Haram in the area, N'Djamena has armed local ethnic militias. However, given the tensions over the fertile region whose territory supports agriculture, pastoralism and fishing, this has served to cause these tensions to escalate into armed violence. Some of these armed ethnic militias accused the Buduma ethnic group inhabiting the Basin of colluding with Boko Haram and promptly attacked them.[72] This was clearly a case of local groups appropriating the discourse of global jihad to increase control of fertile territory. The cases of Mali and Chad remind us that governments in the Sahel need to think of the long-term consequences of arming local ethnic militias in the fight against jihadis.

Another characteristic that all critical terrorism scholars share is exploring the total reality of terrorism by adopting an interdisciplinary perspective[73] when examining the phenomenon. Security after all straddles politics and economics, law and the sociocultural realm.[74] This allows for a far more holistic approach to terrorism in the Sahel where context matters. Consider the fact that much of Niger is dusty and infertile. Climate change has resulted in greater desertification, food insecurity and deteriorating economic conditions.[75] Niger has a very youthful demographic profile with 67 per cent of the population being under twenty-five years of age. The majority of these are unemployed. As a World Bank report has admitted, youth unemployment is contributing to social instability.[76] These unemployed youth are especially vulnerable to recruitment into terrorist groups who pay a monthly stipend to the recruit as well as to his family. Neither is this confined only to Niger. In January 2018, the UN Security Council expressed concern over the negative impact of climate change on security in the entire Sahel region.[77] Across the Sahel, the youth are especially vulnerable to radicalization. Only 56 per cent of the region's children have access to primary school. A smaller percentage go on to secondary school.[78] A UN study has found that those youth who are studying or working are least vulnerable to joining extremist organizations.[79] Clearly, more effort needs to go into fixing the education system, thereby increasing employment opportunities.

In a similar vein, critical terrorism scholar, Lee Jarvis also points out that because terrorism is artificially uncoupled from the processes of its emergence (context), traditional counterterrorism tends to ignore the economic context.[80] In the Nigerian context, this is a fatal omission. Consider the following: while 27 per cent of the population in the largely Christian south live in poverty, the comparative figure in the overwhelmingly Muslim north is a staggering 72 per cent. The north's precarious economic situation has been further undermined by desertification, frequent drought and a rinderpest pandemic. The effects of economic globalization have also worsened the north-south economic divide. The few industries existing in the north are largely textile mills and these have been unable to compete with cheaper Asian imports. Under the circumstances, the number of factories in the main northern city of Kano has fallen from 350 in 1987 to 103 today.[81] These economic grievances have been used by Boko Haram propagandists with great effect in their recruitment strategy. A similar economic dynamic also occurs in Mali. While the average poverty rate in Mali is 64 per cent, it is much higher in the Tuareg-dominated north. Timbuktu has a poverty rate of 77 per cent. For Gao the figure is 78.7 per cent and for Kidal, it is a staggering 92 per cent. As in Niger, Mali's youth unemployment rate is extremely high. In Gao, youth unemployment reached 80 per cent in the first decade of the twenty-first century.[82] It is these economic variables that lay at the core of Tuareg rebellions in 1963–64, 1990–96, 2006–09, and again in January 2012. It was the poor state of northern Mali's economy that compelled Tuaregs there to join Gaddafi's armed forces, and his Islamic Legion in particular, given the financial incentives on offer from Tripoli.[83]

Interdisciplinary insights into, and the demand for, context to truly understand the emergence of terrorism also embrace historical accounts of the phenomenon in the Sahel. Indeed, much of the mainstream scholarship ignores the historical roots of jihad. Consider for instance the jihad embarked upon in the Senegal River Valley in 1673 as well as the jihadi roots of the various Fulani uprisings starting in Futa Jallon in 1725 and ending in Macina in 1818. The formation of the Toucouleur Empire of El Hadj Umar Tall from 1856 to 1861 also had its basis in jihad. The most impressive of these jihads was undoubtedly that of Fulani scholar, Uthman dan Fodio, which began in 1804 and established a caliphate that endured until the arrival of the British in 1903.[84] This brief historical overview is important for two reasons. First, the fact that historically jihad has emerged from within these societies suggests that it is not something alien to these societies and not necessarily imposed on them by global jihadis in the Middle East. Moreover, latter day jihadis in the form of Boko Haram look for inspiration from Uthman dan Fodio's jihad in the nineteenth century and deliberately seek to emulate his campaign in their struggle against Abuja.[85]

It is this context that results in scholars like John Campbell arguing that groups like Boko Haram are the product of local political dynamics and are more focused on the destruction of their respective states rather than waging war against the West.[86] Critics might well respond by noting that there is considerable antipathy directed against the West as evinced by attacks on American and French troops in the region. However, this antipathy has less to do with Islamist ideologies of the 'Great Satan' in reference to the United States and more to do with local dynamics. Consider here the establishment of a US military base in Tamanrasset in southern Algeria and the negative impact this had on the livelihood of local residents. To secure water for the base, a well was sunk in an area 15 km to the north of the base – in the Oued Otoul – and water pumped to the military base. This, however, served to lower the water table and dry up the wells of local residents who were dependent on this water for their livelihood: horticulture. Needless to say, this callous act hardly endeared the American presence to locals – a fact that was exploited by Islamists operating in the area.[87]

Anger against the French in Niger has its origins in 2007 when the French company, Veolia Entertainment became a 51 per cent shareholder in a newly privatized company that controlled 100 per cent of the country's water sector. Shortly after securing its 51 per cent stake, Veolia Entertainment increased water tariffs phenomenally – this, too, in a water-scarce country that also happens to be one of the poorest on the planet. This was followed by widespread unrest.[88] Western countries also earn the ire of local citizens when they prop up rapacious local political elites. The problem is further exacerbated by the fact that Western countries do not have reliable human intelligence on the ground and therefore rely on local intelligence services.[89] These, of course, colour such intelligence reports in the interests of regime security as opposed to the human security of ordinary citizens. Portraying local dissidents and local Islamist insurgencies as part of Global Jihad, Inc., of course, is in the interests of governments in the Sahel.

Identity theorists, whose work examines the manifold roles that identity plays in generating popular support for terrorist organizations, assist with the recruitment of new members and the types of attacks undertaken also support critical terrorist scholars' position on the central importance of identity.[90] Research conducted by Schwartz, Dunkel and Waterman[91] emphasizes how terrorist groups could emerge where there is a confluence of different identities. Cultural identities that stress the collective over the individual, coupled with a fundamentalist and literal interpretation of religious texts, as well as a social identity based on sharp contrasts between the in- and out-groups all contribute to terrorism. Consider here the case of the 4,000- strong Macina Liberation Front (MLF), which instrumentalizes religion (Islam) for reasons of ethnocentric nationalism. This is an ethnic Fulani (also called Peul) movement that seeks to revive the nineteenth-century Macina Empire. There are 20 million Fulani spread across the Sahel and the MLF recruits from among them.[92] The same could be said of the Kanuri-dominated Boko Haram[93] which recruits not only from the 7 million Kanuri in Nigeria, but also from among the 1,1 million Kanuri in Chad, the 850,000 Kanuri in Niger and the 56,000 Kanuri in Cameroon.[94]

In an effort to broaden its appeal, Boko Haram has also reached out to Hausa-Fulani peoples across the region, but the upper echelons of the movements remain Kanuri-dominated. Far from having global jihadi organizations facilitating cooperation among the region's disparate Islamists, it is local kinship networks driving such cooperation. Moreover, far from forming some united Islamic front, the cooperation among Islamists sharing different ethnicities often results in 'short-term, opportunistic alliances to ensure the continuation of the respective groups' activities rather than more substantive long-term bonds of affiliation'.[95]

Insights from critical terrorism studies highlight the fact that terrorism is a product of local conditions. Only by de-linking terrorism from the objective conditions that have given rise to it could one come to the erroneous conclusion that terrorist groups in the Sahel are a recent phenomenon and merely franchises of global terror networks.

Conclusion

The inescapable conclusion of this chapter is that terrorism in the Sahel is the result of local conditions. Those who stress the international dimension over local conditions lack understanding of regional dynamics from politics and the environment to issues of identity and economics.[96] The respected Africanist and specialist on jihadis in Africa, Marc-Antoine Perouse de Montclos opines that it is the *local* balance of power that determines the development of terrorism in the region.[97] He goes on to also point out that stressing the international jihadi connection underestimates the lack of unity among jihadis – that they do not constitute a united front. He notes that dissent within their ranks 'comes from doctrinal disputes as much as from personal rivalries about commands, tactics, the choice of targets, or the distribution of the spoils of war'.[98] The constant mergers and splits among Islamists in the Sahel certainly underscore the point being made.[99]

Even the mergers between local Islamist groups and international jihadi networks are hardly sustainable. The internal dynamics of these groups – for instance, focusing on the Kanuri or Fulani ethnic groups – also prevent a global jihadi narrative from dominating the agenda of Boko Haram or the Macina Liberation Front, respectively. Despite Boko Haram's leader Abubaker Shekau taking an oath of allegiance to ISIS's 'caliph' Abu Bakr al-Baghdadi and renaming the Boko Haram as ISIS West Africa Province, tensions emerged in their relationship that resulted in al-Baghdadi dismissing Shekau in August 2016 and replacing him with Abu Musab al-Barnawi, Muhammed Yusuf's son. Angered, Shekau went off to revive his old organization.[100] Policymakers should exploit these tensions to better manage the terrorist threat in the region.

The preceding observation does not mean that the global jihadi narrative holds no relevance in the Sahel. In the Sahel, militant insurgencies began as sub-state terrorist groups. Western support for the often-corrupt states of the region confronting these insurgencies in the form of counterterrorism assistance results in these sub-state terrorist movements finding support from other external sources as well. This then facilitates the entry of global jihadis into the Sahel in the form of Al Qaeda and ISIS. Instead, Western countries need to problematize the African state, utilizing its leverage over Sahelian governments to open up the democratic space in their respective polities.

Policymakers should ponder why Senegal, though situated in a volatile region, and whose population is 92 per cent Muslim, is free from such radicalization. Perhaps the answer lies in the fact that it is a genuine democracy where the opposition routinely comes to power through elections and where the state attempts to respond to people's needs.[101] This suggests that more holistic solutions are needed for the Sahel's myriad challenges. These holistic solutions should stress better development and governance as opposed to military-centred responses. Even the men in uniform are beginning to accept the fact that the military is a blunt instrument. Recently, Major-General Barre Seguin, Director of Strategy, Plans and Programmes at AFRICOM stated, 'The overarching solution is not the military. If we tend toward military solutions, we're only addressing the symptoms and not the root cause: the political, social, economic and environmental insecurities.'[102] This does not mean, of course, that there is no role for the military in the Sahel. The various terrorist groups in the region must be confronted militarily in order to save the lives of innocent civilians. However, the military must not be the primary instrument of an overarching counterterrorism policy and where force is deployed it must be proportional to and cognizant of the long-term consequences for civilians.

Inclusive state-building will also need to be stressed given the competing ethnocentric nationalisms in the region. As one Tuareg elder in Kidal, northern Mali, stated, 'We need a new definition of the nation that includes us.'[103] Moderate Sufi- Islamic civil society should also be given a role in this state-building project.

Notes

1 'UN Security Council voices concern over security situation in West Africa', *Xinhua*, 12 January 2018. Internet: www.xinhuanet.com/english/2018-01/12/c_1368893314.htm (accessed 13 January 2018).
2 Jeremy H. Keenan, 'Instability and terrorism in Africa's Sahel: A primer', *Just Security*, 26 January 2016. Internet: http://www.justsecurity.org./28972/instability-terrorism-afr icas-sahel-primer (accessed 25 January 2017).
3 Stephen Harrison, 'Securitization initiatives in the Sahara-Sahel region in the twenty-first century', *African Security*, 8, no. 4 (2015): 227–9.
4 Hussein Solomon, *Terrorism and Counter-Terrorism in Africa: Fighting Insurgency from Al Shabaab, Ansar Dine and Boko Haram* (London: Palgrave Macmillan, 2015), pp. 72–3.
5 Tuesday Reitano, 'An evolving threat: The two faces of Sahel terrorism', *The Broker*, 20 January 2016. Internet: http://www.thebrokeronline.eu/Blogs/Sahel-Watch-a-livin g-analysis-of-the-conflict-in-Mali/An-evolving-threat-the-two-faces-of-Sahel-terroris m (accessed 25 January 2017).

6. Ibid.
7. Hussein Solomon, 'The particular role of religion in Islamic State', *The South African Journal of International Affairs*, 2017. Internet: https://dx.doi.org/10.1080/10220461.2016.1272486 (accessed 5 October 2017).
8. Bruce Hoffman and Fernando Reinares, 'Introduction', in Bruce Hoffman and Fernando Reinares (eds), *The Evolution of the Global Terrorist Threat: From 9/11 to Osama Bin Laden's Death* (New York: Columbia University Press, 2014), pp. ix–xiv.
9. 'Eleven soldiers killed in Mali attack', *The Citizen*, 5 March 2017. Internet: http://citizen.co.za/news/news-africa/1448187/eleven-soldiers-killed-mali-attack (accessed 9 March 2017).
10. Antonia Ward, 'Why Africa could provide an "ISIS Renaissance"', *The National Interest*, 11 January 2018. Internet: http://nationalinterest.org/feature/why-africa-could-provide-isis-renaissance-23199 (accessed 11 January 2018).
11. Jamie Detmer, 'North Africa Braces for impact as Islamic State Fighters return', *Voice of America*, 19 December 2017. Internet: https://www.voanews.com/a/north-africa-braces-impact-islamic-state-fighters-return/417-589.html (accessed 11 January 2018).
12. Solomon, *Terrorism and Counter-Terrorism in Africa*, p. 88.
13. ReliefWeb Report, *Chad: Fighting Boko Haram in Chad: Beyond Military Measures*, 8 March 2017. Website: http://reliefweb.int/report/fighting-boko-haram-chad-beyond-military-measures (accessed 9 March 2017).
14. Marc-Antoine Perouse de Montclos, 'Jihad in Sub-Saharan Africa: Challenging the Narratives of the War on Terror', *World Policy Papers* (New York: World Policy Institute, October 2016), p. 9.
15. John Campbell, 'Radical Islamist terrorism in West Africa', *Council on Foreign Relations*, 16 March 2016. Internet: https://www.cfr.org/blog/radical-islamist-terrorism-west-africa (accessed 31 August 2017).
16. Brahima Ouedraogo, 'Jihadists attack north Burkina Faso towns amid film festival', *US News*, 28 February 2017. Internet: https://www.usnews.com/news/world/articles/2017-02-28/suspected-jihadists-attack-norhern-burkina-faso-towns (accessed 3 March 2017).
17. Josue Michels, 'Germany and France Arm West Africans', *The Trumpet*, 23 August 2017. Internet: https://www.thetrumpet.com/18181-germany-and-france-arm-west-africans (accessed 31 August 2017).
18. Connor Gaffey, 'Who is Iyad Ag Ghaly, Mali's veteran jihadi?' *Newsweek*, 29 June 2016. Internet: http://europe.newsweek.com/who-iyad-ag-ghaly-malis-veteran-jihadi-475436? (accessed 9 March 2017).
19. Ibid.
20. Mali: Sahel Coalition Formed, *Strategy Page*, 16 February 2017. Internet: https://www.strategypage.com/qnd/mali/articles/20170216.aspx (accessed 9 March 2017).
21. Michels, 'Germany and France Arm West Africans'.
22. Mali: Sahel Coalition Formed, *Strategy Page*.
23. Jamie Read, 'Burkina Faso: Ansar ul Islam attack leaves a dozen militants dead', *SOFREP News*, 11 December 2017. Internet: https://sofrep.com/93766/burkina-faso-ansarul-islam-attack/ (accessed 11 January 2018).
24. Didier Bamouni, 'Fighting terrorism in Burkina Faso', *DefenceWeb*, 15 February 2017. Internet: http://www.defenceweb.co.za/index/php?view=article&catid=56%3Adiplomscy-a-peace-&id=46811%3Afighting-terrorisminburkinafaso&tmpl=component (accessed 9 March 2017).

25 Connor Gaffey, 'Mali hotel attack: What is the Macina Liberation Front, Mali's Boko Haram', *Newsweek*, 24 November 2015. Internet: http://europe.newsweek.com/mali-hotel-attack-who-are-macina-liberation-front-malis-boko-haram-397727 (accessed 9 March 2017).
26 Connor Gaffey, 'African Jihadi Groups Unite and Pledge Allegiance to Al Qaeda', *Newsweek*, 3 March 2017. Internet: http://europe.newsweek.com/al-qaeda-groups-united-Sahel-563351?rm=eu# (accessed 9 March 2017).
27 Sheikh Beqaj, 'Mali's extremist movements integrate into one organization', *Arabs Today*, 2 March 2017. http://arabstoday.net/en/314/malis-extremist-movements-integrate-into-one-organization-154808 (accessed 9 March 2017).
28 Yonah Alexander, 'Terrorism in North Africa and the Sahel in 2015', *Inter-University Centre for Terrorism Studies*, Potomac Institute for Policy Studies, March 2016. Internet: www.potomacinstitute.org/images/TerrNASahel2015.pdf (accessed 13 December 2016).
29 Ward, 'Why Africa could provide an "ISIS Renaissance"'.
30 Jeremy Keenan, *The Dying Sahara: US Imperialism and Terror in Africa* (London: Pluto Press, 2013), p. 222.
31 'UN Security Council voices concern over security situation in West Africa'.
32 Keenan, *The Dying Sahara: US Imperialism and Terror in Africa*, p. 10.
33 Harrison, 'Securitization initiatives in the Sahara-Sahel region in the twenty-first century', p. 237.
34 'Macron eyes new ties with Africa to better tackle terrorism, migration', *Xinhuanet*, 18 December 2017. Internet: http://news.xinhuanet.com/english/2017-12/18c_1368 32846.htm (accessed 19 December 2017).
35 Detmer, 'North Africa Braces for impact as Islamic State Fighters return'.
36 Ward, 'Why Africa could provide an "ISIS Renaissance"'.
37 Keenan, *The Dying Sahara: US Imperialism and Terror in Africa*, p. 17.
38 Martin Fey, 'View from the Right: Making pseudo-nations safe for democracy is nearly impossible', *Norwich Bulletin*, 16 December 2017. Internet: https:///norwichbulletin.com/opinion/20171216/view-from-right-making-pseudo-nations-safe-for-democracy-is-nearly-impossible (accessed 18 December 2017).
39 Keenan, *The Dying Sahara: US Imperialism and Terror in Africa*, p. 24.
40 Malik Ibrahim, 'America's self-defeating Sahel strategy', *Geopolitical Monitor*, 26 October 2017. Internet: http://www.geopoliticalmonitor.com/america-self-defeating-sahel-strategy/ (accessed 1 November 2017).
41 Ibid., p. 242.
42 Ibid., p. 233.
43 Mali: Sahel Coalition Formed, *Strategy Page*.
44 Ibid.
45 Sangar Ali, 'Italy plans to shift military force from Iraq to Niger', *Kurdistan24.net*, 25 December 2017. Internet: www.kurdistan24.net/en/news/c6a77cda-9661-40c3-9-d66-29cfa800bf91 (accessed 10 January 2018).
46 Amandla Thomas Johnson, 'Britain to join France in West Africa counter-terrorism mission', *Middle East Eye*, 11 January 2018. Internet: www.middleeasteye.net/news/britain-expected-join-west-africa-counter-terrorism-mission-1931687346 (accessed 13 January 2018).
47 Michels, 'Germany and France Arm West Africans'.
48 'Sahel countries set up fund for anti-terror campaign', *Business Day*, 9 January 2018. Internet: https: www.businesslive.co.za/bd/world/africa/2018-01-19-sahel-countries-set-up-fund-for-anti-terror-campaign/ (accessed 10 January 2018).

49 Daphne Benoit, 'Sahel force funding shows Saudi serious on terrorism fight: Analysts', *The Citizen*, 15 December 2017. Internet: https://citizen.co.za/news-africa.1760610/africa-saudi-uae-france-military-conflict/ (accessed 18 December 2017).
50 Ralph Peters, 'Here's what the US is doing in Africa', *New York Post*, 25 November 2017. Internet: https://nypost.com/2017/11/25/what-us-soldiers-like-la-david-johnson-are-doing-in-africa (accessed 11 January 2018).
51 ReliefWeb Report, *Chad: Fighting Boko Haram in Chad: Beyond Military Measures*.
52 Ibrahim, 'America's self-defeating Sahel strategy'.
53 Harrison, 'Securitization initiatives in the Sahara-Sahel region in the twenty-first century', p. 227.
54 'The eyes in the skies: Taking on West Africa's terrorists', *The Economist*, 26 November 2016. Internet: https://www.economist.com/news/middle-east-and-africa/217108 26-america-has-been-revving-up-its-efforts-against-terrorist-groups-taking (accessed 31 August 2017).
55 J. Joseph, 'Critical of what? Terrorism and its study', *International Relations*, 23, no. 1 (2009): 93.
56 J. L. Stump and P. Dixit, 'Towards a completely constructivist critical terrorism studies', *International Relations*, 26, no. 2 (2011): 200.
57 Bob Brecher and Mark Devenney, 'Introduction: Philosophy, politics, terror', in Bob Brecher, Mark Devenney and Aaron Winter (eds), *Discourses and Practices of Terrorism: Interrogating Terror* (London: Routledge, 2010), p. 1.
58 Richard Jackson, Eamon Murphy and Scott Poynting, 'Introduction: Terrorism, the state and the study of political terror', in Richard Jackson, Eamon Murphy and Scott Poynting (eds), *Contemporary State Terrorism: Theory and Practice* (London: Routledge, 2010), p. 1.
59 'Cameroonian Critic jailed', *Mail and Guardian*, 33, no. 44 (3–9 November 2016): 20.
60 Keenan, *The Dying Sahara: US Imperialism and Terror in Africa*, p. 29.
61 Ibid.
62 Ibid., p. 12.
63 'The eyes in the skies: Tracking West Africa's terrorists'.
64 Ibid.
65 Robert Fulford, 'Boko Haram and the broken country that let it thrive', *National Post*, 15 December 2017. Internet: http://nationalpost.com/opinion/robert-fulford-boko-haram-and-the-broken-country-that-let-it-thrive (accessed 18 December 2017).
66 United Nations Development Programme, *Journeys to Extremism in Africa*. UNDP, New York, 2017, p. 5.
67 *Amnesty International* (Nigeria: Human Rights Agenda, 2011–2015), p. 30.
68 R. Jackson, 'Security, democracy and the rhetoric of counter-terrorism', *Democracy and Security*, 1, no. 2 (2005): 147.
69 Richard Jackson, Marie Breen Smyth and Jeroen Gunning, 'Introduction: The case for critical terrorism studies', in Richard Jackson, Marien Breen Smyth and Jeroen Gunning (eds), *Critical Terrorism Studies: A New Research Agenda* (London: Routledge, 2009), p. 1.
70 Marc-Antoine Boisvert, 'Failing at violence: The long-lasting impact of pro-government militias in northern Mali since 2012', *African Security*, 8, no. 4 (2015): 272–98.
71 Ibid., p. 285.
72 'Chad: Fighting Boko Haram in Chad: Beyond military measures', *ReliefWeb*, 8 March 2017. Internet: https://www.reliefweb.int/report/fighting-boko-haram-chad-beyond-military-measures (accessed 9 March 2017).

73 R. Jackson, 'The core commitments of critical terrorism studies', *European Political Science*, 6 (2007): 244.
74 M. Neocleous, 'Security, liberty and the myth of balance: Towards a critique of security politics', *Contemporary Political Theory*, 6 (2007): 133; J. Gunning, 'Babies and bathwaters: Reflecting on the pitfalls of critical terrorism studies', *European Political Science*, 6 (2007): 236.
75 'The eyes in the skies: Tracking West Africa's terrorists'.
76 'Boosting youth employment in Niger', *The World Bank*, 11 June 2013. Internet: www.worldbank.org/eng/news/feature/2013/06/11-boosting-youth-employment-in-niger (accessed 27 January 2018).
77 'UN Security Council voices concern over security situation in West Africa'.
78 'Africa's Sahel region can become hotbed for terrorist recruitment, UN official warns', *UN News Centre*, 25 November 2015. Internet: www.un.org/apps/news/story.aspx?NewsID=52656# (accessed 25 January 2017).
79 United Nations Development Programme, *Journeys to Extremism in Africa*, p. 5.
80 'UN Security Council voices concern over security situation in West Africa'.
81 Solomon, *Terrorism and Counter-Terrorism in Africa*, p. 99.
82 Ibid., p. 69.
83 Ibid.
84 de Montclos, 'Jihad in Sub-Saharan Africa', p. 15.
85 Walter Gam Nkwi, 'Terrorism in West African History: A 21st century appraisal', *Austral: Brazilian Journal of Strategy and International Relations*, 4, no. 8 (July–December 2015): 84.
86 Campbell, 'Radical Islamist terrorism in West Africa'.
87 Keenan, *The Dying Sahara: US Imperialism and Terror in Africa*, p. 17.
88 Ibid., p. 40.
89 Ibid., p. 230.
90 Seth J. Schwartz, Curtis S. Dunkel and Alan S. Waterman, 'Terrorism: An identity theory perspective', *Studies in Conflict and Terrorism*, 32 (2009): 539.
91 Ibid., pp. 537–59.
92 Gaffey, 'Mali hotel attack'.
93 Zacharias P. Pieri and Jacob Zenn, 'The Boko Haram paradox: Ethnicity, religion and historical memory in pursuit of a Caliphate', in James J. Hentz and Hussein Solomon (eds), *Understanding Boko Haram: Terrorism and Insurgency in Africa* (London: Routledge, 2017), p. 42.
94 Kanuri People, *Wikipedia*, 2013. Internet: https://en.wikipedia.org/wiki/Kanuri_people (accessed 25 October 2017).
95 Cristina Barrios and Tobias Koepf, 'Introduction and summary', in Cristina Barrios and Tobias Koepf (eds), *Re-mapping the Sahel: Transnational Security Challenges and International Responses*, Issue Report No. 19 (Paris: European Union Institute for Security Studies, June 2014), p. 6.
96 de Montclos, 'Jihad in Sub-Saharan Africa', p. 3.
97 Ibid., p. 10.
98 Ibid., p. 11.
99 Reitano, 'An evolving threat'.
100 Anneli Botha, Martin Ewi, Uyo Salifu and Mahdi Abdile, 'Understanding Nigerian citizens' perspectives on Boko Haram', *ISS Monograph 196*. Pretoria, Institute for Security Studies, 2016, p. 1.
101 Campbell, 'Radical Islamist terrorism in West Africa'.

102 Kimberly Dozier, 'Too many generals, not enough troops or cash to catch terrorists in the Sahel', *The Cipher Brief*, 20 December 2017. Internet: https://www.thecipherbrief.com/article/africa/many-generals-not-enough-troops-catch-terrorists-sahel (accessed 11 January 2018).

103 Stepahnie Rezard and Michael Shurkin, *Achieving Peace in Northern Mali: Past Agreements, Local Conflicts, and the Prospects for a Durable Settlement* (Santa Monica: RAND Corporation, 2015), p. 36.

JIHAD IN MALI

REGIONAL CONDITIONS, REGIONAL GOALS, GLOBAL IMPORTANCE

Stephen A. Harmon

Introduction

Mali, though considered remote in the popular imagination, the home of fabled Timbuktu, is nonetheless a key country in the Sahara-Sahel region owing to its location astride both north-south and east-west trade routes across the Sahara. The jihad movement in Mali is peripheral, rather than global, so long as the global jihad movement is defined as concentrated in the core countries of the Middle East. From the Middle Eastern perspective, Mali is clearly on the periphery of the Islamic world. From the Islamist perspective, the Malian jihad, like those in neighbouring states, is peripheral and local because it focuses on the 'Near Enemy', the hypocrite regional regimes that claim to be Muslim but fail to establish sharia law. It does not focus on the 'Far Enemy', the United States and its Western allies who support and enable the hypocrite Arab regimes. The 'Far Enemy' is the focus of the global jihad. We know Mali's jihad is peripheral for two reasons.

First, it was caused by local and regional conditions, not by commitment to the global goals of Al Qaeda Central or the ISIS. One such local condition is the ongoing threat of Tuareg rebellion. Four Tuareg nationalist rebellions centred in the northern part of Mali have erupted since it achieved independence from France in 1960. These rebellions were the result of lingering resentments and racism that date from the pre-colonial era and that were exacerbated during the colonial period by aspects of French policy. Another source of Tuareg resentment was that their pastoral economy was destroyed by regional droughts in the late twentieth century.[1] It seems the Saharan Tuareg were the canaries in the coal mine of climate change. Another layer of complexity regarding the Tuareg rebellions lies in the fact that there are major rivalries within the Tuareg, both among clans and within clans (see p. 12). A fifth Tuareg rebellion cannot be ruled out because the underlying conditions have not changed significantly. Other local Malian conditions include social problems such as corruption, smuggling contraband and human trafficking. Malian authorities routinely accept payoffs from smugglers and traffickers and are capable of accepting a cut of the earnings that jihadis make on terrorist activities, including the kidnapping of Western tourists and aid workers.[2]

Yet another local condition is poor economic prospects. Much of Mali's youth sees little hope for the future, and as a result, youths as young as fourteen are turning to the mosques, some of which are led by radical imams.[3] The temptation of easy money in contraband or jihad draws in many young Malians who feel cut off from the cash economy and left out of the social contract. Finally, there is the failure of Mali's democratic institutions to resolve any of these issues. Mali's democracy is a procedural democracy, not a genuine one. In other words, it follows the procedure of democracy, elections, a representative legislature and so on, but it does not follow the spirit of democracy. The political elite remains indifferent, if not predatory, towards the ordinary people. The resulting disillusionment with democratic institutions makes many Malians susceptible to jihadi recruitment.[4]

Second, Mali's jihad is peripheral because jihadi activity in the broader region beyond Mali remains primarily national and regional, rather than global. The Algerian jihad movement is dominated by its most active jihadi organization, Al Qaeda in the Islamic Maghreb (AQIM). Despite its highly publicized affiliation with Al Qaeda Central in 2006, AQIM remains focused on the overthrow of Algeria's (apostate) military government. The roots of the Algerian jihad go back to the Dirty War of the 1990s, and its goal, despite its operations in the Malian Sahara, remains the creation of an islamic state in Algeria.[5] The Algerian jihad's most important contribution to the global jihad began even before the Al Qaeda merger, namely, the funnelling of newly-recruited fighters from North Africa to Iraq to join the Al Qaeda in Iraq (AQI) insurgency opposing the American occupation and Iraq's Shi'a government during the mid-2000s.[6] The Nigerian jihad movement, dominated by Boko Haram, is likewise a national and regional jihad. Boko Haram remains focused on combating the Nigerian security forces, known for their ham-handedness and brutality, and evidence of the presence of Boko Haram fighters in Mali, though cited by many sources, remains anecdotal.[7] Only ISIS, active in parts of Libya and Mali, is genuinely part of the global jihad. But its presence in Mali is likewise limited, although the potential of the Malian jihad movement linking up with ISIS in Libya is worrisome. Therefore, this chapter will argue that while Mali is not, itself, as peripheral as people might think, its jihad movement is a local and/or regional one, not a cog in the wheel of global jihad.

Radicalization of Islam in the north

Although Mali's jihad erupted suddenly in 2012, as far as the outside world was concerned, the process of radicalization in the north of Mali had been going on for some time. Northern Mali, like the rest of the country, had formerly been known for a tolerant and largely non-violent strain of Islam, dominated by Sufi movements that penetrated the region in the eighteenth and nineteenth centuries. But radical Islamism had begun to affect the north, beginning in the late 1990s, via two vectors. One of these was the Pakistani Tablighi Jama'at, the world's largest Muslim proselytizing organization. Tablighi preachers had made contact with Tuareg clans in the Kidal Région,[8] including the noble Kel Adagh, or Ifoghas

Tuareg, and one of its leaders, Iyad ag Ghali. They had also made contact with Fulbe Qur'anic schoolteachers in the Gao Région.[9] The other vector was radical preachers at Wahhabi-funded mosques at Timbuktu and Gao. A Malian branch of the Saudi Wahhabi movement had taken root in the capital Bamako in the 1950s, and it has slowly gained traction in the country's remote north in recent decades. Ag Ghali had radicalized many Tuareg rebels in the Kidal Région, influencing them with jihadi rhetoric, while radical Fulbe preachers, some also influenced by Wahhabi preachers, had radicalized many of their students, especially in towns and villages along the Niger River. Many of Ag Ghali's radicalized Tuareg fighters flocked to his Ansar Dine (Supporters of the Faith) organization based at Kidal, while radicalized Fulbe youths were readily recruited by the Movement for Tawhid and Jihad in West Africa, known by its French acronym MUJAO.[10] These two movements and the jihadi militias they recruited and fielded, under the leadership of AQIM, formed the core of the Malian jihad.

Prior to these radicalization efforts, AQIM had become established in the Kidal Région by the early 2000s, some say as early as the mid-1990s.[11] However, AQIM's interest in Mali had been as a rear base for its fighters, who had found themselves severely hampered by Algerian security forces in their home area of operations, the Kabyle region of northern Algeria, which had earned the nickname 'Triangle of Death' during Algeria's Dirty War. Their chief interest in Mali in the early 2000s had not been prosecuting jihad, but, rather, raising money to buy weapons for their national jihad in Algeria. This they did by ransoming kidnapped European hostages, beginning in 2003, and by profiting from and participating in regional contraband trafficking. This trafficking was in both licit commodities, such as subsidized foodstuffs and supplies and untaxed cigarettes, as well as illicit commodities, such as arms and drugs, along with the trafficking of undocumented labour migrants into and across the Sahara.

Algerian jihadis established themselves in remote areas of northern Mali by posing as businessmen, establishing community links with local Tuareg and Malian Arab (Bidan) families, including marriage ties. They pursued a mix of licit and illicit commerce common in much of Algeria, including the Algeria–Mali border regions, called *trabendo* (from contraband).[12] Once the smuggling routes are established and the infrastructure—trucks and drivers and roads—is intact, and customs officials and security forces are either bribed or intimidated, it is an easy shift from the smuggling of ordinary commodities, such as pasta and tyres, to the trafficking of illicit commodities like drugs, arms, and even labour migrants. An early exemplar of this process was AQIM's 'southern emir' Mokhtar Belmokhtar, born and bred to *trabendo* in his native Algeria and schooled in jihad in the Afghanistan/Pakistan border regions. Belmokhtar established marriage links with Bidan tribes in the north of the Timbuktu Région and made a lifelong career out of the Saharan traffic in untaxed cigarettes, earning the nickname Mr. Marlboro. This nexus of jihadi power and pre-existing business networks changed in degree and in kind after 2007, when the large-scale smuggling of South American cocaine through West African countries, especially Mali, began. Large quantities of cocaine started arriving in the Timbuktu and Gao Régions by truck or by plane around 2007. From there the cocaine was transferred to smaller trucks for shipment north to Algeria and ultimately to Europe. It was trafficked along established routes, one stretching from Gao to Kidal to unmapped, wild-west border towns, such as al-Khalil, and then through Algeria via established *trabendo* routes to the Mediterranean coast. The smuggling was directed by Tuareg and Bidan commercial families, including some who had built business and family ties with Algerian jihadis. AQIM supplied protection for the smugglers and enforced contracts, and also sometimes participated in the traffic directly. The money thus gained was used to buy arms, recruit fighters and stockpile supplies in desert caches. The Bidan trading families typically used their profits to invest in licit enterprises such as businesses and workshops and to build villas at Gao and other regional towns.[13]

The jihad begins

Mali's jihad did not begin in earnest until mid-2012, when AQIM and its affiliates Ansar Dine and MUJAO hijacked what was at that time the fourth Tuareg nationalist rebellion in northern Mali since independence. The Tuareg rebellion was led by the secular-nationalist National Movement for the Liberation of Azawad (MNLA). At first AQIM and its affiliates provided auxiliary support for the MNLA in its seizure of Mali's three northern regional capitals, Timbuktu, Gao and Kidal. But by mid-2012, the jihadis turned on their erstwhile allies, expelling the MNLA from the cities and driving many of them into exile. AQIM and its hitherto little-known affiliates Ansar Dine and MUJAO emerged in control of the entire northern part of Mali, sparsely populated, but comprising well over half of Mali's national territory. The Malian jihad was on in earnest.[14]

Both the Tuareg nationalist rebellion and its subsequent commandeering by the Islamist militias were unintentionally abetted by similarly dramatic political developments in the capital Bamako. In late March of 2012, the democratically elected President Amadou Toumani Touré (ATT) was overthrown in a coup d'état led by Amadou Sanogo, a Malian army captain. ATT, who had mere weeks to go to complete his second, and last, constitutionally permitted term, fled without resistance when mutinous troops overran the presidential palace at Koulouba, overlooking Bamako. Malian troops in the north, who had been pushed back in the first months of the rebellion, now fled the north entirely, abandoning equipment and vehicles and facilitating the Tuareg rebels' seizure of the three undefended northern capitals. The coup-makers, Capt. Sanogo and his men, were based at the Kati Barracks about an hour north-west of Bamako. It was they who had moved on the presidential complex at Koulouba. They were motivated by at least two factors, anger and mistrust towards President ATT and frustration over the decline of the army as a result of underfunding and corruption. Elements of the army, along with many Malians, had become disenchanted with the once popular ATT because he presided over a corrupt regime. His officials, reportedly including the president himself, had colluded with traffickers and smugglers and even jihadis, taking cuts from their *trabendo* and kidnapping operations. They were also angry with the army high command over the humiliating defeats in the north, as well as the weak condition of the army due to underfunding by the government and the 'hollowing out' of units and supplies by internal corruption. They came to Koulouba to demand answers and wound up seizing power almost spontaneously.[15] Amid negative regional and international reactions to the coup, an interim government was hastily agreed upon. The interim government grew out of a deal made with coupist Amadou Sanogo to restore civilian government, if not constitutionality. The deal was brokered by the Economic Community for West African States (ECOWAS). It included an interim president, Dioncounda Traoré, an interim prime minister, Cheikh Modibo Diarra, and a civilian government of twenty-four ministers. Sanogo formally stood down but retained effective control over the army, especially the troops stationed near the capital, throughout most of 2012. With the political situation in the capital still in flux, the Islamist militias turned against the Tuareg secular-nationalist rebellion in June and July and took control of the three northern Régions themselves, with MUJAO holding power at Gao and Ansar Dine, backed by its AQIM patrons, holding Timbuktu and Kidal.[16]

At first neither the ethnic makeup of the Islamist militias nor the degree of their allegiance to AQIM was well known to outsiders. As time passed, answers to these questions emerged. Ansar Dine was largely composed of radicalized Tuareg, under the leadership of Iyad ag Ghali. MUJAO was originally composed of Bidan (nomadic Arabs) from northern Mali, Mauritania and parts of Algeria, though they later recruited from among Malian Fulbe youth and other local ethnicities. Both groups were under significant supervision from AQIM. When they first came on the scene as allies of MNLA, they operated more like regular insurgent movements rather than non-state terrorist groups. After they took over power in Mali's northern regions, they perpetrated a form of state terrorism to stifle resistance and maintain their authority. To this end, they provided some government services and utilities, while imposing a restrictive code regarding dress, smoking, entertainment and social interactions. This code was enforced with public beatings for minor infractions, as well as occasional imposition of the so-called *hudud* punishments for more serious infractions, such as stealing and adultery.[17] After being driven from their urban strongholds by French troops and their allies, beginning in January of 2013 (see later), they dispersed and regrouped abroad in Algeria and Libya or went to ground locally, relying on the community and family ties they had built earlier. As soon as they were dislodged from the cities by Opération Serval, the French-led intervention, they began to act like non-state terrorist organizations, perpetrating suicide bombings and car bombings. But all the while they continued to extract funds through kidnapping for ransom, 'taxing' and 'protecting' the regional contraband traffic and participating directly in that traffic as well.

By late 2012, the international community was rallying to support Mali in the face of the occupation of its northern regions by Al Qaeda-linked Sunni Islamist terrorist groups. With talk of some sort of multilateral intervention in the air, Ansar Dine, especially, seemed to be jockeying to make a deal with the Malian government. However, in early January, the Islamists, including Ansar Dine, appeared to put everything on the line for a massive drive into central Mali. Arriving in 'several dozen' armed Toyota 4 x 4 pick-up trucks—technicals—fighters from Ansar Dine, MUJAO and AQIM seized the central Malian towns of Konna, in the Région of Mopti, and Diabaly, in the Région of Segou. Konna lay within striking distance of Sévaré airbase, the field headquarters of the Malian army. Diabaly lay astride the road to Bamako. The Islamist militias seized Konna and Diabaly on Wednesday, 9 January 2013.[18] The raid was reportedly led by radical Fulbe cleric Amadou Koufa.[19] The Islamist advance into central Mali, orchestrated by AQIM, threatened to move Mali's jihad to a new level. Though still a national jihad, it was definitely attracting global attention.

International military intervention

The terrorists' motorized thrusts led to a massive French military intervention in the form of Opération Serval, which began on Friday, 11 January. French SOF troops hastily deployed from neighbouring countries, including Côte d'Ivoire. This action forced a halt of the Islamists' drive and then a massive retreat. More French troops arrived from the metropole over the next few days to reinforce Bamako and the Sévaré airbase near Mopti City. After driving the jihadis from their forward positions at Konna and Diabaly, Opération Serval quickly liberated the cities of Timbuktu and Gao, beginning on 25 January, driving the Islamist militias into the desert. French President François Hollande arrived at Sévaré on 2 February, and was greeted by interim president Traoré and his ministers. He then made an appearance at Timbuktu to receive the accolades of the people.[20] Gao, and its strategic bridge over the Niger, was liberated on 26 January. As was the case in Timbuktu, little resistance was put up by the Islamists, at least at first. But the struggle had not ended; it had merely entered a new phase. On 8 February, Gao's first ever suicide bombing rocked the city, followed by rocket attacks on the first responders. Days later MUJAO fighters re-entered Gao, crossing the river in canoes, and engaged Malian troops who had taken up positions in the city. With the help of French troops, this new resistance was soon quelled. The cities had fallen quickly, but the Islamists just as quickly found ways to regroup. MUJAO, for example, switched from perpetrating state terrorism at Gao during the time that they controlled it to non-state terrorism, including suicide bombings, once they had been driven from power. Kidal would prove more complicated. First of all, the French refused to allow Malian soldiers to participate in the liberation of Kidal. Supported by Malian troops during the liberation of Konna and Diabaly as well as of Timbuktu and Gao, the French had been alarmed by reports of reprisals, beatings and killings of captured terrorist suspects. Such reprisals were perpetrated by Malian troops, humiliated by their defeat the previous year and angered by the excesses of the jihadis perpetrated against the Malian people. Instead, the French preferred to have the support of Chadian troops, who were more disciplined and properly trained for desert combat. The French also allowed remnants of the rebel

MNLA to occupy Kidal City as the Islamists fled. The Malian army and elements of the Malian public, already angered by France's refusal to permit Malian security forces to participate in the liberation of Kidal, were outraged that the French would allow unrepentant MNLA rebels into the town.[21]

The subsequent fighting in the hinterland of the Région of Kidal proved to be the most difficult and deadly of the entire operation. The Amettetaï Valley, north of Kidal City and south-east of the strategic airbase at Tessalit, proved to be the site of the war's heaviest fighting. AQIM and Ansar Dine had been storing caches of weapons and food in the valley for years.[22] Abou Zeid's *katiba* (battalion) made a stand in the valley, as more French troops arrived from Gao, and over a thousand Chadian troops brought up from Méneka, east of Gao, were also deployed. As the French blocked the western end of the Amettetaï Valley, the Chadians began to push in from the eastern end on 29 February, ultimately losing twenty-six soldiers, killed in the battle for the valley. The forces of AQIM's southern emir Abou Zeid were trapped and crushed, and he, along with many of his fighters, were killed, though many escaped to melt into the desert oases. It took a total of ten days to clear the valley, during which numerous caches of weapons and food were discovered and destroyed. French sources estimated that they and the Chadians eventually killed over 400 jihadis in the Région of Kidal, eliminating an estimated 90 per cent of Al Qaeda's operational strength. With the Amettetaï Valley cleared, Abou Zeid's *katiba* defeated and other key points, including Tessalit and Alguelhok, occupied by the French and Chadians, it could be said that the battle for northern Mali was over.[23] Serious problems remained, however. First, the jihadis had been defeated, but not eliminated. They went to ground, blending in with local populations and falling back on their family ties and commercial alliances with the Tuareg and the Bidan of the far north. With the Algerian border still porous, they drifted across the desert into Niger and Libya, where they regrouped to plan new attacks. One such attack was the 13 January seizure of the In Amenas natural gas facility in eastern Algeria, near the border with Libya.[24] In addition, the secular MNLA had also regrouped and had seized control of Kidal City and most of the Région of Kidal, including the capital. This fact rankled Malians, making them feel their sovereignty had been but partially restored. Perhaps most significantly, Mali was still ruled by an ineffective and unpopular interim government. It would be necessary to organize and conduct elections for a new president and national assembly.

New elections

Presidential elections were set for late July, allowing just five months for campaigning and for the logistics of holding the first and second rounds of voting. Despite criticism that holding elections so soon was ill-advised, Mali's main allies, the United States and France, wanted an early poll because they felt the restoration of a legitimate government was necessary before large quantities of foreign military aid could be brought to bear. Former prime minister Ibrahim Boubacar Keita, who had been a candidate for president in the cancelled 2012 elections, won the presidency in a second-round runoff with a substantial majority. The international community judged the poll 'free and fair', and the new president was sworn in on 4 September 2013.[25]

However, neither the expulsion of the Islamist militias from the cities of the north nor the restoration of Mali's electoral democracy did much to alleviate the country's ongoing difficulties. Islamist terrorist groups were still active in the north; the MNLA remained armed and in the field and occupying significant territory in Kidal; government corruption and military weakness persisted; smuggling and trafficking resumed, if they were ever interrupted; and popular disillusionment with democratic governance among ordinary Malians continued. AQIM, for its part, was not defeated, but, rather, had gone underground and was still able to inflict damage.[26] By July of 2013, Belmokhtar's al-Moulathamin (The Veiled Ones, a reference to the *litham*, a facial veil worn by Tuareg men) had merged with remnants of MUJAO to form al Mourabitoun (The Sentinels), and some of their cadres had returned to the Gao area. France began to draw down its troop presence in Mali in anticipation of its pivot to its new Saharan counter-terrorist initiative Opération Barkhane. Barkhane, which rolled out in mid-2014, was based in Chad and aimed at controlling terrorist activity in a broader swathe of territory than just northern Mali. Its mandate extended from the Lake Chad area, where Boko Haram was threatening three former French colonies, Chad, Cameroon and Niger, to north-western Niger, where France had uranium interests. While France also maintained some troop presence in Mali, a new UN peacekeeping mission, the Multidimensional Integrated Stabilization Mission in Mali (MINUSMA), followed up on Opération Serval. MINUSMA began deployment on 1 July 2013, with some 6,000 troops, out of a proposed total strength of over 12,000.[27] It was supported by the European Union Training Mission to Mali (EUTM), whose job it was to rebuild combat units of the Malian army. The first of these units, the *Waraba* (Old Lion) Battalion, was officially inaugurated in early April of 2013, composed of remnants of the old Malian army.[28]

Even the most optimistic analysts regarding Mali's future, however, must have been given pause in mid-May of 2014 when an incident in Kidal laid bare two of the above-mentioned issues, MNLA's hold on Kidal and the inability of Mali's armed forces to do anything about it. Malian Prime Minister Moussa Mara, who had been appointed only the previous month, rekindled tensions between the Government of Mali (GOM) and the MNLA with an 'ill-advised' visit to Kidal, which remained under MNLA control. The stated purpose of Prime Minister Mara's trip was to show support for government soldiers stationed there. Fighting promptly broke out between the bodyguards that accompanied Mara and rebel troops that controlled the city. The minister was forced to retreat to safety even as the renewed fighting threatened the ongoing peace talks. This premature attempt to establish an official GOM presence at Kidal City resulted in a debacle, as a subsequent attempt to retake the city a week later by a Malian army column led by Gen. El-Hajj Ag Gamou failed. MNLA reinforcements, allegedly supported by AQIM remnants, outfought the Malian force, forcing it to retreat, leaving dozens of Malian soldiers dead. The incident was yet another humiliating defeat for the Malian army, whose troops, some of whom had been trained by the EUTM, fled, abandoning weapons and vehicles. It also solidified the MNLA's power over Kidal. Rather than weakening the nationalist rebels, as intended, the incident strengthened them. As a result of this humiliating defeat, the Malian army abandoned all its remaining positions in the Kidal Région, including Aguelhok and Tessalit, as well as those in areas north and east of Gao, including Anéfis and Ménaka, leaving only MINUSMA forces and a modest number of French troops in the north. Mali was effectively cut in two again, as it had been before Opération Serval.[29]

Ethnic and Islamist militias

Prime Minister Mara's Kidal mission and the failure of Gen. Gamou's follow-up attempt led to a return of government reliance on ethnic-based militias as proxy fighters. These ethnic militias included the pro-government Groupe Autodéfense Touareg Imghad et Alliés (GATIA), founded in August of 2014 and composed of Imghad (non-noble) Tuareg. Gamou, the only Tuareg member of Mali's general staff, became the leader of GATIA. Imghad Tuareg had sided with the government against the Ifoghas (noble) Tuareg in earlier fighting, including in 2012, when the Ifoghas, including MNLA, sided with the Islamists to take over the north.[30] The creation of GATIA in the summer of 2014 marked the return to a government policy of arming ethnic militias to fight Tuareg rebels, as had been done in 1994. GATIA soon joined with the pro-government Platform Coalition. It had an estimated 1,000 fighters, including some *ishumar* Tuareg who had been refugees in Libya and had served in Muammar Gaddafi's Islamic Legion, and thus had desert combat experience. GATIA is against separatism and jihadism and represents a serious obstacle to the ambitions of both Islamists and Azawad nationalists.[31] Along with other pro-GOM armed groups, GATIA had replaced Mali's military in the north after regular troops were unable to hold their own. The existence of GATIA, composed of Tuareg fighters loyal to Mali, undermines the MNLA's claim to be the spokesmen of all the Tuareg. As a result, the separatist groups (the MNLA and others) did their best to prevent GATIA from securing official representation at any future peace talks.[32]

The Islamist militias in the Sahara-Sahel region had also undergone changes by mid-2014. They still included AQIM and its affiliates MUJAO and Ansar Dine, but al Mourabitoun was operating in Algeria, while its leader Belmokhtar had, reportedly, decamped to the Fezzan (Libya). Meanwhile, Ansar Dine-linked groups were still active in the Régions of Timbuktu and Kidal. The range of these groups was from Mauritania eastward through central and southern Algeria into south-west Libya and southwards into Mali, Chad, Niger and Nigeria. MUJAO, in particular, was still recruiting new fighters all across West Africa, posing a 'direct threat' to all bordering countries.[33] By late 2014, the people of Timbuktu still feared a return of the Islamist militias, as only MINUSMA and a few French troops were keeping them out. The presence of Islamist militias was making life very dangerous for MINUSMA; some thirty-one peacekeepers had been killed and ninety-one wounded since July of 2013, making it the most dangerous UN peacekeeping unit (for the peacekeepers themselves) in the world.[34]

A peace settlement

Just as international actors called for democratic elections in Mali in 2013, hoping for a resolution to Mali's problems, these same actors by early 2015 pushed for a peace accord that would include the GOM and the secular-nationalist rebel groups who had started the rebellion, but not the transnational jihadi groups. Renewed fighting among pro-government and rebel groups had erupted in late April of 2015 when the pro-government fighters of the Platform Coalition, which included GATIA, attacked and seized Ménaka, east of Gao, from rebel fighters.[35] What united these disparate groups of the Platform Coalition was their desire to fight the noble rebel Tuareg (Ifoghas), who were represented by the CMA (Coordination of Azawad Movements), also known as the Coordination Coalition, which consisted of the MNLA, along with splinter and related anti-government groups.[36] Tuareg rebels of the recently formed Coordination Coalition (CMA) responded with attacks as far south as Ténenkou, in the Région of Mopti, and ambushes of army convoys near Timbuktu. Continuing fighting in early May between the Coordination Coalition and Platform Coalition fighters left twenty more soldiers and twenty-five rebel fighters dead. This renewed fighting was a result of various groups jockeying for position as international pressure mounted for a comprehensive peace agreement.[37]

Two preliminary agreements, one on 15 May and the other on 5 June, initialled by the representatives of the agreed groups, became the basis for a proposed peace agreement negotiated in Algiers. The agreement, called the Algiers Accords, included concessions, such as a stipulation that CMA fighters be included in a future security force for the north, and that northern residents be granted better representation in government institutions. These concessions convinced the CMA to sign the proposed comprehensive agreement. At last, with great fanfare, the Algiers Accords were signed on 15 June 2015. Negotiated under the auspices of the Algerian government, the final accords also called for greater autonomy for the northern regions and promised to allow limited access to the north for the Malian army in exchange for promises of renewed government development assistance.[38] The terms of the Algiers Accords were similar to the terms on which the rebellions of the 1990s and the 2000s had been settled. As with those earlier agreements, the problem would prove to be not the terms themselves, but their incomplete and under-resourced implementation.

Unsurprisingly, renewed fighting among ethnic militias broke out in August of 2015 near the town of Anéfis, on the main *wadi* linking Gao and Kidal, a major trafficking route. This new fighting, a violation of the Algiers Accords, had erupted between GATIA, which had since become part of the Algiers Platform Coalition, allied with the GOM, and the CMA, which by this time had become the main rebel umbrella group. Anéfis, in MNLA hands since the Kidal debacle of May 2014, was seized by GATIA in August, but MUNISMA handed it back to MNLA and its CMA supporters on 18 September.[39] The restoration of Anéfis to CMA control triggered a new round of talks among the ethnic militias on both sides, pro-government and pro-rebel. These new 'bottom-up' negotiations, held at Anéfis beginning on 15 October 2015, and lasting three weeks, brought together the CMA alliance and the Platform Coalition group in a 'surprising détente'. After the talks, a series of honour pacts was signed on behalf of the various Tuareg factions involved in the new negotiations.[40] These negotiations touched on issues such as trafficking, power sharing and intercommunal rivalries, issues that the Algiers negotiations had been unwilling or unable to tackle. The new negotiations and the honour pacts they generated were subsequently endorsed by the United Nations in Security Council Resolution 2295 of June 2016. The resolution encouraged the three parties now involved, the GOM and the Platform and Coordination armed groups, to 'continue to engage constructively' to accelerate the Algiers agreement's implementation and to abide by earlier ceasefires. The resolution also authorized a more 'pro-active and robust mandate' for its MINUSMA peacekeeping mission, including allowing it to respond to asymmetric (terrorist) threats. The Anéfis meetings were said to 'represent a re-appropriation by some local actors of a peace process until now largely driven by external partners'.[41]

However, the larger problem for peace in Mali was that neither the Algiers Accords nor the Anéfis honour pacts included the Islamist terrorist movements, who had not been welcomed at either set of talks. These movements were still active, and even expanding their areas of operations. According to a US Department of State travel warning, as of mid-2015, most, if not all, of the transnational jihadi groups were still operating in Mali, including Ansar Dine, MUJAO and AQIM, as well as Belmokhtar's al Mourabitoun.[42] The travel warning had been issued in response to an attack on 7 March 2015, on La Terrasse nightclub in Bamako's Hippodrome neighbourhood, which was frequented by expats. Two European nationals and three Malian citizens were killed. Eight other Malians were wounded in the attack. The attack on La Terrasse, which was carried out by al Mourabitoun, was followed by another more serious incident at Hotel Byblos in Sévaré. This attack, which resulted in a siege and hostage-taking, occurred on 8 August 2015, leaving thirteen dead, including five UN workers, as well as some of the attackers.[43] This renewed activity by transnational jihadi groups had begun in early 2015, partly due to resurgent terrorist organization in the Fezzan area of Libya, especially the Ubari Valley, which observers had begun calling the 'new safe haven' for terrorists.[44] Other jihadi groups were also taking shelter in southern Libya at this time, including al Mourabitoun. The extreme mobility of these attacks was indicative of the facility with which the jihadi groups could cross the desert from Libya to Mali in their technicals.[45]

Furthermore, attacks by jihadi terrorist groups had been spreading to central and southern Mali. Notably, a new ethnic-based Islamist terrorist group had formed in central Mali in January 2015. The Macina Liberation Front (MLF), or Katiba Macina, had allied with Ansar Dine. The MLF was founded by Sheikh Amadou

Koufa, a Fulbe *marabout* (cleric) who, as mentioned earlier, had commanded the Islamist militias during their joint raid on Konna in January of 2013. The new group was composed of radicalized Fulbe youth from the Macina area of central Mali. It was based near Nampala between Timbuktu and Segu. The MLF started out as an activist group demanding sharia law in regional towns and nomadic Fulbe camps, punishing leaders in communities that did not adhere to their moral and social agenda.[46] From there it progressed to terrorist-style attacks on hotels and other civilian targets, and eventually became part of the coterie of Sunni jihadi groups active in the Sahel, though notably concentrated in the Macina region. Several of the Islamist militias may also have had an ethnic base. In addition to Katiba Macina, which is Fulbe, there is also Ansar Dine, which is composed of Islamist Malian Tuareg, and al Mourabitoun, which is largely Arab, including Malian, Algerian and Tunisian Arabs, along with some Malian Tuareg. An interview source in late 2015 mentioned fears among many Malians of an increase in the number and size of these ethnic-based militant Islamist groups. Fighters of such groups, the source said, could easily blend in with the local population when necessary and thus cause little initial alarm.[47] During the year or so following the Algiers Accords, Ansar Dine fighters, for example, were still finding shelter and support from Tuareg communities, whether in northern towns or remote camps, even if they had to pay for it. While their movements on main roads were restricted by MUNISMA and remaining French troops, these terrorists could still attack caravans using IEDs or roadside bombs, thus endangering military convoys and trucks carrying aid supplies for local civilians. MUJAO was still active and recruiting in the Région of Gao, as well as in Niger and Burkina Faso. More mobile groups like al Mourabitoun were still roving back and forth across the desert from northern Mali to the Libyan Fezzan.

Realignment of the jihadi militias

As always, the fissiparous nature of the transnational jihadi organizations continued to result in new alliances and formations, such as the already mentioned Macina Liberation Front (MLF).[48] Another was a spin-off group from MUJAO led by Adnan Abu Walid al-Sahraoui, who, as his nom de guerre indicates, is a veteran of the Polisario refugee camps in western Algeria. Sahraoui, an associate of Belmokhtar, had formerly been active with MUJAO. He broke with AQIM and MUJAO in May of 2015, along with some of his fighters, and declared support for ISIS 'Caliph' Abu Bakr al-Baghdadi, renaming his group Islamic State in the Greater Sahara (ISGS). Since then Sahraoui and his group have been active in the so-called Liptako-Gourma corridor straddling the border regions of Mali, Burkina Faso and Niger, an area that includes an important transit route between Mali and Libya. His fighters have embedded in local communities and, like MLF, have leveraged local social, ethnic and political tensions and rivalries to build support and recruit. Sahraoui and his group were most recently in the news when they were named as responsible for the deaths of four US SOF troops in Niger in October of 2017.[49]

Perhaps the most significant recent development among the transnational jihadi groups in the Sahara-Sahel region is the announced merger of four previously known groups into a new umbrella group called the Group for Support for Islam and Muslims *(Jama'ah Nusrah al-Islam wal-Muslimin*, JNIM). The new alliance announced itself in a highly publicized seventeen-minute video on 2 March 2017. It is said to represent a merger of Ansar Dine, Katiba Macina, al Mourabitoun and AQIM.[50] Pictured in the video were Iyad ag Ghali (Ansar Dine), Amadou Koufa (Katiba Macina), Deputy Amir Hassan al-Ansari (al Mourabitoun) and the Saharan 'judge' of AQIM, Abu Abderrahman al Sanhaji. These men appear to be the operational commanders of JNIM, while Ag Ghali is presumed to be the group's emir. In the video, Ag Ghali renewed his allegiance to AQIM emir Abdelmalek Droukdel.[51] Days later, on 14 March, Droukdel endorsed the merger, calling 'all jihadi groups to follow the example ... and to unite' under the banner of Al Qaeda. On 19 March, Al Qaeda Central issued an official statement offering the new group its congratulations. The reason for the merger remains unclear, though some observers have suggested that it may be in response to AQIM's concerns over the presence of ISIS-linked groups in the Sahara-Sahel region, including Sahraoui's ISGS. JNIM subsequently claimed responsibility for attacks in central Mali in late March and early April, including one near the Burkina border. Conspicuous by his absence in the announcement video was the old smuggler/terrorist Belmokhtar, emir of al Mourabitoun, who sent his deputy instead. His absence fuelled rumours that he was either dead or holed up in his hideout in Libya's Fezzan region. There have been no videos or audio recordings of Belmokhtar since unconfirmed reports of his being killed in airstrikes in Libya in 2015. Belmokhtar, no stranger to mergers and rebrandings, generally shuns photo-ops and propaganda videos, unlike his colleague Ag Ghali, who appears to court them.[52]

Also not specifically mentioned in the video is the AQIM branch called the Katiba Grand Sahara, not to be confused with the islamic state-affiliated ISIS in the Greater Sahara. Katiba Grand Sahara formed in late 2015 in the northern part of the Région of Timbuktu. The group has carried out kidnappings and hotel bombings, some in conjunction with other *katiba*, including al Mourabitoun. As noted earlier, AQIM has deep community and marriage ties with local Arab tribes in the desert area north of Timbuktu. An AQIM fighter who carried out a VBIED attack on the Hotel La Palmeraie in Timbuktu in February of 2016 was said to be of the Oulad Idriss clan of Bérabiche. The hotel was being used by Nigerian police attached to MINUSMA. The Oulad Idriss clan is among those reported to have significant marriage ties with AQIM.[53]

Terrorist attacks continue

The Algiers Accords of June 2015, and especially the subsequent Anéfis 'honour pacts', led to a decline in fighting among the secular Tuareg armed groups. But the transnational jihadis continued, and even increased, their attacks on civilians and on Malian, French and MINUSMA troops. The first high-profile attack after the June 2015 Accords came on 7 August at Hotel Byblos at Sévaré, mentioned earlier (p. 14). The Hotel Byblos attack appeared to signal a shift on the part of jihadis to softer targets like hotels and nightclubs. In a more daring attack, the Radisson Blu Hotel in Bamako was attacked on 20 November, leaving more than two dozen dead. During that attack, more than one hundred guests were temporarily held hostage by Islamist terrorists. Belmokhtar's al Mourabitoun ultimately claimed responsibility for the attacks at both the Byblos and the Radisson Blu. The Radisson Blu attack got the attention of the world media as earlier attacks had not, coming as it did in the capital in a luxury hotel frequented by foreigners.[54]

AQIM, along with its affiliates, had clearly changed strategy since 2012. It no longer sought to control territory, but, rather, it developed a regional strategy that included attacks on capitals of regional countries that were supporting France's Opération Barkhane. This strategy had the double benefit of punishing France for its 2013 intervention in the Malian north and also showing that AQIM could hit targets across a broad area. Following up on the Radisson Blu attack in Bamako, as if to underscore its new strategy, AQIM in early 2016 attacked hotels in or near two neighbouring capitals, Wagadugu in Burkina Faso and Grand Bassam in Côte d'Ivoire, some 40 km from the capital, Abidjan. On 15 January, gunmen stormed the Cappuccino restaurant and the Splendid Hotel in the heart of Wagadugu. There were thirty killed and fifty-six wounded. The Grand Bassam Resort was struck on 14 March, leaving sixteen dead. AQIM quickly claimed responsibility for both attacks. There was no doubt that the attacks on luxury hotels frequented by foreigners underscored the continuing instability in the Sahel. The hotel attacks on the capitals of Mali, Burkina Faso, and Côte d'Ivoire demonstrated AQIM's region-wide integration. The attack on the Splendid Hotel in Wagadugu, popular with aid workers and Barkhane soldiers and staff, was put together by militants in Mali and carried out with vehicles with licence plates from Niger, showing that it was a truly regional operation. The hotel attacks also pointed out vulnerabilities in other West African governments besides Mali.[55]

Attacks by Islamist militants continued in Mali and neighbouring states throughout 2016, focusing on MUNISMA and Malian army bases and posts. A MINUSMA police base was captured on 5 February 2016, by AQIM fighters. The base was recaptured by Malian troops supported by UN helicopters; however, a Malian army officer was killed in the incident. Militants attacked a MINUSMA base in Kidal on 12 February, killing five UN peacekeepers and wounding thirty others. Six more peacekeepers were wounded by a mine near Kidal on 1 March. In a return to the hotel attacks of late 2015, the Nord-Sud Hotel in Bamako, which was serving as a base for personnel attached to the EUTM training mission, was attacked on 21 March. One Malian soldier was wounded, one assailant was killed, and two more captured. Similarly, AQIM fighters carried out a VIBED attack on the Hotel La Palmeraie near Timbuktu in February of 2016. The hotel was then housing Nigerian police affiliated with MINUSMA. On 12 April, three French soldiers with Opération Barkhane were killed and another wounded in a bomb attack by unknown assailants. Attacks on UN peacekeepers, some fatal, continued throughout May and June at Aguelhok, Sévaré and Gao. A significant mass-casualty attack took place on 19 July on a Malian army post at Nampala, near the Mauritanian border and not far from the headquarters of Katiba Macina, killing seventeen Malian soldiers and wounding thirty-five. Both Ansar Dine and the Katiba Macina claimed responsibility. This attack served to further weaken public confidence in the army. Taken as a whole, Islamist militant attacks in 2016 in Mali represent a sharp rise over those in 2015, increasing by some 150 per cent. At least 257 attacks occurred in Mali and neighbouring states in 2016. One significant difference regarding attacks in 2016 compared to 2015 is that in 2015 many of the attacks were by secular-nationalist Tuareg rebels, not transnational jihadis. The attacks in 2016 were largely perpetrated by Islamist militants. This difference indicates that the Algiers Accords of mid-2015 and the Anéfis honour pacts of late 2015, both of which excluded the terrorist groups, seem to have been taking hold.[56]

Attacks by transnational jihadis continued at a significant pace in 2017, with some sixty attacks by early April. A particularly deadly suicide attack on a Malian army base at Gao on 18 January 2017, carried out by al Mourabitoun, killed sixty and wounded over a hundred. The Joint Operational Mechanism base housed government soldiers and members of former rebel groups who had signed the peace agreement and who were preparing to begin joint patrols, as stipulated in the Algiers Accords. French Interior Minister Bruno Le Roux termed the bombing a 'highly symbolic attack'. West Africa analyst Sean Smith said the attack 'strikes at the very heart of the Algiers peace agreement'. Bombers forced their way into the camp at 9.00 am, just as hundreds of soldiers were forming up. The attack, said to be in retaliation for cooperating with France, represents a setback for peace efforts. UN peacekeeping chief Hervé Ladsous remarked, 'If the security situation continues to deteriorate, then soon there won't be any peace to keep in Mali.'[57]

Encouraging signs of movement in the peace process between the GOM and the Tuareg nationalist rebels notwithstanding, the Islamist militants continued their attacks in 2017, not only in Mali, but in neighbouring countries like Niger. A new hotel attack on 18 June by Al Qaeda militants at a resort near Bamako targeted EU training mission personnel. The attack killed five people, including Malian and foreign victims. An Al Qaeda hostage video released in early July shows that its affiliates remain the main jihadi threat across the Sahara-Sahel region. It also shows that they are still relying on ransom money to fund their operations.[58] Perhaps the most shocking of the Islamist attacks, at least for American television audiences, was the 4 October 2017 ambush in Niger at a village near the Malian border that killed four US SOF troops (see earlier, p. 18). Three of the four US dead were Green Berets. Four Nigerien soldiers were also killed. The ambush took place near the small village of Tongo-Tongo. A total of twelve US troops, eight of whom were Green Berets, were involved in the incident, as well as thirty Nigerien soldiers. The US troops were in Niger as part of a US training mission. They and their Nigerien colleagues had participated in reconnaissance and training missions associated with Operation Flintlock, a US-led regional counter-terrorism training initiative that dated to the mid-2000s.[59] Reportedly, the attackers, as well as other terrorists, had many 'accomplices' in Tongo-Tongo. The *chef de village* was arrested by Nigerien authorities after the ambush. Most US and Nigerian defence analysts have attributed the ambush to fighters linked to Adnan Abu Walid al-Sahraoui and his Islamic State in the Greater Sahara (ISGS) brigade.[60] Sahraoui's ISGS, though having declared support for ISIS and its global agenda, nonetheless tends to operate much like the other regional jihadi militias, most of whom have declared support for Al Qaeda and its Northwest African affiliate AQIM. They establish local commercial and family ties, they insert themselves in between pre-existing ethnic and clan rivalries, and they extract revenge for the collaboration with US and French counterterrorism and security initiatives. They do not attack the United States or its Western allies directly, as Al Qaeda and ISIS have done.

A report by *Reuters* appeared about a week after the Tongo-Tongo affair, saying the attack was led by Doundou Chefou, a Fulbe herdsman turned jihadi terrorist. Chefou, a leader of fighters with the ISGS, was, like most of his men, an ordinary, non-radicalized Fulbe pastoralist who took up arms a decade ago, trying to protect his cattle from Tuareg cattle raiders. His trajectory illustrates that violent extremism in the Sahel is 'ever more enmeshed in long-standing ethnic and clan conflicts'.[61] If true, this picture resembles the situation of Tuareg rebels in northern Mali in 2011, as the Mali War was about to break out. The Tuareg were motivated by ethnic tensions with the black majority of southern Mali, and by clan tensions, as evidenced by the rivalry between the Ifoghas (noble) Tuareg and the Imghad (free client) Tuareg. These tensions and rivalries among the Tuareg were successfully exploited by AQIM. Involvement by AQIM was based on navigating the interstices among various ethnic and clan groups and exploiting local rivalries by posing as the defenders of the victimized groups. This tactic has been widely used by both ISIS and Al Qaeda and their affiliates, not only in Mali and the Sahara-Sahel region, but in Libya as well, and in the Middle Eastern core countries of Syria and Iraq.

Conclusion

The internationally sponsored peace process that culminated with the Algiers Accords of June 2015, along with the locally negotiated Anéfis 'honour pacts', have, for now, brought the Tuareg nationalist rebellion of 2012 under a measure of control. It was the Tuareg rebellion that had allowed the Islamist jihad to gain a purchase in the first place and ultimately to take over half of the country. The Islamist militias, though driven from power in the urban centres of the north by the French–Chadian intervention of January 2013, are continuing their attacks and expanding their areas of operations as we speak. They also continue to both fracture and realign. Despite ideological support and branding from the 'global' jihad and declarations of loyalty to Al Qaeda Central from Malian and other Sahara-Sahelian jihad movements, these Northwest African movements remain national and regional in focus, not global. Their goals are to establish islamic states in their countries of origin, such as Algeria and Mali. In other words, they place their focus on the 'Near Enemy', the 'hypocrite' regimes that claim to be Muslim but do not enforce sharia law or adhere to the principles of political Islam. Their goals, therefore, do not include attacking the 'Far Enemy', the United States and its Western allies, which is the stated goal of Al Qaeda and, ultimately, ISIS.

Yet the jihadi movements in the Sahara-Sahel region are of global importance because, like the truly globally focused jihad movements, they have proven resistant to the strategies and tactics that the United States and its Western allies have arrayed against them. The cycle of terror in the Sahara-Sahel region, as recent history has shown, cannot be controlled or eliminated by military means – not national armed forces, not France and its allies, and not a large UN peacekeeping force. Instead, the underlying factors that predate and create the conditions for the success of the jihadi movements must be confronted. These factors include widespread trafficking in contraband and undocumented labour migrants, pervasive corruption in local governments and their security forces, unresolved ethnic and clan tensions that date back to the colonial era and before, and, perhaps most importantly, the relentless pressure of the extractive economy and asymmetrical international economic competition that has long characterized Africa's relations with the West. These factors cannot be addressed by military means – certainly not by military means alone. They must be addressed through diplomatic, educational and developmental initiatives. While such international projects can be helpful, the impetus must come from within the region and the countries directly involved, especially from Mali, the key to the Sahara-Sahel region.

Notes

1 For background on the Tuareg nationalist rebellions against the Malian central government, as well as the devastation of the Tuareg community and livelihood and the resultant long-term refugee status that befell many of them, see Baz Lecocq, *Disputed Desert* (Leiden: Brill, 2010); also Stephen A. Harmon, *Terror and Insurgency: Contraband, Corruption, Jihad and the Mali War of 2012-2013* (Farnham: Ashgate, 2014), pp. 23–33, 93–108.
2 Isaline Bergamaschi, 'The fall of a donor darling: The role of aid in Mali's crisis', *Journal of Modern African Studies*, lviii, no. 3 (2014): 350; Bruce Whitehouse, 'What went wrong in Mali?' *London Review of Books*, xxxiv, no. 16 (30 August 2012), pp. 17–18.
3 Interview 206, Thiam, Bamako, 30 December 2015.
4 Harmon, *Terror and Insurgency*, pp. 78–94.
5 Jean-Pierre Filiu, *From Deep State to Islamic State: The Arab Counter-Revolution and Its Jihadi Legacy* (New York: Oxford University Press, 2015), pp. 83–115.
6 Jean-Pierre Filiu, 'The local and global jihad of al-Qa'ida in the Islamic Maghrib', *Middle East Journal*, lxiii, no. 2 (2009): 221.
7 Jacob Zenn, 'Boko Haram's international connections', *Combatting Terrorism Center at West Point*, vi, no. 1 (January 2013): 1. Available at https://ctc.usma.edu/boko-harams-international-connections/ (accessed 17 July 2018).

8   Here 'Région' refers to the political subdivisions of Mali, what other countries might call a province. Elsewhere I use the term 'region' in the conventional sense to denote a local vicinity or a broader general area, as in the Sahara-Sahel region.
9   William Lloyd-George, 'The man who brought the black flag to Timbuktu', *Foreign Policy*, 22 October 2012. Available at https://foreignpolicy.com/2012/10/22/the-man-who-brought-the-black-flag-to-timbuktu/ (accessed 17 July 2018); Steve Metcalf, 'Iyad Ag Ghali – Mali's Islamist leader', *BBC News*, 17 July 2012. Available at https://www.bbc.com/news/world-africa-18814291 (accessed 17 July 2018). The Fulbe, also called Fulani, are an ethnic group of the Sahel, including Mali. They were traditionally cattle herders, and some of them still practise a semi-nomadic lifestyle. Others have settled in towns, generally adopting Islam in the process. Many of these Muslim Fulbe have become *marabouts*, clerics and teachers.
10 Tim Lister, 'Six reasons events in Mali matter', *CNN.com*, 17 January 2013. Available at https://www.cnn.com/2013/01/16/world/africa/mali-six-reasons/index.html (accessed 17 July 2018); Bergamaschi, 'The fall of a donor darling', p. 348.
11 J. Peter Pham, 'Foreign influences and shifting horizons: The ongoing evolution of al-Qaeda in the Islamic Maghreb', *Orbis*, lv, no. 2 (2011): 249. Available at https://www.sciencedirect.com/science/article/pii/S0030438711000068 (accessed 17 July 2018).
12 Ibid., p. 247.
13 Harmon, *Terror and Insurgency*, pp. 143–54.
14 Christopher S. Chivvis, *The French War on al-Qa'ida in Africa* (New York: Cambridge University Press, 2016), p. 72.
15 Harmon, *Terror and Insurgency*, pp. 85–93, 185–191.
16 Chivvis, *The French War*, pp. 69–72.
17 Morten Boas, 'Guns, money and prayers: AQIM's blueprint for securing control of Northern Mali', *Combatting Terrorism Center Sentinel*, vii, no. 4 (28 April 2014): 4. Available at https://ctc.usma.edu/guns-money-and-prayers-aqims-blueprint-for-securing-control-of-northern-mali/ (accessed 18 July 2018).
18 Isabelle Lasserre and Thierry Oberlé, *Notre Guerre Secrète au Mali: Les nouvelles menaces contre la France* (Paris: Fayard, 2013), p. 91; Roland Marchal, 'Briefing: Military (Mis)Adventures in Mali', *African Affairs*, cxii, no. 448 (July 2013): 486–97; Robin Poulton and Raffaella Greco Tonegutti, *The Limits of Democracy and the Postcolonial Nation State: Mali's Democratic Experiment Falters, while Jihad and Terrorism Grow in the Sahara* (Lewiston: Edwin Mellon, 2016), p. 237. Chivvis, *The French War*, p. 94.
19 Interview 206, p. 2. Amadou Koufa led the afternoon prayer at a Konna mosque during the Islamists' brief occupation of the town.
20 Chivvis, *The French War*, pp. 123–5.
21 Harmon, *Terror and Insurgency*, pp. 210–12; Chivvis, *The French War*, pp. 127–8, 132.
22 Interview 107, Maïga, Bamako, 24 September 2012, Part 1.
23 Lasserre and Oberlé, *Notre Guerre Secrète au Mali*, p. 58.
24 Ibid., p. 61.
25 'Mali election: IBK and Soumaila Cissé in run-off', *BBC Africa.com*, 2 August 2013. Available at https://www.bbc.co.uk/news/world-africa-23549738 (accessed 17 July 2018); Chivvis, *The French War*, p. 150.
26 Boas, 'Guns, money and prayers', p. 1.
27 Chivvis, *The French War*, pp. 143–4, 152–4; Harmon, *Terror and Insurgency*, p. 238.
28 Chivvis, *The French War*, p. 147.

29 'Mali: Tuareg rebels "defeat government army in Kidal"', *BBCNews.com*, 22 May 2014, p. 2. Available at https://www.bbc.co.uk/news/world-africa-27511448 (accessed 18 July 2018); Andrew McGregor, 'The fox of Kidal: A profile of Mali's Tuareg general, al-Hajj ag Gamou', *Aberfoyle International Security.com*, 30 November 2016. Available at http://www.aberfoylesecurity.com/?m=201611 (accessed 18 July 2018); Harmon, *Terror and Insurgency*, p. 227; Chivvis, *The French War*, p. 152.
30 See Lecocq, *Disputed Desert*, passim, for discussion of Tuareg clan structure and social status.
31 Ibid., pp. 227–94 for discussion of the Tuareg Teshumara (*ishumar*) refugee movement.
32 Baz Lecocq, 'Mali: This is only the beginning', *Conflict and Security*, Summer/Fall 2013, p. 62. Available at https://biblio.ugent.be/publication/4106838/file/6801526.pdf (accessed 18 July 2018); Kassim Koné, 'A Southern view on the Tuareg Rebellions in Mali', *African Studies Review*, lx, no. 1 (2017): 60. Available at Project MUSE, muse.jhu.edu/article/655350 (accessed 27 July 2018); Stephanie Pezard and Michael Shurkin, *Achieving Peace in Northern Mali: Past Agreements, Local Conflicts, and the Prospects for a Durable Settlement* (Santa Monica: Rand Corporation, 2015), pp. 56–7; Andrew Morgan, 'Mali peace deal in danger as fierce fighting flares', *The Guardian*, 15 May 2015, p. 3. Available at https://www.theguardian.com/world/2015/may/15/mali-peace-deal-violence (accessed 18 July 2018).
33 Bakary Guèye, 'West Africa: Mali violence worries African neighbours', *All Africa*, 29 January 2018, p. 1. Available at http://allafrica.com/stories/201501301582.html (accessed 18 July 2018).
34 Andrea M. Walther-Puri, 'Security sector assistance in Africa, but where is the reform?' in Jessica Piombo (ed.), *The US Military in Africa: Enhancing Security and Development?* (Boulder: First Forum Press, 2015), p. 85; Guèye, 'West Africa: Mali violence', p. 1; Charlie English, 'Women of Timbuktu find their voice again after nightmare of jihadi rule', *The Guardian*, 25 December 2014. Available at https://www.theguardian.com/world/2014/dec/25/women-timbuktu-shape-city-future-mali (accessed 20 July 2018).
35 'Assault by pro-govt militia a threat to peace in Mali: UN', *Business Standard*, 28 April 2015. Available at https://www.business-standard.com/article/pti-stories/assault-by-pro-govt-militia-a-threat-to-peace-in-mali-un-115042801180_1.html (accessed 20 July 2018).
36 Interview 206, pp. 1, 9; Poulton, *The Limits of Democracy*, p. 196, n. 185. Poulton and Tonegutti give an excellent breakdown of the Tuareg rebel groups and alliances, p. 264.
37 Morgan, 'Mali peace deal', p. 2.
38 Katrin Matthaei, 'Leader of troubled Mali seeking renewed international support', *DW.com*, 22 October 2015. Available at http://www.dw.com/en/leader-of-troubled-mali-seeking-renewed-international-support/a-18799352 (accessed 20 July 2018).
39 Ibid.
40 Emmanuel Kendemeh, 'Mali peace negotiations expected to resume', *Cameroun Tribune*, 21 September 2015, p. 1. Available at http://allafrica.com/stories/201509211329.htm l (accessed 20 July 2018); Obi Anyadike, 'The new Jihadist strategy in the Sahel', *IRIN Briefing*, 4 February 2016, p. 8. Available at http://allafrica.com/stories/20160208060 6.html (accessed 20 July 2018); International Crisis Group, 'Mali: Peace from below', Briefing 115, Africa, 14 December 2015, p. 1. Available at https://www.crisisgroup.org/africa/west-africa/mali/mali-peace-below (accessed 20 July 2018); 'Mali: Islamic terrorists

go total gangster', *Strategy Page*, 18 October 2015, p. 5. Available at https://www.strategypage.com/qnd/mali/articles/20151018.aspx (accessed 20 July 2018).
41 United Nations, Security Council Resolution 2295. UN Security Council, 29 June 2016. Available at https://www.un.org/press/en/2016/sc12426.doc.htm (accessed 20 July 2018); International Crisis Group, 'Mali: Peace from below', p. 2.
42 US Department of State Mali Travel Warning, 7 May 2015 (site no longer available).
43 Susana D. Wing, 'A new hope for peace, but old challenges remain in Mali', *IPI Global Observatory*, 10 March 2015, p. 1. Available at http://theglobalobservatory.org/2015/03/hope-peace-talks-mali-bamako-unrest/ (accessed 20 July 2018); 'Mali hotel siege: Several killed in Sévaré, four UN workers saved', *BBC News*, 9 August 2015, p. 1. Available at https://www.bbc.com/news/world-africa-33833363 (accessed 20 July 2018).
44 Harmon, *Terror and Insurgency*, p. 246; 'Mali's foreign minister appeals for international intervention in Libya to combat terrorism', *New Europe*, 14 January 2015, p. 2. Available at https://www.neweurope.eu/article/malis-foreign-minister-appeals-international-intervention-libya-combat-terrorism/ (accessed 20 July 2018).
45 Interview 204, Maïga, 28 December 2015, Bamako, p. 2.
46 'Mali: Islamic terrorists', p. 2.
47 Interview 206, p. 3, 10.
48 'Mali: Islamic terrorists', p. 4.
49 William Assanvo and Ibrahim Maiga, 'Mali's jihadist merger – desperate or dangerous?' *All Africa*. Institute for Security Studies, 3 April 2017. Available at http://allafrica.com/stories/201704030744.html (accessed 20 July 2018). p. 1; Andrew Lebovich, 'The real reason U.S. troops are in Niger', *Foreign Policy Magazine*, 27 October 2017, pp. 3–4. Available at http://foreignpolicy.com/2017/10/27/the-real-reason-u-s-troops-are-in-niger/ (accessed 23 July 2018); Idrissa Fall and Bagassi Koura, 'Niger: New details emerge about attack that killed U.S. soldiers', *AllAfrica.com*, 23 October 2017, p. 1. Available at https://allafrica.com/stories/201710230170.html (accessed 23 July 2018).
50 Saad Eddine Lamzouwaq, 'ISIS, AQIM, and Polisario: How do terrorist threats in the Sahel affect Morocco?' 2 June 2017, p. 1. Available at https://www.moroccoworldnews.com/2017/06/218501/isis-aqim-and-polisario-terrorist-threats-sahel-affect-morocco/ (accessed 23 July 2018).
51 This swearing of allegiance to AQIM Grand Amir Droukdel would indicate that Ag Ghali represents a Saharan branch of AQIM, not its overall leadership.
52 Assanvo and Maiga, 'Mali's jihadist merger', p. 1; 'Quatre organizations djihadistes du Sahel fusionnent: La lecture qu'il faut en faire', *Setal.net*, Senegal, 3 March 2017, p. 1. Available at https://www.dakaractu.com/Quatre-organisations-djihadistes-du-Sahel-fusionnent-La-lecture-qu-il-faut-en-faire_a127474.html (accessed 23 July 2018); Alex Falconer, 'The al-Qaeda affiliates merger in Mali', *Fair Observer*, 28 March 2017, p. 1. Available at https://www.fairobserver.com/region/africa/al-qaeda-mali-algeria-maghreb-international-security-news-71098/ (accessed 23 July 2018); Anyadike, 'The new jihadist strategy', p. 6.
53 Rida Lyammouri, 'AQIM never really abandoned Timbuktu, Mali', Blog, Maghreb and Sahel: Sand Tea and Guns, 6 February 2016, p. 2. Available at https://maghrebandsahel.wordpress.com/2016/02/06/aqim-never-really-abandoned-timbuktu-mali/ (accessed 23 July 2018).
54 Drew Hinshaw, 'Mali hostage crisis ends with 27 people dead, including five attackers, military officials say', *Wall Street Journal*, 20 November 2015. Available at https://ww

w.wsj.com/articles/ongoing-shooter-operation-reported-at-radisson-blu-hotel-in-mali-1448011876 (accessed 23 July 2018).
55 Anyadike, 'The new jihadist strategy', pp. 1–2.
56 Bruce Whitehouse, 'Is Mali heading back to the abyss?' Blog: Bridges from Bamako, 31 July 2016. Available at https://bridgesfrombamako.com/2016/07/31/is-mali-heading-back-to-the-abyss/ (accessed 23 July 2018); Adama Diarra, 'Mali president fires defense minister after gunmen seize village', *Reuters*, 4 September 2016, p. 1. Available at https://www.reuters.com/article/us-mali-politics/mali-president-fires-defense-minister-after-gunmen-seize-village-idUSKCN11A0CG (accessed 23 July 2018); Assanvo and Maiga, 'Mali's jihadist merger', p. 3; Lamzouwaq, 'ISIS, AQIM, and Polisario', p. 1.
57 Assanvo and Maiga, 'Mali's jihadist merger', p. 3; Souleymane Ag Anara, 'Al Qadea says Mali attack punishment for cooperation with France', *World News.com*, 18 January 2017, pp. 1–2. Available at http://news.trust.org/item/20170118172004-bamo0/ (accessed 23 July 2018); 'Suicide attack at military camp in Mali kills scores', *New York Times*, 18 January 2017, pp. 1–2. Available at https://www.nytimes.com/2017/01/18/world/africa/suicide-attack-at-military-camp-in-mali-kills-scores.html (accessed 23 July 2018); Yacouba Cissé, 'Death toll in Mali suicide blast rises to at least 60', *Washington Times*, 18 January 2017, pp. 1–2. Available at https://www.washingtontimes.com/news/2017/jan/18/death-toll-in-mali-suicide-blast-rises-to-more-tha/ (accessed 23 July 2018).
58 'Mali attack: Gunmen kill five at tourist resort', *BBC News*, 19 June 2017. Available at https://www.bbc.com/news/world-africa-40322039 (accessed 23 July 2018); 'Hostages shown in al-Qaeda Mali video as Macron flies in', *BBC News*, 2 July 2017, pp. 1, 5. Available at https://www.bbc.com/news/world-africa-40472162 (accessed 23 July 2018).
59 Harmon, *Terror and Insurgency*, p. 135.
60 Fall and Koura, 'Niger: New details', p. 1; Lebovich, 'The real reason', pp. 1–2.
61 'How a herdsman became the jihadist who killed US soldiers in Niger', Voice of America, 1 November 2017, p. 3. Available at https://www.voanews.com/a/niger-herdsman-jihadist-us-soldiers/4111534.html (accessed 23 July 2018).

NIGERIA

THE RISE AND 'FALL' OF BOKO HARAM

Caroline Varin

Introduction

For nearly a decade, Boko Haram, also known as *Jama'atu Ahlis Sunnah Lidda'awati w'al Jihad*, has been waging a low-intensity war against the Nigerian state, using both classic military tactics (invasion/occupation of territory), terrorist tactics (hit-and-run, shootings, bombings, kidnappings) and, most recently, suicide bombings. Since its rise in 2009, Boko Haram has killed over 20,000 people, injured scores more and displaced nearly two million Nigerians.[1] While most of its activity has been concentrated in the north-east of the country, Boko Haram's attacks have reached all corners of Nigeria, and across the border in Niger, Cameroon and Chad. The Lake Chad Basin has been most severely impacted, exacerbating existing hardship for the population and the local environment.

Boko Haram has been branded an 'Islamist terrorist group' by the Nigerian government and the international community. This has enabled the group to tap into the global jihadi network that has been growing these past few decades: Boko Haram was one of many organizations that joined forces between 2010 and 2013 with transnational terrorist organizations such as Al Qaeda, AQIM and Al Shabaab, giving them a global platform and ideological credibility, and in 2015 it pledged allegiance to ISIS, a move it has since rescinded.

Despite the media's portrayal of Boko Haram as a part of a transnational Islamist threat, however, the group was initially perceived as a local problem. Indeed, Nigeria has a history of violent non-state actors and religious fanaticism, with feuds between religious cults and between farmers and herders of opposing faiths.[2] For some, Boko Haram is symptomatic of identity politics and social cleavages that have characterized the country since the colonial era.[3] This has been exacerbated by the gross inequalities between the north and the south of the country that have long been ignored by leaders and have aggravated existing feelings of political alienation[4] and the government's endemic miscalculations in dealing with the growing threat.

In its early life, Boko Haram was portrayed as a problem from north-east Nigeria, funded and propped up by local politicians who held a personal grudge against President Goodluck Jonathan. This narrative dominated the Nigerian press until

President Jonathan began to appeal for foreign support to counter the 'terrorist threat' in 2013. The current regional impact of Boko Haram is undeniable, but its international reach is certainly questionable. The way in which Boko Haram is portrayed – as a local insurgency, a terrorist group, a sociopolitical movement and so on – can influence the way it is addressed but also gives it credibility to further its own agenda and pursue alliances with like-minded organizations at home or abroad. To a large extent this has shaped the evolution of the group, regardless of whether it started off as a 'Nigerian' phenomenon.

This chapter reviews Boko Haram's ties to the global jihadi network. It argues that, while a lot of learning has been shared between the different groups as a result of regional and technological opportunism, there has been limited ideological alignment between the leaders of these jihadi groups and many obstacles to obtaining any international traction for Boko Haram. Rather, Boko Haram's leadership under founder Muhammad Yusuf and his successor Abu Shekau has been preoccupied primarily with local dynamics and goals. Likewise, the different strategies adopted by Presidents Jonathan and then Buhari have been key in shaping the rise and fall of Boko Haram. Since Buhari won the elections in 2015, the President has spearheaded a military campaign to defeat the group, or at least reduce its potency. As a result, there were 850 fewer fatalities in 2017, a fall from 3,000 killings in 2016 and a dramatic drop from its peak of 12,000 deaths caused by Boko Haram in 2015.[5]

Nonetheless, the impact of the near-decade-long war cannot be underestimated. The UNHCR estimates the number of internally displaced people to be over 2.5 million, with many stuck in IDP camps in squalid conditions, ignored by the government. This has also caused a crisis in food security as farmers and herders have left their land, forcing 5 million Nigerians to face acute food shortages.[6] According to UNICEF, 75 per cent of water infrastructure in the region has been damaged or destroyed, leaving 3.6 million people without access to clean water.[7] While the Nigerian government offensive – supported by the United States, the United Kingdom, France, and regional and the Sahel G5 countries, among others, any victory will be short-lived if the living conditions of northerners, especially those impacted by the war, are not redressed.

The rise of Boko Haram

The conditions that would lead to the rise of an extremist religious group were overwhelmingly present in Nigeria, with early indications that the country would be embroiled in some way or another in a sociopolitical upheaval with religious undertones.

From a historical perspective, the asymmetric process of integration developed by the British in the colonial era emphasized the differences within the regions and laid the foundations upon which modern Nigeria was built, favouring a Christian south over the Muslim north. A power struggle between the major political parties and along religious lines has since defined the political arena with democratically elected leaders repeatedly overthrown and replaced by military coups.

The political unrest has been exacerbated by increasing sectarian violence, as local political leaders have subsidized various religious groups to rally voters. According to Murray Last: 'Boko Haram (…) follows a pattern that goes back at least 200 years in Northern Nigeria, and has a logic to it.'[8] Among the worst cases of extremist violence in the country are the Maitatsine riots that took place between 1980 and 1985 and during which close to 10,000 people in Kano were killed in clashes between the fundamentalist group and government forces. Many scholars have drawn comparisons between Maitatsine and the rise of Boko Haram, which appear to match each other in 'intensity, organization and spread'.[9] Toyin Falola explains the Maitatsine riots as 'a consequence of Islamic fundamentalism on the one hand, and of the political decadence and economic troubles of the 1970s on the other'.[10] The competition for religious ideology has been pervasive on all sides: in 1987, Christians in Kafanchan, Kaduna state, 'wantonly destroyed the property of local Muslims'[11] and in 2014, Human Rights Watch denounced the murder of 150 Muslims killed in 'Christian rampages'[12] in Kuru Karama, in Jos. Between 1999 and 2003, over 10,000 people were killed in religious clashes,[13] and the murder of hundreds of Muslims by Christian militias in May 2004 forced President Obasanjo to declare a state of emergency in the Middle Belt. Between May 2011 and June 2013, a further 785 people were killed in religious violence unrelated to Boko Haram. Abimbola Adesoji understands the prevalence of fundamental Islamist groups in Nigeria 'in terms of the dominance of Islam and its adherents in the region; it could imply the prevalence of factors and circumstances that made the region prone to extremism. Among such factors and circumstances are poverty and illiteracy, the existence and seeming proliferation of radical Islamic groups and recurrent violent religious crises'.[14] These characteristics explain the rise of fundamental religious groups in general in the country and the ensuing and recurrent sectarian violence.

To make matters worse, the leaders of Nigeria have failed again and again to stem the violence and redress the inequalities that mar the country. Despite rising national income and an average GDP growth of 5.4 per cent in 2013,[15] development in Nigeria has been asymmetric and concentrated overwhelmingly in the south. The disparities between the north and the south are quantified by the Gini Index, which rates Nigeria among the most unequal thirty-five countries in the world with a coefficient of 48.8. Overall, the living standards in the country have dropped to levels unseen since Nigeria's independence in 1960 and the poverty rate has continued to increase in the last decade. The poorest half of the population receives less than 10 per cent of the national income.[16] Sixty-one per cent of the Nigerian population fall under the poverty line, but that burden is disproportionally felt in the north, for example, in Sokoto state where 86.4 per cent of residents are under the poverty line.[17] Access to education is a further illustration of the vast differences between the regions. In Borno, the heart of Boko Haram's insurgency, the literacy rate is fifteen per cent compared to Lagos in the south, where ninety per cent of residents are fully literate.[18] An estimated seven to nine million children nationally are out of school, of which nearly half are from a nomadic background and have limited access to education. These trends are subsequently reflected in the level of youth unemployment that reached fifty-four per cent among under thirty-year-olds in 2012,[19] and again the north shows the highest level of unemployment in the country. The problem is compounded by the high levels of corruption that continue to plague every sector across Nigeria and exacerbate the differences between the population and the political elite.

The main leaders of Boko Haram – Mohammed Ali, Mohammed Yusuf and Abu Shekau – have all capitalized on the government's inability to redress inequalities and provide basic services to its population in the north. With the legitimacy of the political elite was undermined by allegations of corruption and mismanagement, the vacuum of power offered an opportunity for charismatic preachers to recruit their members, promising a better life built on their interpretation of fundamental Islam.

Boko Haram has been active since at least 1995, when three Islamic organizations from the University of Maiduguri merged under the leadership of the preacher Muhammad Ali. There is an oversupply of fiery preachers from all faiths in Nigeria, so when Ali – a former mujahedeen who had fought in Afghanistan[20] – declared the state irredeemable and started to build his own community in Kanama, he did not elicit any reaction from the government until 2004, when the security forces besieged Ali's mosque and killed 200 members including the leader. This could have been the end of Boko Haram, except that the survivors returned to Maiduguri where they reassembled under the leadership of the charismatic preacher Mohammed Yusuf, who had himself just come back from a self-imposed exile in Saudi Arabia. Mohammed Yusuf transformed the organization from a tiny cult into a popular religious community. Drawing from the tradition of 'missionary Islam', Yusuf set about providing services where the government failed to do so. This included food and shelter, and facilitating marriages for members of the group. He quickly built a cohesive social group around him. Members shared a common aim to rid Nigeria of a corrupt and abusive government that had evidently failed its people, and to return the country to a state of religious purity.[21] Boko Haram's spokesperson Abu Qaqa said in 2012 that 'our objective is to place Nigeria in a difficult position and even destabilize it and replace it with Shari'a; ... to take Nigeria back to the pre-colonial period when the Sharia law was practised'.[22] As a result of these political aspirations, Yusuf received financial support from his followers and allegedly was given funds from some Saudi Salafists and individuals in Libya and Algeria – although these claims have been disputed.[23]

Yusuf's religious message became increasingly political as he sought to influence the gubernatorial election and obtain the implementation of Sharia law in Borno state. Pushed by his more belligerent deputy Abubakr Shekau, Yusuf's proselytizing adopted a more jihadi discourse, although the preacher himself never openly encouraged jihad. Nonetheless, the members of the group became increasingly violent: they targeted police stations to kill security officials and steal their weapons, broke into prisons to release militants and assassinated a number of political and religious figures.[24] The Nigerian security forces responded to the increase in violence and set up a joint military anti-crime operation to bring the group and its preacher to heel, as they had done in the Maitatsine riots. In July

2009, within forty-eight hours the army had killed 800 Boko Haram members and arrested hundreds of others, including Mohammad Yusuf who subsequently was killed in police custody. The extrajudicial killing transformed Yusuf into a martyr, as he became a symbol of the excessive police and military brutality. This state of affairs united both surviving Boko Haram members and the civilians in an ideological and military campaign against Nigeria's brutal security forces and unaccountable political system. The virulent Abubakr Shekau took over the leadership of the group and turned it into a deadly nemesis.

Boko Haram's unchecked rise and gratuitous brutality under Shekau's leadership between 2010 and 2016 reveals the government's inability to learn from the past, the continued incompetence of the armed forces and the severity of the sociopolitical problems that seem to have just increased in the past thirty-five years. But it is also indicative of a wider trend of Islamist jihadi groups whose popularity and military clout have increased in the last decade, particularly on the axis from Nigeria, across the Maghreb and into the Middle East and South Asia.

Boko Haram and the Islamic Republic of Azawad

The events that played out in Mali in 2012 suddenly transformed the playing field for Islamist jihadi groups across Africa. North Africa and the Sahel region have long experienced the threat of Islamist insurgents, well before the advent of Al Qaeda on the international scene. Since 1996, Algeria has suffered terrorist attacks from the Salafist Group for Preaching and Combat (GSPC) that sought to establish an islamic state in the country. The GSPC is an offshoot of the Armed Islamic Group (GIA), which fought a violent insurgency against the secular Algerian state in the 1990s. Neither group had transnational aspirations until 2008, when the GSPC merged into Al Qaeda in the Islamic Maghreb (AQIM).

AQIM has continued to target Algeria, carrying out suicide missions and hijackings, and taking hostages, attacking security personnel and even foreign workers. It has also expanded its reach, increasing its activities in the Sahel and sending combatants to Iraq and Afghanistan to help the Islamist insurgency. According to a 2013 Rand report, under the leadership of Abdelmalek Droukdal, AQIM's ambitions became regional rather than just local, reflecting the leader's desire to create an Islamist Caliphate beyond Algeria's borders.[25] Although this appears in line with Al Qaeda's goals, Chivvis and Liepman describe the alliance as a 'marriage of convenience' between leaders who share a common jihadi and anti-Western ideology that justifies the use of force.[26] For AQIM, however, the foreign enemy is France rather than the United States, and while the Al Qaeda brand gives the group legitimacy, both organizations operate with entirely separate chains of command.

Unlike Al Qaeda, Droukdal's organization has not particularly targeted Western interests in the region or abroad. Indeed, bin Laden's obsession with pursuing the United States does not appear to have inspired any of its local partners. AQIM has maintained its focus on building a North African Caliphate, grabbing the opportunity to install itself in northern Mali when the regime collapsed in 2012. The terrorist group emerged in an environment with gross levels of poverty, unemployment and inequality, all within an expanse of land with very limited government presence – something reminiscent of the ascent of Boko Haram in Nigeria. This created an opportunity for criminal and insurgent activities, which go hand in hand in the Sahel. Indeed, AQIM has built a fortune from kidnap and ransom and smuggling operations led by Mokhtar Belmokhtar who commanded the southern faction of the GSPC.

AQIM's big moment came in 2012 when it successfully established control over northern Mali. It effectively hijacked the Tuareg insurgency after the separatist group known as the National Movement for the Liberation of Azawad (MNLA) declared the independence of Azawad in northern Mali. The Tuaregs had fought to have their own state since 1960 and took advantage of a military coup against President Touré and the ensuing political chaos in March 2012 to capture Timbuktu and claim it as their capital. To achieve this feat, the MNLA allied itself with the local Islamist group Ansar Dine, also primarily made up of Tuaregs, although its goal is the implementation of Sharia law throughout Mali.[27] The Tuareg rebellion was initially successful but quickly turned sour as Islamist groups Movement for Oneness and Jihad in West Africa (MUJAO) and AQIM stepped into the power vacuum.

MUJAO is also a Mali-based Tuareg Islamist organization that was previously associated with AQIM but broke off in 2011, allegedly over the marginalization of black African members. MUJAO claimed to spread Islamist law in black Africa.[28] In this complicated interplay of Islamist and secular groups in the 2012 Mali rebellion, it is important to take note of the many interests and ideologies that compete with one another. While the MNLA insurgency was inward-looking and seeking to create an independent secular Tuareg state, Ansar Dine sought to implement Sharia law in that state, and turned to MUJAO and AQIM for support. The latter grabbed this opportunity to overwhelm the MNLA and push them out of the new Azawad state; they subsequently imposed Sharia law and created the first islamic state of the twenty-first century.

By December 2012, AQIM and its allies had firm control over northern Mali and began to develop their model of statehood. They opened training camps for like-minded terrorists and threatened to become the 'Tora Bora of Africa',[29] attracting jihadis from around the world and providing them with a safe haven. In early 2013, the insurgents began to move south towards Bamako, the capital of Mali, demonstrating their intention to expand their territory. The unexpected success of an Al Qaeda-affiliated insurgency and their occupation of territory less than 2,500 km from Spain presented a real and immediate threat to the security of Europe and the rest of Africa. Indeed, in January 2013 a terrorist hub had clearly appeared at Europe's doorstep.

The creation of the first Islamist state of this century was a turning point for two reasons: first, for over twelve months, Al Qaeda in the Islamic Maghreb (AQIM) and its sister group, the Movement for Unity and Jihad in West Africa (MUJAO), were able to forge links with Islamist groups worldwide whose leaders met freely in Timbuktu and Gao while their militants exchanged ideas in terrorist training camps, learnt to fix Kalashnikovs, make bombs and launch rockets.[30] Second, it set a precedent by which other organized groups could aspire to create their own Islamist state by overthrowing the existing structure in their home territory. Since 2012, we have seen this taking place relatively successfully, even if short-lived in parts of Iraq and Syria and in northern Nigeria.

Between April 2012 and January 2013, Islamist groups were for all intents and purposes in military control of a territory the size of France, which also enabled them to accumulate capital. Northern Mali had long been the gateway for the drug trade, particularly marijuana and cocaine, in Africa and Europe, and enjoyed deep trafficking networks across the region. The relationship between drug traders and terrorists is complex, but reports suggest that AQIM derived a large proportion of its wealth by providing drug convoys with security across its territory, in exchange for materials including vehicles, medical supplies, weapons and electronics.[31] This could explain the supply of weapons across the region and into the hands of Boko Haram. Drug and cigarette smugglers also provided important regional connections to MUJAO through their established presence in Gao and networks across the Sahel and into the Middle East. It is common knowledge that the leader of Nigerian Islamist group Ansaru and former deputy to Yusuf, Khalid al-Barnawi, was involved with cigarette smuggler turned terrorist Mokhtar Belmokhtar.[32] During the brief period of their rule in northern Mali, the Islamists developed their criminal networks including drug and human trafficking, smuggling of arms and cigarettes, and kidnap for ransom – this strategy was later utilized by Boko Haram. These enterprises provided them with an independent source of revenue to finance training camps in Mali and invite like-minded organizations to meet in Gao.

There has been anecdotal and hard evidence of Nigerian militants travelling to northern Mali in 2012 and 2013. According to researcher Jacob Zenn who conducted interviews in Mali in 2014, there were a significant number of Nigerians present in the country during this time who fought with MUJAO, although they did not necessarily identify publicly as members of Boko Haram.[33] A poster with Ansaru's logo, another Islamist group in Nigeria with known ties to Boko Haram, was found in Belmokhtar's compound in Gao.[34] In Timbuktu, AQIM ran a sophisticated training camp for multinational terrorists, the majority of whom were Nigerians, 'all of them members of Boko Haram'.[35] Over a nine-month period, 'hundreds of Boko Haram members' stayed at these camps where they 'learned to fix Kalashnikovs and launch shoulder-fired weapons'.[36] These centres provided perfect conditions for exchanging battlefield skills and ideologies. A video posted on a jihadi online forum by Boko Haram in 2012 also appears to have been filmed in Mali. It is unique in that Shekau is dressed in military fatigues and praises the 'Soldiers of God in the Islamic State of Mali…our brothers and sheikhs in the Islamic Maghreb' and the backdrop is a vast desert reminiscent of northern Mali, unlike the first five videos released by Shekau where he is seated in a room dressed in Islamic robes.[37] He also speaks in Arabic as opposed to his usual Hausa dialect. Zenn adds that Boko Haram's media and military strategies changed significantly in 2013, suggesting a period of learning that could be the result of Boko Haram fighters' experience in the occupation of northern Mali and exposure to other like-minded terrorist groups. He gives the example of 4X4s mounted with weapons, a tactic of desert warfare utilized in Gao in 2012 and seen again in Nigeria in 2013.[38]

Territorial expansion and ISIS

Boko Haram's rapid territorial expansion began in 2014, shortly after the Malian experience. At first, Boko Haram simply moved into villages in the north-east of Borno state where there was little, if any, police presence. Some of the villages are so dispersed that there 'is not a friendly walled city within a week's journey'.[39] This power vacuum offered an irresistible opportunity for the group to easily claim territory and consolidate its position. Town by town, the militants expanded their hold across the state and into parts of Yobe and Adamawa, walking into areas from which the government was virtually absent.

Boko Haram was able to gain territory principally for two reasons: first, thanks to their new access to weapons and ammunitions looted from the arsenal of the defunct Libyan armed forces following the overthrow of Gaddafi, which improved their strike capability; and second, the total absence of the military in these areas and the general lack of resistance to the advance of the militants. Rocket launchers and armoured vehicles stolen or, according to some sources, bought from Nigerian military personnel,[40] completed an arsenal that included small arms, automatic weapons, rifles, grenades and mortars.

The establishment of an Islamic capital in the mountainous border town of Gwoza, Borno state, in August 2014 marked a turning point for Abu Shekau's ambitions. In September, Shekau claimed leadership of an Islamic Caliphate in Nigeria and in March 2015 declared Boko Haram to be the West African branch of ISIS.[41] This shift away from traditional hit-and-run tactics to position warfare was a risky gamble as it prompted a swift reaction from the Nigerian government and armed forces. Shortly thereafter in March 2015, the Nigerian army, allegedly with the help of foreign private military providers, had retaken the town and forced Boko Haram out of their stronghold.[42] Meanwhile, Boko Haram sought to expand its territorial claims across the borders into Cameroon and Chad. This additional miscalculation would later help cement the military collaboration between the neighbouring countries.

Throughout 2014, Boko Haram's operational successes indicated that it had both the intent and capacity to create a separatist state in north-east Nigeria. This was hardly a surprise as Abu Shekau has long been referring to the nineteenth-century Islamic Sokoto Caliphate in northern Nigeria led by Usman dan Fodio that he sought to emulate. Having gathered enough recruits, Boko Haram was able to shift from typical asymmetric warfare, including a combination of guerrilla and terrorist tactics, to direct assaults on cities and military positions. Furthermore, as Boko Haram expanded its territory, it increased its manpower by forcing men and boys into its army while the women were kidnapped and taken as slaves and hostages, constraining the men to follow and obey. A secondary but important result of Boko Haram's military successes has been the humiliation and demoralization of the Nigerian security forces and the Jonathan government, temporarily weakening any opposition to the group's territorial incursions. Abu Shekau was thereby able to inflate the public perception of Boko Haram's powers and capabilities and increase its credibility in the eyes of like-minded organizations such as ISIS.

Boko Haram's pledge of allegiance to ISIS followed an intense courtship that had begun a year earlier, according to Jacob Zenn.[43] Despite the symbolic significance of this alignment, it is debatable whether the support of ISIS was at all advantageous for Boko Haram. There is evidence of increased knowledge-sharing between the two organizations, particularly in the use of social media, but access to weaponry does not seem to have improved and Boko Haram certainly did not attract more followers as a result of its allegiance. This may be because of the language limitations – Boko Haram followers typically speak Fulani, not Arabic, making it difficult for foreigners to integrate with the terrorist group. In addition, travel to northern Nigeria is more complicated than to Syria or Libya for example, and Boko Haram's camps are typically located in remote areas such as the Sambisa Forest and the Mandara mountains and not very comfortably placed. Another explanation could be that Boko Haram is really inward-looking with local ambitions in the area around Lake Chad; they would thus appeal to Islamists with similar sociopolitical interests whereas those with religious ambitions have other more appealing and more easily located groups to turn to. This is despite the widened media campaign launched by Boko Haram and ISIS through ISIS media channels where Islamists were encouraged to join the West African Caliphate.[44] Ironically, there have been more reports of Nigerians being arrested on the way to Libya to join ISIS, rather than of their migrating to the north of the country.[45] Considering the standard of living for militants in Boko Haram's camps, it is unsurprising that they lack appeal to all but the most desperate. Zenn describes ISIS's role as a 'narrative development' in Boko Haram's existence. They provide support for media use, recommendations for strategy and targeting, with funding, recruitment and training notably in Libya.[46] However, the decision to hold territory may have been more opportunistic than strategic, just like the expansion of attacks across the northern and eastern borders are born more out of necessity than a deliberate desire to expand transnationally. In fact, these two manoeuvres were arguably counterproductive as they prodded the neighbouring countries and the Nigerian government to take a more proactive military approach to counter the mounting threat of Boko Haram. This is not dissimilar to ISIS's recent decline in Syria and Iraq.

Other links to Islamist groups

Before the association with ISIS, Boko Haram was linked to Al Qaeda, which remains the more influential Islamist group in North Africa. Boko Haram leader Muhammad Yusuf praised bin Laden repeatedly in his speeches and claimed to have sent dozens of members to Algeria and Mauritania to train with Al Qaeda in the early 2000s.[47] In his first video released in 2010, Shekau continued this line and directed his statement to 'leaders of Al Qaeda and its affiliated groups in Algeria, Iraq, Somalia and Yemen' and later his spokesman claimed that 'Al Qaeda are our elder brothers. During the lesser Hajj, our leader travelled to Saudi Arabia and met Al Qaeda there. We enjoy financial and technical support from them. Anything we want from them we ask them'.[48] However, it is important to note that Al Qaeda never officially recognized Boko Haram as a direct offshoot and appeared critical of the ideological divergence between the two groups – notably Boko Haram's use of indiscriminate killing of other Muslims. This has also been a point of contention internally for the group and led to the formation of splinter groups such as Ansaru and, more recently, the West African Province faction led by Shekau's 'son' Abu Musab al-Barnawi.[49]

In 2012, Ansaru emerged as a direct competitor to Boko Haram in northern Nigeria. It appeared more closely aligned to AQIM, from whom it received training and funding, and was involved in the 2012 occupation of Mali. This new Islamist group announced its creation publicly by releasing flyers in Kano describing itself as a humane alternative to Boko Haram: it only targeted the Nigerian government and Christians, and would not attack Muslims except in self-defence. In June 2012, the group released a video dubbed in English and Hausa in which its self-proclaimed leader Abu Usamarul Ansari – a nom de guerre for Boko Haram member Khalid al-Barnawi – outlined the ideological stand of Ansaru as prescribed in its charter and explained its schism with Boko Haram.[50] Although ideologically close to Boko Haram, Ansaru carried out its attacks using its individual signature, which focused primarily on the kidnappings of foreigners. The differences were accentuated by Ansaru's claim to defend the interests of Muslims across West Africa and in Africa as a whole, contrary to Boko Haram's apparent local ambitions at the time. The group's success was short-lived, however, and Ansaru has not publicly claimed responsibility for any attacks since at least May 2013, when a known militant appeared in a video celebrating the suicide attack on the Arlit uranium mine in Niger. The most likely scenario cited is that Ansaru merged with Boko Haram following the disruptions caused to its international networks by the French-led intervention in Mali.[51] Since then, Boko Haram has increased its tempo of attacks and adopted distinctly more sophisticated weaponry, providing evidence of its strengthened international connections and development as a violent ideological organization, probably influenced by Ansaru's achievements and the reintegration of key members into Boko Haram's nucleus. Most notably, since 2012, Boko Haram's strategy overwhelmingly includes kidnappings, with thousands of men, women and children forcibly abducted and integrated into the Islamist group's ranks, a modus operandi favoured by Ansaru.

Another influential Islamist group in Africa, which surpassed Boko Haram in the number of people killed in 2017, is Al Shabaab, based in Somalia. Until 2010, Al Shabaab had portrayed itself first and foremost as a nationalist Islamist resistance movement whose primary objective is to drive out the foreigners from the country. This changed in 2010 when the militants declared their affiliation with Al Qaeda and began launching transborder attacks, notably in Kenya. The group has specifically targeted hotels and restaurants in Mogadishu, as well as both foreign and local political figures. Al Shabaab claimed responsibility for the attack on the 2013 Westgate shopping mall in Nairobi that killed sixty-three people and injured a further 175, and their assault on a university in Garissa, in the northeastern province of Kenya left 148 students dead.[52] Several members of Boko Haram were allegedly sent to training camps run by Al Shabaab, where they were taught to build improvised explosive devices (IEDs) and how to best use suicide bombers.[53] Mamman Nur, for example, another important personality in Boko Haram, is from Cameroon and allegedly trained with Al Shabaab.[54] However, Al Shabaab appears to have faced a similar crisis as Boko Haram, over whether to maintain its alignment with Al Qaeda or join ISIS. This has led to reports of factionalism within the organization that have only recently been reversed, coinciding with ISIS's good fortune.[55] In fact, Al Shabaab remains as inward-looking as Boko Haram, but is ideologically opposed to the massacre of Muslims and in addition has been silently killing defectors who turn to other Islamist groups.[56] For this reason, future association between Boko Haram and Al Shabaab remains an unlikely occurrence, even if the former rejoins the ranks of Al Qaeda.

The fall of Boko Haram

President Buhari declared in December 2015 that the enemy was 'technically defeated'. Since his election, the Nigerian armed forces have taken a more proactive approach to the insurgency than under the presidency of Goodluck Jonathan. As mentioned earlier, there were 850 fewer fatalities in 2017, over 2,000 fewer than in 2016 and a significant decrease from the 12,000 deaths caused by Boko Haram in 2015.[57] In addition, Boko Haram members have been pushed out of their strongholds in the towns and are mainly entrenched in the Sambisa Forest and Mandera mountains, areas that are difficult to access. However, the group has since adapted and resorted to tried-and-tested guerrilla tactics ensuring its survivability. Its recent use of suicide attacks – especially using female and underage victims in the Lake Chad region and in neighbouring countries – has been an effective tool of terror against the local population, and is difficult to prevent.

The 'fall' of Boko Haram can be attributed to three factors: first, the improved military operations conducted by the Nigerian armed forces and their collaboration with neighbouring countries; second, the defeat of ISIS in Iraq and Syria, courtesy of the international community; and third, the splinter groups that have emerged and divided the power of Abu Shekau's organization.

First, the Nigerian armed forces, supported by foreign contractors, have been largely responsible for turning the tide on Boko Haram. Before the 2015 presidential elections, President Jonathan contracted a number of companies, notably African-based private military companies such as STTEP and Pilgrims to help the Nigerian army defeat the terrorist group. The mission allegedly included posting 100 men in Nigeria at a price of USD$400 per day.[58] It thereafter morphed into 'an aggressive strike force'[59] and contractors assisted the Nigerian forces in combat, despite assurance by the Nigerian government that they serve mainly as 'technical advisors'. One contractor revealed that mercenaries were sometimes embedded with the Mobile Striking Force, but that their main role was limited to training and mentorship.[60]

The episode was short-lived, however, as President Buhari did not apparently renew any of the contracts begun by his predecessor. Ex-military commander Buhari has, instead, focused his attention on building up the Nigerian armed forces with the help of foreign governments. British military and civilian experts present in Nigeria provide the security forces with cutting-edge technology and analysis along with a substantial funding package that had been denied to Jonathan.[61] Until the elections, the United States had also been reluctant to assist the country militarily, despite its strong influence in Nigeria. But in 2017, the Pentagon notified Congress that it had sold over USD 593 million worth of military equipment to Nigeria, including advanced infantry tactics with the specific objective of countering Boko Haram.[62]

The Counterterrorism Strategy developed in ECOWAS and the Multinational Joint Task Force (MNJTF) have also played a part towards regional coordination, with neighbouring countries deploying soldiers and supporting the Nigerian effort across borders. The MNJTF has a 10,000-strong force made up of soldiers from Chad, Niger, Nigeria, Cameroon and Benin, improving bilateral missions, intelligence- sharing and, most important, cross-border pursuits.[63]

The military defeat of ISIS in Syria and Iraq has also weakened Boko Haram's influence and aspirations as it lost its major political supporter. From its peak in 2014 when it occupied roughly one-third of Iraq and half of Syria, the terrorist group has since lost nearly all its territory and 80 per cent of its funds.[64] This has been achieved only as a result of a robust cooperation between the Iraqi government and the international community, which arguably took too long to achieve. By destroying ISIS's dreams of forming a caliphate, the international community of states sent a message to the world that non-state actors would not be allowed to claim territorial sovereignty. Sooner or later, it would intervene. This message was equally meant for Boko Haram whose military defeat has disrupted, albeit not annihilated, them. Nonetheless, the 'fall' of ISIS has meant the end of the training camps for terrorists in Syria and Iraq (although they are allegedly still operating in Libya) and the disruption of communication streams between the two organizations, and it has weakened the media campaign of Boko Haram: Jason Burke, author of *The New Threat: The Past, Present and Future of Islamic Militancy* points out that by September 2017, governance-related media published by ISIS came to an abrupt end and its social media propaganda has been significantly reduced.[65] While this won't have a major impact on Boko Haram, whose leadership has always been inward-looking and concerned with local objectives, it does slow down its international appeal and arguably some of its local legitimacy. In fact, ISIS has also been the source of internal disruption as Boko Haram's leadership has been split on whether to pursue its 'allegiance' with the losing terrorist group, and Abu Shekau has complained that he has been unable to communicate directly with ISIS leader Abu Bakr al-Baghdadi.[66]

Rumours of factions forming within Boko Haram's inner circle have been circulating since August 2016.[67] A statement issued by ISIS announced that its West African 'province' was no longer under the leadership of Abu Shekau and, instead, was led by Abu Musab al-Barnawi.[68] This prompted a leadership battle with reports of clashes between the two factions in remote areas of Borno state in late 2017. According to Boko Haram expert Freedom Onuoha, the factions have also been operating a propaganda war against one another, with Barnawi's allies accusing Shekau of being un-Islamic in his targeting of Muslims, and condemning his tactics. Mamman Nur, a known associate of al-Barnawi and former member of Boko Haram explained the ideological difference: 'In the Qur'an, Allah forbids Muslims from killing one another…and He also taught against killing in secret. If it is a serious punishment, it must be public for people to know and witness it. But once you see killings in secret, there is something fishy, and this is what we noticed with Shekau.'[69] While the splitting of Boko Haram's main group may weaken Abu Shekau, it does not lessen the threat of Islamist groups to the Nigerian population. To the contrary, a turf war has emerged between the factions with an increase in kidnappings and attacks on the local population. In addition, negotiations to free the Chibok girls kidnapped in 2014 have been further complicated as each of the factions is believed to be holding some of the girls.[70]

Boko Haram has in the past resurged from its ashes, adapting to new environments and reinventing its purpose and strategy as it encounters obstacles and opportunities. In military terms, the organization operates with a few thousand 'hard' militants, and a supporting crew of a couple more thousand recruits and slaves. This makes up a small army but hardly a military might to be reckoned with. Its hit-and-run strategy, use of suicide bombers and indiscriminate violence arguably causes more terror that the actual number of casualties. This also undermines the legitimacy of the government by highlighting its inability to control the territory and secure its citizens. The group has benefited from the confusing and scaremongering stories typically present in the Nigerian press and the wild accusations thrown around by some unscrupulous politicians. Indeed, the hint of rumours that 'Boko Haram is approaching' can provoke widespread civilian displacement, clogging up the already burdened refugee camps. Likewise, allegations of sleeper cells in Nigeria's main cities and the incidents of suicide bombers have contributed to the sect's ongoing imprint on the national mindset beyond the north-east.

Conclusion

Boko Haram's rise and fall were principally due to local conditions, failures of the Nigerian government and opportunities seized by the group's leaders. It remains but one among many jihadi groups, in Nigeria and in the wider region. Arguably, its fate has been influenced, if not decided, by international dynamics including the wave of jihadi groups in Africa and the Middle East that have enjoyed considerable success in the early twenty-first century and shared their learnings and experience liberally, thanks to the failures of the Malian, Syrian and Iraqi governments, to the opportunities offered by globalization and to the visibility they have been given by the global media.

Neither ISIS nor Boko Haram will disappear in the near future. Even if they are defeated militarily, the roots of Islamist radicalization will continue to flourish in Nigeria and beyond, feeding off the frustrations of a population that feels outdone by its politicians and fellow citizens. Addressing problems such as inequality and economic opportunity will help deter radicals from becoming insurgents by offering them viable alternatives. A focus on displacing the supply chains by clamping down on weapons smuggling and controlling borders can provide ongoing oversight and controls over regions identified as 'risky'. Investment in critical infrastructure such as roads and training to security officials to maintain good relations with locals will further assist in controlling the threat of an insurgency. And, of course, the problem of internally displaced people living in squalid refugee camps must be addressed as a matter of urgency. Unfortunately, the presidential elections in 2019 are likely to distract the government from necessary policy implementation and, instead, prompt it to focus on the 'easier' and more visible strategy of pursuing Boko Haram militarily.

Notes

1 Mark Wilson, 'Why January is Boko Haram's deadliest month', *BBC News*, 25 January 2018. Available at http://www.bbc.co.uk/news/world-africa-42735414.
2 Caroline Varin, *Boko Haram and the War on Terror* (California: Praeger ABC-Clio, 2016).
3 Olabanji Akinola, 'Boko Haram insurgency in Nigeria: Between Islamic fundamentalism, politics, and poverty', *African Security*, 8, no. 11 (2015): 1–29. Daniel Egiegba Agbiboa, 'The Nigerian burden: Religious identity, conflict and the current terrorism of Boko Haram', *Conflict, Security & Development*, 13, no. 1 (2013): 1–29.
4 Alafuro Epelle and Uranta Iwarimie, 'Political economy of violence: Interpreting the Nigerian Boko Haram', *Mediterranean Journal of Social Sciences*, 5, no. 10 (2014): 528. Seth Kaplan, 'How inequality fuels Boko Haram', *Foreign Affairs*, 5, no. 2 (2015). https://www.foreignaffairs.com/articles/africa/2015-02-05/how-inequality-fuels-boko-haram.
5 Heidelberg Institute for International Conflict Research (HIIK) *Conflict Barometer*, 2018. Available at https://hiik.de/conflict-barometer/current-version/?lang=en.
6 Ibid.
7 Ibid.
8 Cited in John Azumah, 'Boko Haram in Retrospect', *Islam and Christian-Muslim Relations*, 26, no. 1 (2015): 33–52 (p. 34).
9 Abimbola O. Adesoji, 'Between Maitatsine and Boko Haram: Islamic fundamentalism and the response of the Nigerian State', *Africa Today*, 57, no. 4 (2011): 99–119. Mike Smith, *Boko Haram* (London, 2015).

10 Toyin Falola, *Violence in Nigeria* (Rochester, 1998), p. 138.
11 Ibid., p. 4.
12 Andreena Narayan, 'Christian-Muslim violence in Nigeria warrants probe, rights group says', *CNN.Com*, 23 January 2014. Available at http://edition.cnn.com/2010/WORLD/africa/01/23/nigeria.massacre.probe/index.html.
13 Freedom Onuoha, 'The Islamist challenge: Nigeria's Boko Haram crisis explained', *African Security Review*, 19, no. 2 (2010): 54–67.
14 Adesoji, 'Between Maitatsine and Boko Haram'; Smith, *Boko Haram*.
15 Data.worldbank.org. 2015. 'GDP Growth (Annual %) | Data | Graph'.
16 Adegoke Yetunde, 'Disparity in income distribution in Nigeria: A Lorenz curve and Gini index approach', *Universal Journal of Management and Social Sciences*. Available at http://cprenet.com/uploads/archive/UJMSS_12-1254.pdf.
17 National Population Commission (NPC) [Nigeria] and ICF International, 2014. Nigeria Demographic and Health Survey 2013. Abuja, Nigeria, and Rockville, Maryland, USA: NPC and ICF International.
18 Leena Koni Hoffmann, *Who Speaks for the North? Politics and Influence in Northern Nigeria*, Chatham House Africa Programme. http://www.chathamhouse.org/sites/files/chathamhouse/field/field_document/20140703NorthernNigeriaHoffmann.pdf.
19 Tunji Akande, 'Youth unemployment in Nigeria: A situation analysis', *The Brookings Institution*. http://www.brookings.edu/blogs/africa-in-focus/posts/2014/09/23-youth-unemployment-nigeria-akande.
20 Kyari Mohammed in Marc-Antoine Pérouse de Montclos, *Boko Haram* (Leiden: African Studies Centre, 2014), p. 10.
21 Daniel Egiegba Agbiboa, 'The social dynamics of the "Nigerian Taliban": Fresh insights from the social identity theory', *Social Dynamics*, 41, no. 3 (2015): 415–37. Cited in Johannes Harnischfeger, 'Boko Haram and its Muslim critics: Observations from Yobe State', in Marc-Antoine Perouse de Montclos (ed.), *Boko Haram: Islamism, Politics, Security and the State in Nigeria* (Leiden: African Studies Center, 2004), p. 51.
22 Cited in Varin, *Boko Haram and the War on Terror*.
23 Pérouse de Montclos, *Boko Haram*, p. 140.
24 Virginia Comolli, *Boko Haram* (London: C Hurst & Co, 2014).
25 Christopher S. Chivvis and Andrew Liepman, 'North Africa's Menace: AQIM's evolution and the U.S. policy response | RAND', *Rand.Org*. http://www.rand.org/pubs/research_reports/RR415.html.
26 Ibid.
27 Jude Cocodia, 'Nationalist sentiment, terrorist incursions and the survival of the Malian State', in Caroline Varin and Dauda Abubakar (eds), *Violent Non-State Actors in Africa* (London: Palgrave, 2017).
28 alakhbar.info, 'Alakhbar | Sahel: MUJAO À La Conquête Des "Jeunes De L'afrique Noire"', 2012. Available at http://fr.alakhbar.info/3512-0-Sahel-MUJAO-a-la-conqute-des-jeunes-de-lAfrique-noire.html.
29 Chivvis and Liepman, 'North Africa's Menace'.
30 Jacob Zenn, 'Boko Haram's international connections, Combating Terrorism Center at West Point', *Ctc.Usma.Edu*, 2013. Available at https://www.ctc.usma.edu/posts/boko-harams-international-connections. Freedom Onuoha, *A Danger not to Nigeria Alone- Boko Haram's Transnational Reach and Regional Responses* (Abuja: Friedrich-Ebert-Stiftung, 2014).
31 FCO, *Traffickers and Terrorists: Drugs and Violent Jihad in Mali and the Wider Sahel*, Foreign and Commonwealth Office, 2013. Available at https://www.gov.uk/govern

ment/uploads/system/uploads/attachment_data/file/256619/Oct_2013_Traffickers_and_Terrorists.pdf.
32. Jacob Zenn, 'Leadership analysis of Boko Haram and Ansaru in Nigeria', *Combating Terrorism Center, CTC Sentinel*, 7, no. 2 (2014): 23–9.
33. Jacob Zenn, 'Nigerians in Gao: Was Boko Haram really active in Northern Mali?' *African Arguments*, 2014. Available at http://africanarguments.org/2014/01/20/nigerians-in-gao-was-boko-haram-active-in-northern-mali-by-jacob-zenn/.
34. L. Staveland, 'Ny islamistgruppe kan være tilknyttet Al-Qaida', *Aftenposten*, 2013. Available at https://www.aftenposten.no/verden/i/qn5eo/Ny-islamistgruppe-kan-vare-tilknyttet-Al-Qaida#.UtKWlfZRF0E.
35. David Blair, 'Timbuktu: Al-Qaeda's terrorist training academy in the Mali Desert', *Telegraph.Co.Uk*, 2013. Available at http://www.telegraph.co.uk/news/worldnews/africaandindianocean/mali/9860822/Timbuktu-al-Qaedas-terrorist-training-academy-in-the-Mali-desert.html.
36. Habeeb Pindiga, 'Nigeria: Boko Haram training camps found in Mali'. Available at http://allafrica.com/stories/201302060749.html.
37. Zenn, 'Nigerians in Gao'.
38. Ibid.
39. Andrew Walker, *Eat the Heart of the Infidel* (London: Hurst & Company, 2016), p. 31.
40. Frances Martel, 'Nigeria arrests soldiers supplying arms to Boko Haram – Breitbart', *Breitbart*, 2016. Available at http://www.breitbart.com/national-security/2016/02/10/nigeria-arrests-soldiers-supplying-arms-to-boko-haram/.
41. BBC News, *ISIS 'Accepts' Boko Haram's Allegiance*, 2015. Available at http://www.bbc.com/news/world-africa-31862992.
42. BBC News, *Boko Haram HQ in Nigeria 'Retaken'*, 2015. Available at http://www.bbc.com/news/world-africa-32087211.
43. J. Zenn, '"Boko Haram and the Islamist insurgency in West Africa" testimony before the U.S. House of representatives, committee on foreign affairs, terrorism, non-proliferation, and trade subcommittee', The Jamestown Foundation. Available at https://gallery.mailchimp.com/28b6673fcc2022a1dd557acae/files/Jacob_Zenn_Written_Testimony_Feb_24_2016.pdf.
44. Ibid.
45. Ibid.
46. Ibid.
47. P. Zimet, *Boko Haram's Evolving Relationship With al-Qaeda – GCSP*, 2017. Available at https://www.gcsp.ch/News-Knowledge/Global-insight/Boko-Haram-s-Evolving-Relationship-With-al-Qaeda.
48. Ibid.
49. J. Zenn, *Boko Haram: Abu Musab al-Barnawi's Leadership Coup and Offensive in Niger – Jamestown*, 2016. Available at https://jamestown.org/program/boko-haram-abu-musab-al-barnawis-leadership-coup-and-offensive-in-niger.
50. Varin, *Boko Haram and the War on Terror*.
51. Ibid.
52. Usman Tar, 'Al-Shabaab: State collapse, warlords and Islamist insurgency in Somalia', in Caroline Varin and Dauda Abubakar (eds), *Violent Non-State Actors in Africa* (London: Palgrave, 2017).
53. Onuoha, *A Danger not to Nigeria Alone*, p. 6.

54 Counter Extremism Project, 'Mamman Nur', 2014. Available at http://www.counterex tremism.com/people/mamman-nur.
55 C. Gaffey, *This Is Why Al-Shabaab Is Not Joining ISIS*, 2016. Available at http://www.newsweek.com/al-shabab-not-joining-isis-418656.
56 Ibid.
57 Heidelberg Institute for International Conflict Research (HIIK), *Conflict Barometer*, 2018. Available at https://hiik.de/conflict-barometer/current-version/?lang=en.
58 Ibid.
59 Colin Freeman, 'South African mercenaries' secret war on Boko Haram', *Telegraph.Co.UK*, 2015. Available at http://www.telegraph.co.uk/news/worldnews/africaandindianocean/nigeria/11596210/South-African-mercenaries-secret-war-on-Boko-Haram.html.
60 Beegeagle's Blog, 'Boko Haram and "mercenaries" in Borno – the myth, the reality; Hearing it from A PMC operative', 2015. Available at https://beegeagle.wordpress.com/2015/03/18/boko-haram-and-mercenaries-in-borno-the-myth-the-reality-hearing-it-from-a-pmc-operative/.
61 Varin, *Boko Haram and the War on Terror*.
62 M. Myers and M. Myers, *Army Troops, Special Forces Train Nigerian Infantry for Fight against Boko Haram, ISIS*, 2018. Available at https://www.armytimes.com/news/your-army/2018/02/23/special-forces-troops-train-nigerian-infantry-for-fight-against-boko-haram-isis/.
63 S. Solomon, *As Nigeria's Regional Task Force Strengthens, Pressure Mounts on Boko Haram*, 2018. Available at https://www.voanews.com/a/nigeria-boko-haram/4254565.html.
64 R. Monsour, *ISIS Is Still in Business*. Chatham House, 2018. Available at https://www.chathamhouse.org/expert/comment/isis-still-business.
65 J. Burke, 'Rise and fall of ISIS: Its dream of a caliphate is over, so what now?', *The Guardian*. Available at https://www.theguardian.com/world/2017/oct/21/isis-caliphate-islamic-state-raqqa-iraq-islamist.
66 F. Onuoha, *Split in ISIS-Aligned Boko Haram Group*, 2016. Available at http://studies.aljazeera.net/en/reports/2016/10/split-isis-aligned-boko-haram-group-161027113247008.html.
67 Ibid.
68 BBC News, *Boko Haram Splits over Leadership*, 2016. Available at http://www.bbc.co.uk/news/world-africa-369733.
69 K. Adamu, 'Security risk management and the feud amongst Salafi jihadists in Nigeria', *LinkedIn*, 27 August. Available at https://www.linkedin.com/pulse/security-risk-management-feud-amongst-salafi-jihadists-kabir-adamu.
70 Onuoha, *Split in ISIS-Aligned Boko Haram Group*.

LIBYAN JIHADISM

FROM GADHAFI AND TRIBALISM TO THE ARAB SPRING AND TRIBALISM

Anneli Botha

Historically Libya has been synonymous with 'terrorism'; it has ranged from being a state sponsor of international terrorism, facilitating terrorism in the region, to a target of acts of domestic terrorism. The central argument in this chapter will be that although external actors – most notably Al Qaeda and ISIS – have used and manipulated state failure, the underlying motivating factor for people to get involved in terrorism rests with domestic circumstances, similar to other countries around the world that have experienced the devastating consequences of terrorism. Historic, geographic and ethnic divisions, followed by state repression and a closed political landscape facilitated the involvement of Libyan nationals as foreign fighters in other conflicts. It also facilitated both the coup d'état that brought Muammar Gaddafi to power and forty-two years later, the one that brought about his removal from power.

It is important to remember that Gaddafi had been a target of Islamic extremism during his rule, resulting in his becoming the target of a number of assassination attempts. It was clear even then that Islamists would define the post-Gaddafi era. Since the root of terrorism rests in domestic circumstances, the political and ethnic origins of marginalization and frustration need to be presented first. Gaddafi, as a sponsor of international terrorism, used terrorism as an extension of his foreign policy. His being a victim of domestic terrorism also created the foundation of the revolution in 2011.

Political background

King Muhammad Idris bin Muhammad al-Mahdi as-Senussi (1951 to 1969) derived his power from the Sanusi Order. It was founded by Sayyid Muhammad bin Ali al-Sanusi who devoted himself to spreading Islam against European infiltration into Arab countries during the nineteenth century. Sanusi established the first residential settlement (*zawiya*) at Al-Bayda in Cyrenaica, also referred to as Barqa (the eastern coastal region of Libya with modern Benghazi as its capital), in 1843, from where he proclaimed that he would protect *dar al-Islam* (house of Islam) from *dar al-harb* (house of war). At the time, Libya was confronted by tribal conflicts. Al-Sanusi mediated disputes among tribes and developed cohesion between the provinces through Islam. The order's success was based on its ability to develop mutually beneficial political and economic relationships with the surrounding tribes. As explained by Joffé: 'Conditions in Cyrenaica were especially conducive to the growth of a political–religious movement such as the Sanusiyyah [since] it was cut off by deserts from neighbouring countries, it had a homogenous population, it had a tribal system which embraced common traditions and a strong feeling of community of blood. The country was not dominated by the towns, and the Ottoman administration exercised very little control over the interior.'[1]

When the Italians entered Libya in 1911, they were unable to create a stronghold due to the influence of the Sanusi. By the end of World War II, the Sanusi order had successfully used religion to defend Libya against colonialism, but could not complete its control over Tripolitania.[2] This division between Cyrenaica and Tripolitania would continue to define Libya's history (to be discussed later).[3] The collapse of the Sanusi order in Libya was stimulated by two events: First, the Sanusi government gave in to Western interests during the 1950s and 1960s, allowing British and American military bases on Libyan soil in exchange for subsidies. This move was particularly unpopular among the younger generation that had not experienced the positive role of the Sanusi order against colonialism.[4] Second, the discovery of oil in 1959 had created an emerging middle class. In the absence of an economic programme for development, corruption within government, and failure to adequately distribute wealth acquired from the oil contributed to growing dissent. Consequently, Gaddafi gained a foothold with his nationalist ideologies.[5]

On 1 September 1969 a small group of army officers led a bloodless military coup d'état in which Colonel (then Captain) Muammar Gaddafi deposed the monarchy. The country was ruled by a Revolutionary Command Council that introduced a new Constitution. Gaddafi initially legitimized his rule with the assistance of the ulama (religious authority) through speaking at mosques and consulting with religions leaders, and by presenting himself as a true representative of Islam by closing down churches, flying the green flag of Islam, adopting the Muslim calendar, banning alcohol, gambling and nightclubs, and even equating the sporting of the Western-style necktie with wearing the emblem of the cross.[6] Using religion, Gaddafi called for the eradication of corruption, which is, in principle, against Islam. Gaddafi, further, awarded prominent positions in the education and legal sectors of government to religious leaders. However, with the introduction of the Green Book and the start of the Cultural Revolution in 1973 that presented Gaddafi with a vision for Libya, the influences of traditional institutions – including religious authorities – were to be eradicated and replaced with egalitarianism, socialism, Arabism and anti-imperialism.

The Cultural Revolution also paved the way for a political system known as 'direct democracy', which continued to operate till the 2011 Revolution. Between 1973 and 1979, direct democracy included popular congresses and committees, in principle allowing the country to be directly governed by its citizens, unimpeded by political parties and bureaucratic institutions.[7] But in reality, by

January 2011, Gaddafi had come to believe that democracies are meant to be dictatorships, and vice-versa: 'A system where you have a party, a president and a government is ridiculous.'[8] Instead, then, 'direct democracy' meant dictatorship through Gaddafi's clan based in Sirte. When confronted by religious scholars, Gaddafi proclaimed that his ideas were a more progressive interpretation of Islam, undermining the authenticity of the hadith: Gaddafi arrogated to himself the right to interpret the sacred text (ijtihad) in accordance with his distinctive view of socialism. With the introduction of the Green Book, Gaddafi moved away from the sharia as the guide to social and political affairs by stating: 'The Glorious Quran is the Sharia of Our New Socialist Society.' Second, Gaddafi attempted to break the authority of the ulema by stating that Islamic law, which was based on the hadith, and of which the ulema were custodians, was flawed, and, instead, implemented a virtually unsupervised revolutionary court system. This was staffed by Revolutionary Committee members who were not bound by the country's penal code – unsurprisingly, a series of abuses ensued. By claiming superiority over religious affairs, Gaddafi placed himself on a direct collision course with religious institutions, allowing political Islam to gain a foothold in Libya. As Gaddafi established a monopoly on political participation and expression, Islam offered an ideological framework and institutions to channel protest against Gaddafi from the 1980s.[9]

Quelling opposition from religious scholars, Gaddafi responded through a 1975 decree that prohibited public discussion of political matters by religious authorities. One of Gaddafi's casualties was Sheikh Muhamad Abd al-Bishti, a very prominent Salafi preacher who was originally appointed by King Idris. Although al-Bishti did not preach jihad, he was the first to publicly denounce Gaddafi's rule as illegitimate, bringing him into direct confrontation with Gaddafi. After being arrested from Al-Qasr mosque in Tripoli in 1980 he was tortured and killed by Libyan security forces. On his becoming a martyr, his sermons inspired jihadi cells across the country. These small cells operated independently, meeting in secret in houses or shops, while spreading the message of jihad through pamphlets, cassettes and videos. This oppression at home also influenced militants to join the *mujahideen* (fighters) fighting against the Soviet Union in Afghanistan. Awad al-Zuwawi who visited Afghanistan in the early 1980s brought the idea of jihad back with him. He in turn influenced Sheikh Muhammad al-Ushbi who led a group in eastern Libya in 1986 against Gaddafi. The group was implicated in the assassination of Ahmed Musbah al-Warfali (a leading Revolutionary Committee member). Although some of its members were publicly executed, the defeat of the Soviet Union in Afghanistan and the group's growing revival in Libya and broader region introduced a growing confidence among Islamist extremists. For example, in 1989 Sheikh Fahkih, an imam of a mosque in Benghazi, established Harakat al-Jihad (The Jihad Movement) and launched his own jihad. Fahkih and others were killed in the uprising led from Benghazi. This uprising led to a heavy security response that included mass arrests, including that of al-Zuwawi who was killed in the Abu Salim prison massacre in 1996 (the commemoration of this day sparked the Arab Spring fifteen years later).[10]

Ethnic divisions

Libya is historically and geographically divided between Tripolitania, Cyrenaica and Fezzan; and on ethnic terms between Arabs, Berbers and Toubous in which a deeply tribal system remained a reality.[11] Cyrenaica stretches from Sirte to Egypt and southward to the Saharan border with Chad. This region is also home to several hundred tribes (the largest concentration in all of Libya), of which almost every tribe has branches elsewhere in Libya.[12] Throughout history, eastern Libya, most notably Benghazi, Derna and Ajdabia had been the epicentre of opposition inside Libya, but also the origin of foreign fighters. For example, according to the 'Sinjar Records' of the 595 foreign fighters who travelled to Iraq between August 2006 and August 2007, 18.8 per cent (the second highest) originated from Libya.[13] Of these, fifty-two of the 112 Libyans on the list came from Derna as well as Benghazi (especially the Laythi neighbourhood),[14] begging the question: Why? Considering that the Sanusi order was established in Cyrenaica, Gaddafi led his revolution from Benghazi. Being the origin of any major political developments, it should, therefore, not come as a surprise that for this reason, Gaddafi expected resistance to his rule to come from the east. Consequently, from the day he took power, Gaddafi started to marginalize this region, which, instead of diminishing the threat, planted the seed for growing frustration that at the end resulted in the birthplace of Islamist extremism and later the Arab Spring. Gaddafi started by removing Sanusi officers from the military, dismantling Sufi orders and transferring land from Saadi notables to tribes of lesser status. Gaddafi also started to move government offices from Benghazi to Tripoli and later, in 1977, to his hometown of Sirte. Instead, as will be explained later, Gaddafi's reign was marked by key political and security appointees emanating from his extended family and his kinsmen from Sirte, thereby exacerbating the divide between Cyrenaica and Tripolitania. Economically, although two-thirds of Libyan oil production comes from Sirte and eastern Benghazi, oil revenues had very little effect on the living conditions and infrastructure of locals.[15]

Although the 2011 Revolution in Libya was not the product of tribal divisions but, rather, the result of political and socioeconomic marginalization of the broader Libyan public by Gaddafi, tribal conflict emerged as a facilitator and influenced the forming of militias, especially in western and southern Libya, after the removal of Gaddafi. According to Libyan historian Faraj Abd al-Aziz Najm, there are approximately 140 tribes in Libya, but only around thirty of those are considered to have any political significance. Some of these tribes are built around ethnic or family lines, and others around cities and regions.[16] Historically, the coastal region of Libya was divided into two distinct provinces before the time of the Romans: Tripolitania in the west around Tripoli and Cyrenaica around Benghazi. As the 2011 Revolution gained momentum, Libya was again divided along these lines, with the area around Benghazi under opposition control and the rebels taking the flag of the former Cyrenaican monarchy. The three Gaddafi strongholds were Bani Walid, 170 km south of Tripoli, Sirte on the Mediterranean coast and Sebha, capital of the country's south-west region.[17]

Although the objective of this section is not to discuss all the tribes in detail, a broad context is needed to describe the most influential tribes and their relationship with Gaddafi. The Warfala, Libya's largest tribe, the Tarhuna and the Qadhadhfa, Gaddafi's tribe, used to be especially powerful under him. It is, however, important to note that the Qadhadhfa (Gaddafi's tribe) is one of the smaller tribes – traditionally from the port of Sirte midway between Tripoli and Benghazi down into the Sahara – and not very powerful before Gaddafi came to power. When in office, Gaddafi paid much attention to tribal membership, consolidating alliances and ensuring that no single tribe held a monopoly on key positions of local and administrative power, in an attempt to secure his supra position and the national monopoly of power for his own clan. It is not disputed that Gaddafi relied on his tribe to keep him in power through appointing representatives to key positions and, in turn, the tribe became wealthy under his rule. Gaddafi entrenched the tribal divide by promoting his hometown of Sirte against neighbouring Misrata. He filled other important but less strategic positions with the Warfala tribe, which enjoys blood ties to the Qadhadhfa. A third tribe from which regime members were recruited was the Magarha.[18] Tribal elders of the Warfala announced early during the Arab Spring that they were turning against Gaddafi. It is important to note that the tribe launched a coup d'état against Gaddafi in 1993 with the support of the Magarha tribe, demanding greater representation in government. When the coup attempt failed, a number of leaders were killed, imprisoned and driven into exile, but the tribe remained well represented in the military. The Magarha, the second largest tribe in Libya, has had mixed relations with Gaddafi's government, being involved in the 1993 coup attempt,[19] but along with the Warfala and the Qadhadhfa, it occupied high-ranking positions in Libya's security forces up until the Arab Spring. The Magarha is originally from the interior, but its members moved to the coast as the tribe became politically more influential. Despite historically supporting Gaddafi, the Warfala withdrew their alliance with Gaddafi in objection to the brutal treatment directed at the opposition during the Arab Spring uprisings.[20]

Mashashiya (around Al-Awaniya and Zawiyat al-Bagul in Nafusa Mountains, western Libya) was another tribe that supported Gaddafi after he took land from Arab and Berber tribes hostile to his government and gave it to the Mashashiya in a bid to dampen anti-regime hostilities in the region.[21]

Among the tribes that led the uprising against Gaddafi were the Zuwaya, the Misrata, al-Awaqir and the Obeidat, all based in the east. The Zuwaya is a small tribe largely based in the oil-producing regions of the east and interior. Being vocal opponents of Gaddafi, its main interest was most probably to protect and demand greater benefits from oil revenues. The Misrata are said to be the largest tribe in eastern Libya, based in the towns of Misrata, Benghazi and Darnah. The al-Awaqir is predominately based in the city of Al-Bayda that had historically been at the centre of opposition against the Ottomans and, later, the Italian occupation. Also included is the Obeidat tribe from Tobruk.[22]

After Gaddafi's death in October 2011, the rebels began seeking retribution for being discriminated against. For example, all 30,000 residents of the former

Gaddafi stronghold of Tawergha were arrested, chased away or killed by rebel troops from neighbouring Misrata.[23] Conflict between the Toubou and Zuwaya (an Arab tribe favoured by Gaddafi) tribes around Kufra in south-eastern Libya (historically linked to Cyrenaica via tribal linkages and commerce) is expected to remain a challenge. Traditionally based along Libya's southern border with Niger and Chad, the Toubou was historically marginalized even before Gaddafi came to power in 1969 (the Kingdom of Libya's citizenship laws, enacted in 1954, made it difficult for non-Arab tribes to be assimilated into mainstream Libyan Arab society). Different cultural traditions and language as well as the inability to be accepted and integrated into broader Libyan society strengthened the Toubou's ethnic identity, but at the same time its repression under Gadhafi. Therefore, none of Libya's rulers were successful in building an inclusive national identity.[24]

With Gaddafi being a supporter of Egypt's Gamal Abdel Nasser and his idea of Pan-Arab nationalism, the Toubou as also other non-Arab ethnic groups were marginalized, especially the Amazigh, whose language and books were banned. During this phase, African tribes, for example the Toubou and the Tuareg, were also isolated and even denied citizenship. However, when Libya became more pan-African, Gaddafi began to reconsider groups that had initially been marginalized, such as the Amazigh, the Toubou and the Tuareg (by providing assistance to the Tuareg in their self-determination conflict in neighbouring countries). During this period more Libyans might have been under the impression of living in an inclusive society, speaking of a form of nationalism, but the real impact of Gaddafi's Arab nationalism agenda came to the fore during and after the Arab Spring, which allowed those previously marginalized to settle old scores.[25]

Gaddafi managed Libya's ethnic division – especially in the south, where tribal ties were far more powerful than on the Mediterranean coast – by playing one tribe or clan off against the other to weaken their power or through threats of violence, awarding economic privileges to some and exploiting family loyalties, to ultimately divide and rule. During the period before the Arab Spring, legal disputes between communities were predominately settled in tribal talks rather than in court, knowing, however, that security forces would intervene should these community-based conflicts turn violent. In the absence of a central government and the subsequent power vacuum, a Pandora's box was opened by allowing long-standing tribal rivalries and divided communities to act out using copious weapons at their disposal.[26] It is equally important to note that 'in March 1997, the Libyan parliament passed a "code of honour" which enabled the imposition of collective punishment against tribes and clans – usually through the withdrawal of government services – whenever they engaged in activities against the regime'.[27]

In an attempt to bring tribes into the fold of his new security strategy against Islamist movements, Gaddafi replaced revolutionary committees with Popular Councils (Sha'abiat) in 2000. This new decentralized administration transferred considerable power to tribal leaders. Consequently, with the transferring of security operations to local authorities, Islamist movements found it difficult to spread their reach beyond Cyrenaica. However, without the administration following through with an economic policy to address the rising decline in standard of living, Islamist organizations managed to survive. In April 2006 the Mujahideen of Libya emerged in Derna calling on supporters around the world to return to Libya. In another communique, Abu Baraa al-Libi, signed as 'leader of Al Qaeda in Libya'. Growing urbanization in Derna and other towns implied that a growing number of people lived outside the conservative tribal control; rising unemployment among soldiers and security crackdowns extended the recruitment opportunities to Islamist organizations.[28]

Desertification and difficulties associated with their traditional way of life forced many Toubou to move north, putting them at odds with other Arab tribes, particularly the Zuwaya, in the areas of southern Libya surrounding the oasis towns of Sabha and Kufra. During Gadhafi's Arabization campaigns, the regime's interventions typically favoured the Zuwaya over the Toubou, supporting local Arab tribal suppression of minority groups that competed for resources and control of Saharan trade routes. This support fuelled the Toubou's and other minority groups' anti-government sentiment, which still lingers today. Unless the fledgling government finds a way to deal effectively with the Toubou, Zuwaya, Berbers, Tuaregs and other tribal groups in southern Libya, there is a very real chance that it will foster not just further tribal violence, but also opposition to the central government.

Porous borders with neighbouring countries, discontent and the availability of arms made the region one of the most challenging to post-Gaddafi government. In Zuwara (port city in north-western Libya), conflict broke out between ethnic Berbers (who were not allowed to speak their own language under Gaddafi) largely opposed to Gaddafi and their Arab neighbours in settlements to the south who remained loyal to Gaddafi. In another example, in February 2012, a long-standing rivalry between the Toubou (a black African ethnic group) and the Arab Zuwaya tribes turned violent in Al Kufra over control of territory linked to oil and water resources. The Toubou was also involved in the tribal conflict in Sabha.[29]

Libya and international terrorism

After Gaddafi came to power, he quickly gained the reputation of being unpredictable, leading to tension with neighbouring states who accused Gaddafi of using oil revenues to fund terrorist groups and sending assassination squads to silence Libyan enemies and dissidents abroad. For example, between 1980 and 1981 eleven Libyan dissidents were assassinated abroad. Justifying the designation of Libya as a state sponsor of terrorism, Gaddafi in September 1986, declared: 'I will do everything in my power to divide the world into imperialists and freedom fighters. Any violent action against one of the "imperialist" states is just and welcome. Those perpetrating these attacks are not "terrorists", but rather "freedom fighters", because national liberation can only be achieved through armed struggle.'[30]

This policy materialized as Libya was implicated in assassination attempts on the lives of heads of state from Egypt (both Presidents Anwar Sadat and Husni Mubarak), Chad (President Habre), Sudan (Jaafar al Numayri), Zaire (President Mobutu Sese Seko), Tunisia (Habib Bourguiba), Jordan (King Hussein) and Morocco (King Hassan II). Attempts were also made to foster instability in Algeria, Senegal, Togo, Burkina Faso, and among the Tuareg in the Sahel.[31] Gaddafi encouraged the Tuareg (nomadic tribe found predominately in south-western Libya, southern Algeria, Niger, Mali and Burkina Faso) and aided the establishment of the Popular Front for the Liberation of the Greater Arab Central Sahara in 1980 with a political wing and a military training camp near Bani Walid. Through providing weapons and training to the Tuareg, Gaddafi's aim had been to influence the Tuareg to demand self-determination under Libyan influence from existing Sahelian states. After the 2011 Revolution, it was also the Tuareg soldiers of Sahelian origin that looted Libyan armouries and went to Mali, where they led an insurgency and helped establish a short-lived semi-state in the north known as Azawad.[32]

During the 1970s, 1980s and 1990s, Libya was regarded as a one-stop resource – providing funding, training, safe haven and operational support in the form of travel documents and so on. – to any terrorist organization representing any ideological background from the Irish Republican Army (IRA) and the Japanese Red Army to insurgents from Guatemala and El Salvador, and Colombia's M-19 terrorist organization. Tripoli also maintained relationships with terrorist groups in Pakistan, Bangladesh and the Philippines.[33] Gaddafi even went so far as to send Libyan troops to areas of international conflict or assist organizations he sponsored in the form of military instructors, specialized units or combat regulars.[34] According to Craig Black, Gaddafi supported an estimated fifty terrorist organizations and subversion groups, in addition to more than forty radical governments in Africa, Asia, Europe and America.[35]

Libya was also directly implicated in acts of international terrorism, starting with the bombing on 21 December 1988 of Pan Am flight 103 over Lockerbie, Scotland, that killed all 243 passengers and 16 crew, as well as 11 more people on the ground. Indictments for murder were issued against Abdelbaset al-Megrahi, a Libyan intelligence officer and Lamin Khalifah Fhimah, the Libyan Arab Airline station manager in Luqa Airport, Malta. These two suspects were, however, handed over to Scottish police only on 5 April 1999 following UN sanctions against Libya and prolonged negotiations with Gaddafi.[36]

The second was the mid-air bombing of Union de Transports Aériens (UTA) flight 772 over Niger near Agadez on 19 September 1989 in which 171 passengers and crew were killed, including Bonnie Pugh, the wife of the US ambassador to Chad, Mahamat Soumahila, the Chadian Planning Minister and six Italian nationals.[37] In the third attack on 5 April 1986, three people were killed and 230 injured when *La Belle* discothèque was bombed in West Berlin, Germany. The discotheque was known to be frequented by U.S. soldiers, and two of the dead and seventy-nine of the injured were American servicemen. The incident was suspected to be in retaliation to the sinking of two Libyan boats by the United States in the Gulf of Sirte.[38]

The 9/11 terrorist attack and the impending 2003 US invasion of Iraq contributed to the realization that President George W Bush was serious about going after countries hostile to the United States. Consequently, in March 2003, days before the invasion of Iraq, Gaddafi contacted President Bush and British Prime Minister Tony Blair about Libya's willingness to dismantle all Weapons of Mass Destruction (WMD) programmes. Further redeeming itself, in 2003, Libya accepted responsibility for the 1988 bombing of Pan Am 103, over Lockerbie, Scotland.[39] Consequently, on 12 September 2003, United Nations Security Council lifted sanctions against Libya. Libya in turn agreed to pay upto US$10 million to each of the families of the 270 victims of Pan Am flight 103.[40] Despite being an ally of extremist and terrorist organizations in other parts of the world (representing a vast ideological spectrum) and even actively using terrorism as an extension of Libya's foreign policy, Gaddafi had to, increasingly, deal with growing resentment within his borders. Not even being a supporter of the Palestinian cause would shield Gaddafi from Islamist extremists within Libya who were driven by local frustrations.

Domestic terrorism in Libya

Internal political opposition strengthened in 1975 as two members of the Revolutionary Command Council launched an attempted coup as a sign that even within the regime, Gaddafi was not untouchable.[41] One of the many inconsistencies in the Gaddafi regime's policies had been supporting international Islamist extremist groups involved in spreading instability, while being implicated in repressing domestic Islamist groups. Despite being a devout Muslim, Gaddafi distrusted religious organizations becoming involved in politics, breeding factionalism and undermining his revolutionary objectives. As part of eliminating any threat to his ideology and leadership, Gaddafi had attacked the Islamists as 'agents of reaction and obstacles to the progress of the Revolution'. Religious groups were offended by Gaddafi's efforts to concentrate religious power in his own hands and to make himself the sole interpreter of the Quran.[42] In one of these inconsistencies, Gaddafi financially supported Chechens as it clandestinely transferred tens of millions of dollars by shipping most of the money via Turkey, where Libyan intelligence used couriers and channels to launder money.[43] On the other hand, Gaddafi had been one of the few leaders in the Middle East to issue an arrest warrant for Osama bin Laden.[44]

The domestic situation in Libya changed in the 1990s as other countries in the region started to experience the effects of Al Qaeda and the return of foreign fighters from Afghanistan. Following the uprising in Benghazi in 1996 many had to flee Libya into exile, escape to Afghanistan or face being arrested. It is estimated that between 800 and 1000 Libyan nationals joined the jihad in Afghanistan from 1984 until 1989.[45] Receiving training in, for example, Al-Masada (the Lion's Den) near Jaji, Khaldan and Darunta,[46] the majority of Libyan fighters fought under the command of Abd al-Rasul Sayaf in the tribal area between Afghanistan and Pakistan.[47]

Extremists established the Islamic Martyrdom Movement, founded in 1993 by Amir al-Haim and including Libyan veterans that had returned from Afghanistan.[48] Following repression by Revolutionary Committees, a number of organizations established operational armed units and political wings, including al-Jamaa al-Islamiya al-Muqatila (Islamic Combat Group or ICG), Ansar Allah (Partisans of God) and Harakat al-Shuhada al-Islamiya (Islamic Martyrs' Movement or IMM). On 23 April 1995, ICG led by Abdallah Sadek stated: 'The abolition of the apostate regime and the salvation of the Muslim people of Libya from its ordeal cannot be achieved without wounds, suffering, sacrifices and the expenditure of resources. The Islamic Combat Group appeals to all Muslims to take their places in this battle alongside the Mujahideen.' In March 1996 ICG claimed responsibility for an attempt to assassinate Gaddafi by bombing his motorcade in Sirte. In response, the Libyan Air Force bombed Jebel Akhdar in north-eastern Libya from where ICG cells allegedly operated. Additionally, the ICG received active support from tribes in the Derna region.[49]

On 8 August 1996, Ansar Allah, another Salafi group, was founded, aiming at restoring the Caliphate. It was also actively operating from the Cyrenaica region, which had historically been associated with the Salafi movement. The Islamic Martyrs' Movement led by Mohammed al-Hami claimed responsibility for a number of operations in Benghazi, Sebha and Tobruk.[50]

Libyan Islamic Fighting Group (LIFG)

The LIFG was founded in Cyrenaica, where it was operational between 1996 and 1999,[51] by Libyans who had fought in Afghanistan, led by Abu Munder al-Saidi, the spiritual leader and Awatha al-Zuwawi.[52] Influenced by the repressive nature of the Gaddafi regime, the LIFG intended to overthrow the regime and install a sharia-based government. The LIFG embraced the global jihadi agenda of Al Qaeda, but the origin of LIFG was domestic.[53] In its first communique, LIFG described Gaddafi's administration as 'an apostate regime that has blasphemed against the faith of God Almighty', and declared its intention to overthrow it 'as the foremost duty after faith in God'. Since its inception, the LIFG made four attempts on Gaddafi's life between 1994 and 1997.[54] While in Afghanistan, the LIFG established their own camp near Nangahar, close to the Pakistani border. Due to the securitization of Libya, leaders were forced to direct their followers from afar, not being able to organize and operate inside Libya. Members were trained by getting into fights with gangs and criminals in rough neighbourhoods in cities.[55]

Being closely associated with Al Qaeda, some senior members also belonged to Al Qaeda's senior command structure. In 1994, Abdelrahman Al-Hattab, a former engineering student in Libya and one of the founding members of LIFG and Afghan mujahideen explored opportunities to dispatch LIFG fighters to Algeria. Relationships between the GIA in Algeria and the LIFG were tense from the outset and reached breaking point when Abdullah Al-Libbi was killed by the GIA following a factional conflict within the GIA.[56] LIFG members have also been implicated in the planning of the May 2003 bombings in Casablanca, Morocco.[57] With the support of Al Qaeda, LIFG fighters set up their own camps in Afghanistan. For example, in Shahid Cheikh Abu Yahya, located about thirty km north of Kabul, LIFG welcomed volunteers associated with other organizations aligned with Al Qaeda.[58]

In September 2009, prominent members of the LIFG imprisoned in Libya issued a 417-page document renouncing the use of violence, supported by Saif al-Islam al-Qadhafi through his Qadhafi International Charity and Development Foundation (QDF). Abdelhakim Belhadj, and Abd al-Wahhab Muhammad Qaid, alias Abu Idris al-Libi, the elder brother of Abu Yahya al-Libi, were among those who renounced violence, and by 1 September 2010, more than 700 prisoners accused of having ties with Islamist militant groups had been released under the reconciliation programme.[59] Following the 2011 Revolution, many of the former leaders turned to politics.[60] One faction, led by Abd al-Hakim Bilhaj, the LIFG's former emir and the former commander of the Tripoli Military Council, formed the al-Watan Party. Other former members joined the Umma al-Wasat, led by Sami al-Saadi, the LIFG's key ideologue who had once authored a seminal anti-democratic tract. Al-Saadi was joined by another central figure in the LIFG, Abd al-Wahhab al-Ghayid (brother of the late Abu Yahya al-Libi), who ran successfully as a parliamentary candidate in the southern city of Murzuq.[61]

Libyans also held senior positions in Al Qaeda, often connected with the LIFG. First, Nazih Abdul-Hamed Nabih al-Ruqai' alias Abu Anas al-Libi spent time in Sudan with Osama bin Laden in the early 1990s. Al-Libi was wanted by the United States for being a key planner of the 1998 bombings of US embassies in Kenya and Tanzania. Al-Libi's background includes being a computer specialist with Al Qaeda after he studied electronic and nuclear engineering, graduating from Tripoli University.[62] On 5 October 2013 the US Delta Force captured al-Libi in Tripoli, Libya, to stand trial for his alleged involvement in the 1998 US embassy bombings, but he died of liver cancer before he could stand trial.[63] Mohamed Hassan Qaid, alias Abu Yahya al-Libi or Hasan Qayad, Yunis al-Sahrawi and Hassan Qaed al-Far, travelled to Afghanistan in the early 1990s, but was sent back to study Islam in Mauritania. He returned to Afghanistan, but was arrested by Pakistani authorities. Al-Libi, however, managed to escape from US custody in Baghram, Afghanistan, in July 2005 to become the most recognizable Libyan national associated with Al Qaeda. Being in the inner circle of Al Qaeda, he headed a Libyan contingent of fighters in the Afghanistan/Pakistan region.[64] At the time of his death (in a US missile strike in North Waziristan) in June 2012, Al-Libi was regarded as Al Qaeda's second-in-command after Ayman al-Zawahiri.[65]

Jamal Ibrahim Ashtiwi al Misrati, alias Atiyah Abd al-Rahman or Atiyah Allah, participated in the war in Afghanistan during the 1980s, where he learned how to work with explosives. In 1993 Atiyah Allah left Afghanistan for Algeria to serve as a liaison between Al Qaeda in Afghanistan and the Armed Islamic Group (GIA). Instead of accepting him, the GIA detained Atiyah Allah. Five months later, he, along with a few other Libyan prisoners, escaped to return to Afghanistan to be in Al Qaeda's inner circle (serving as Osama bin Laden's emissary).[66] He served as

Al Qaeda's liaison with Abu Musab al-Zarqawi in Iraq and likely shuttled between Iran and Afghanistan, all the while forging new relationships with other jihadist groups and leaders.[67] Atiyah Allah again returned to Algeria as liaison with the Salafist Group for Combat and Preaching (GSPC), the forerunner of Al Qaeda in the Islamic Maghreb (AQIM). He also acted as a liaison with Pakistan, brokering a deal not to execute attacks in Pakistan in return for protection of Al Qaeda members in Pakistan.[68]

An important takeaway from this account of the activities of the above-mentioned architects of the spread of global jihad was the fact that these Libyan nationals were initially radicalized in their homeland. As a result of domestic circumstances, these and others left Libya to other jihadi hotspots where they sharpened their resolve while building new networks, just to close the circle for some when they returned to Libya to influence a new generation.

The Arab Spring and the subsequent instability

Building on the historical context of the domestic circumstances discussed, Libyan authorities used the international context and the language of the 'War on Terror' to justify further repression. This counterterrorism argument was used as a new justification for an old practice, enshrined in Libyan law to prohibit the formation of associations or political parties outside the existing political framework and the repression of all political dissent.[69] The Libyan authorities decisively dealt with dissidents inside and outside the country under circumstances suggesting that they were extrajudicially executed by members of the security forces or by agents working on behalf of the Libyan authorities.[70] Under these circumstances of domestic repression Libyan authorities ultimately sowed the seeds for the Arab Spring to be planted in what was to be left of their own nation.

Being reduced to a bystander in the political system, Gaddafi increasingly closed the political landscape. Being politically marginalized for reasons often associated with geographic and tribal affiliations became increasingly unacceptable till a relatively small spark set the revolution in motion. Both King Idris and, forty-two years later, Gaddafi were unaware of the growing frustration.[71] As Gaddafi became more isolated, he became less tolerant of criticism, repressing Islamic extremist groups and imposing brutal control over ethnic and tribal minorities. The Muslim clergy viewed Gaddafi as a heretic for his reinterpretation of the Quran and military officers were enraged by Gaddafi's plans to raise a people's militia to replace the regular army. In reality, the Libyan public – especially intellectuals and students – increasingly experienced the darker side of Gaddafi's rule, witnessing a series of hangings carried out at the country's universities. Instead of countering extremism, it facilitated radicalization. For example, Abdel Wahab Mohamed Qaid, the elder brother of Abu Yahya al-Libi, one of the leaders of the LIFG who later became a leader in the 2011 Revolution explained that he was drawn into politics by the Libyan student movement of the mid-1980s. Recalling that as a medical student at the University of Benghazi, he was appalled by the Gaddafi government's use of torture and public hangings to quell dissent, he said: 'I started to realize the scale of the oppression'.[72]

Similar to neighbouring Tunisia and Egypt, Libya's introduction to the Arab Spring started with a small incident: on 15 February 2011 people took to the Benghazi police headquarters to protest against the arrest of Fathi Tarbil, a human rights lawyer who had represented some of the 1000 families of prisoners who had been killed by security forces in Abu Salim prison in 1996. Although the protests were initially peaceful, the arrival of the military and the use of sharp point ammunition against protesters led to the protesters reaching a tipping point where personal survival and years of repression and marginalization tipped the scale. Within a few hours it became clear that this demonstration would not go away, especially after members of the security forces also joined the protesters.[73] Being completely out of touch with the sentiments of Libyans, Gaddafi stated in an interview with BBC on 28 February 2011 that 'he was loved by all his people and denied that there had been any protests in Tripoli. His people would die to protect him. [He also] said true Libyans had not demonstrated but those who had come on to the streets were under the influence of drugs supplied by Al Qaeda.'[74]

However, the death of Gaddafi on 20 October 2011 created a power vacuum that led to a new phase in Libya's history as an exporter of instability and terrorism. All actors including ISIS and Al Qaeda capitalized on the power vacuum created and the unlimited weaponry available. Gaddafi, for example, managed to import an estimated US$10 million worth of arms every year from 1992 to 2003 despite the arms embargo. In 2003 the arms embargo was lifted and according to the UN estimates, Libya spent approximately 30 billion dollars on weapons. The largest portion came from Russia (US$22 billion); the United Kingdom (US$ 170 million) and the EU between 2005 and 2009. Libya also bought military hardware from China and Turkey.[75] Weaponry ended up in the hands of smugglers, insurgents and Islamist extremists.[76] For example, according to the United States, a small number of Soviet-made SA7 missiles from Libya had reached the black market in Mali, where AQIM had been active. The Tuareg bought from Libya surface-to-air missiles, which the MNLA said it had used to shoot down a Malian Air Force MIG-21 jet in January 2012.[77] In another example, Ibrahim Ag Bahanga, a leader of the National Movement for the Liberation of Azawad (MNLA) was killed as he was smuggling weapons across the border from Libya and hiding them on the border with Algeria and Niger. Furthermore, the return of fighters from Libya, especially to Mali, was among the main factors that contributed to the 2012 crisis in Mali.[78]

By 2015, Libya had been torn apart between two rival factions – one based in the central city of Misrata and allied with some Islamists and the other based in the eastern cities of Tobruk and Bayda and allied with an anti-Islamist military leader, Gen. Khalifa Haftar. Initially a governor of Tobruk from 1981 to 1986, he turned against Gaddafi in 1987.[79] In 2014, Haftar staged an offensive against the Tripoli government with the support of tribes in eastern Libya and attacked military bases and the parliament building in Tripoli.[80] Complicating the security situation, an estimated 1,700 different armed groups in Libya competed for power and according to the UN, in April 2015, an estimated 100,000 to 300,000 actively participated in the conflict. Considering that approximately 30,000 Libyans participated in the revolution that overthrew Gaddafi in 2011, the escalation is considerable.[81] Although the Salafi ideology is historically well established in Libya, the Arab Spring also brought with it a split between an older generation of Salafis that has embraced political participation (for example, LIFG leadership) and a new generation that rejects democracy.[82]

Growing instability led to a number of struggles over identity, power and resources across Libya, most notably oil reserves, with nearly 80 per cent of the country's oil production (and armed groups) based in eastern Libya.[83] The most covered included ISIS, Ansar al-Sharia Libya (ASL) and Abu Salim Martyrs Brigade (ASMB). All three groups came into direct conflict with one another in 2015.[84] Both ASMB and ASL's appeal is mostly local, whereas ISIS became subsequently involved in attacks in Europe. While this chapter predominately focuses on Islamist militias, it is important to note that militias in western and southern Libya, as well as in the capital Tripoli also emerged with different structures and objectives in mind. For example, according to Lacher, militias in north-western Libya identified with specific neighbourhoods, towns and cities – most notably Zintan and Misrata – rather than being driven by ideology, tribal membership or ethnicity. Its main focus was to secure territory without a clear political agenda. In contrast to the west, in the south, southern – for example, Fezzan – militias were defined based on ethnic and tribal identity that can be traced back to the animosity discussed earlier between Arabs and Tubus (Kufra and Sabha).[85]

Abu Salim Martyrs Brigade (ASMB)

In addition to the older generation (also imprisoned by Gaddafi) who accepted democracy, a second younger generation of Salafi jihadis emerged. This faction included the sons of the first generation, who witnessed the crackdown and torture of their fathers under Gaddafi or who were incarcerated themselves and radicalized by their experiences. Some went to Afghanistan and Iraq after 2001 and were imprisoned by coalition forces, and then repatriated to Libya by British and American intelligence services. In the aftermath of the 2011 Revolution, this second generation of jihadis re-emerged as leaders of revolutionary brigades in Benghazi and Derna. For example, Abd al-Hakim al-Hasadi formed the Derna Brigade, one of the first groups to take up arms in the revolution and which later became the Abu Salim Martyrs' Brigade.[86] Al-Hassadi also fought in Afghanistan, on the side of the Taliban, from 1997 to 2002 and personally met Ayman al-Zawahiri and Abu Musab al-Zarqawi. Explaining the consequences of state repression, al-Hassadi explained: 'We went to Sudan, to Syria, to Egypt. But they followed us everywhere. Europe was impossible to get into. So you had to go to Afghanistan. It was controlled by the Taliban, so it was the safest place for us.'[87] Sufyan bin Qumu, another veteran of the LIFG, met Osama bin Laden in Sudan and fought with the Taliban before being arrested by Pakistani authorities and turned over to the United States. Qumu later had a fallout with the brigade, most probably as a result of his explicit links to Al Qaeda. Lastly, Abd al-Basit Azuz, a former Afghan mujahideen, who fled Libya for Syria in the 1990s lived for a period in the United Kingdom before moving to the Afghanistan–Pakistan border in 2009. He was also allegedly personally dispatched by Ayman al-Zawahiri to Libya at the time of the 2011 Revolution to establish an Al Qaeda presence in Derna.[88]

In addition to attacks on the Supreme Security Committee (SSC), ASMB was also implicated in establishing training camps for volunteers to travel to Syria while also getting involved in transnational organized crime such as drug smuggling and illicit weapons trafficking. On 11 April 2012, Fathi al-Sha'iri, the new ASMB commander was integrated into the SSC, while a more militant faction integrated into Ansar al-Sharia.[89]

Ansar al-Sharia Libya (ASL)

Ansar al-Sharia Libya (ASL) can best be described as an umbrella organization that emerged in 2011 from the Abu Obayda Bin Aljarah Brigade, Malik Brigade and February 17th Martyrs Brigade. Its stronghold was established in the north-eastern city of Benghazi (led by Muhammad Ali al-Zahawi), from where it expanded its reach to Sirte, Derna and Ajdabiya. Al-Zahawi was a former political prisoner under Gaddafi and assumed command of the Rafallah Sahati Brigade (fighting in Misrata). On the political front, al-Zahawi was one of the founders of the High Authority for the Protection and Achievement of the February 17 Revolution and the Society for Islamic Dawa and Reform. In Derna, Sufyan bin Qumu along with hard-line members of ASMB, who refused to be integrated in SSC, formed Ansar al-Sharia in April 2012. Despite their similarities, Ansar in Benghazi denies any linkages to Qumu's Ansar al-Sharia Brigade in Derna.[90]

ASL refused to swear allegiance to Abu Bakr al-Baghdadi, but, instead, established connections with other Al Qaeda affiliates in North Africa. ASL attracted the attention of terrorism experts when the group was implicated in the 11 September 2012 attack on the U.S. consulate in Benghazi that killed Ambassador Chris Stevens and three other American citizens, although the organization denied its involvement. According to information, Ahmed Abu Khattala, a commander of Ansar al-Sharia, led the embassy attack. As a result he was arrested on 15 June 2014 in a raid in Libya by US Delta Force special operations and charged for playing a significant role in the attack.[91] According to Youssef Jihani, a senior member of the organization: 'All of America's policies are hostile to Islam. If America is waging war against Al Qaeda, then Al Qaeda has a right to defend itself. We oppose American policies because they are stained in Muslim blood.'[92] Despite the Benghazi incident, the primary focus of ASL had been on Libya, provided that Libya is governed by its interpretation of sharia. Although members of the group denied involvement in attacks against Muslim shrines around Libya, it did take over the Jalaa Hospital, the city's main emergency hospital in providing security.[93] Further enhancing its local foundation and reach, the organization focused on *da'wa* (missionary activities) through charity work and providing social services, ranging from security patrols to garbage collection. Additionally, ASL also established a cultural centre for women, a medical clinic and religious schools.[94]

Driven by these local circumstances, Ansar al-Sharia was successful in attracting foreign fighters from Tunisia, Algeria and other African countries to facilitate attacks in either their countries of origin or other theatres of operation.[95] The former included relationships with organizational counterparts in Tunisia, Egypt and Al Qaeda in the Islamic Maghreb (AQIM). For example, Tunisian security officials have pointed to operational, financial and logistical links between ASL and Ansar al-Sharia in Tunisia (AST), with the latter receiving weapons from its Libyan counterpart. Abu Iyadh, the leader of AST was allegedly also present in Libya after AST founded a terrorist organization in Tunisia in August 2013. In the same report Algerian security sources also claimed that Iyadh attended a secret meeting hosted by ASL in Benghazi in September 2014 with representatives of AST, AQIM and various Moroccan and Egyptian jihadi factions.[96] According to French intelligence Mokhtar Belmokhtar also met with ASL fighters in Ubari, southern Libya.[97] Allegedly ASL provided training in military training camps in Benghazi to Al-Murabuutin Brigade members involved in the January 2013 attack in Amenas.[98]

In spite of its unwillingness to swear allegiance to ISIS, ASL was also implicated in providing assistance – from logistical support to establishing mobile training camps around Benghazi – to individuals seeking to travel to Syria.[99] Commentators also attributed the first vehicle-borne improvised explosive device (VBIED) attack on 12 December 2013 directed at a military checkpoint in Bersis (east of Benghazi) that killed thirteen people and injured seventeen others to Ansar al-Sharia (although no group claimed responsibility).[100] According to Fadhl al-Hassi, a Libyan military commander, Mohamed al-Zahawi died in January 2015 from wounds sustained in an airstrike in October 2014.[101] Since al-Zahawi's death, members of ASL increasingly defected to ISIS. For example, in 2014, Abu Sufyan Bin Qumu, the leader of ASL's Derna branch became the first high-ranking ASL member to pledge allegiance to ISIS.[102] He was followed by Abu Abdullah Al-Libi, ASL's chief Sharia jurist who pledged allegiance to ISIS on 30 March 2015. On 27 May 2017, the group announced that it was formally dissolving itself amid heavy losses, but in a statement called on revolutionary forces and Shura councils in Benghazi to unite in order to form a united front.[103]

Majlis Shura Shabab al-Islam (MSSI) and ISIS

Insurgents in Libya capitalized on the popularity of ISIS at the time when it established *Majlis Shura Shabab al-Islam* (the Islamic Youth Shura Council) or MSSI on 4 April 2014. In October 2014 MSSI announced that Derna was now part of the ISIS 'caliphate'. In a statement on 22 June, MSSI proclaimed its support for ISIS and Abu Bakr al-Baghdadi: 'It is incumbent on us to support this oppressed Islamic State that is taken as an enemy by those near and those far, among the *kuffar* (infidels) or the *munafeqin* (hypocrites) or those with *marda al-nafous* (deceased souls) alike.'[104] In November 2014 al-Baghdadi recognized the annexation of Libya through MSSI that implied the nullification of MSSI as a local group, the creation of Wilayat Libya of ISIS and the appointment of *wulat* (governor).[105]

Consequently ISIS dispatched a team led by Wissam al-Zubaydi, alias Abu Nabil al-Anbari and Abu al-Mughirah al-Qahtani, a senior ISIS commander who had been a former policeman in Saddam Hussein's regime, to become the *wulat* in Libya on 9 September 2015.[106] Anbari was also assisted by Abu al-Baraa el-Azdi, a Saudi preacher who became Derna's top religious judge. When declaring allegiance to Abu Bakr al-Baghdadi, the 'Mujahideen of Libya' was divided into three provinces: Barqa, Tripoli and Fezzan (south-west Libya).[107] Al-Zubaydi established a shadow authority by infiltrating and subverting Al Qaeda's network in Libya that resonated in Abu Salim Martyrs' Brigade (ASMB) and ASL, penetrating other militias, and incorporating organized crime syndicates under ISIS's banner to increase their independence and the viability of establishing a form of government. In Libya this state-building process equalled similar initiatives in Syria and Iraq to include tax-collection offices, police, courts and even an immigration office to support foreign recruits. Around the same time, the caliph's deputy, Abdurrahman al-Qaduli, alias Abu Ali al-Anbari also visited Libya as a sign of ISIS's commitment to its new Wilayat.[108] Al-Zubaydi was killed in a US airstrike on 13 November 2015.[109]

Utilizing social media, the organization also issued statements, through Facebook, from its sharia committee about individuals (including members of the former Libyan government, other rebel forces, and random citizens) who had 'repented' and joined the group. As to those not falling in line, MSSI instituted *hudoud* (criminal punishments under sharia) in mid-July, going so far as to perform public executions.[110] ISIS expanded from Derna after October 2014, when the group officially announced the expansion of its caliphate to Libya. In addition to Derna, Sirte (hometown of Gaddafi) became the third city to fall into the hands of ISIS in February 2015. MSSI was popular in Derna and Benghazi, eastern Libya, as expected, but its spreading to Sirte, in western Libya, in mid-2015 was not anticipated.[111] In his analysis of the spread of ISIS in Libya Dr Khaled Hanafy Aly, from the Al-Ahram Foundation, explained that ISIS's expansion capitalized on local frustration and challenges across the region, and presented a well-known organization to these individuals, thereby establishing a regional representation. Secondly, ISIS used tribal differences, most notably support from former regime loyalists, including those belonging to the Qadhadhfa (Gaddafi's tribe) that was displaced after the fall of Gaddafi, socially excluded and marginalized, to further fill its ranks: 'The Islamic State has become a "banner" for those Libyan tribesmen to express local grievances, tribal and religious, and change the political equation in their favour after the 2011 revolution.'[112] ISIS has used tribes as pillars in the statement: 'Tribes have long histories and [are] socially embedded institutions [that] make them more durable than [Libya's] shallow-rooted political parties.'[113]

Similar to being the prime supplier of suicide bombers in Iraq, Derna again produced the first suicide bombers in early November 2014 in Tobruk in which one person was killed and fourteen injured. ISIS also carried out a car bombing outside Labraq air force base in Al-Bayda, killing four. The Derna wing further claimed that it had previously dispatched nine suicide bombers from Egypt, Libya and Tunisia to carry out attacks against Libyan security forces in and around Benghazi. It included a twin attack on a Libyan special forces camp in Benghazi on 23 July and an attack on a military checkpoint near Benina airport on 2 October. An ISIS-linked Twitter account also suggested the Tripoli wing was responsible for car bomb attacks in early November outside the Egyptian and UAE embassies in the capital.[114] ISIS controlled Sirte for more than a year, but lost control of it at the end of 2016, resulting in fighters fleeing Sirte to move around Libya in small groups or settle in sleeper cells making it hard to locate and eliminate them. Instead of providing public services, the main focus of ISIS had been to recruit foreign fighters (from Egypt, Tunisia, Yemen, Sudan and, most notably, Europe) and they preferred to use Libya as a base and resource to plot and stage attacks on the West.[115]

Regional impact of the Arab Spring

Aaron Zelin, in a report on foreign fighters in Libya published by The Washington Institute for Near East Policy, estimated that between 2,600 and 3,500 foreigners joined or attempted to join jihadi groups in Libya in comparison to 4,000 and 5,000 foreign fighters in Iraq from 2003 to 2011.[116] Baker and Singleton estimated that approximately 5,000 foreign fighters flocked to Libya, including many who first fought in Syria/Iraq in the aftermath of the Arab Spring.[117] Although it is impossible to produce specific figures, it is accurate to say that Libya till 2018 was the fourth-largest theatre of conflict (after Syria, Afghanistan in the 1980s and Iraq in 2003) to mobilize foreign fighters especially from neighbouring Tunisia (largest contributor), Morocco, Algeria, Egypt, Sudan, Mali and Niger. Libya also attracted more fighters, as ISIS started to suffer defeat in Syria and Iraq, from Syria, Iraq, France, Belgium, Spain, United Kingdom, United States, Canada, Saudi Arabia, Palestinian Authorities, Jordan and Qatar. Libya also attracted fighters from countries confronted with terrorism, namely Nigeria, Somalia, Kenya and Yemen. Other African countries represented were Senegal, Ghana, Chad, Eritrea, Gambia, Rwanda, Burundi and Ethiopia. India, Nepal, Bosnia and Philippines were also represented.[118] It is, however, equally important to note that Libyan fighters operational in other conflict areas returned to Libya after receiving training and practical experience

The impact of the Libyan crisis also manifested in operations in Europe. In late 2015, hundreds of Libyan ISIS jihadis returned to Libya from Syria. Many were from Katibat al-Battar, an elite unit of troops and trainers, who also facilitated external operators such as Abdelhamid Abaaoud, a Belgian national who was implicated as the on-the-ground leader of the Paris attacks.[119] The Libya connection was also established in the attacks in Britain on 22 May 2017, and Germany on 19 December 2016. Libya's foreign fighter network and the insights it offers regarding the future trajectory of jihadism in North, East and West Africa, as well as Western Europe, are of great concern.[120]

Libyan territory has also become the go-to location for regional jihadis. For example, Ayman Saadi, a Tunisian national arrested on 30 October 2013 in the Tunisian city of Monastir received training near Benghazi and Derna with the aim of fighting in Syria, but ended up being tasked by Libyan militants with a plot in his own country. His ultimate objective was to carry out a suicide mission in Tunis on 31 October 2013. Other organizations in the region also gained momentum to execute attacks through receiving training, logistical support and strategic direction from Libya. According to an article in June 2014, fighters from various organizations, including Ansar al-Sharia in Tunisia, Al Qaeda in the Islamic Maghreb (AQIM) and Ansar al-Sharia in Libya, were moving across the Tunisian–Libyan border areas to bring in arms and recruit young men to fight in Mount Chambi situated on the border between Algeria and Tunisia.[121] Libya also served as a safe haven for fighters and leaders of jihadi organizations alike when security forces in the said countries started to close in.

On 15 January 2018, Ghanaian security forces arrested three returnees from Libya for allegedly planning a terrorist attack. One of the suspects, Ishmael Ali Musa, was alleged to have connections to ISIS in Libya. The men were found in possession of grenades, ammunition and explosives that security officials suspected were smuggled into Ghana – traditionally not associated with Islamist extremism and terrorism – from Libya.[122]

Conclusion

It would be a mistake to assess the threat associated with ISIS to Libya, the broader region and Europe in historic isolation. Considering that Libya has had a long history of being not only a state sponsor of terrorism, but also a target of domestic terrorism and exporter of foreign fighters to Afghanistan since the 1980s and Iraq following the 2003 war, there is a need to understand the domestic circumstances. To risk one's freedom, life and limb inside Libya and/or travel to another country confronted with similar risks requires particular local circumstances and frustrations. Similar to the assessment of conflict and terrorism in other parts of the world, everything starts with a history of domestic political, social and economic circumstances. Another issue addressed in this chapter was understanding why Islamist extremism – including foreign fighters and other forms of revolt – started in eastern Libya: government repression, political isolation, tribal marginalization (between Tripolitania and Cyrenaica) and attempts by Gaddafi to monopolize religion provided the necessary incentives to facilitate radicalization and, later, recruitment into terrorist organizations. Under Gaddafi, Libya managed, to a large extent, to export Islamist extremists to other conflict areas. Localized ethnic divisions further contributed to Libya becoming a powder keg after the removal of Gaddafi, especially in western and southern Libya with the forming of militias driven by the need to ensure geographic domination and the protection of tribal interests in the new dispensation. The void created by the removal of Gaddafi also opened old rivalries between the different tribes, allowing ISIS to use this lack of cohesion to enhance its foothold in Libya at a time when the organization was experiencing growing pressure and military defeat in Iraq and Syria. These divisions are expected to continue and prevent real efforts towards stability and nation building – two concepts that have been illusive to Libyans in recent history.

Notes

1. George Joffé, *Islamist Radicalisation in North Africa: Politics and Process* (New York: Routledge, 2012), p. 10.
2. George Joffé, 'Islamic opposition in Libya', *Third World Quarterly*, 10, no. 2 (1988): 616–18.
3. Ibid., pp. 615–31.
4. Alia Brahimi, 'Islam in Libya', in G Joffé (ed.), *Islamist Radicalisation in North Africa: Politics and Process* (New York: Routledge, 2012), Kindle Edition, p. 11.
5. Joffé, 'Islamic opposition in Libya', pp. 615–31.
6. Brahimi, 'Islam in Libya', p. 12.
7. Ibid.
8. Cornell University, Gaddafi's Arabic etymology of democracy, Middle East & Islamic Studies Collection Blog, Available at http://blogs.cornell.edu/mideastlibrarian/2011/02/18/libya-revolution-feb-17/ (accessed 25 January 2018).
9. Brahimi, 'Islam in Libya', pp. 13–14.
10. Dirk Vandewalle, *Libya since 1969: Qadhafi's Revolution Revisited* (Springer, 2016), p. 93.
11. Jean-Pierre Filiu, *From Deep State to Islamic State: The Arab Counter-Revolution and Its Jihadi Legacy* (Oxford University Press, 2015), p. 242.
12. Frederic M. Wehrey, *The Struggle for Security in Eastern Libya*. No. 160. (Washington DC: Carnegie Endowment for International Peace, 2012). Available at http://carnegieendowment.org/files/libya_security_2.pdf (accessed 9 February 2018), p. 4.
13. Michael Griffen, *Islamic State: Rewriting History* (London: Pluto Press, 2016), p. 12.
14. Aaron Y. Zelin, 'The Islamic State's First Colony in Libya', *The Washington Institute for Near-East Policy*, 10 October 2014. Available at http://www.washingtoninstitute.org/policy-analysis/view/the-islamic-states-first-colony-in-libya (accessed 13 January 2018).
15. Wehrey, *The Struggle for Security in Eastern Libya*, p. 5.
16. Mansouria Mokhefi, 'Gaddafi's regime in relation to the Libyan tribes', *Al-Jazeera Network*, 20 March 2011. Available at file:///Users/Anneli/Desktop/Gaddafi%20Relations%20with%20Tribes.pdf (accessed 24 January 2018).
17. Shatha Sbeta, 'The Libyan conflict is not a tribal conflict', *Arab Millennial*, 26 May 2016. Available at https://arabmillennial.net/2016/05/26/the-libyan-conflict-is-not-a-tribal-conflict/ (accessed 23 January 2018).
18. Craig R. Black, 'Muammar Gaddafi and Libya's strategic culture', in B. Schneider and J. Post (eds), *Know thy Enemy: Profiles of Adversary Leaders and their Strategic Cultures* (USAF Counterproliferation Center, 2003), pp. 247–70 (p. 252).
19. Peter Apps, 'Factbox: Libya's tribal, cultural divisions', *Reuters*, 25 August 2011. Available at https://www.reuters.com/article/us-libya-tribes/factbox-libyas-tribal-cultural-divisions-idUSTRE77O43R20110825 (accessed 24 January 2018).
20. Mansouria Mokhefi, 'Gaddafi's regime in relation to the Libyan tribes'.

21 *Human Rights Watch*, 'Libya: Opposition forces should protect civilians and hospitals', 13 July 2011. Available at https://www.hrw.org/news/2011/07/13/libya-oppositi on-forces-should-protect-civilians-and-hospitals (accessed 24 January 2018). Ruth Sherlock, 'Libya's uneasy uprising: Tribal feuds, clan rifts and deepening political turmoil threaten to undermine the war against Gadhafi', *Maclean's*, 23 August 2011. Available at http://www.macleans.ca/news/world/an-uneasy-uprising/ (accessed 24 January 2018).
22 Apps, 'Factbox: Libya's tribal, cultural divisions'.
23 Valerie Stocker, 'Tribal feuds, local conflicts engulf Libya', *Deutsche Welle*, 12 October 2013. Available at http://www.dw.com/en/tribal-feuds-local-conflicts-engulf-libya/a-17154021 (accessed 23 January 2018).
24 Stratfor, 'Libya's tribal conflicts', 5 December 2012. Available at https://worldview.st ratfor.com/article/libyas-tribal-conflicts (accessed 23 January 2018).
25 Sbeta, 'The Libyan conflict is not a tribal conflict'.
26 Marie-Louise Gumuchian, 'Libya struggles to contain tribal conflicts', *Reuters*, 8 April 2012. Available at https://www.reuters.com/article/us-libya-violence/libya-struggles -to-contain-tribal-conflicts-idUSBRE83702Z20120408 (accessed 23 January 2018).
27 Mokhefi, 'Gaddafi's regime in relation to the Libyan tribes'.
28 Olivier Roy and Antoine Sfeir, *The Columbia World Dictionary of Islamism* (Columbia University Press, 2007), p. 212.
29 Gumuchian, 'Libya struggles to contain tribal conflicts'.
30 Boaz Ganor, 'Libya and terrorism', 1992. Available at https://www.ict.org.il/UserFiles/ Libya%20and%20Terrorism.pdf (accessed 15 January 2018), p. 2.
31 Christopher Boucek, 'Libyan state-sponsored terrorism: An historical perspective', *Terrorism Monitor*, 3, Issue 6 (5 May 2005). Available at https://jamestown.org/ana lyst/christopher-boucek/ (accessed 15 January 2018).
32 Frederic M. Wehrey, *The Struggle for Security in Southern Libya* (Washington DC: Carnegie Endowment for International Peace, March 2017). Available at https://carnegi eendowment.org/files/CP304_Wehrey_Libya_Final.pdf (accessed 9 February 2018), p. 7.
33 Boucek, 'Libyan state-sponsored terrorism'.
34 Ganor, 'Libya and terrorism'.
35 Black, 'Muammar Gaddafi and Libya's strategic culture', p. 256.
36 Peter Ross, 'Remembering Lockerbie 20 years on', *The Scotsman*, 21 December 2008. Available at https://www.scotsman.com/lifestyle/remembering-lockerbie-20-years -on-1-1302316 (accessed 20 December 2017).
37 *New Straits Times*, 'Plane with 171 aboard explodes', 21 September 1989. Available at https://news.google.com/newspapers?id=k1lPAAAAIBAJ&sjid=G5ADAAAAIBAJ&p g=5662,1311458&dq=uta+bombing&hl=en (accessed 20 December 2017).
38 Steven Erlanger, '4 Guilty in fatal 1986 Berlin disco bombing linked to Libya', *New York Times*, 14 November 2001. Available at http://www.nytimes.com/2001/11/14/w orld/4-guilty-in-fatal-1986-berlin-disco-bombing-linked-to-libya.html (accessed 16 August 2001).
39 *Nuclear Threat Initiative*, 'Libya country profile', January 2015. Available at http://www.nti.org/learn/countries/libya/nuclear/ (accessed 10 February 2018).
40 *UN News Centre*, 'Security council lifts sanctions against Libya imposed after Lockerbie bombing', 12 September 2003. Available at http://www.un.org/apps/news/st ory.asp?NewsID=8225#.Wn75iJP1WuU (accessed 10 February 2018).
41 Brahimi, 'Islam in Libya', p. 12.
42 Black, 'Muammar Gaddafi and Libya's strategic culture', p. 257.

43 Yossef Bodansky, *Chechen Jihad: Al Qaeda's Training Ground and the Next Wave of Terror* (New York: HarperCollins, 2008), p. 31.
44 Black, 'Muammar Gaddafi and Libya's strategic culture', p. 258.
45 Vandewalle, *Libya since 1969*, p. 94.
46 Dallas E. Shaw, *Libyan Former Foreign Fighters and Their Effects on the Libyan Revolution* (Marine Corps Command and Staff College, Quantico, 2012), p. 14, 16.
47 Vandewalle, *Libya since 1969*, p. 94.
48 Ray Takeyh, 'Qadhafi and the challenge of militant Islam', *Washington Quarterly*, 21, no. 3 (1998): 159–72.
49 Olivier and Sfeir, *The Columbia World Dictionary of Islamism*, pp. 211–12.
50 Ibid., p. 212.
51 Jason Pack, Rhiannon Smith and Karim Mezran, 'The origins and evolution of ISIS in Libya', *Atlantic Council* (2017), p. 7. Available at https://www.atlanticcouncil.org/wp-content/uploads/2017/06/The_Origins_and_Evolution_of_ISIS_in_Libya_web_0705.pdf.
52 Jarret M. Brachman, *Global Jihadism: Theory and Practice* (New York: Routledge, 2008), p. 114.
53 Vandewalle, *Libya since 1969*, p. 94.
54 Mary Fitzgerald, 'Islamic militant group pledges support to anti-Gadafy rebels', *The Irish Times*, 29 March 2011. Available at https://www.irishtimes.com/news/islamic-militant-group-pledges-support-to-anti-gadafy-rebels-1.585344 (accessed 8 February 2018).
55 Vandewalle, *Libya since 1969*, p. 95.
56 Alison Pargeter, *The New Frontiers of Jihad: Radical Islam in Europe* (University of Pennsylvania Press, 2008), pp. 70–1.
57 *State Department Press Releases and Documents,* 'State Department Announces Steps to Reduce Terrorist Threat', 28 December 2004. Available at https://wfile.ait.org.tw/wf-archive/2004/041228/epf212.htm (accessed 8 February 2018).
58 Shaw, *Libyan Former Foreign Fighters*, pp. 14;16.
59 Salah Sarrar, 'Ex-Islamists walk free from Libyan jail', *Reuters*, 1 September 2010. Available at https://af.reuters.com/article/topNews/idAFJOE68003B20100901 (accessed 8 February 2018).
60 Maggie Michael and Hamza Hendawi, 'A Benghazi power, Libya militia eyed in attack', *Associated Press*, 18 September 2012. Available at https://web.archive.org/web/20120921015158/http://bigstory.ap.org/article/benghazi-power-libya-militia-eyed-attack (accessed 18 January 2018).
61 Wehrey, Insecurity and governance challenges in Southern Libya, pp. 10–11.
62 *Al-Jazeera America*, 'Libyan accused in 1998 US embassy bombings dies before trial', 3 January 2015. Available at http://america.aljazeera.com/articles/2015/1/3/allibi-embassy-bombing.html (accessed 8 February 2018).
63 Benjamin Weiser and Michael S. Schmidt, 'Qaeda suspect facing trial in New York over Africa embassy bombings dies', *The New York Times*, 3 January 2015. Available at https://www.nytimes.com/2015/01/04/us/politics/qaeda-suspect-facing-trial-in-new-york-dies-in-custody.html (accessed 8 February 2018).
64 Michael Moss and Souad Mekhennet, 'Rising leader for next phase of Al Qaeda's war', *The New York Times*, 4 April 2008. Available at http://www.nytimes.com/2008/04/04/world/asia/04qaeda.html?_r=1&oref=slogin (accessed 19 January 2018).
65 *BBC News*, 'Al Qaeda commander Abu Yahya al-Libi killed – US officials', 5 June 2012. Available at http://www.bbc.com/news/world-asia-18334377 (accessed 10 June 2012).
66 Halimullah Kousary and Abdul Basit, 'Threat group profiles', in Rohan Gunaratna and Douglas Woodall (eds), *Afghanistan After the Western Drawdown* (Rowman & Littlefield, 2015), pp. 153–4.

67 Brachman, *Global Jihadism,* 15–16.
68 Kousary and Basit, 'Threat group profiles', p. 154.
69 *Amnesty International,* 'Libya: Time to make human rights a reality', April 2004. Available at https://www.amnesty.org/en/documents/MDE19/002/2004/en/ (accessed 15 December 2017).
70 *Amnesty International,* '"Libya of tomorrow": What hope for human rights?' 23 June 2010. Available at https://www.amnesty.org/en/documents/MDE19/007/2010/en/ (accessed 15 January 2011), p. 87.
71 Dirk Vandewalle, *A History of Modern Libya* (New York: Cambridge University Press, 2012), pp. 68–9.
72 David D. Kirkpatrick, 'Political Islam and the fate of two Libyan brothers', *The New York Times,* 6 October 2012. Available at http://www.nytimes.com/2012/10/07/world/africa/political-islam-and-the-fate-of-two-libyan-brothers.html (accessed 19 January 2018).
73 *Cornell University,* 'The Libyan revolution, F.B.-17 (February 17th), Arab Spring: A research & study guide'. Available at http://guides.library.cornell.edu/c.php?g=31688&p=200751 (accessed 25 January 2018).
74 BBC News, 'Libya protests: Gaddafi says, "All my people love me"', 28 February 2011. Available at http://www.bbc.com/news/world-africa-12603259 (accessed 25 January 2018).
75 Andrew Feinstein, 'Where is Gaddafi's vast arms stockpile?' *The Guardian,* 26 October 2011. Available at https://www.theguardian.com/world/2011/oct/26/gadaffis-arms-stockpile (accessed 10 February 2018).
76 Mohammad-Mahmoud Ould Mohamedou, 'AQIM: Maghreb to Mali, and back, open democracy', 19 April 2013. Available at https://www.opendemocracy.net/mohammad-mahmoud-ould-mohamedou/aqim-maghreb-to-mali-and-back (accessed 10 January 2018).
77 BBC News, 'Mali crisis: Key players', 12 March 2013. Available at http://www.bbc.com/news/world-africa-17582909 (accessed 15 January 2018).
78 Grégory Chauzal and Thibault van Damme, 'The roots of Mali's conflict', *Clingendael Institute,* March 2015. Available at https://www.clingendael.org/pub/2015/the_roots_of_malis_conflict/ (accessed 10 January 2018).
79 Filiu, *From Deep State to Islamic State,* p. 186.
80 Erin Banco, 'ISIS establishes stronghold in Derna, Libya', *International Business Times,* 11 October 2014. Available at http://www.ibtimes.com/isis-establishes-stronghold-derna-libya-1721425 (accessed 8 February 2018).
81 Alessandra Bajec, 'How strong is ISIS in Libya?', *Muslim Village,* 17 April 2015. Available at https://muslimvillage.com/2015/04/17/76953/strong-isis-libya/ (accessed 19 April 2015).
82 Wehrey, *The Struggle for Security in Eastern Libya,* p. 9.
83 Ibid., p. 3.
84 *The Conversation,* 'Political chaos in Libya makes it a haven for radical terrorist groups', 25 May 2017. Available at https://theconversation.com/political-chaos-in-libya-makes-it-a-haven-for-radical-terrorist-groups-78281 (accessed 8 February 2018).
85 Wolfram Lacher, 'Fault lines of the revolution', German Institute for International and Security Affairs, May 2014. Available at https://www.swp-berlin.org/fileadmin/contents/products/research_papers/2013_RP04_lac.pdf (accessed 24 July 2018), p. 17.
86 Wehrey, *The Struggle for Security in Eastern Libya,* p. 10.

87 Abigail Hauslohner, 'With Libya's ascendant Islamists: "Don't get the wrong idea"', *TIME*, 30 March 2012. Available at http://content.time.com/time/world/article/0,8599,2110520,00.html (accessed 9 February 2018).
88 Wehrey, *The Struggle for Security in Eastern Libya*, p. 10.
89 Ibid., p. 11.
90 Ibid.
91 *BBC News*, 'US seizes Benghazi raid "ringleader" Ahmed Abu Khattala', 18 June 2014. Available at http://www.bbc.com/news/world-us-canada-27893831 (accessed 25 June 2015).
92 Michael and Hendawi, 'A Benghazi power'.
93 Ibid.
94 Ludovico Carlino, 'Ansar al-Shari'a: Transforming Libya into a land of Jihad', *Terrorism Monitor*, 12, no. 1 (2014). Available at https://jamestown.org/program/ansar-al-sharia-transforming-libya-into-a-land-of-jihad/#.U-L_L4358QY (accessed 1 February 2014).
95 Bajec, 'How strong is ISIS in Libya?'.
96 Carlino, 'Ansar al-Shari'a'.
97 Aaron Y. Zelin, 'Libya's jihadists beyond Benghazi', *Washington Institute for Near East Policy*, 12 August 2013. Available at http://www.washingtoninstitute.org/policy-analysis/view/libyas-jihadists-beyond-benghazi (accessed 9 September 2013).
98 *Agence France-Presse*, 'UN security council adds Libya's Ansar Al-Sharia to terror list', *I24 News*, 20 November 2014. Available at http://www.i24news.tv/en/news/international/africa/51583-141120-un-security-council-adds-libya-s-ansar-al-sharia-to-terror-list (accessed 30 November 2014).
99 Bajec, 'How strong is ISIS in Libya?'.
100 Carlino, 'Ansar al-Shari'a'.
101 Ulf Laessing, 'Leader of Libyan Islamists Ansar al-Sharia dies of wounds', *Reuters*, 23 January 2015. Available at https://www.reuters.com/article/us-libya-security/leader-of-libyan-islamists-ansar-al-sharia-dies-of-wounds-idUSKBN0KW1MU20150123 (accessed 15 February 2015).
102 Aya Elbrqawi, 'Libya: Derna cries for help', *AllAfrica*, 1 December 2014. Available at http://allafrica.com/stories/201412020345.html (accessed 10 December 2017).
103 Eric Knecht, 'Libyan Islamist group Ansar al-Sharia says it is dissolving', *Reuters*, 28 May 2017. Available at https://uk.reuters.com/article/uk-libya-security/libyan-islamist-group-ansar-al-sharia-says-it-is-dissolving-idUKKBN18N0YZ (accessed 30 May 2017).
104 Zelin, 'The Islamic state's first colony in Libya'.
105 Ibid.
106 Kyle Orton, 'Demise of an ex-Saddamist in Libya', *The Syrian Intifada*, 21 July 2015. Available at https://kyleorton1991.wordpress.com/2015/07/21/demise-of-an-ex-saddamist-in-libya/ (accessed 23 January 2018).
107 Paul Cruickshank, Nic Robertson, Tim Lister and Jomana Karadsheh, 'ISIS comes to Libya', *CNN*, 18 November 2014. Available at http://edition.cnn.com/2014/11/18/world/isis-libya/ (accessed 8 February 2018).
108 Kyle Orton, 'Analysis: "The end of the beginning for the Islamic State in Libya"', *The Henry Jackson Society*, 7 December 2016. Available at http://henryjacksonsociety.org/2016/12/07/analysis-the-end-of-the-beginning-for-the-islamic-state-in-libya/ (accessed 23 January 2018).
109 Orton, 'Demise of an ex-Saddamist in Libya'.

110 Zelin, 'The Islamic state's first colony in Libya'.
111 Orton, 'Analysis'.
112 Bajec, 'How strong is ISIS in Libya?'
113 Seth Kaplan and Bassma Kodmani, 'To rebuild Libya, start from below', *Foreign Policy*, 15 June 2015. Available at http://foreignpolicy.com/2016/06/15/to-rebuild-libya-start-from-below/ (accessed 15 December 2017).
114 Cruickshank, Robertson, Lister and Karadsheh, 'ISIS comes to Libya'.
115 *The Conversation*, 'Political chaos in Libya makes it a haven for radical terrorist groups'.
116 Aaron Y. Zelin, 'The others: Foreign fighters in Libya', *The Washington Institute for Near East Policy* (2018), p. 3. Available at http://www.washingtoninstitute.org/uploads/PolicyNote45-Zelin.pdf (accessed 25 January 2018).
117 Edwin Bakker and Mark Singleton, 'Foreign fighters in the Syria and Iraq conflict: Statistics and characteristics of a rapidly growing phenomenon', *Foreign Fighters under International Law and Beyond* (The Hague: TMC Asser Press, 2016), p. 12.
118 Zelin, 'The others: Foreign fighters in Libya', p. 3.
119 Orton, 'Analysis'.
120 Zelin, 'The others: Foreign fighters in Libya', p. 1.
121 Omar Shabbi, 'Jihadists coordinate on Tunisian-Algerian border', *Al-Monitor*, 13 August 2014. Available at http://www.al-monitor.com/pulse/fr/originals/2014/08/tunisia-algeria-coordinate-fight-terrorism-border.html#ixzz54iQRwm2m (accessed 15 December 2017).
122 *Jihadology*, 'Eye on jihadis in Libya weekly update: 23 January 2018'. Available at http://jihadology.net/2018/01/23/eye-on-jihadis-in-libya-weekly-update-23-january-2018/ (accessed 25 January 2018).

JIHAD AND THE UNITED KINGDOM

Paul Gill, Zoe Marchment, Bettina Rottweiler and Sanaz Zolghadriha

The year 2017 in the United Kingdom perfectly encapsulated the centre-periphery debate at the heart of this book. Four jihadi-inspired terrorist attacks in the United Kingdom (UK) resulted in thirty-five fatalities, and the number of injured came close to 400. The perpetrators included individuals born and bred in the UK, with no first-hand experience of foreign conflicts but inspired by actions abroad, a Libyan-born refugee who had travelled back and forth between the UK and his country of origin, religious converts, first-generation immigrants from Pakistan, members of the Saudi-born extremist group al-Muhajiroun, a failed asylum seeker from Morocco and a recent refugee from Syria. The year also witnessed several serious plots disrupted by UK intelligence involving UK-born citizens, who had trained, and/or were directed from, foreign theatres of conflict. Meanwhile, approximately 1400 UK citizens reside in Syria as members of ISIS. This list demonstrates the complex import from, and export to, the jihadi centre within the UK. There is no simple answer and the ratio of whether a behaviour or event was primarily influenced by foreign or domestic sources is likely to vary from case to case.

So where do we go from here? Generally, research on terrorism and political violence focuses on one of three units of analysis: the individual terrorist, the terrorist organization or the community that the terrorist group claims to represent. Let's take these units of analysis as a starting point to weigh evidence of import and export dynamics. Generally speaking, studies on individual terrorists seek to ascertain the factors that drive individuals to engage in terrorism. Various analyses have focused on pathological dispositions to violence,[1] authoritarian personalities,[2] general socialization factors,[3] suicidal personalities,[4] altruism,[5] vengeance,[6] quests for personal significance,[7] religious fanaticism,[8] revenge for personal suffering,[9] and despair.[10] Studies on the organizational dimension generally offer rational-choice style explanations. Various analyses emphasize strategic utility,[11] power balances in asymmetric war,[12] terrorism's ability to produce system collapse,[13] and its role as a signalling act.[14] Bloom[15] emphasizes tactical choice and its relationship with domestic political competition and the search for public support. Studies on the societal dimension of terrorism focus on factors such as degrees of political freedom and poverty,[16] regime type,[17] social injustice,[18] and attachment to political Islam.[19] Hafez[20] outlines that a sense of victimization and threat, combined with symbolic narratives venerating martyrdom and legitimate leaders consenting to violence, leads to societal support for certain types of terrorist tactics.

Many research projects within the study of Al Qaeda or ISIS violence point towards jihadi narratives as sources of support (at the community level), enablers for violence (at the individual level) and a set of practical codes and constraints (at the group level). Their acceptance and presence are often treated as a given prerequisite. This chapter seeks to disaggregate the import and export of jihadi narratives (and their effects) from a UK perspective. The above-mentioned studies collectively contribute to our knowledge of jihadi-inspired violence, but the literature lacks a framework that ties the individual, organizational and societal dimensions together to explain the causal interactions among them. More specifically, we have little understanding of how the import and export of jihadi narratives impact upon these three levels of analysis. Where exactly are such import/export dynamics crucial? First, we look at the critical, yet differing, roles that various foreign-born epistemic authority figures (and the nominally non-violent groups they led) have had within the UK. Second, we explore evidence for community support for jihadi narratives and goals within the UK, and place these levels within their comparative context. Third, we examine the impact of the importation of Jihad from the centre, and the effect it has had within the UK. This section will consider the importation of core narratives, and the importation of direction for violent plots. Before concluding this chapter, the final section focuses on UK citizens who travelled outside of the UK for training, or to participate in related conflicts.

Marketing martyrdom: The role of epistemic authority figures

The direction for violent plots within the United Kingdom has come from multiple levels of influence. Many foreign-born religious leaders from various groups have used the UK as their base to provide the broad call to arms and legitimating ideology and martyrdom narratives, without which there would be no violence. Such religious/political entrepreneurs frame the necessity of violence and seek to increase the social allure of violence to both the constituency they claim to represent and, at a more micro level, potential attackers.

The UK has a long and changing history with these types of individuals. For example, in the initial aftermath of their victory in Afghanistan against the Soviets in the late 1980s, 'many of those who had been to London before, or knew others who had, returned once again … seeking refuge' as Afghanistan returned to internal turmoil.[21] At this time, the list included leadership from the Libyan Islamic Fighting Group and the Algerian Front Islamique du Salut as well as individuals linked to Osama bin Laden. According to Pantucci, 'for most of these activists the priority was to instigate action in the Muslim world'.[22] The London-based Arabic newspaper *Al-Quds al-Arabi* published an interview with Osama bin Laden in 1996, where he announced that after the United States had stationed troops in the Gulf, it had 'entered into a confrontation with a nation whose population is 1 billion Muslims'.[23] This was not limited to the print world. The URL www.azzam.com was registered in Britain in the 1990s. Its main purpose was to disseminate

English-language extremist material related to the key Afghan mujahedeen ideologue, Abdullah Azzam. Much later, al-Shabaab's website was also apparently run from the UK. The website formed part of a network that was 'providing at least the ideological backdrop, if not the practical support, to young Britons, who were trying to join al-Shabaab'.[24]

Abu Qatada

Among this predominantly London-based milieu, several individuals and groups are worthy of greater mention. The first is Abu Qatada. He was 'renowned throughout the Muslim world as a prominent academic and cleric … he served as a one-stop shop for the itinerant body of post-Afghanistan jihadis who had scattered around Europe while helping support active wars'.[25] In particular, he used his base in the UK to help influence the Algerian jihad. From London, he wrote for the Ansar al-Jihad newsletter and acted as a fundraiser. He also issued fatwas in support of the Group Islamique Armee (GIA).[26] One such fatwa condoned the killing of the wives and children of 'apostates' in Algeria. This occurred two months after GIA's first suicide bombing. At that stage, the group was in its third year of a bloody insurgency that had killed over 30,000 people. Up to that point, that initial suicide bombing was the single most deadly attack of the insurgency, killing forty-two and injuring over 300. The vast majority of victims were civilians, although a police headquarters was the intended target. The claim of responsibility depicted the headquarters as a 'base for torture and killing'.[27] However, in the concluding paragraph of this claim, the group maintains that the death of and injuries to civilians was a major error for which 'the group is obliged to ask for pardon'.[28] Abu Qatada's fatwa intended to provide complete religious pardon for the atrocity.

This depicts a process whereby UK-based individuals sought to influence the jihad within the core. Abu Qatada's inability to speak English fluently meant that a limited impact occurred upon British Muslims. His influence lay elsewhere. 'For men like this, London was simply a backdrop against which they would carry out their activities overseas. Their targets and interests remained abroad, and their fatwas and commandments mostly concerned activities that occurred beyond Britain's borders.'[29]

Omar Bakri Mohammed

The first organized group worthy of mention is Hizb ut-Tahrir (HT), which has used the UK as a base since the 1980s. Syrian-born Sheikh Omar Bakri Mohammed initially led the group in the UK, after being arrested and deported from Saudi Arabia. Bakri arrived in London in 1986, where he started organizing HT activities almost immediately, and he personally takes credit for HT's success in the UK.[30] The group's stated goal is to use Islam to defeat Western powers upon the Caliphate's establishment elsewhere. Unlike Abu Qatada's group, it has had a major and long-lasting impact upon the jihadi sphere within the UK. Indeed, many violent British jihadis were at one time linked with HT. Baran[31] describes

HT's British chapter as the 'nerve centre for the international movement', although the group itself has not disclosed the location of its global leadership. The British branch, however, 'has been speaking in defence of the group as a whole over the last couple of years, and speaks confidently on the group's beliefs, goals, and methods as one might expect the global leadership to do'.[32] Certainly, the group's media operations are largely based out of the UK, including websites, regular magazines and books. All of the group's communiques emanate from the UK,[33] including the al-Khilafah magazines and leaflets, which are distributed across the world. There is evidence to suggest that the English-language version differs from those translated and published elsewhere with local-based reporting from various Muslim countries omitted from English-language versions. HT's YouTube videos are also produced in the United Kingdom with translations later spliced in for non-English-speaking audiences.[34] HT acknowledges that it removed some of its overseas literature from its British website for fears that if it were 'read out of its context [some] might see it as offensive'.[35]

In 1996, Bakri left HT. Pantucci[36] alleges that Bakri's departure was on ideological grounds. Bakri 'began saying that the group should start trying to convert the United Kingdom to Islam, rather than simply focusing on recruiting people to support HT efforts to take over Muslim majority nations'. Bakri intended to shift the focus therefore from the international core of jihad to the domestic struggle. This obviously led to a great deal of tension and resulted in his departure. After Bakri left the group, HT 'embarked on a period of semi-clandestine recruitment and re-growth, not emerging back into the limelight until the campaign against the government of Uzbekistan'[37] in the early 2000s. HT's goal of focusing on the jihad abroad has therefore remained steady in the wake of Bakri's departure.

Very soon after his departure from HT, Bakri set up al-Muhajiroun (translated as 'The Emigrants') with the help of Anjem Choudary.[38] The group's name alludes to those who accompanied the Prophet Muhammad after his expulsion from Mecca. 'Just as The Emigrants helped Muhammad establish a base for his new religion in Medina, a base from which he and his followers later conquered Mecca and much of the Arabian Peninsula, so Bakri and his students hoped their organization might play a similar role in bringing Islamic rule to Britain.'[39] The group's stated goal is to 'overthrow the British government without using violence, and to establish an Islamic state in the UK based on Sharia law'. Upon the ISIS's establishment, the plan is to 'continue to conquer other countries, removing the obstacles in the way of establishing the Sharia until we have the domination of Islam globally'.[40]

During his leadership, Omar Bakri was an expressive supporter of Al Qaeda-related activities. However, this largely depended upon the location in which the violence occurred. On occasions, Bakri has explained that he does not support jihadi violence in the United Kingdom and the United States because of a covenant of security that exists between Muslims and non-Muslims in these countries.[41] Elsewhere, however, he has played active roles in facilitating and promoting violence. He sees the violent jihadis 'around the world in Lebanon, Somalia, Sudan, Afghanistan, Palestine, Bangladesh, Pakistan' as being in 'one hundred percent agreement in matters with us'.[42] On one occasion, he applauded the US

Embassy suicide bombings in Africa in 1998 because US troops were present in the Gulf fighting Muslims.[43] At other times, he legitimized foreign fighters engaging in battle in Chechnya, Kashmir and Afghanistan. Bakri also claimed that he recruited Bilal Ahmed – England's first suicide bomber, who took part in the Kashmir insurgency and detonated his bomb in December 2000. Omar Bakri also released statements on behalf of Osama bin Laden and once in 1999 published a letter to bin Laden imploring him to act against the West.[44] He praised the 9/11 hijackers as the 'magnificent 19' and referred to the attacks as a 'Towering Day in World History'.[45] On its first anniversary, al-Muhajiroun convened a meeting of 'radical mullahs' at Finsbury Park Mosque to argue for jihad. Bakri stated: 'The people at this conference look at September 11 like a battle, as a great achievement by the mujahideen against the evil superpower.'[46]

A mixed method analysis of al-Muhajiroun conducted by Kenney et al.[47] demonstrates the significant impact Omar Bakri's leadership had upon the network. A social network analysis demonstrated the centrality of Bakri to key al-Muhajiroun operations and conduct. His impact, however, declined after two major incidents: first, when he left Britain for Lebanon shortly after the 7/7 attacks (he was later prohibited from returning by British authorities); second, when two successor groups to al-Muhajiroun (al-Ghurabaa and the Saved Sect) were proscribed as illegal. The latter incident led to a 45 per cent decline in total connections within the al-Muhajiroun network. First-hand interviews and participant observation of al-Muhajiroun protests, locations where they proselytized Islam, educational lessons and internet chat rooms demonstrated that 'Bakri's leadership has changed from direct oversight of al-Muhajiroun to symbolic, geographically removed leadership'.[48]

Kenney et al.[49] argue that since Bakri's departure, al-Muhajiroun has gone through two quick generational shifts. First, several al-Muhajiroun veterans based in Britain replaced Bakri as day-to-day emirs. These individuals created the 'Ahlus Sunnah wal Jamaah' internet discussion forum Islam4UK. Islam4UK conducts political protests and roadshows 'largely without Bakri's direct involvement'.[50] This group similarly invoked the previously mentioned covenant of security: 'As Muslims in Britain, we live among you under a covenant of security; in return for our lives and wealth being protected we are not permitted to attack the lives and wealth of the non-Muslims with whom we live.'[51] These new leaders have directly replaced Bakri's provision of Islamic theology lectures and jurisprudence. The last generation have had little to no direct contact with Omar Bakri and joined al-Muhajiroun through one of its successor organizations and later set up their own such as Muslims Against Crusades and Supporters of Sunnah.[52].

Abu Hamza al-Masri

The next individual of note is the radical cleric from Egypt, Abu Hamza al-Masri. Croft[53] depicts him as a 'key radicalizing influence' in the domestic jihadi scene in the UK. In the late 1980s, he went on Hajj to Mecca and studied under the mujahideen leader and ideologue Abdullah Azam.[54] After moving back to the UK, he acted as a translator for wounded mujahideen fighters from the Afghanistan battle in the late 1980s. Abu Hamza visited Bosnia three times in the early 1990s, visited Afghanistan in 1991 and returned to the UK in 1993. He was the official spokesman for al-Ansar's organizational newsletter that supported the Algerian jihad, and acted as press secretary for the Islamic Army of Aden-Abyan.[55] In 1994, he leveraged his growing infamy from participating in two foreign conflicts to develop the Supporters of Sharia group in London. It became a 'crucial intersection between jihad in the Muslim world and its Western support network'.[56] Abu Hamza claims the formation of this group was to 'give the message to the average Muslims [from those who participated in Bosnia, Afghanistan and elsewhere] … we are established to defend the Shari'ah, the Islamic law, and also to defend the people who are defending Islamic law…we also give people advice to go for training to help fellow Muslims, and not to be deceived by the Western European society'.[57] Later, he became leader of the notorious Finsbury Park Mosque in 1997. His activities 'transformed the mosque into one of the major stops on the European jihadi trail'.[58] The mosque acted as a 'secure retreat for rest and recreation after a tour of duty in the holy war'.[59] There, Pantucci[60] outlines, 'Videos and newsletters could be purchased, read or watched which provided grim updates from jihadi battlefields around the world. Returning warriors would regale newer recruits with tales of adventure and experiences fighting or training on the frontline, while posters would offer sign-up sheets for those who were eager to go abroad.' On different occasions, Abu Hamza stated his readiness to train suicide bombers for the Chechen insurgency, his belief that 9/11 was an act of self-defence,[61] facilitated travel to various conflict zones and sought to set up a jihadi training camp in Oregon, United States.[62] While he undoubtedly had a large impact in English-speaking jihadi circles, his impact with non-English-speaking populations has been negligible.[63]

Therefore, the various cases outlined above demonstrate the variance in UK-based epistemic authority figures and how their groups have influenced both the domestic and international jihadi scenes. Usually this influence is a direct outcome of their personal affordances (language, social networks, battlefield experience) and personal strategic goals. The next section looks at the levels of support for various themes associated with the jihadi movement within the UK.

Support for jihadi narratives

Opinion polls in many states illustrate that small minorities justify suicide bombings and other acts of jihadi violence. This is the constituency that jihadi-inspired groups aim to gain support from. It is also the constituency from which much smaller numbers will become radicalized to the point of engaging in militancy. Opinion polls conducted by ICM Research for *The Guardian* newspaper in England reveal that in March 2004, 13 per cent of polled British Muslims could justify any future Al Qaeda suicide bombing on the United States. Directly after the 2005 7/7 Tube bombings in London, 5 per cent of British Muslims polled could justify future attacks by British suicide bombers in the UK. In an ICM poll of Muslims in Britain in June 2009, 11 per cent of those surveyed felt that it was right for the Taliban to attack or target British/NATO soldiers in Afghanistan. Two per cent agreed with the Taliban using suicide bombers in Pakistan. Populous opinion polls undertaken for *Times* in England reveal that, of the British Muslims polled in December 2005, 7 per cent could justify suicide bombings in the UK, 16 per cent in Israel, 15 per cent in Iraq and 13 per cent in Chechnya. An opinion poll close to one year after the 7/7 bombings showed that 13 per cent of polled British Muslims considered the 7/7 perpetrators as martyrs. Sixteen per cent would justify suicide bombings in the United Kingdom against military targets, 11 per cent against government buildings/workers, 10 per cent against the police and 7 per cent against civilians. This poll illustrates that those who provide support do not just lend support without thinking about the methods used and intended target. Here, the supporters more readily justify attacks on traditionally legitimate targets, such as the military or political targets. In more recent academic polling of a representative survey of individuals of Muslim heritage in the UK between the ages of 18 and 45, it was found that 2.4 per cent showed some sympathy for violent protest and terrorist acts. Among other factors, sympathy was higher for those born in the UK, and those who spoke English at home.[64]

For a comparison, let's look at the evidence in other countries. Kazim et al.'s[65] survey shows that 15.3 per cent of Pakistani respondents supported suicide bombing and that 37.2 per cent saw it as an act of martyrdom. Much higher numbers expressed approval for suicide bombings in other conflicts such as in Palestine (48.4 per), Kashmir (47.3 per cent) and Lebanon (50.7 per cent). The Pakistani respondents, therefore, saw differing levels of legitimacy and this was dependent upon the cause the suicide bombing was associated with. Respondents seemingly more readily accept suicide bombings in far-off conflicts than suicide bombings within Pakistan that could potentially harm the respondents themselves. This dynamic is repeated in the single-country case studies analysed below. Haddad's[66] survey of perceptions of suicide bombing in Lebanon showed that 70 per cent of Lebanese Sunni Muslims and 81 per cent of Shi'a Muslims supported suicide bombings targeting Israel. A major Pew Research Centre poll of 60,000 Muslims living in the United States showed that 5 per cent justified suicide bombings. Of those under thirty years of age, 15 per cent saw justification.

The Program on International Policy Attitudes survey in September 2008 for BBC's World Service, in which respondents relayed their feelings about Al Qaeda, allows for a direct comparison. Of those polled, 20 per cent in Egypt, 19 per cent in Pakistan, 16 per cent in Indonesia, 7 per cent in Lebanon, 4 per cent in the UK and 2 per cent each in the US and Turkey expressed positive feelings.[67] Pew's 'Global Attitudes Project', in May 2006, asked the question: 'Can suicide bombing of civilian targets to defend Islam be justified?' Muslim respondents from states in which suicide bombers have emerged, showed a significant minority who justify suicide bombing. Examples include Jordan (29 per cent), Egypt (28 per cent), Turkey (17 per cent), Great Britain (15 per cent), Pakistan (14 per cent) and Indonesia (10 per cent). From the previous surveys outlined, we may be able to infer that if the question asked specifically about military or political targets, then the positive expressions of support would be higher. It should also be noted that the justification for suicide bombing is already embedded within that particular question. If either no justification or a different justification is given, or if a specific target is mentioned, the results are likely to be much different.

One of the most interesting observations we can extract from this opinion poll research is the disparity between those who can justify or support violence and the actual numbers who become violent. This vast difference needs explaining. The huge disparity indicates that attitudinal affinity with a cause is not a sufficient explanatory variable for participation. Moskalenko and McCauley[68] accurately distinguish between these two states of mind by developing both an Activism Intention Scale, which assesses an individual's readiness to participate in legal and non-violent political action and a Radicalism Intention Scale, which assesses willingness to participate in political action that is illegal or violent. Clearly, there is a difference between passively accepting and justifying acts of suicide bombing and engaging in suicide bombings. For an adequate explanation, other factors than attitudinal affinity are at work concurrently.

Importing the jihad and its effect on the individual terrorist

This section looks at the main impacts that the importation of jihad from the centre has had upon jihad within the UK, which has been inextricably linked to the importation of jihadi ideals from the centre since the beginning. This has come in many forms. This section narrows its analysis to the importation of both, core narratives and the direction for violent plots.

The failed attacks on the London transport system on 21 July 2005 illustrate the broader network that violent operators tend to inhabit. The levels of foreign and domestic influence differ across different aspects of the plot. The subsequent investigation of the failed attacks led to several convictions and highlighted a number of associations within a wider network than the suicide bombers themselves. In this example, the detonators of all four bombers (Yasin Omar, Osman Hussain, Muktar Said Ibrahim and Ramzi Mohammed) failed to ignite the explosives. Prosecutors of the failed bombers allege that both Muktar Said Ibrahim and Ramzi Mohammed devotedly followed Abu Hamza al-Masri (whose accepting attitude towards suicide bombings will be covered later in this chapter). Seized documents belonging to the failed bombers included speeches by al-Masri, Osama bin Laden and Sheikh Abdullah al-Faisal (formerly an extreme cleric based in the UK but who was deported in 2007 due to his actions), as well as footage of various suicide bombings, jihadi executions and videos that provided explosives training. Muktar Said Ibrahim also allegedly received hands-on bomb-making training in Pakistan between December 2004 and March 2005.

The second level of influence captures all individuals that provide the space for face-to-face interaction which further normalizes martyrdom narratives, increases a sense of in-group identity and provides a location to physically and mentally prepare to become a violent jihadi. On one occasion, Omar Bakri Mohammed, for example, clearly explained how the radicalization process works: 'We find young men in university campuses or mosques, invite them for a meal and discuss the situation for on-going attacks being suffered by Muslims in Chechnya, Palestine or Kashmir. We…make them understand their duty to support the Jihad struggle verbally, financially and, if they can, physically in order to liberate their homeland.'[69] This depiction places the import of jihadi narratives as crucial. However, other extremist preachers give a different side to the story. Al-Muhajiroun's leader in the UK, Anjem Choudary, outlined that the group tailors its message to local concerns to increase its appeal: 'We go to the areas looking at the problems they have, a lot of places have a lot of problems with the youth, with prostitutes, drugs, alcohol, and [what we do is] really tap into that and present Islam as an alternative … we don't really talk about the judicial system and jihad … we talk more about the social system, economics, etc.'[70]

Similarly, recruiters Atilla Ahmet and Mohammed Hamid, who were convicted in September 2007 and February 2008, respectively, did not engage in any violent acts. However, their provision of a safe space for would-be 21/7 attackers to condition themselves, originally normatively and mentally, and later, physically, for martyrdom acted as a crucial cog in the psychological process of becoming a violent jihadi. Those who run jihadi websites and those who upload the jihadi literature and propaganda would also fall into this category. For example, in 2008 Blackfriars Crown Court in England convicted Aabid Hussain Khan. Two years earlier, police at Manchester International Airport had arrested him upon his arrival from Pakistan. The conviction itself related to the items he returned to Britain with and items stored on his laptop. The presiding judge referred to the seized artefacts as 'amongst the largest and most extensive ever discovered'. They included thousands of files of propaganda glorifying acts of political violence and suicide bombing, training manuals, maps and logistical videos of potential targets, and maps of transport infrastructure, in the United Kingdom and the United States. In total, the soft-copy materials came to 1.3 terabytes of data across thirty-three hard drives, ninety floppy disks, multiple USB drives and MP3 players, 450 audiotapes, 188 videos and over 600 CDs and DVDs (Simcox et al., 2010). Newspaper reports depicted Khan as a 'cyber groomer', while the Crown Prosecution Service referred to him as a 'Terrorist Mr. Fix-It'. Further evidence revealed that Khan arranged travel to Pakistan for budding jihadis looking to train. Khan also administered the at-Tibyan website, which provided translations of Al Qaeda recruitment documents. Khan therefore played multiple roles that could potentially facilitate violent acts, including suicide bombings.

The third level is that of ideological support networks. Here, the influence from abroad becomes more actively engaged in ideological debate, religious observation and physical preparation. According to the Metropolitan Police, Ahmet and Hamid hosted meetings in the latter's home in East London. During these meetings, Hamid encouraged the small assembled audience 'to murder people who do not believe in the Islamic faith'. The group also frequently engaged in discussion about preparing for life as fighters in terms of discipline and training. These meetings were typically strewn with references of, and from, foreign jihadi conflicts. Two of the failed 21/7 suicide bombers attended these meetings while Hamid was also in telephone contact with the other two failed bombers. Again, behaviours within this group depiction are not causal and no behaviour within this setting is in itself violent. Instead, the physical and spiritual preparation facilitates an individual, who may later engage in terrorist violence, by providing a more internalized militant group identity that is deemed to be religiously and ideologically justified. The numbers within this network are still larger than those of individuals who join operational support networks and/or operational cells. The behaviours and conditioning apparent within the ideological support network may facilitate transition to the smaller, more intense and more intentionally violent groups, but they neither cause terrorist violence by themselves nor even promise that an individual will become more deeply embedded within a plot.

The next level captures those who were intrinsic to the actual attempted violent act. Whereas earlier levels provide face-to-face or online justification and glorification of terrorism, those in this level provide the expertise needed to actually carry out a suicide bombing. Those who trained Muktar Said Ibrahim in bomb-making in Pakistan, and the convicted Adel Yahya's expertise, provided (in theory at least) the practical skills necessary to successfully detonate a bomb.

Lone-actor terrorists typically do not have such complicated levels of interaction. However, that leaves them open to greater influence from foreign bodies, who disseminate their message via the internet. For example, on 14 May 2010, Roshonara Choudhry stabbed Stephen Timms, a Labour Party member of Parliament, causing him serious bodily injury. In the subsequent trial, the court heard a draft letter of Choudhry addressed to her mother that was found on her computer. The letter stated that she hated living in Britain and did not want to spend the rest of her life in a non-Muslim country. She said that she could not live under the British government, which she described as an 'enemy of Islam', and that she could not pay taxes to it or work as a teacher in its education system. Investigators established that Choudhry began downloading Anwar al-Awlaki's videos and sermons in the autumn and winter of 2009, when she began spending long periods of time in her bedroom. Her parents believed that she was studying, but in reality, she was downloading extremist material, including more than 100 hours of al-Awlaki's sermons. It was supposedly during this time that Choudhry made the decision to engage in a violent attack. During her police interview, Choudhry responded to a question concerning the transition from immersing herself in religion to committing violence. Her response stated: 'Because as Muslims we're all brothers and sisters and we should all look out for each other and we shouldn't sit back and do nothing while others suffer. We shouldn't allow the people who oppress us to get away with it and to think that they can do whatever they want to us and we're just gonna [sic] lie down and take it.' Choudhry referred to a specific YouTube video of Sheikh Abdullah Azzam that made her understand that 'even women are supposed to fight' and that she had an obligation to turn towards violence.

When we examine how violent jihadis within the United Kingdom justify their violence, we often see the direct importation of narratives from the core of jihad. For example, the drafting of a last will and testament acts as a point of little return for the terrorist. In terms of the narratives contained within these testaments, often the individuals draw a line of descent from the martyrs of the past to themselves. This places the individual within a path-dependent historical narrative, on a pedestal with the martyrs and heroes of the past. The testament of the leader of the 7 July attacks, Mohammad Siddique Khan stated, 'I am directly responsible for protecting and avenging my Muslim brothers and sisters ... I myself make due to Allah to raise me amongst those whom I love like the prophets, the messengers, the martyrs and today's heroes.' We know from elsewhere that the success of other terrorists spurs individuals on the fringe forward. One of the 7/7 bombers, Hasib Hussain was open in school about his support and reverence for the 9/11 bombers.[71] Newspaper reports suggest two of the 7/7 bombers were present at a party celebrating 9/11 in Beeston, Leeds.[72] Police found pictures of the four 7/7 bombers and Mohammed Siddique Khan's last will and testament in a house belonging to one individual charged in the transatlantic airplane plot. Following the failed attacks, a fortnight after the 7 July 2005 suicide bombings on London's transport infrastructure, police raided the dwellings of the perpetrators. According to newspaper reports of the court proceedings, the police found video images of beheadings, cassettes of bin Laden's speeches, images of a suicide bomber attacking a US barracks in Saudi Arabia, CD-ROMs including one of a course on Jihad, and a videotape of a speech by the radical cleric Abu Hamza suggesting that suicide bombers are martyrs.

The narratives of violence also typically place a call to arms for other potential recruits to follow the same path. No one attacker can realistically think that his or her one bombing will achieve the stated aims of the group; therefore, this type of narrative attempts to placate the individual to assume that others will follow in trying to achieve the goal. The British suicide bomber Asif Hanif stated: 'You Muslims are sitting in your houses, watching whatever is happening here to your Muslim brothers in Palestine. We want to be martyrs for Allah and we want you to be martyrs for Allah as well.' Often, last wills and testaments also seek to coalition-build by linking their attack with the conflicts and insurgencies of others. Bilal Abdulla, the Glasgow airport suicide bomber, addressed his will to the 'soldiers of Islam in the country of the Two Rivers', a moniker Al Qaeda regularly applies to Iraq.

Finally, these testaments also tend to displace responsibility onto the targets of violence themselves. By blaming others, the individual absolves him/herself of blame for the deaths of innocents and cites the deaths of innocent Muslims in core conflict areas. The will of 7/7 attacker Shehzad Tanweer announced: 'For the non-Muslims in Britain, you may wonder what you have done to deserve this. You are those who have voted in your government who in turn have oppress[ed] our mothers and children, brothers and sisters ... Your government has openly supported the genocide of more than 150,000 innocent Muslims in Fallujah.' He continued that suicide bombings will continue until 'you [Britain] pull all your troops out of Afghanistan and Iraq. Until you stop all financial and military support to the US and Israel and until you release all Muslim prisoners from Belmarsh'. The shoe bomber Richard Reid stated: 'Your government has killed 2 million children in Iraq … Your government has sponsored the rape and torture of Muslims in the prisons of Egypt and Turkey and Syria and Jordan with their money and their weapons … I don't know … what I done as being equal to rape and to torture, or to the deaths of the 2 million children in Iraq'. Nicky Reilly's handwritten note following his attempted suicide bombing of a restaurant in Exeter was more clearly aimed at the British government and their policies and the British public: 'Everywhere Muslims are suffering at the hands of Britain, Israel and America. We are sick of taking all the brutality from you. You have imprisoned over 1,000 Muslims in Britain alone in your war on Islam … In Britain it's OK for a girl to have sex without marriage and if she gets pregnant she can get an abortion so easily. When you are getting drunk on Friday and Saturday night your behaviour is worse than animals. You have sex in nightclub toilets. You urinate in shop doorways. You shout your foul and disgusting mouth off in the street … Britain and USA and Israel have no real rules'.

These testaments directly show the impact that foreign conflicts and their motivations have had on individual plotters in the United Kingdom. As Tony Blair described the leader of the 7/7 plot: He 'may have been born here. But his ideology wasn't'.[73]

Exporting violent activists

There is a long list of UK citizens, who planned or travelled outside of the UK to gain the requisite training and/or participate in foreign conflicts. Perhaps the earliest expression of this was by the little-known UK-based group Jam'iat Ihyaa Minhaaj Al-Sunnah (JIMAS). Established in 1984, JIMAS was crucial for many Britons who travelled to foreign theatres of conflict. The group explained to its followers that 'you don't feel at home in Britain, but you can't go "home" to a country you have never visited. So, we have a third identity for you – a Pan-national Islamism that knows no boundaries and can envelop you entirely'.[74] From 1989 onwards, JIMAS sent up to 100 British nationals to fight in Afghanistan, Kashmir, Bosnia, Burma and the Philippines. Among those influenced by JIMAS was Britain's Omar Saeed Sheikh, who was a very experienced jihadi by the time he was convicted for kidnapping the journalist Daniel Pearl.[75]

Pantucci[76] estimates the number of Britons who fought for jihad in the Balkans in the 1990s to be in the hundreds. At least five Britishers died in Bosnia during this time. Six Britishers were arrested in Yemen in 1998 for organizing a terrorist attack on US forces. The Yemeni prosecutor in the case stated, 'This offense started in London in the offices of SoS [Supporters of Sharia] which is owned by Abu Hamza and who exports terrorism to other countries.'[77] Other activities that led to convictions include Waheed Ali and Mohammed Shakil's attempts to join training camps in Pakistan. The leader of the 7/7 plot, Siddique Khan, attended a terrorist training camp in Pakistan; as did two of the 21/7 plotters. Omar Sharif attempted a suicide bombing in a Tel Aviv bar in 2003. Some seventy or eighty British individuals including some suicide bombers appeared in the Iraqi insurgency.[78] Just like most countries on the periphery, the UK has also witnessed a mass export of jihadis into Syria in the past decade. Some, like Mohammed Emwazi, played key operational and propaganda roles in the early days of the newly established Caliphate. Others, like Junaid Hussain, played an active role in encouraging ISIS-related attacks in the West.

Of course, violent operators are only one necessary component of a terrorist campaign. Funding also plays a large role for complex terrorist organizations. Again here, we can find multiple examples of British-based organizations exporting their finances to aid foreign conflict theatres. Kalim Siddiqui set up the Muslim Parliament in 1992. In the Parliament's initial manifesto, they describe jihad 'as a basic requirement of Islam and living in Britain or having British nationality by birth or naturalization does not absolve the Muslim from his or her duty to participate in jihad: this participation can be active service in armed struggle abroad and/or *the provision of material or moral support to those engaged in such struggle anywhere in the world*'.[79] True to its commitment, the Muslim Parliament later set up an 'Arms for Bosnia', which was later rebranded as the 'Jihad Fund' and collected money for those fighting in Algeria, Kashmir and elsewhere.[80]

Conclusion

The illustrations demonstrate the complexity in assessing the relative importance of import and export dynamics at the heart of this book. The notion is too reductive to be useful. What we can say absolutely for certain is that specificity matters. The importance of these dynamics will differ from case to case and behaviour to behaviour. To sum this up, we look at the case of Umar Farouk Abdulmutallab. On 25 December 2009, Abdulmutallab boarded Northwest Airlines Flight 253 from Amsterdam to Detroit. He ignited an incendiary device shortly before arrival in Detroit in an attempt to destroy the plane and 289 individuals on board. Fortunately, there were no fatalities or serious injuries. Abdulmutallab reportedly became very pious in his religion during his teenage years in Nigeria. He spent his free time reading the Quran and earned the nickname 'Alfa'. Over 300 internet postings under the handle 'farouk1986' were identified. Abdulmutallab spoke of love, his future ambitions, and his inner struggle between liberalism and extremism as a devout Muslim. In January 2005, Abdulmutallab confessed:

'I am in a situation where I do not have a friend. I have no one to speak to, no one to consult, no one to support me and I feel depressed and lonely. I do not know what to do and then I think this loneliness leads me to other problems…I get lonely sometimes because I have never found a true Muslim friend.'[81]

Abdulmutallab's postings display his gradual ideological changes towards more devout Islamic opinions and practices, and his views on violence and extremism, without specific mention of his own choice to follow such behaviours. However, when Abdulmutallab enrolled in mechanical engineering at University College

London in September 2005, his religious beliefs began attracting attention. Abdulmutallab became head of the campus branch of the Islamic Society in 2006, inviting controversial speakers and former Guantanamo Bay inmates to attend functions. He regularly attended prayers at London mosques monitored by the British security services. He was seen 'reaching out' to known extremists and was noted as being 'on the periphery' of various investigations. He was not, however, considered a threat by British counterintelligence.

In June 2008, Abdulmutallab graduated and was granted a multiple entry tourist visa to the United States. The following January, Abdulmutallab enrolled at the University of Wollongong, Dubai, to study a business course. In August 2009, he dropped out and travelled to Yemen, to study at the Sana's Institute for Arabic Language. At this time Abdulmutallab attempted to return to England, but his student visa request was refused. Abdulmutallab later explained that he travelled to Yemen to meet radical Imam Anwar al-Awlaki, after studying his preachings. While attending a mosque in Yemen, Abdulmutallab was introduced to 'Abu-Tarak', who was allegedly a member of Al Qaeda, and during daily discussions, they discussed various ways to attack the United States. In October 2009, Abdulmutallab travelled to the Shabwa Province and attended an Al Qaeda training camp, purportedly under the direction of al-Awlaki. In November 2009, Abdulmutallab agreed to become involved in an aerial martyrdom attack against the United States. It was also during this time that Abdulmutallab contacted his parents and hinted at his involvement in a movement. His father contacted CIA officials at the United States embassy in Nigeria, expressing concerns for his son. Abdulmutallab claimed to have met the bomb-maker, a Saudi Arabian individual, while in Yemen. The device, consisting of Pentaerythritol Tetranitrate (PEIN) and Triacetone Triperoxide (TATP), weighed approximately 200 grams. The device had no metal parts, and therefore, would not alert airport security. Detonation was to be achieved by injecting liquid acid into the PEIN and TATP at a time of choosing. The device was designed to be part of Abdulmutallab's underwear. Prior to leaving Yemen, Abdulmutallab recorded a video. The video showed Abdulmutallab at a desert training camp shooting at targets including a Jewish star, the British Union Jack flag, and the initials 'UN'.

In Abdulmutallab, we have an example of an individual who, prior to being in the UK, displayed a lot of attitudinal affinity with the jihadi cause, but little of the propensity or capability that was needed. In the UK, his initial social isolation in a new country led to his developing social networks in these local milieus. The social networks led to new ties in other countries and strong links with those engaged in violence. These links offered him the direction and capability for violence. All of this occurred as a chain of behaviours. The importance of foreign or domestic influences ebbed and waned depending upon what phase of the sequence he was in. Ultimately, each acted as a force multiplier making the next stage more likely. As we noted at the outset of this chapter, *there is no simple answer to the issue and the ratio of whether a behaviour or event was primarily influenced by foreign or domestic sources is likely to vary from case to case*. The Abdulmutallab case demonstrates that it is also likely to vary within a single case.

While the above may hold true for most, if not all, of the countries examined in this book, there are some features of the United Kingdom's experience that may hold it as an outlier in some respects. Its experience as a colonial power and home to multiple iterations of immigration flow into the country immediately sets it apart. More specifically related to terrorism, however, is the fact that it is widely acknowledged that the United Kingdom's engagement in Iraq elevated the terror threat domestically. A former head of MI5 is on record as stating that these actions 'undoubtedly increased' the terror threat and that within a year of the invasion, MI5 was 'swamped' with investigative leads. She continued: 'What Iraq did was produce fresh impetus on people prepared to engage in terrorism ... The Iraq war heightened the extremist view that the West was trying to bring down Islam. We gave bin Laden his jihad.'[82]

Notes

1. Harvey Gordon, 'The suicide bomber: Is it a psychiatric problem?' *Psychiatric Bulletin*, 26, no. 8 (2002): 285–7.
2. David Lester, Bijou Yang and Mark Lindsay, 'Suicide bombers: Are psychological profiles possible?' *Studies in Conflict and Terrorism*, 27, no. 4 (2004): 283–95.
3. Scott Atran, 'Genesis of suicide terrorism', *Social Science Review*, 299 (2003): 1534–9.
4. Ariel Merari, *Driven to death: Psychological and social aspects of suicide terrorism* (Oxford: Oxford University Press, 2010).
5. Jean-Paul Azam, 'Suicide bombing as inter-generational investment', *Public Choice*, 122, no. 1 (2005): 177–98.
6. John Rosenberger, 'Discerning the behavior of the suicide bomber: The role of vengeance', *Journal of Religion and Health*, 42, no. 1 (2003): 13–20.
7. Arie W. Kruglanski, Xiaoyan Chen, Mark Dechesne, Shira Fishman and Edward Orehek, 'Fully committed: Suicide bombers' motivation and quest for personal significance', *Political Psychology*, 30, no. 3 (2009): 331–57.
8. Daniel Pipes, 'Despair and hopelessness do not motivate suicide bombers', in Lauri S. Friedman (ed.), *What Motivates Suicide Bombers?* (Michigan: Greenhaven Press, 2005), pp. 19–23.
9. Avishai Margalit, 'The suicide bombers', *The New York Review of Books*, 50, no. 1 (2003).
10. Ilene R. Prusher, 'Despair and hopelessness motivate suicide bombers', in Lauri S. Friedman (ed.), *What Motivates Suicide Bombers?* (Michigan: Greenhaven Press, 2005), pp. 24–33.
11. Robert A. Pape, *Dying to Win: The Strategic Logic of Suicide Terrorism* (New York: Random House publishers, 2005).
12. Gal Luft, 'The Palestinian H-Bomb', *Foreign Affairs*, 81, no. 4 (2002): 2.
13. Mohammed M. Hafez, *Suicide Bombers in Iraq: The Strategy and Ideology of Martyrdom* (Washington: United States Institute of Peace Press, 2007).
14. Bruce Hoffman and Gordon H. McCormick, 'Terrorism, signalling and suicide attack', *Studies in Conflict and Terrorism*, 27, no. 2 (2004): 243–81.
15. Mia Bloom, *Dying to Kill: The Allure of Suicide Terror* (New York: Columbia University Press, 2005).
16. Alberto Abadie, 'Poverty, political freedom and the roots of terrorism', *American Economic Review*, 96, no. 2 (2004): 50–6.
17. Sara Jackson Wade and Dan Reiter, 'Does democracy matter? Regime type and suicide terrorism', *Journal of Conflict Resolution*, 51, no. 2 (2007): 329–48.
18. Bloom, *Dying to Kill: The Allure of Suicide Terror*.

19. Simon Haddad, 'A comparative study of Lebanese and Palestinian perceptions of suicide bombings: The role of militant Islam and socio-economic status', *International Journal of Comparative Sociology*, 45, no. 5 (2004): 337–63.
20. Mohammed M. Hafez, 'Rationality, culture, and structure in the making of suicide bombers: A preliminary theoretical synthesis and illustrative case study', *Studies in Conflict and Terrorism*, 29, no. 2 (2006): 165–85.
21. Raffaello Pantucci, *'We Love Death as You Love Life': Britain's Suburban Terrorists* (Oxford: Oxford University Press, 2015), p. 46.
22. Ibid.
23. Shiraz Maher, *Salafi-Jihadism: The History of an Idea* (Oxford: Oxford University Press, 2017).
24. Pantucci, *'We Love Death as You Love Life': Britain's Suburban Terrorist*, p. 250.
25. Raffaello Pantucci, 'The Tottenham Ayatollah and the hook-handed cleric: An examination of all their jihadi children', *Studies in Conflict & Terrorism*, 33, no. 3 (2010): 226–45.
26. Ibid., p. 227.
27. Associated Press, 'Radical group threatens more suicide commandos during Ramadan', 5 February 1995.
28. Ibid.
29. Pantucci, *'We Love Death as You Love Life': Britain's Suburban Terrorists*, p. 133.
30. Ibid., p. 91.
31. Zeyno Baran, *Hizb ut-Tahrir: Islam's Political Insurgency* (Nixon Center, 2004).
32. John Horton, 'Hizb-ut Tahrir: nihilism or realism?' *Journal of Middle Eastern Geopolitics*, 23 (2006): 74.
33. ICT, 'The mode of operation of Hizb ut Tahrir in an open society', The International Institute for Counter-Terrorism, 2004. Available at https://www.ict.org.il/Article/135/The%20Mode%20of%20Operation%20of%20Hizb%20ut%20Tahrir%20in%20an%20Open%20Society#gsc.tab=0 (accessed 21 January 2010).
34. Mohamed Nawab Mohamed Osman, 'The transnational network of Hizbut Tahrir Indonesia', *South East Asia Research*, 18, no. 4 (2010): 735–55.
35. Maher, *Salafi-Jihadism: The History of an Idea*, p. 24.
36. Pantucci, *'We Love Death as You Love Life': Britain's Suburban Terrorists*, p. 116.
37. ICT, 'The mode of operation of Hizb ut Tahrir in an open society', pp. 3–4.
38. Catherine Zara Raymond, 'Al Muhajiroun and Islam4UK: The group behind the ban', International Centre for the Study of Radicalization and Political Violence, London, 2010, pp. 18–19.
39. Michael Kenney, John Horgan, Cale Horne, Peter Vining, Kathleen M. Carley, Michael W. Bigrigg, Mia Bloom and Kurt Braddock, 'Organizational adaptation in an activist network: Social networks, leadership, and change in al-Muhajiroun', *Applied Ergonomics*, 44, no. 5 (2013): 739–47.
40. Raymond, 'Al Muhajiroun and Islam4UK: The group behind the ban', p. 7.
41. Ibid.
42. Ibid., p. 11.
43. L. Harding, 'New terror laws: Muslims who find a haven in London', *The Guardian*, 26 August 1998.
44. John Horgan, *Walking Away from Terrorism: Accounts of Disengagement from Radical and Extremist Movements* (London, 2009).
45. Raymond, 'Al Muhajiroun and Islam4UK: The group behind the ban', p. 7.
46. Stuart Croft, 'British Jihadis and the British War on terror', *Defence Studies*, 7, no. 3 (2007): 317–37.
47. Kenney et al., 'Organizational adaptation in an activist network'

48 Ibid., p. 743.
49 Ibid.
50 Ibid.
51 Raymond, 'Al Muhajiroun and Islam4UK: The group behind the ban', p. 7.
52 Kenney et al., 'Organizational adaptation in an activist network', p. 743.
53 Croft, 'British Jihadis and the British War on terror', p. 321.
54 Pantucci, *'We Love Death as You Love Life': Britain's Suburban Terrorists*, p. 112.
55 Ibid., p. 113, 122.
56 Pantucci, 'The Tottenham Ayatollah and the hook-handed cleric', p. 229.
57 Pantucci, *'We Love Death as You Love Life': Britain's Suburban Terrorists*, pp. 113–14.
58 Ibid., p. 117.
59 Sean O'Neill and Daniel McGrory, *The Suicide Factory: Abu Hamza and the Finsbury Park Mosque* (HarperCollins UK, 2006).
60 Pantucci, *'We Love Death as You Love Life': Britain's Suburban Terrorists*, p. 125.
61 D. Dronfield, 'Suicide attacks were self-defence – Outspoken cleric', *Press Association*, 14 September 2001.
62 Pantucci, *'We Love Death as You Love Life': Britain's Suburban Terrorists*, p. 127.
63 Ibid., p. 129.
64 Kamaldeep Bhui, Nasir Warfa and Edgar Jones, 'Is violent radicalization associated with poverty, migration, poor self-reported health and common mental disorders?' *PloS One*, 9, no. 3 (2014): e90718.
65 Syed Farez Kazim, Zarmeneh Aly, Haider Khan Bangash, Bhisham Pardeep Harchandani, Affan Bin Irfan, Syed Muhammad Javed, Rana Khalil-ur-Rehman, Haider Naqvi and Murad Moosa Khan, 'Attitudes towards suicide bombing in Pakistan', *Crisis*, 29, no. 2 (2008): 81–5.
66 Haddad, 'A comparative study of Lebanese and Palestinian perceptions of suicide bombings'.
67 Program on International Policy Attitudes, 2018. Available at http://www.pipa.org/.
68 Sophia Moskalenko and Clark McCauley, 'Measuring political mobilization: The distinction between activism and radicalism', *Terrorism and Political Violence*, 21, no. 2 (2009): 239–60.
69 Croft, 'British Jihadis and the British War on terror', p. 321.
70 Raymond, 'Al Muhajiroun and Islam4UK: The group behind the ban', p. 15.
71 House of Commons, Report of the official account of the bombings in London on 7 July 2005 (London, 2006).
72 E. Vuilliamy, 'When I heard where the bombers were from I felt sick', *The Guardian*, 24 June 2006.
73 Croft, 'British Jihadis and the British War on terror', p. 328.
74 Pantucci, *'We Love Death as You Love Life': Britain's Suburban Terrorists*, p. 94.
75 Ibid., pp. 95–7.
76 Ibid., p. 107.
77 Ibid., p. 125.
78 Ibid., p. 157.
79 Ibid., p. 86.
80 Ibid., p. 100.
81 Cited in Paul Gill, *Lone-Actor Terrorists: A Behavioural Analysis* (London, 2015), p. 70.
82 BBC News, 'Iraq inquiry: Ex-MI5 boss says war raised terror threat', 20 July 2010. Available at https://www.bbc.co.uk/news/uk-politics-10693001.

CONFRONTING ORIENTALISM, COLONIALISM AND DETERMINISM

DE-CONSTRUCTING CONTEMPORARY FRENCH JIHADISM

Joseph Downing

Introduction

In March 2012 Mohammed Merah went on a killing spree in Toulouse and Montauban. Merah, born in Toulouse to Algerian parents, was from a dysfunctional and xenophobic family.[1] While his actions were extremely serious, which he nominally claimed under the banner of an Islamist movement, no one could have surmised that this would be the beginning of a wave of spectacularly gruesome, effective, often well organized but mainly unrelated terror attacks that would rapidly propel France from a calm, if not wholly unproblematic, part of the fringe of global jihad to the most restive periphery in Europe. While touched by Islamist unrest in Algeria in the 1990s and Al Qaeda activity in the 2000s, France had remained mostly untouched by mass-casualty attacks while having Europe's largest Muslim population.[2] However, culminating in the Charlie Hebdo, 13 November 2015 Paris attacks, and the Bastille Day Nice attack, the country with the continent's largest Muslim population was thrust under the spotlight.[3] Politicians, scholars and policy makers alike suddenly found themselves in the spotlight where answers were demanded about a large range of themes relating to jihadism touching French soil. These questions centred on two key questions, one causal, and one institutional. First, there has been a huge amount of attention lavished on ascertaining causal links as to exactly how and why these attacks could take place, regardless of their being in the main unrelated. As such, the hunt quickly began for the 'magic formula' for what turns a normal French citizen of Muslim origin or confession into someone who suddenly wants to commit acts of mass murder.

This causal question unfortunately opened up a Pandora's box of answers that seek to create Franco-centric grand theories for French jihadism. These draw heavily on latent orientalism and intellectual ineptitude that tried to explain a fringe social phenomenon with recourse to far wider social and historical forces.[4] France here is not alone – it shares not only general social and historical problems with other European states with large post-migration Muslim populations, but also the same problematic approaches to discussing Islamist terrorism that often situates terror perpetuated by someone who acts under an Islamist banner as part of the wider 'clash of civilizations'[5] between an aggressive Islam and a secular, liberal Europe. Thus, France's colonial skeletons were brought out of the closet and dusted off and given causal primacy as the reason for France's recent jihad phenomenon.[6] Yes, France shares issues around a bloody colonial history in the Islamic world and contemporary intervention in the region with European countries like the UK. Both the UK and France were party to the Sykes-Picot agreement, which laid the foundations of the current Israel–Palestine conflict. Additionally, France fought a bloody war against independence forces in Algeria, which France incorporated not as an overseas colony but as a department of metropolitan France itself, which included torture and mass killings in both urban and rural areas, facts well known and understood by French Muslims, but facts of history that are yet to be publicly acknowledged and dealt with in a broader sense. However, it remains unclear how these historical facts act to push young men and women from a range of backgrounds in France to commit themselves to jihad. For example, Hussey[7] argues that the current wave of French Muslims involved in jihadi movements is part of a 'French intifada' with roots in the anti-colonial struggle that represents a coherent, continuous and uninterrupted historical arch from the FLN's[8] mobilization in the Kasbah of Algiers to the white and black converts who took up the call to travel to Syria to fight to create a utopian caliphate. This is highly problematic scholarship, based in part on 'research' he conducts on participants outside bars in the Maghreb[9] and within this makes causal explanations that are presented as taking primacy over the meticulous scholarship on French Muslims which demonstrates that they overwhelmingly identify as French and French first, and want desperately to be part of the contemporary social incarnation of the historical colonial oppressor

The second key causal argument goes that France's recent social, economic and political failures create a black and Arab underclass, poorly educated and ripe for the picking by crafty jihadi ideologues.[10] Again, in terms of social facts, it is true that the low-skilled jobs that sucked in migrant labour after the Second World War have gone – replaced in global nodes such as London and Paris by high-skilled service jobs, and in places less connected to the global system, by nothing but unemployment and residual social welfare hand-outs. Additionally, even at the nodes of the new knowledge capitalism, such as Paris, discrimination, poor schools and social decay have shut out many French Muslims from the knowledge economy, leaving them to suffer the same fate as their compatriots in capitalist peripheries, facing lives of low wages, poor working conditions and welfare hand-outs or more lucrative employment in the highly developed, sophisticated, well-organized and hugely lucrative drugs trade. This explanation focuses on the romanticized figure of 'soldiers of Allah' pushed out of French society by economic marginalization and social discrimination.[11] This, however, has significant colonialist and paternalist overtones – while under conditions of social marginalization or economic difficulties, the rational white man seeks betterment or accepts his lot, the irrational Muslim, whether black, white or Arab takes these same conditions as a cue to commit mass murder to seek his salvation in the afterlife. This chapter seeks to rebuff these explanations, drawing heavily on the concepts supplied by critical terrorism studies (CTS) and the Copenhagen school of securitization.

Conceptual approaches to de-constructing orientalism in French security studies: Critical terrorism studies and securitization

In making an argument that the current scholarship on French jihadism is overly orientalist in its position, and overly concerned with problem-solving in providing causal explanations, a broader discussion is opened up on how the study of terrorism needs to be conducted in the contemporary era. Here, the de-constructivist approach of CTS offers particular insights into both how the processes of terrorism studies have been conducted and, importantly, how they should normatively be conducted. CTS emerged out of a well-thought-out critique of the empirical, conceptual and ontological weaknesses of conventional terrorism studies.[12] In particular, Burnett and Whyte[13] present an important summary of many of the key arguments that evolve from this agenda and highlight key concerns around issues of terror 'experts' who know little about the contexts in which they operate, have never met or researched terrorists and are closely involved with state security approaches to terror from a 'problem-solving' perspective.[14] This is an important starting point for this study in particular – one of the reasons my personal research agenda shifted towards examining the construction of terror events was in part because of constant request for comment about French terror events based on my prior expertise on Muslim communities in France as if these two extremely divergent sets of knowledge were one and the same. Indeed, Jackson's[15] observations that the emergence of the widespread term 'Islamic terrorism' owes much to the assumptions that underpinned the orientalist scholarship on Islam and the Middle East that blossomed from the nineteenth century onwards, captures well the intellectual and conceptual underpinnings of why a scholar of Muslim minorities would be quizzed about terror events.

Bringing this discussion of literature back to the analysis at hand, a key means by which CTS seeks to fight back against such intellectual follies is by adopting an overtly social constructivist stance vis-à-vis terror events.[16] An important nuance of this approach is not to negate the empirically irrefutable violence involved in terror events – as not to obfuscate the objective deaths, suffering and horror of mass killings, but, rather, as a means to understand that the meanings rendered to such events are not objective. As such, when it comes to knowledge creation about terror events, one is not dealing with ideologically neutral knowledge on an ideologically neutral subject,[17] but, rather, one is embroiled in deeply political and ideological ground and as creators of knowledge scholars need to be aware of this. This is not to say, however, that the creation of good scholarship on terror is at all a simple and straightforward task. Sageman[18] makes a very pertinent observation in this regard that academics often suffer from an information deficit about terror events where intelligence agencies do not want to share information with academics. This is, however, only part of the story of such methodological and data issues. Many terrorists die in the conduct of violence, and thus are not available for post-facto interviews about their motivations, ideological rationale or connection to transnational networks. For example, it still remains unclear how and why the individual responsible for the Nice attack, Mohamed Lahouaiej-Bouhlel became involved in jihadi terrorism as he had no previous or current affiliations with any Islamist groups nor was he on the radar of either the French or Tunisian security services. However, although there are, increasingly, biographical studies of and interviews with jihadis published in reports in France, these do not get the attention, acclaim or press coverage of the orientalist take on terrorism studies. In short, orientalism and essentialism offer simple and accessible explanations for terror, which as we will see in this chapter are founded and disproved by examining closely the evidence we have that paints a far more nuanced picture.

This is particularly problematic given the already 'securitized' status of French Muslims, which further essentialism only serves to buttress. This opens up a broader discussion, however, that requires conceptual explanation in that how security threats are constructed, which gives significant insight into why French jihadism would have been constructed in the ways that it has, for example as a product of a colonial legacy or domestic political failings. In understanding how the de-construction and nuancing of group identity is important in a security context, it is important to consult the Copenhagen school of securitization.[19] Here, security threats are not objective truths, rather they are socially constructed as such via discursive 'speech acts' that render narratives about security plausible and salient, and thus possible to be then subjected to emergency politics.[20] The Copenhagen school's key normative aim is to undo this process of 'securitization' through 'de-securitization' and de-construct security threats.[21] One of the key ways in which they prescribe this is through the de-construction of group identities to give individual faces to security threats[22] – exactly the kind of humanization of Muslim terror victims that is created through the data analysed here. This is especially important given the context in which this study situates itself where how Islam and Muslims are securitized in France has direct consequences for the ways in which jihadism is conceptualized. Importantly, prior to the recent explosion of terror attacks on French soil, French Muslims have been the subject of significant discursive construction as existential threats both to France's secular political order and to its liberal social habits. This is not important per se because it explains why French Muslims commit terror attacks as some commentators would have it[23] but it is important to understand the context out of which scholarship is produced and what dominant ideas shape the context in which Muslims are discussed. The securitization of Islam in Europe is well covered in the literature.[24] Of particular importance to this study is the observation that the securitization of Islam in Europe is present in both speech and rhetoric, specifically the link between Islam and political violence.[25] The most important place to situate a discussion of the de-securitization of Muslims in terms of the speech acts and narratives generated about their position vis-à-vis such phenomena is thus at this nexus between Muslims and political violence. France is a country where Islam has been set up as a counterpoint, and antithesis, to the liberal, democratic republican values upon which the French polity is founded.[26] Importantly, this has not been a unified process, but, rather, has taken on numerous forms across time and space, especially in the French context. As such, the position of French Muslims is consistently undercut by elite public narratives that persistently frame French Muslims as 'incomplete citizens'.[27] Discussions of these dynamics of Muslim diasporas have received attention in some very specific ways in the literature. El Hamel[28] examines the role of the politicization and mediatization of the Muslim headscarf (hijab) as one of the defining features of debates about the position of Muslims under the secular republic. Here, of particular importance is the observation, again, about the essentializing rhetoric explicit in such coverage – here, Muslims are Muslims when publicly religious, and as also highlighted by Crourcher,[29] present a problem to a secular republic and society and thus require control and regulation, often in very reactive, ad-hoc and erratic ways.[30] It is worth noting that this occurs in the face of repeated large-scale studies that demonstrate without any doubt that France is a place where the vast majority of Muslims are trying hard to fit in, rather than the commonly repeated mantra that they are intent on 'opting out' and existing, often portrayed in hostile terms, outside of society.[31] Thus, it is no surprise if these are the dominant conceptions and narratives that dictate how French Muslims are constructed, that they bleed over into the problematic theoretical explanations of the causes for French jihadism. It is to this question that this chapter now turns, in employing a CTS approach to de-construct and rebut these explanations.

A question of misplaced causality: De-constructing the grand theories of French jihad

A key tenet of CTS is to employ a de-constructivist approach to terror events and the explanations that are given for individuals becoming involved in terrorism. Here, it is thus important to question overarching 'grand theories'-type explanations that assert universal truths as causes of jihadism. This has, however, not been done with the explanations given for the recent jihadi violence in the French case. Therefore, what have emerged have been extremely Franco-centric grand theories that seek to root French jihad in both the colonial and historical legacy of France as a colonial power and in the contemporary political and social failings of the French state to both politically accommodate Islam and to socioeconomically enfranchise large parts of its Muslim population. While these explanations may seem logical and discursively coherent, as both a troubled colonial history and significant social and political problems do exist, this chapter argues that they fail the de-constructive and causal tests required by both the CTS literature and the standards of rigorous and robust social science methodologies more broadly. Such a de-construction must, importantly, be rooted in the social, religious and economic contexts of French Muslims.

Arguably one of the reasons that such grand theories have become so popular and, even to the general public, plausible is that these are often the language of both the jihadis and the broader movements like Al Qaeda or ISIS. In the opinion of such groups, it is the duty of Muslims worldwide to fight against the Western domination of the international system and the moral decadence of domestic political systems whose morality does not conform to their particular extreme world views.

Addressing the question of jihadism in France in recent years requires questioning both the extent of the problem and the explanations commonly used to explain jihadism in France. To do this we need to examine the numbers of French Muslims who are engaged in jihadi activity. This runs into a significant difficulty in France when we come to contrast the numbers of French jihadis to the size of the French Muslim population. This is because nobody, the French government included, actually can accurately say how many Muslims are in France. This is because of the specifics of the French system, where the collection of ethnic or religious statistics about the population are forbidden by law.[32] As such, the French census does not ask questions about religion or ethnicity. This means that anyone interested in the subject has to rely on estimates that are calculated via indirect forms of estimation. For example, the Pew Research Centre estimates the French Muslim population to be 5.72 million in 2016, 8.8 per cent of the population.[33] However, as mentioned, this cannot be proven or disproven by any official source, hence the number is open to all kinds of contestation and uncertainty from those on both the left and right of French politics. Interestingly, in the past decade both Azouz Begag, researcher at the CNRS, and the far-right 'National Front'[34] political party argued that a more accurate estimate of the Muslim population in France was between 15 and 20 million, that is, between 22 per cent and 30 per cent of the French population of 66.9 million.[35] Additionally, the French population is uncertain about numbers according to a poll that showed a tendency to overestimate the Muslim population at around 31 per cent of the population, so around 20.74 million Muslims.[36]

Muslims as a category in France, as in the rest of Europe, share many characteristics with ethnic categories like black and white.[37] That is to say, it is a category that can relate as much to inter-subjective, non-religious forms of identification (such as ethnic, national and/or cultural) as much, if not more, as it refers to an individual who believes in and practises a religion. Even among those who identify as Muslims and do practise the religion, there is a large variation in forms of practices and level of adherence to dogma, as well as variations between different types of folk Islam that originate in North Africa, West Africa or the Comoro Islands. Additionally, there are estimated to be between 70,000 and 110,000 converts to Islam in France from a variety of cultural, religious and socioeconomic backgrounds. Already, the complexity of this sociocultural and doctrinal patchwork should set alarm bells ringing vis-à-vis simplistic causal explanations that lack nuance.

Thus, as there is significant uncertainty with regard to the number of Muslims in general in France, there is also significant variation in the numbers of possible radical Muslims in France and also by extension the number of possible violent jihadis in France. This uncertainty is born out of reasons somewhat different from the general doubts about the Muslim population, because as CTS literature states[38] it is extremely difficult to gather data about jihadis due to the clandestine nature of their activities. Additionally, making estimates about how many violent radicals, as opposed to peaceful ultra-conservative Muslims, there might be, is even more difficult as this involves predicting violence prior to the act, thus bringing a problematic pre-crime approach to the study of terrorism, where individuals are deemed future terrorists without significant criminal evidence or charges.[39] However, these difficulties do not stop politicians or scholars from making estimates about their numbers in France. Manual Vals, former prime minister, estimates that there were 15,000 individuals being monitored in France for radicalization, yet only 1400 are currently under judicial prosecution for terror offences.[40] However, as the issues with the terminology are numerous, and Vals also does not give further details on these numbers, they mean very little. However, Samir Amghar, researcher at the University Libre de Bruxelles estimates that there are between 20,000 and 30,000 'ultra-orthodox' Muslims in France, less than 1 per cent of the practising Muslim population of France.[41] This figure of the ultra-orthodox Muslim population does not in any way imply that these 20,000–30,000 French Muslims are violent or likely to commit acts of jihad. Thus, the number of jihadis in France, even if it was put as Vals states at 15,000, is less than 1 per cent of the French Muslim population. Thus, this corroborates Khosrokhavar's[42] findings that radicalization is 'ultra-minoritiaire', that is to say, a phenomenon at the fringes.

Thus, the overarching 'grand theories' of radicalization begin to look extremely lacking. That is, methodologically explaining French jihadism using these grand theories centres on explaining statistical anomalies, less than 1 per cent of the French Muslim population become jihadis, with recourse to phenomena that affect much larger parts of the Muslim and, indeed, non-Muslim French population and this does not generate the same results of mass murder. Hussey's[43] contention that the current wave of jihadism has a coherent and cogent link with a problematic colonial past in Muslim countries thus causally fails to explain why the rest of the over 5 million Muslims are not answering the call of jihad. Additionally, Kepel's[44] argument that the current wave of jihadis has its roots in France's recent political intolerance of Islam on the left and right and its inability to deal with socioeconomic segregation is again causally naïve and has not been subjected to the de-construction asserted by CTS. In short, if these rather general and overarching social grievances are to be evaluated for their causal primacy, then surely the counterfactual question of how the explanation does not also tell us why the vast majority of Muslims affected by similar issues in France are not also involved in radical jihadi movements. For example, in an interview given to security forces after being stopped from travelling to Syria, Chérif Kouachi expressed an incoherent world vision, and expressed that he was actually thankful to be stopped and thus unable to carry out jihad.[45] Thus, the overarching, Franco-centric world view that it is a combination of political failings and historical indignities that causes individuals to take up arms fails to explain not only why some do not commit jihad but also why some actually do.

The damage done by these kinds of explanations is the result of not simply bad social science methods, which produce inaccurate causal relationships and thus poor policy responses, but they also serve to securitize French Muslims even more. If one is to take at face value the possibility that French Muslims can be turned into mass murderers through things that they have no control over, for example, colonial history or dysfunctional national politics, then it means that every French Muslim is a potential jihadi and thus should be under suspicion. This involves two key issues. First, it effectively leads to a 'pre-crime'[46] approach to be applied to French Muslims, whereby they are immediately under suspicion of being jihadis simply because of being Muslim, however nominally. This is a worrying process that was highlighted by both Amnesty International[47] and Human Rights Watch,[48] who identified France's state of emergency as focusing specifically on Muslim communities and placing individuals under house arrest or detention for sometimes nebulous connections to individuals accused of being radicals. Here, law enforcement caught up individuals in their net whose lives were disrupted and who never had a formal charge bought against them for any terror or related offences. However, the damage here is arguably also done at a broader and more discursive level within society, if we are to take the assumptions of the Copenhagen school of securitization that security threats are not objective realities but, rather, are constructed as such through discourse emanating from actors endowed with authority.[49] Here, the broader popularity and mainstreaming of these explanations thus acts in a similar way to the 'pre-crime' approach of law enforcement because it casts its explanatory net very wide and thus pulls in extremely large numbers of the French Muslim population. If we are to take a speculative guess that even 30 per cent of the French Muslim population don't agree with France's colonial past and have disagreements with the dysfunctions of French politics, exactly as many of their non-Muslim counterparts do, we are talking about 1.7 million French Muslims under suspicion for the crimes of only several thousand. This is clearly not good enough from an explanatory perspective and would struggle to gain such mainstream acceptance or credibility in many other areas of the social or natural sciences. Thus, clearly here we have prime examples of the empirical, conceptual and ontological weaknesses, and the focus on problem-solving, that the CTS literature highlights so clearly as key problems with conventional terrorism studies.[50]

Nuancing and identifying the soldier of Allah: The diversity of the French jihad

We have thus seen so far that the grand, Franco-centric theories of French jihad do little to advance our understanding of the characteristics of this phenomenon and, indeed, who these jihadis actually are, no matter how fringe a phenomenon French jihadism actually is. This is where a key feature of CTS becomes extremely important in furthering this endeavour. CTS, in addition to being de-constructivist, also aims to free itself from the problem-solving focus of traditional terrorism studies. This is a problem with the current global attempts to understand who jihadis are because of the focus on trying to present causal mechanisms for radicalization and, thus, solutions to 'radicalization'. There are many problems with this – notably problems with defining the dominant terms like 'radicalism' and 'extremism' and, perhaps more importantly, the inability of scholars to give definitive answers as to how radicalization takes place.[51] This flies in the face of the dominant assumptions of those who believe radicalization occurs due to Salafist readings of the Koran and the Sunnah[52] or colonial history and ongoing Western domination of the third world.[53] Importantly, it is not simply that jihadism in France is the result of an overspill from the Algerian Civil War in the 1990s – while some trace its lineage back to this conflict and the resulting upheaval, others do not.[54] Indeed, this is also a key problem with the grand theories – in focusing on politics or history they attempt to provide explanations that affect all jihadis but also, importantly, for which there are, at least, world solutions that could, so the argument goes, be implemented to solve the jihadi problem. For example, if only France would deal with its colonial past and stop intervening in the Muslim world, and fix its dysfunctional domestic politics, then jihadism would surely evaporate.

Rather, it seems that on the examination of the evidence available, jihadism in France as a fringe social movement is not to do with Islam per se but shares much more in common with other forms of radicalizations and political violence like those of the far right and ultra-nationalists.[55] Thus, this ties up with broader observations that the conceptual distinction between 'religious' terrorism and other forms of terror and violence is difficult to sustain as they share so many commonalities in terms of the lack of previous religious practice or knowledge, and the perplexing diversity of motivations and social backgrounds of those committing violence.[56] As such, when delving into exactly who French jihadis are, it is clear that the stunning variation in socioeconomic backgrounds, previous activities and even paths towards radicalization paints a far more complex and nuanced picture. Thus, freeing ourselves from this problem-solving focus enables an understanding of this diversity and thus of the phenomena more broadly. What stands out from studies that seek to understand the backgrounds and motivations of French jihadis is the diversity of their socioeconomic backgrounds, with many coming from middle-class backgrounds.[57] What is also striking is the diversity of opinions and motivations that emerge from the few first-hand accounts of French jihadis that emerge in specific studies.[58] The strength of this particular account comes from its comparative design that examines jihadis in tandem with those in France drawn to secular, nationalist causes such as Basque and Corsican separatism. This research design thus does a lot to escape the essentialist and particularist assumptions about jihadism being a religious backlash against a secular society. Indeed, these motivations do emerge in some of the testimonials of the jihadis themselves, albeit in somewhat paradoxical and unexpected ways. Both Paul and Abdel are cited as turning to radicalism after their early years in which they experienced neither discrimination nor poverty, and neither were they raised in particularly religious households – Paul is a convert to Islam and Abdel is the child of non-practising Muslim parents.[59] In fact, Abdel went as far as to enrol in a cinema school.

This points to a broader trend that confounds many of the assumptions about the securitization of Islam in France that overtly religious and practising Muslims are an existential threat to society as many of those involved in jihadi activity discover religion in their late teens or early twenties in a very de-contextualized and diffuse way that also does not add credence to the idea that there is a problem with French mosques producing radicalization. Rather, these processes are very much individualized and thus present significant difficulties to those who seek to apply the 'problem-solving' approach to radicalization and jihadism that seeks early warning systems for its detection and prevention, whether these are religious organizations or intelligence and security services who seek to anticipate and contain jihadis. Thus, there is no 'silver bullet' for the issues of radicalization nor how those radicalized then go on to commit violence. However, this does not mean that contextual factors are irrelevant to a discussion of recent French jihadism. But they are not the causal factors of jihad; rather, they are contexts that lend themselves to the occurrence of certain kinds of violence. It is to making this argument that the final section of this chapter turns in examining the institutional and banal contexts of insecurity that have to take such deadly and efficient turns.

Enabling jihad to be so effective in France: Institutional and banal security problems

Given their essentialist and orientalist foundations, the theories of French jihad that see it as something that is the result of abstract and immediate historical and political grievances fail to examine the broader social and institutional context in which jihadism sits. This is not surprising conceptually, as discussing the less romantic security failings affecting France do little to buttress a grand 'clash of civilizations' narrative but, rather, bring the discussion back to more worldly features of the security landscape. However, even when such contextual factors are brought into the picture their causal roles are significantly over-egged. Senni[60] in an opinion piece makes the case that it is the lack of social mobility present in the suburbs that is at fault as the key 'push' factor towards jihadism. It is impossible, however, to address these questions of banal security problems without discussing the vectors of broader insecurity so often brought into discussions about terror in France – the poor suburbs of French cities, the *banlieues*. Much has been written on the daily grind of poor housing, poor education and high crime in these areas of French cities over the past three decades, much of it very good sociological work providing nuanced accounts of the ethnically and socially diverse inhabitants of these areas, fighting dominant stereotypes that these areas are populated by threatening, tracksuit-wearing, drug- dealing young men.[61] Indeed, the first wave of 'securitization' directed at post-migration communities in France referenced the class and race differential between these individuals and French society and did not see religious differences as such as a key 'problem'. However, around the early 2010s, scholarship began to take a worrying orientalist turn (perhaps the most well known is Kepel's 2012 *Banlieue de la République*[62]) and began to put forward a threatening assessment of an 'Islam' that was gradually dominating and taking over the politics and social relations of these areas. This has reached a worrying crescendo in light of recent attacks in France, with these areas becoming widely labelled in the press as the heartlands from which jihadis rise and attack the French state.[63]

However, Zappi in Le Monde[64] is correct to question these narratives, arguing that the jihadi has become the new 'scarecrow' of the suburbs. Thus, it is not pursuing the economic and social problems of the suburbs that causes jihadism – as we have already seen that the backgrounds of those who have sought to depart France to fight in Syria and Iraq are staggeringly diverse socioeconomic backgrounds that show no clear route back to residency in the suburbs. Indeed, the Nice attacker Mohamed Lahouaiej-Bouhlel had never lived in a suburban housing estate and one of the Kouachi brothers that carried out the Charlie Hebdo attacks, Chérif, was raised in a children's home far outside of Paris. A 2014 report also cited that 67 per cent of French jihadis have come from middle-class backgrounds, and only 16 per cent come from deprived backgrounds.[65] Therefore, the causal link between poor areas of French cities as repositories for radicalizations and jihadism clearly does not stand up to closer scrutiny.

However, this does not mean that the more 'banal' security issues neglected by the French state are not important in facilitating the occurrence of terror attacks. An aspect of where the suburbs do come into play is their ability to act as vectors of general insecurity that affect the broader security landscape in France. This becomes extremely important when examining where the arms used in terror attacks came from, and also how and why they came to be found in France and what this demonstrates about the banal security failings of the French state. Here, journalists have done important work in tracking where the arms came from – both the arms used in the Charlie Hebdo attack and those used in the Paris attacks came from the former Yugoslavia, and were brought into France via the firearms 'black market'.[66]

However, this black market does not exist to supply the tiny number of jihadis in France seeking heavy weapons. Rather, owing to the mutations in the French drugs trade, these heavy weapons have become common currency in all kinds of crime in France, something that the French state has not kept pace with. Also, it is the new, and largely unchecked 'narco-banditisme'[67] that not only supplies France's cannabis,[68] but is also a significant social phenomenon that provides employment, belonging and one of the few avenues for any kind of social mobility to working class young men in the suburbs. This is not, however, a strictly Muslim or North African controlled trade, as can be seen by reports from Marseille that demonstrate the diversity of warring clans who, alongside North Africans, are gypsy and black groups.[69] These heavy arms are used both as weapons of enforcement in regular 'score settling' killings[70] and as weapons of choice in armed robberies.[71] Thus, the banality of the use of such weapons, for example in the robbery of a jewellery store in otherwise calm and touristic Saint Tropez,[72] demonstrates these banal security failings and that if those robbing small businesses can gain access to, and use, such dangerous weapons, it does not require a jihadi mastermind to gain access to the same. Thus, this secular failing to get a grip on the illegal trade in military weapons has nothing to do with colonial legacies, nor with the specifics of Islam or Salafism as violent ideological movements.

Similar arguments about secular failings enabling jihadism to be devastatingly effective in France can also be seen in the failings of the central French intelligence services. Thus, in addition to banal security problems, France also has problems institutionally. The institutional context in France has rightly come under significant scrutiny in the past several years. It is important to begin by saying that security forces, including those in France, cannot stop all terror attacks.[73] However, this also does not mean that France's intelligence landscape has not contributed to the ability of jihadis to operate in France and carry out such complex attacks. In the wake of the recent upsurge in jihadi attacks, France has had to review its intelligence services with a view to improving their effectiveness. This has thrown up some significant failings that demonstrate that by being ineffective, the intelligence services have indirectly contributed to the ability of jihadis to carry out such deadly attacks in France by consistently slipping through the law enforcement net. These failings are numerous and cannot be narrowed down simply either to personnel failings to share intelligence nor to structural, institutional issues but, rather, are a combination of both. Key, however, is a bureaucratic atrophy that stifles dynamism, cooperation and effectiveness.[74] Chrisafis[75] cites a report commissioned by a parliamentary committee investigation into intelligence issues after the Paris attacks that finds a 'global failure' of the country's intelligence services. France has six intelligence services who report to different ministries.[76] This provides a 'Balkanised' institutional context where the duplication of roles and separation of services into different branches hampers co-working and breeds the kind of institutional mistrust that is hardly ideal when seeking to thwart internal security threats. Indeed, many of the attacks involved in recent French terror episodes were known to intelligence services but lapses in communication prevented their being accurately tracked.[77]

Some of these issues can be seen at the most basic level with the monitoring system used in France for internal security threats, the 'fiche S'. The S-list (Fiche S, 'atteinte a la surete de l'etat) is part of a system of categories in which individuals who are deemed wanted by the authorities are placed. Created in 1969, the entire system of lists has contained over 400,000 names in its history, including organized crime figures, escapees from prison and political and social activists including anarchists and ecologists, in addition to terror subjects.[78] As such the list contains twenty-one categories, which correspond to the reasons that the individuals are placed on the list.[79] The 'S' section, which refers to those deemed a specific security danger to the state, has sixteen subsections detailing why individuals have come to the attention of the authorities, with S14 corresponding to those returning from Iraq and Syria.[80] His or her being placed on this list, however, does not come with automatic obligations for the law and order authorities to watch or detail a particular individual. Thus this is clearly not a user-friendly system, with individuals of different threat levels placed in the same category, without any specific obligations placed upon law enforcement to monitor them. In an attempt to answer some of these problems, Macron's most recent attempt at improving France's security landscape has involved proposing the creation of a central anti-terrorist 'task force'.[81] He proposed the creation of a new central authority dedicated solely to the investigation and prevention of terrorism that reports directly to the president and seeks to unify the fight against terror. Whether or not this just further reproduces the duplications and bureaucratism of the existing system remains to be seen.

Conclusion

This chapter set out to dispel the causal myths about jihadism so commonly prevalent in France. Using the de-constructivist tools of CTS it has been argued that both deterministic explanations relying on France's colonial history and structural arguments about jihadism being a function of France's dysfunctional domestic politics do not hold water. Thus the de-construction of the empirical and ontological failings of the current Franco-centric 'grand theories' of French jihadism has shown that these theories commit two key empirical and conceptual errors. First, they essentialize and homogenize the French Muslim population, which is actually extremely diverse socially, culturally and doctrinally. This is turn leads to essentialist and paternalistic assumptions about French Muslims that smack of colonialism. Second, the grand theories seek to root current French jihadism in extremely broad and far-reaching social phenomena that affect huge numbers of French citizens, both Muslim and non-Muslim, without acknowledging that jihadism remains an anomaly. Here, grand theories do little to explain such a fringe phenomenon. Thus, these explanations do little to aid in the understanding of the field of French jihadism. Indeed, not only is the current field notably poor from an explanatory perspective, but the conceptual rationale employed also actually serves to further securitize the French Muslim population, already one of the most securitized in Europe.[82] This is because arguing that broad social forces that affect much larger communities are the root cause of politically motivated mass murder inadvertently makes every socially marginalized Muslim a potential terrorist, waiting for a cue to self-radicalize and commit acts of violence.

Indeed, the second key argument of this chapter adds to the critique of these theories because when one examines the remarkable diversity of French jihadis it becomes clear that they come from a range of backgrounds, many of which are not disadvantaged nor marginalized. The emphasis of CTS literature on moving away from the obsession of problem-solving in traditional terrorism studies is the conceptual bedrock of this analysis because it enables the nuancing of exactly who the jihadi is and being able to argue that the road to jihadism is extremely diverse, to the point of requiring an individual approach to understanding how and why each individual chooses to become involved in such movements. This presents significant problems for those who still seek to provide 'silver bullet' theories of frameworks for identifying and dealing with jihadism across both Europe and the broader world because actually examining the biographies of jihadis demonstrates that no single factor will provide such a solution.

Finally, this chapter also seeks to outline the more general features of the security landscape that contribute to the operation of French jihadism and its being so deadly and effective. Institutionally, the French state was overly complex and bureaucratic in its approach to monitoring a range of terror threats, which enabled the networks involved, transnational in nature as they were, to plan and carry out attacks on French soil. Additionally, the French state has an extremely poor record in dealing with banal security concerns and has thus overlooked the proliferation of heavy grade military weapons onto the streets of French cities through organized crime networks.

Notes

1 The children of the Merah family were regularly battered by their father, and Mohamed's brother and sister were both anti-Semitic Islamist radicals. This is covered in detail in Mohamed's brother's book: Abdelghani Merah and Mohamed Sifaoui, *mon frère ce terroriste: un homme dénonce l'islamisme* (Édition Calmann-lévy, 2012).
2 Conrad Hacket, '5 facts about the Muslim population in Europe', 2017. [online] http://www.pewresearch.org/fact-tank/2017/11/29/5-facts-about-the-muslim-population-in-europe/ (accessed 5 January 2018).
3 Laurence Bindner, 'The jihadists' grievance narratives against France', *The International Centre for Counter-Terrorism – The Hague*, 8, no. 7 (2018): 1–24.
4 See inter alia Andrew Hussy, *The French Intifada: The Long War between France and Its Arabs* (New York: Farrar, Straus and Giroux, 2014); Giles Kepel and Antoine Jardin, *Terreur dans l'hexagone* (Paris: Editions Gallimard, 2015); Giles Kepel, *Terror in France: The Rise of Jihad in the West* (Princeton: Princeton University Press, 2017); and François Burgot, *Comprendre L'islam politique* (Paris: La découverte, 2016).
5 Samuel Huntingdon, 'The clash of civilizations?' *Foreign Affairs*, 72, no. 3 (1993): 22–49.
6 Hussy, *The French intifada* and Burgot, *Comprendre L'islam politique*.
7 Hussy, *The French intifada*.
8 The Front de Libération National was the main anti-colonial, pro-independence organization that fought French rule in Algeria prior to its independence in 1962.
9 On pages 349 and 350 Hussey discusses at length a conversation with a Tunisian called Omar outside 'the bars and semi-brothels in rue Ibn Kadloun and rue Oum Khaltoum' who while not identifying as a Salafist is quoted as saying 'I can't get to France. There's nothing else here now. Why not fight for God?' This kind of assertion does not question radicalization nor account for why a large number of those in Tunisia who left to fight in Iraq and Syria were actually very well educated and socially mobile.
10 Kepel and Jardin, *Terreur dans l'hexagone* and Kepel, *Terror in France*.
11 Kepel, *Terror in France*.
12 Richard Jackson, 'The core commitments of critical terrorism studies', *European Political Science*, 6 (2007): 244. https://doi.org/10.1057/palgrave.eps.2210141.Jeroen

Gunning, 'A case for critical terrorism studies?' *Government and Opposition*, 42, no. 3 (2007): 363-93; Lee Jarvis, 'The spaces and faces of critical terrorism studies', *Security Dialogue*, 40, no. 1 (2009).
13 Jonny Burnett and Dave Whyte, 'Embedded expertise and the new terrorism', *Journal for Crime, Conflict and the Media*, 1, no. 4 (2005): 1-18.
14 Jackson, 'The core commitments of critical terrorism studies'.
15 Ibid.
16 Ibid., Gunning, 'A case for critical terrorism studies?' and Jarvis, 'The spaces and faces of critical terrorism studies'.
17 Burnett and Whyte, 'Embedded expertise and the new terrorism'.
18 Marc Sageman, 'The stagnation in terrorism research', *Terrorism and Political Violence*, 26 (2014): 565-80.
19 Jeff Huysmans, 'The question of the limit: Desecuritisation and the aesthetics of horror in political realism', *Millenium Journal of International Studies*, 27 (1998): 569-89; Barry Buzan, Ole Weaver and Jaap de Wilde, *Security: A New Framework for Analysis* (London: Lynne Reinner, 1998); and Paul Roe, 'Securitisation and minority rights: Conditions of de-securitisation', *Security Dialogue*, 35, no. 3 (2004): 279-92.
20 Michael C. Williams, 'Words, images, enemies: Securitisation and international politics', *International Studies Quarterly*, 47 (2003): 511-31.
21 Huysmans, 'The question of the limit'; Roe, 'Securitisation and minority rights', and Ken Booth, *Theory of World Security* (Cambridge: Cambridge University Press, 2007).
22 Bezen Coskun, *Analysing Desecuritisation: The Case of the Israeli-Palestinian Peace Education and Water Management* (Cambridge: Cambridge University Press, 2011); Lene Hansen, 'Theorizing the image for security studies: Visual securitisation and the Muhammad cartoon crisis', *European Journal of International Relations*, 17, no. 1 (2011); and Bahar Rumelili, 'Identity and desecuritisation: The pitfalls of conflating ontological and physical security', *Journal of International Realtions and Development*, 18 (2013): 52-74.
23 Inter alia Andrew Hussey, *The French Intifada: The Long War between France and Its Arabs* (New York: Farrar, Straus and Giroux, 2014), Kepel and Jardin, *Terreur dans l'hexagone*, François Burget, *Comprendre L'islam politique* (Paris: La découverte, 2016) and Kepel, *Terror in France*.
24 Jocelyne Cesari, 'The securitisation of Islam in Europe', *CEPS*, 15 (2009) [online]. Available at: http://aei.pitt.edu/10763/1/1826.pdf (accessed 06 March 2017), Jocelyne Cesari, 'European conundrum: Integration of Muslims or securitisation of Islam?' *World Review*, 2 December 2013 [online]. Available at https://berkleycenter.georgetown.edu/essays/european-conundrum-integration-of-muslims-or-securitisation-of-islam (accessed 12 April 2017); Luca Mavelli, 'Between normalisation and exception: The securitisation of Islam and the construction of the secular subject', *Millennium: Journal of International Studies*, 41, no. 2 (2013); Joseph Downing, Jennifer Jackson-Preece and Maria Werdine-Norris, 'The security threat posed by "outsiders" is becoming a central theme of French politics in the aftermath of Charlie Hebdo', EuroppBlog, 15 April 2015 [online]. Available at http://blogs.lse.ac.uk/europpblog/2015/04/15/the-security-threat-posed-by-outsiders-is-becoming-a-central-theme-of-french-politics-in-the-aftermath-of-charlie-hebdo/ (accessed 6 March 2017); and Clara Eroukhmanoff, 'The remote securitisation of Islam in the US post-9/11: Euphemisation, metaphors and the "logic of expected consequences" in counter-radicalisation discourse', *Critical Studies on Terrorism*, 8, no. 2 (2015): 246-65.

25 Cesari, 'European conundrum'; Downing, Jackson-Preece and Werdine-Norris, 'The security threat posed by "outsiders"'; and Eroukhmanoff, 'The remote securitisation of Islam in the US post-9/11'.
26 Cesari, 'The securitisation of Islam in Europe'.
27 Jennifer Fredette, *Muslims in France – Discourse, Public Identity, and the Politics of Citizenship* (Philadelphia: Temple University Press, 2014).
28 Chouki El Hamel, 'Muslim Diaspora in Western Europe: The Islamic Headscarf (Hijab), the media and Muslims' integration in France', *Citizenship Studies*, 6, no. 3 (2002): 293–308.
29 Stephen M. Croucher, 'French-Muslims and the Hijab: An analysis of identity and the Islamic veil in France', *Journal of Intercultural Communication Research*, 37, no. 3 (2008): 199–213.
30 Michael E. Samers, 'Disapora unbound: Muslim identity and the erratic regulation of Islam in France', *Population, Space and Place*, 9, no. 4 (2003): 351–64.
31 Stéphanie Giry, 'France and its Muslims', *Foreign Affairs*, 85, no. 5 (2006): 87–104.
32 Alec Hargreaves, *Multi-ethnic France: Immigration, Politics, Culture, and Society*, 2nd edn (London: Routledge, 2007).
33 Hacket, '5 facts about the Muslim population in Europe'.
34 The far-right French political party the 'Rassemblement national' was known as the *Front national* until 2018.
35 Azouz Begag, 'Arithmétique migratoire, Azouz Begag: Il y a 15 à 20 millions de musulmanes en France' [online]. Available at https://www.dailymotion.com/video/xiwsnc (accessed 5 January 2018), and E. Jacob, 'La population musulmane largement surestimée en France' [online]. Available at http://www.lefigaro.fr/actualite-france/2016/12/14/01016-20161214ARTFIG00214-la-population-musulmane-largement-surestimee-en-france.php (accessed 5 January 2018).
36 Jacob, 'La population musulmane largement surestimée en France'.
37 Olivier Roy, *L'Islam mondialisé* (Paris: Éditions du Seuil, 2004).
38 Sageman, 'The stagnation in terrorism research'.
39 Jude McCulloch and Sharon Pickering, 'Pre-crime and counter-terrorism: Imagining future crime in the "war on terror"', *The British Journal of Criminology*, 49, no. 5 (2009): 628–45.
40 France 24, 'Des attentats déjoués "tous les jours" en France et 15,000 personnes radicalisées', 2016 [online]. Available at http://www.france24.com/fr/20160911-terrorisme-france-attentats-dejoues-tous-jours-15000-personnes-radicalisees-valls (accessed 6 January 2017).
41 Jean Lois Dell'Oro, 'Combien y a-t-il de djihadistes en France et quells sont leurs profiles?' 2015 [online]. Available at https://www.challenges.fr/france/combien-y-a-t-il-de-djihadistes-en-france-et-quels-sont-leurs-profils_45504 (accessed 6 January 2018).
42 Farhad Khosrokhavar, *La radicalisation* (Paris: éditions de la Maison des sciences de l'homme, 2014).
43 Hussey, *The French Intifada*.
44 Kepel, *Terror in France*.
45 Angelique Chrisafis, 'Charlie Hebdo attackers: Born, raised and radicalised in Paris', 2015 [online]. Available at https://www.theguardian.com/world/2015/jan/12/-sp-charlie-hebdo-attackers-kids-france-radicalised-paris (accessed 6 January 2018).
46 McCulloch and Pickering, 'Pre-crime and counter-terrorism'.
47 Amnesty International, 'Upturned lives: The disproportionate impact of France's state of emergency', 2016 [online]. Available at https://www.amnesty.org/en/documents/eur21/3364/2016/en/ (accessed 30 December 2017).

48 Human Rights Watch, 'Abuses under the state of emergency', 2016 [online]. Available at https://www.hrw.org/news/2016/02/03/france-abuses-under-state-emergency (accessed 30 December 2017).
49 Buzan, Weaver and de Wilde, *Security* and Huysmans, 'The question of the limit'.
50 R. Jackson, 'Security, democracy and the rhetoric of counter-terrorism', *Democracy and Security*, 1, no. 2 (2005): 147. J. Gunning, 'A case for critical terrorism studies?' *Government and Opposition*, 42, no. 3 (2007): 363–93. doi:10.111 1/j.1477-7053.2007.00228 and Jarvis, 'The spaces and faces of critical terrorism studies'.
51 Khosrokhavar, *La radicalisation* and Alex P. Schmid, 'Radicalisation, de-radicalisation, counter-radicalisation: A conceptual discussion and literature review', ICCT Research Paper, 2013 [online]. Available at https://s3.amazonaws.com/academia.edu.documen ts/31064974/ICCT-Schmid-Radicalisation-De-Radicalisation-Counter-Radicalisa tion-March-2013.pdf?AWSAccessKeyId=AKIAIWOWYYGZ2Y53UL3A&Expires=1 514896672&Signature=5q%2BiYm%2BYT4f%2FvYIr0pkqohXDTnA%3D&response -content-disposition=inline%3B%20filename%3DAlex_P._Schmid._Radicalisation_ De-Radica.pdf (accessed 2 January 2018).
52 Kepel and Jardin, *Terreur dans l'hexagone*.
53 Burgat (2016).
54 Pierre Puchot and Romain Caillet, *Le combat vous a été prescrit* (Paris: Stock, 2017).
55 Olivier Roy, *Jihad and Death: The Global Appeal of Islamic State* (London: Hurst, 2017).
56 Jeroen Gunning and Richard Jackson, 'What's so "religious" about "religious terrorism"?', *Critical Studies on Terrorism*, 4, no. 3 (2011): 369–88. doi:10.1080/175391 53.2011.623405.
57 Dounia Bouzar, Christophe Caupenne and Sulayman Valsan, *Recherche-Action sur la mutation du processus d'endoctrinement et d'embrigadement dans l'islam radical*, Centre de prevention contre les derives sectaires, 2014 [online]. Available at http:// www.cpdsi.fr/articles-et-rapports/la-metamorphose-operee-chez-le-jeune-par-les -nouveaux-discours-terroristes/ (accessed 29 December 2017).
58 Xavier Crettiez and Sèze Romain, 'Saisir les mécanismes de la radicalisation violente: pour une analyse processuelle et biographique des engagements violent', Rapport de recherehce pour la mission de recherche droit et justice, 2017 [online]. Available at http://www.gip-recherche-justice.fr/wp-content/uploads/2017/08/Ra pport-radicalisation_INHESJ_CESDIP_GIP-Justice_2017.pdf (accessed 3 January 2017).
59 Ibid., p. 38.
60 Aziz Senni, 'Les banlieues, des fabriques de djihadiste? La faute aux politiques. Il est terms d'agir', 2016 [online]. Available at http://leplus.nouvelobs.com/contribution /1500213-les-banlieues-des-fabriques-de-djihadistes-la-faute-aux-politiques-il-est-te mps-d-agir.html (accessed 5 January 2017).
61 Loïc Wacquant, *Urban Outcasts: A Comparative Sociology of Advanced Marginality* and *Badlands of the Republic: Space, Politics and Urban Policy* (Cambridge, UK: Polity Press, 2007).
62 Giles Kepel, *Banlieue de la République: Société, politique et religion à Clichy-sous-Bois et Montfermeil* (Paris: Editions Gallimard, 2012).
63 Hussey, *The French Intifada*.
64 Sylvia Zappi, 'Le djihadiste, nouvel épouvantail des banlieues françaises', 2015 [online]. Available at https://www.lemonde.fr/banlieues/article/2015/10/22/le-djiha diste-nouvel-epouvantail-des-banlieues-francaises_4794877_1653530.html.

65 Bouzar, Caupenne and Valsan, *Recherche-Action sur la mutation du processus d'endoctrinement et d'embrigadement dans l'islam radical*.
66 Eléanor Douet, 'Attentats à Paris: des armes utilisées par les terroristes identifiéees en Serbie', 2015 [online]. Available at https://www.rtl.fr/actu/debats-societe/attentats-a-paris-des-armes-utilisees-par-les-terroristes-identifiees-en-serbie-7780673680 and France Info, 'Attentats terroristes en France: quelles armes ont été utilisées?', 2016 [online]. Available at https://www.francetvinfo.fr/faits-divers/terrorisme/attaques-du-13-novembre-a-paris/enquete-sur-les-attentats-de-paris/attentats-terroristes-en-france-quelles-armes-ont-ete-utilisees_1374239.html (accessed 5 January 2018).
67 Stéphane Sellami, 'Le vrai visage du narco-banditisme à Marseille', *Le Parisien*, 2016 [online]. Available at http://www.leparisien.fr/faits-divers/le-vrai-visage-du-narco-banditisme-a-marseille-02-05-2016-5760745.php (accessed 29 December 2017).
68 France has the largest per capita cannabis consumption figure in Europe, in Gavin Harris, 'Mapped: The countries that smoke the most cannabis', 2017 [oneline]. Available at http://www.telegraph.co.uk/travel/maps-and-graphics/mapped-the-countries-that-smoke-the-most-cannabis/ (accessed 5 January 2018).
69 Sellami, 'Le vrai visage du narco-banditisme à Marseille'.
70 Nina Valette, 'Un homme tué par des tirs de Kalachnikov à Marseille le soir du réveillon', 2018 [online]. Available at https://www.francebleu.fr/infos/faits-divers-justice/un-homme-tue-par-des-tires-de-kalachnikov-a-marseille-le-soir-du-nouvel-1514771178 (accessed 5 January 2018).
71 Ouest France, 'Braquage à la Kalachnikov: 500 000 E de bijoux volés', 2018 [online]. Available at https://www.ouest-france.fr/societe/faits-divers/saint-tropez-braquage-l-arme-lourde-500-000-eu-de-bijoux-voles-5481474 (accessed 5 January 2018).
72 Ibid.
73 Damien Van Puyvelde, 'We can't expect intelligence services to prevent every terrorist attack', 2015 [online]. Available at https://theconversation.com/we-cant-expect-intelligence-services-to-prevent-every-terrorist-attack-36676 (accessed 5 January 2018).
74 Eric Delbecque, 'Une "task force" anti-terroriste à l'Elysée peut elle empêcher des attentats?' 2017 [online]. Available at http://www.huffingtonpost.fr/eric-delbecque/task-force-macron-terrorisme_a_22108783/ (accessed 7 January 2018).
75 Angelique Chrisafis, 'Paris attacks inquiry finds multiple failings by French intelligence agencies', 2016 [online]. Available at https://www.theguardian.com/world/2016/jul/05/paris-attacks-inquiry-multiple-failings-french-intelligence-agencies (accessed 7 January 2018).
76 Ibid.
77 Christophe Cornevin and Caroline Piquet, 'Attentats: la longue traque d'une nebuleuse terroriste franco-belge', 2016 [online]. Available at http://www.lefigaro.fr/actualite-france/2016/03/25/01016-20160325ARTFIG00296-attentats-la-longue-traque-d-une-nebuleuse-terroriste-franco-belge.php (acessed 3 January 2017).
78 Samuel Laurent, 'Terrorisme: qu'est-ce que la <<fiche S>>?', 2015 [online]. Available at http://www.lemonde.fr/les-decodeurs/article/2015/08/31/terrorisme-peut-on-sanctionner-les-personnes-faisant-l-objet-d-une-fiche-s_4741574_4355770.html (accessed 3 January 2018).
79 Ibid.
80 Ibid.
81 Delbecque, 'Une "task force" anti-terroriste à l'Elysée peut elle empêcher des attentats?'
82 Cesari, 'European conundrum'; Downing, Jackson-Preece and Werdine-Norris, 'The security threat posed by "outsiders"'; and Eroukhmanoff, 'The remote securitisation of Islam in the US post-9/11'.

EXPORTING JIHAD FROM THE STREET-LEVEL GROUPS IN THE LOW COUNTRIES

Marion van San

Introduction

By the end of 2012 around 693 young men and women from the Low Countries[1] left for Syria and Iraq in order to join the armed struggle. In Belgium there were three overlapping recruitment networks that have been active in sending Belgian residents to the battlefields. A certain number of young men and women who left the Netherlands to join the armed struggle in Syria and Iraq belonged to three different networks which in terms of individuals and ideology partly overlapped with each other but could not be reduced to a homogeneous network.[2]

While most young men who joined these networks were inspired by the global jihad movement, we can understand why so many left for Syria and Iraq only when we know more about the local conditions in which they grew up and the extent to which this has affected their 'radicalization'. To this extent, what has happened in the Low Countries over the past decade suggests that it is the 'periphery' that *exports* in person to the 'centre'. Once at the 'centre', reports suggest, neighbours, classmates and family members who had followed one another to the battlefields, formed similar groups again as they had done in Belgium and the Netherlands, although the conflict between Jabhat al-Nusra and ISIS also created a clear dividing line and resulted in the fact that some friends became enemies.

In any case, the example of transition from relative inert political activism by some of the networks in Belgium and the Netherlands shows peripheries' receptiveness to the idea of an exported jihad from the centre as Roy suggested.[3] But the history of the networks also shows that local conditions affect group formation and the process of radicalization. The developments that took place in the networks and the consequences that has had, namely, a large proportion of young people leaving for Syria or Iraq, seem to be an example of Devji's observance that *the jihad*, instead of being exported from the centre to the periphery, is being imported back from the periphery to the centre.[4]

Belgian recruitment networks

On a per capita basis, Belgium is the top source of Western fighters in Syria and Iraq. In total, 413 Belgian fighters have left for the war zones.[5] Most of them have joined ISIS. The country has often been called the hotbed of jihadi recruitment. Belgian fighters often came from Brussels and Antwerp, although a relatively high number also left from Vilvoorde, a provincial town between Antwerp and Brussels. Fighters also left from other cities (like Maastricht, Ghent etc.) but they were a small number compared to those from the big cities.

The main reason why so many young men and women left from the triangle of Brussels-Antwerp-Vilvoorde had to do with three overlapping recruitment networks that have been active in sending Belgian residents to the battlefields: Sharia4Belgium, the so-called Resto Tawhid network and the Zerkani network. Belgian historian and Arabist Pieter Van Ostayen and journalist Guy Van Vlierden registered the numbers of the many Belgian men and women who left for Syria and Iraq since 2012 and what their affiliation with these networks was. According to them, it seems that at least ninety-seven people were in touch with Sharia4Belgium (located in Antwerp) before their departure. A total of seventy-two individuals who departed were in touch with the Brussels Zerkani network. An overlap existed, mainly in the circles of the Brussels recruiter Jean-Louis Denis, from the so-called Resto Tawheed network. He worked together with Sharia4Belgium and the Zerkani network, and had influenced at least fifty-eight people who tried to or succeeded in reaching the battle zone.[6]

Sharia4Belgium, a radical Islamic organization in Antwerp, inspired by the pan-Islamic group Hizb ut-Tahrir and later by Al-Muhajiroun, was established in March 2010. The organization originated under the influence of the British extremist Anjem Choudary, whose organization Sharia4UK was banned in January 2010. Choudary invited Fouad Belkacem, son of Moroccan immigrants, who was born in Antwerp, to London and put him in charge of a new organization: Sharia4Belgium. The creation of the organization marked the start of the development of Choudary's international network, the Global Sharia Movement. Choudary visited Belgium several times to give lectures to the members of Sharia4Belgium. He also gave lessons via Skype and Paltalk. It was part of the strategy to equip Sharia4Belgium as well as possible on propagating the ideology of jihadi Salafism. Sharia4Belgium members also had close contacts with Omar Bakri Mohammed, a leading British Islamist militant at the head of an Al Qaeda-affiliated group, who could have been involved in the London attacks in 2005. There were also contacts with the Jordanian-Palestinian Salafist ideologue al-Maqdisi, who had been a major influence in the development of jihadism. In addition, they were also inspired by jihadi ideologues Anwar al-Awlaki and Sayyid Qutb.[7]

Sharia4Belgium had a clear hierarchy, with leading figures, active members and regular supporters. Membership of the group was not formally regulated and was highly fluid in nature, but there was a solid core.[8] Around the core there was a group that joined lectures, attended demonstrations or expressed sympathy on the internet. The network around it was initially built up by informal networks of friendship and acquaintances. People who lived in the neighbourhood and felt attracted by the ideology joined the meetings. But also Facebook and other social media like YouTube also played a role in building up the network. After the organization gained more and more public awareness, Muslims from outside Antwerp also joined its activities.[9]

It was clear that the organization had one leader, although the members preferred to call him their spokesperson: Fouad Belkacem. He was without any doubt the spiritual leader of the group. He had a special status within the group because of his knowledge of Islam. But in addition, he was appreciated by the group because he dared to stand up against the 'infidels'. Although Belkacem was in charge, he was assisted by a few confidants. Within the organization, the 'Shura', which meant 'the top', was often referred to.[10] The connection with Vilvoorde arose when Sharia4Belgium members from Antwerp went to the mosque in Vilvoorde to hand out flyers and when Belkacem started to preach at various places in Vilvoorde. Furthermore, there were good contacts with Brussels, especially with Jean-Louis Denis, a former restaurant owner, who had converted to Islam and who would hand out food to the poor at Brussels North Station, where he probably recruited youngsters for the armed struggle in Syria.[11]

The core group of Sharia4Belgium included, according to the security forces, only six to twenty members in the beginning, in the age range of twenty to thirty years. It is estimated that there were more or less a hundred sympathizers.[12] At the riots in Borgerhout and Sint Jans Molenbeek in 2012, hundreds of youngsters were present. Probably not all these youngsters belonged to the support groups of Sharia4Belgium, but it shows that the organization was able to mobilize large groups of people.[13] From the beginning of its formation, Sharia4Belgium created a form of 'spectacle activism' and aimed mainly at generating media attention by provocation.[14] It organized so-called Streetda'wa to tell youngsters about the virtues of Islam. It disrupted lectures and debates and insulted and threatened politicians.[15] It began spreading its weekly lectures over the internet to reach a wider audience. Its central message in most of these videos was that there was a war going on against Islam and Muslims and Muslims had to defend the honour of Allah and his messenger Mohammed.

It was clear that members of Sharia4Belgium were not unsympathetic towards the armed struggle in Syria. Lectures were given about the suffering of their brothers and sisters in Arab countries, and on the possible role they could play in alleviating their suffering, by Fouad Belkacem as well as other members of the organization. Martyrdom was glorified and going abroad for jihad was framed positively as an act of altruism towards oppressed Muslims.[16]

The group had a few visible members who were involved in the public debate, but there were also members in the background, who must have had an important influence on the fact that the group changed from a group of activists into a group who glorified the jihad and finally joined the armed struggle in Syria and Iraq. One of the heavyweights behind the scenes from the very early days of the organization, Nabil Kasmi, travelled several times to Lebanon where he was trained by Omar Bakri Mohammed.[17] Belgian investigators discovered that he had already travelled to Syria for at least a short while after his visit to Lebanon in April 2012. In addition to Omar Bakri, he certainly had very extensive contacts abroad. A Facebook account that belonged to him, but seemed to have been long abandoned when Van

Vlierden and Van Ostayen retrieved it in August 2015, gives a highly intriguing insight into the kind of groups where support was sought for the *jihadification* of the Syrian war. Kasmi himself had only twelve friends on that account, but their subsequent connections led to an amazingly wide range of organizations (Hizb ut-Tahrir, al-Shabaab, the Syrian Islamist resistance group Ahrar as-Sham, etc.) while the friends of his friends spanned a geographical area consisting of at least forty countries. It goes without saying that being connected on Facebook with Kasmi or one of his friends does not mean that these individuals or organizations have ever been implicated in terrorism. But a strong impression exists that the Lebanon-based Al Qaeda cell to which Kasmi belonged had actively tried to build up as broad a network of potential supporters for its plans in Syria as possible. After Kasmi's final departure from Belgium on 20 August 2012, he managed to get at least five other members of Shariah4Belgium into the ranks of Jabhat al-Nusra. Three of them had previously tried to join Al Qaeda in the Arabian Peninsula in Yemen, but had been arrested there and sent back to Belgium.[18] The sister of one of the core members was married to a man who had been sentenced to three years in prison for plotting attacks in 2006, as part of a terrorism process in Brussels against the GICM-group (the Moroccan Islamic Combatant Group). In addition, four members of the organization were condemned in a terrorism trial in Antwerp for planning a terrorist attack and recruiting young men for the jihad in Chechnya.

The growth of Sharia4Belgium was mirrored by the rise of several smaller networks. One of them was *Resto du Tawhid*, an organization led by Jean-Louis Denis. Resto du Tawhid was active around the Brussels North railway station, distributing food aid to needy Muslims. However, it became clear that Resto du Tawhid was not just about charity, especially when it turned out that a lot of young men from the network of Denis had left for Syria. Not only did Denis connect Sharia4Belgium and Resto du Tawhid, but he also provided a key connection between Sharia4Belgium, operating mainly in Flanders, and the so-called Zerkani network, based in and around the Molenbeek district of Brussels.[19]

The Zerkani network was named after Khalid Zerkani, a forty-two-year-old Moroccan man, who used to be a cleaner living in the Brussels municipality of Molenbeek. Zerkani may have been trained in the famous Afghan-Pakistani terrorist camps.[20] The secret service had kept an eye on him for many years. Zerkani, always surrounded by many youngsters, preached at the attic of a house in Molenbeek, in illegal mosques and in sports clubs. It was obvious that he had an important influence on them, although he was much less eloquent than Fouad Belkacem.[21] Zerkani not only tried to convince young men up to the point that they were willing to sacrifice themselves, but also encouraged them to commit petty crimes in order to pay for their journey to death.[22] Two young men of the Zerkani network have played a direct role in the terrorist attacks in Paris in November 2015, while another one participated in the terrorist attacks in Brussels in March 2016 and was also suspected of being the bomb-maker for both plots.[23] Moreover, Zerkani did not recruit only for the Syrian jihad: prior to this, he was linked to at least seven people convicted in Belgium for their cooperation with al-Shabaab.[24]

Zerkani's modus operandi could hardly differ more from that of Fouad Belkacem. The latter was notorious for his highly visible actions, such as public demonstrations and preaching sessions in crowded shopping streets. Zerkani's organization had no website, no logo and no distinctive name. Recruiting was done under the guise of offering community sporting activities, while further indoctrination happened in old-fashioned back rooms. While Shariah4Belgium's leader Fouad Belkacem participated in televised debates and disseminated his sermons via YouTube, even the grainiest picture of Zerkani is extremely hard to locate. Whereas the Zerkani network operated more like a criminal gang and drew in a lot of unemployed people from the Brussels Canal Zone and a significant number with criminal backgrounds but little or no Islamic background, Sharia4Belgium had recruits from different backgrounds, from Antwerp, Vilvoorde and Brussels, including from all layers of the Muslim population.[25] The young men who were joining Sharia4Belgium were a diverse group. The families in which they grew up often belonged to the lower social class. An exception to this were three brothers, who all left for Syria, whose father had built a fortune by trading in tropical timber. But the fact that most young people grew up in families with low-skilled parents does not mean that they were facing a gloomy future. A number of them had studied in school and at least one at the university, and some of them had well-paying jobs. Others had dropped out of school or had a criminal past.

A remarkable characteristic of the Antwerp-based and mainly Dutch-speaking Shariah4Belgium is that it ostensibly lacked any link with older networks of the Belgian jihad. This could not be more different from the Zerkani network, which operated almost exclusively in French-speaking circles in Brussels and had connections with several people who have been convicted for terrorism. Malika El Aroud, Europe's most notorious female terror convict, and Nizar Trabelsi (who was convicted for plotting against the US Air Force base in the Belgian town of Kleine Brogel and later rendered to the United States) was found with a mobile phone in prison, adding to existing suspicions of a plot to set him free.[26]

Although Sharia4Belgium and the Zerkani network had their dissimilarities, they were connected to a certain degree. The arrest of a Sharia4Belgium convict in connection with the Brussels attacks in April 2016 may have resulted from members of both networks having met each other at the Syrian front as well as in Belgium. The man at the intersection of the two groups was Jean-Louis Denis.[27] Denis was particularly successful as a recruiter, attracting people who wanted to join the jihad. However, he lacked the necessary contacts to get his recruits across Syrian borders. Therefore, he often relied on the social network structures that Zerkani had built.[28]

Dutch recruitment networks

From the Netherlands a significantly smaller number of fighters left for Syria and Iraq than from Belgium. In total, 280 Dutch foreign fighters have left for Syria and Iraq. Most of them left from the region of The Hague (The Hague-Delft-

Zoetermeer). The three most important recruitment networks (Behind Bars, Straat Dawah and Sharia4Holland) were active in this area. In addition, there was a radical preacher from Zoetermeer who had much influence on young Muslims. Around seventy young men, who were part of the three networks from the region of The Hague, left for Syria, starting from the end of 2012.[29] It is not entirely clear how youngsters from the region of The Hague ended up in the three networks, but a controversy about a mosque in The Hague in the period between 2006 and 2008 would probably have played an important role. The mosque had a solid reputation and was popular among youngsters because the imam dared to criticize the government. But when the mosque became the talk of the town for preaching against integration, closed Islamic marriages and stimulated the radicalization of young Muslims, it began to moderate its tone. When the mosque denied access to young men who had left the Netherlands to join the armed struggle abroad, but who were arrested and sent back to the Netherlands, more and more youngsters turned against it.[30]

Several youngsters who had turned their backs on the mosque founded Behind Bars in May 2011. They organized demonstrations in front of embassies against the captivity of Muslim prisoners who they considered as victims of the so-called War on Terror. The hard core of the group had contacts with other networks in Delft and Gouda, and there were also connections with a group of young men from Zoetermeer.[31] The second network was *Straat Dawah*, with various young men from *Behind Bars*, and supplemented by others. The network, which was created in June 2011 after a demonstration organized by *Behind Bars* in front of the Dutch Parliament against the ban on the face veil, generated a lot of attention in the Dutch media.[32] The young men who joined *Behind Bars* and *Straat Dawah* regularly came together to pray, to follow lectures, to watch films on YouTube or just to be around brothers in faith. The informal leader of the group was Azzedine Choukoud. Although the young men were a diverse group and there was disagreement among them on certain issues, they managed to establish a wide network of Salafist youth in the Delft-Zoetermeer-The Hague triangle. The third network was *Sharia4Holland* that can be seen partly as a spin-off of the Belgian *Sharia4Belgium*.[33] Sharia4Holland was launched at the end of December 2010. In the following period Sharia4Holland, Behind Bars and Straat Dawah, and Sharia4Belgium organized various demonstrations.

The group around Azzedine Choukoud became more and more involved in debates about Muslims and the war in Syria after the creation of the news channel *De Ware Religie* [The True Religion] in May 2013. Sharia4Belgium did not exist anymore at that time and the members of the hard core – except Belkacem who was in jail at the time – had already gone to Syria. The provocative tenor of the writers made sure that they remained constantly in the attention of the media.[34] In addition, they were also active on Facebook and Twitter. They discovered that social media were an excellent way to establish contacts with others, to discuss issues with like-minded people and to disagree with those who criticized them. As the war in Syria progressed they also began to show the heroic side of the fighters more and more on social media and used it to correct the image of the foreign fighters in the Dutch media.[35] In addition to Facebook and Twitter they also posted films on YouTube with impressions of protests, streetda'wa and sermons by important preachers.[36] They continued to do so until the core group was arrested in August 2014.

It seemed that the networks from The Hague had much less connection with the international jihad movement than the Belgian networks. There were different 'veterans' within the group who had previously tried to go to jihad areas (such as Afghanistan, Chechnya and Somalia) and had been jailed in the Netherlands and abroad because of their terrorist activities. The networks also found inspiration in international preachers who were linked to Al Qaeda. On *De Ware Religie*, texts from prominent jihadist spiritual leaders, such as Anwar al-Awlaki, Ahmad Musa Jibril, an American radical preacher, Abu Adnan, an Australian preacher known as 'the Australian supporter of Anwar al Awlaki', Dutch preacher Abduljabbar van de Ven and Fouad Belkacem were spread.[37] *De Ware Religie* also openly sympathized with Al Qaeda and ISIS.[38]

The departure of Belgian and Dutch fighters to Syria and Iraq

The departure of both Belgian and Dutch fighters took place in three phases. The first peak concerned the first wave of jihadi foreign fighters leaving in the initial stage of the conflict (in the fourth quarter of 2012 and the first quarter of 2013): the departure of the hard core. In the fourth quarter of 2013 and the first quarter of 2014 another peak can be seen. But this wave was much more diverse than the first one that consisted almost exclusively of hard core members. Hard core members still left but in addition there were also a large group of jihad supporters, who had no physical ties with the Belgian and Dutch networks, leaving in this period. The third peak coincides with the proclamation of the Caliphate by Abu Bakr al-Baghdadi, on 29 June 2014. Strikingly, from that moment on, more women left as also entire families.[39] That so many Belgian and Dutch young men had left for Syria in the fourth quarter of 2012 and the first quarter of 2013 had everything to do with the presence of Houssein Elouassaki, Sharia4Belgium member from Vilvoorde, who left for Syria in the beginning of September 2012 and joined *Majlis Shura al-Mujahideen*. *Majlis Shura al-Mujahideen* was a militia that was established by Firas al-Absi, a Syrian veteran of the jihad, who fought in Afghanistan in 2000–1. Elouassaki was one of the first Western fighters who had joined the group. Despite his age, he was 22 years old at that time, he became the emir of a brigade of foreign fighters within *Majlis Shura al-Mujahideen*, which grew to include Belgian, Dutch and French fighters. Contacting a Belgian young man who was already accepted as a *mujahid* in Syria was far easier than trying to get into groups like the al-Qaeda affiliate *Jabhat al-Nusra*, which strictly vetted recruits. From that moment more and more Belgian and Dutch young men left for Syria to join the group of Elouassaki. Van Ostayen estimates that at least seventy-seven fighters from Belgium have been members of *Majlis Shura al-Mujahideen* at some point. The first were recruits of Shariah4Belgium. The arrival of Sharia4Belgium members in Syria early on in the civil war had a snowball effect on recruitment. As members arrived they encouraged their friends back home to join.[40] Dutch young men also joined *Majlis Shura al-Mujahideen*, although it is unclear how big this group was. Zerkani's early recruits landed within *Katibat al-Muhajireen*, which was led at the time by the ethnic-Chechen commander Tarkhan Batirashvili, better known as Abu Omar al-Shishani.[41] At a later stage, some of them also ended up under the *Majlis Shura al-Mujahideen* command. Soon after the establishment of the ISIS, al-Absi and al-Shishani pledged allegiance to the ISIS leader, Abu Bakr al-Baghdadi. But as was the case with the Shariah4Belgium recruits, several Zerkani members joined the rival *Jabhat al-Nusra*, also known as Al Qaeda's branch in Syria. Most of them, however, joined ISIS.

Sharia4Belgium

While most young men who joined one of the Belgian or Dutch networks were inspired by the global jihad movement, we can understand why so many young men – and later women – involved in the six networks left for Syria and Iraq, only when we know more about the local conditions in which they grew up and the extent to which this has affected their 'radicalization'. Therefore, we focus on the case of Sharia4Belgium, because it sheds light on the mechanisms that led to the departure of so many Belgian young men and women to Syria and Iraq.

Most young men and women who were part of the group were in some way connected to each other. There were five families who had several sons belonging to the organization. In addition, there were several other connections between the young men: they were cousins, brothers-in-law or friends. Some had grown up in the same neighbourhood or had been to school together. Sometimes youngsters were introduced by their neighbours, friends or family members, or women got married to men who were involved in the organization, and became involved in it themselves. As far as we have been able to find out, most youngsters came from moderate Islamic families or were converts to Islam, but there is also evidence that there were quite a few parents who supported the extremist ideas of their children.

Although the organization was housed in one of the poorest districts of Antwerp and some of its followers had a lower social class background, this was not the case for all of them. A number of them had studied in school, and at least one at the university, and some of them had well-paying jobs. The image that only disadvantaged young men and women joined the organization is not correct.

What brought them together was their frustration about how they could experience their faith as Muslims in Belgium. Belkacem and his confidants constantly emphasized that there was a war going on against Islam and Muslims. As the discourse of the organization became more provocative, politics, the media, Muslim organizations and the justice system reacted more aggressively against them. For the organization this was only a confirmation of the fact that everyone was against them. As a result, the links between the group members were becoming stronger and the resistance against the hostile society was becoming more intense.

Sharia4Belgium was not only involved in public debate but also taught its members about Islam. It organized ideological and religious as well as combat training five times a week. The lessons were obligatory: the recruits were urged to show up via text messages, and when they were absent, sanctions followed. The lessons were provided by the core members of the organization. There were sometimes guest speakers from Vilvoorde and Brussels, and several lectures were provided by 'brothers' from the UK. The members also watched videos about training camps, lectures of radical preachers and beheadings. To increase the spread of the ideas, the lectures were recorded on video and posted on the website of the organization. Because the days were filled with all kinds of activities and expulsion threatened when members missed certain activities, youngsters were involved 24/7 in Sharia4Belgium. They had to give up everything else (school, work, contact with family members etc.) to belong to the group. Parents spoke about their sons and daughters becoming more and more involved in the activities of the group and described the growing distance between them and their children. As a result, the youngsters who were involved in the organization became more and more isolated from the rest of society.[42]

Although Sharia4Belgium was especially active in Antwerp, it also started to spread its message among young men in Vilvoorde, Elouassaki's hometown. From August 2011 Belkacem preached in Vilvoorde in parks and in the areas surrounding schools to attract youngsters. Since the end of 2012 an increasing number of members of Sharia4Belgium had left for Syria. This began to happen from the moment Houssein Elouassaki started to contact his friends in Belgium to tell them that he had joined the armed struggle. *But other core members of the group* also tried to convince the other members that as Muslims it was required of them to go to Syria and join the armed struggle. Those who were already in Syria called their friends back home and told them how great it was to be a soldier of Allah and encouraged them to join them. As a result of the strong group dynamics there were only a few who resisted against it. The more young men left for Syria, the greater became the pressure on others, who were still in Belgium, to leave as well. Some returnees stated that being part of Sharia4Belgium had been their mental preparation to leave for Syria as joining jihad was seen as a duty.

Conclusion

The networks in Belgium and the Netherlands that were responsible for the recruitment of young men and women for the jihad in Syria and Iraq were all inspired by the global jihad movement. Scholars like Anwar al-Awlaki and Sayyid Qutb were a source of inspiration like other Salafist ideologues or Al Qaeda affiliated groups. The example of transition from relative inert political activism by some of the networks in Belgium and the Netherlands shows peripheries' receptiveness to the idea of an exported jihad from the centre, suggested by Roy.[43]

But the history of the networks also shows that local conditions affected group formation and the process of radicalization. Most young men and women grew up in the same neighbourhoods, went to the same schools, were related to each other (sometimes through marriage) and were attracted by the same ideology. The developments that took place in the networks and the consequences that has had, namely that a large proportion of young people left for Syria or Iraq, seem to be an example of Devji's observance that *the jihad* was being imported from the periphery to the centre.[44] Once at the 'centre', neighbours, classmates and family members who had followed one another to the battlefields formed similar groups again as they had done in Belgium and the Netherlands.

We know now that the radicalization of the young men and women who belonged to one of the networks often turned out into violent extremism from the moment they joined the armed struggle. In a certain way they had already developed radical beliefs through the classes and lectures within their networks. But they were further trained ideologically in Syria and Iraq, where they learnt that infidels were inferior and where the men were sent to training camps, where they learnt to use weapons. We also know now that *Majlis Shura al-Mujahideen* within a few weeks became a gang of murderers who kidnapped, tortured and beheaded their victims. We know that several members of *Katibat al-Muhajireen,* who belonged to the group of Zerkani in Belgium, became involved in plotting and executing the attacks in Paris in 2015 and in Brussels in 2016. The common ideology of the men and women played an important role in what they were doing, but there was something more, namely the role of friends, comrades and family members, who challenged, encouraged and confirmed them in their role as foreign fighters in an ongoing process of radicalization, within the context of a horrible war.[45]

The enormous amount of propaganda that was distributed, as the war progressed, by Western youngsters via social media spread the message that their brothers and sisters were getting killed by not only the troops of Assad but also by foreign troops, in order to destroy Islam. In the communities of like-minded people, where these messages were spread and dissident voices were disabled, more and more young men and women became convinced to join the armed struggle.[46] Probably most of them were not aware that the war would run out of hand to that extent. But as the war progressed, it seemed that young Europeans were more and more willing to participate in violent actions. De Swaan described in *The Killing Compartments* that the more perpetrators get used to violence, the more they are prepared to go a step further. He wondered why some of them carried out the orders eagerly in such situations, while others did that with a certain indifference and still others refused to follow the orders. These differences in behaviour between people in the same situation could, according to De Swaan, be explained only by the differences in their personal dispositions.[47]

Understanding why so many young men and women from the Low Countries joined the armed struggle in Syria and Iraq is a complicated process and we do not know yet all the details about their involvement in the atrocities of ISIS. It seems that their departure is an example of Deviji's observance that the jihad, instead of being exported from the centre to the periphery, is being imported from the periphery to the centre. But to be certain about that, much more research needs to be done.

Notes

1. Collective name for The Netherlands, Belgium and Luxembourg, so-called because much of their land surface is at or below sea level.
2. Martijn de Koning, Ineke Roex, Carmen Becker and Pim Aarns, *Eilanden in een zee van ongeloof. Het verzet van activistische da'wa-netwerken in België* (Amsterdam: Universiteit van Amsterdam, 2014), p. 168.
3. Olivier Roy, *Globalised Islam: The Search for a New Ummah* (New York: Columbia University Press, 2004).
4. Faisal Devji, *Landscapes of the Jihad: Militancy, Morality, Modernity* (London: Hurst, 2005).
5. Thomas Renard and Rik Coolsaet, eds, *Returnees: Who Are they, Why Are they (not) Coming Back and How should We Deal with Them? Assessing Policies on Returning Foreign Terrorist Fighters in Belgium, Germany and the Netherlands* (Brussels: Egmont-Royal Institute for International Relations, 2018).
6. Pieter Van Ostayen and Guy Van Vlierden, *The Role of Belgian Fighters in the Jihadification of the Syrian War. From Plotting Early in 2011 to the Paris and Brussels Attacks* (Brussels/Berlin: European Foundation for Democracy/Counter Extremism Project, 2016). Available at http://europeandemocracy.eu/wp-content/uploads/2017/02/The-Role-of-Belgian-Fighters-in-the-Jihadification-of-the-Syrian-War.pdf.
7. Joas Wagemakers, *A Quietist Jihadi: The Ideology and Influence of Abu Muhammad al-Maqdisi* (Cambridge: Cambridge University Press, 2012).
8. de Koning, et al., *Eilanden in een zee van ongeloof*.
9. Ibid., pp. 78–9.
10. Shura is an Arabic word for 'consultation'. The Quran encourages Muslims to decide their affairs in consultation with those who will be affected by that decision.
11. When Fouad Belkacem was apprehended in Belgium and Abu Quasim, the leader of Sharia4Holland, was apprehended in the Netherlands, Choudary immediately placed the following contributions on his website: 'Belgium war against Islam and Muslims!' 13 January 2012; 'Holland regime uses oppressive measures against Sharia4Holland', 27 May 2012.
12. de Koning, et al., *Eilanden in een zee van ongeloof*, p. 48.
13. Ibid., p. 77.
14. Ibid., p. 149.
15. Press release, Sharia4Belgium, 5 May 2012.
16. Thomas Hegghammer, 'Terrorist recruitment and radicalization in Saudi Arabia', *Middle East Policy*, 8, no. 4 (2006): 48.
17. Ostayen and Vlierden, *The Role of Belgian Fighters in the Jihadification of the Syrian War*, p. 12.
18. Ibid., 14.
19. Pieter van Ostaeyen, 'Belgian radical networks and the road to the Brussels attacks', *CTC Sentinel*, 9, no. 6 (2016): 9.
20. 'Tribunal de Première Instance Francophone de Bruxelles', issued on 29 July 2015.
21. Mark Eeckhaut, 'Khalid Zerkani, de Kerstman die ronselde voor Syrië. Megaproces tegen Syriestrijders van start, *De Standaard*, 7 May 2015.
22. 'Tribunal de Première Instance Francophone de Bruxelles', issued on 29 July 2015.
23. Guy Van Vlierden, 'The Zerkani network: Belgium's most dangerous jihadist group', 2016. Available at https://jamestown.org/program/hot-issue-the-zerkani-network-belgiums-most-dangerous-jihadist-group/.

24 'Tribunal de Première Instance Francophone de Bruxelles', issued on 29 July 2015.
25 van Ostaeyen, 'Belgian radical networks and the road to the Brussels attacks', p. 10.
26 Van Vlierden, 'The Zerkani network'.
27 'Tribunal de Première Instance Francophone de Bruxelles', issued on 29 July 2015.
28 Van Vlierden, 'The Zerkani network'.
29 Reinier Bergema and Marion van San, 'Waves of the black banner: A comprehensive study on the Dutch jihadist foreign fighter contingent in Syria and Iraq', *Studies in Conflict and Terrorism* (2017). Available at https://www.tandfonline.com/doi/abs/10.1080/1057610X.2017.1404004.
30 de Koning, et al., *Eilanden in een zee van ongeloof*, p. 171.
31 Ibid., p. 175.
32 Ibid., p. 176.
33 Ibid.
34 Ibid., p. 225.
35 Marion van San, *De Nederlandse Syriëgangers. 'Kanonnenvlees' of 'helden van de Lage Landen'?*, (Utrecht: FORUM, 2014). Available at https://www.researchgate.net/publication/283666972_FORUM_Inleiding_FORUM_De_Nederlandse_Syriegangers_'Kanonnenvlees'_of_'helden_van_de_Lage_Landen'.
36 de Koning, et al., *Eilanden in een zee van ongeloof*, p. 227.
37 Requisitory Prosecutor 'Contextzaak'.
38 Ibid.
39 Bergema and Van San, 'Waves of the black banner'.
40 van Ostaeyen, 'Belgian radical networks and the road to the Brussels attacks', p. 8.
41 Van Vlierden, 'The Zerkani network'.
42 Marion van San, 'Belgian and Dutch young men and women who joined ISIS: Ethnographic research among the families they left behind', *Studies in Conflict & Terrorism*, 41, no. 1 (2018): 39–58.
43 Roy, *Globalised Islam*.
44 Devji, *Landscapes of the Jihad*.
45 Beatrice de Graaf, *De vlam van verzet. Nederlandse strijders in het buitenland, vroeger en nu* (Utrecht: Verzetsmuseum Amsterdam, 2014).
46 Marion van San, 'Striving in the way of God: Justifying jihad by Belgian and Dutch young Muslims', *Studies in Conflict & Terrorism*, 38, no. 5 (2015): 328–42.
47 Abram De Swaan, *The Killing Compartments: The Mentality of Mass Murder* (Yale University Press, 2015), p. 212.

SCANDINAVIAN JIHAD

Marco Nilsson

Introduction

How global has the 'Scandinavian jihad' become and what are its local particularities? Sageman has written that 'participants in the global jihad are not atomized individuals but actors linked to each other through complex webs of direct and mediated exchanges'.[1] However, these links and webs of exchange among people and ideas also potentially form the foundation of very localized experiences of jihad, shaped by the subtle interplay of various international connections and local dynamics. Challenging traditional assumptions about the relationship between peripheral countries and the core of global jihad in the Middle East, Devji has argued that 'the jihad, instead of being exported from the centre to the periphery, will be imported from the periphery to the centre'.[2] The empirical question of the nature of *the jihad* waged by citizens and residents of Sweden, Denmark and Norway can be examined by analysing links to groups articulating a global rhetoric of jihad, such as Al Qaeda and ISIS, and by tracing flows, for example, of money, ideas and manpower, across borders. These connections often lead to the war zones of, for example, Syria and Iraq, which have become the centre of gravity of present-day global jihad. However, they can also be traced to other countries in Europe and more locally focused struggles in the Middle East.

In Scandinavia, radicalization processes have been affected both by political developments in the Middle East and elsewhere and by local events in Scandinavia. Some veterans of the Afghan jihad of the 1980s ended up in Scandinavia, and the local struggles in Egypt, Algeria and Somalia attracted attention in the 1990s, but it was the 9/11 attacks and the ensuing US military campaigns against Afghanistan and Iraq that would inspire a new generation of radicals. Other seemingly smaller events, such as the Israeli warfighting in Gaza in 2009, contributed to increasing levels of radicalization.[3] However, the most noteworthy external event in recent years was the Syrian civil war, which after 2012 dramatically increased the number of Scandinavian foreign fighters. At least 300 foreign fighters in Syria came from Sweden, while about 137 and eighty-one came from Denmark and Norway, respectively.[4] The most prominent domestic event, affecting Sweden and Denmark in particular, was the 2005 publication of the Mohammed caricatures in the Danish newspaper *Jyllands-Posten*. This event for the first time seemed to legitimize local attacks in Scandinavia rather than foreign fighting, drawing both global and local attention to Scandinavia from radical circles. However, Norway has not experienced the same magnitude of domestic terror plots as have Sweden and Denmark.

There is a distinct global dimension to the Scandinavian jihad because, as in many other European countries, recruiters often link distant conflict zones and Scandinavia, apparently importing ideas and exporting manpower. Nesser, Stenersen and Oftedal have argued that 'it is symptomatic that Sweden experienced its first suicide bombing after Swedish foreign fighters climbed the ranks of ISIS's forerunner Al Qaeda in Iraq (AQI).'[5] However, beneath this seeming lack of local ideological concerns and the focus on foreign ideas imported by people with connections to foreign conflict zones often lie home-grown social anxieties and local events that merge with ideology to produce the particular characteristics of jihad in any specific place and time.

Recruiters' activities explain 'why seemingly non-political and non-ideological people (such as petty criminals) end up engaging in political violence with the ideology of Al Qaeda and ISIS'.[6] They are well aware of how the local context has a crucial impact on the recruitment process. Wiktorowicz holds that potential recruits must have a cognitive opening that makes them question their previous beliefs,[7] and a personal crisis is a very potent such opening.[8] However, cognitive openings are very local in nature, as in recruitment sessions not only the values and beliefs of potential recruits but also their perceptions of their experiences as part of a particular society are manipulated.

In practice, this often means that the targets' local and individual experiences are framed such that they can be connected to events and processes in other countries. This means that one's individual experiences of, for example, relative socioeconomic deprivation in Scandinavia can be perceived as connected to sectarian conflicts in Syria and Iraq, and even to perceived global threats against the abstract global community of *Ummah*, that is, the Islamic nation. External events such as wars do not matter, regardless of how many casualties they cause, unless they are contextualized in a neatly packaged message by the recruiter such that they are perceived as meaningful to the local receiver. It is this fusion of local experiences, foreign conflicts, and global ideology and connections that has, through aligning local and global frames, recently produced hundreds of foreign fighters who have travelled to Syria, and resulted in varying levels of domestic terror threat.

The local nature of attacks in Europe is also evident in the terror tactics. As many Europeans have attended terrorist training camps, often receiving training in bomb-making, it is sometimes seen as surprising that 'firearms have become more common than bombs'.[9] However, local circumstances (e.g., access to black markets for firearms) and tactical considerations, and not only imported ideas, affect how attacks are executed. For example, while suicide bombings may have been a useful military tactic in Syria and Iraq, they are not necessary to cause many casualties when attacking democracies where there are many unprotected targets.[10] Moreover, while terrorists may copy tactics from other countries, where suicide tactics are more common to mark one's belonging to an identity group, a lack of technical skills can make them less effective, which may have been the case with the Stockholm suicide bombing in 2010 that killed only the perpetrator.[11]

Local circumstances also affect the level of domestic terror threat. After the publication of the Mohammed caricatures in *Jyllands-Posten* in 2005, most domestic terror plots were connected to that newspaper. Unlike the recent increase in domestic terrorist plots in, for example, France, following its visible participation in the military campaign against ISIS, the number of plots in Scandinavia decreased at least temporarily after the higher levels of local activity related to the *Jyllands-Posten* caricatures between 2008 and 2011.[12] Moreover, while there has been an increase in funding from ISIS to conduct attacks in Europe, most of the money has gone to what could be called the semi-peripheral countries of global jihad, such as France and the UK, rather than to the more peripheral countries in Scandinavia.[13] However, the number of Scandinavian jihadi foreign fighters travelling to foreign conflict zones such as Afghanistan, Somalia, Iraq and Syria steadily increased since the 9/11 attacks in 2001, only to subside dramatically in 2016 when access to ISIS-controlled territories became limited.[14]

The present analysis is divided into five sections. To determine the global extent of the Scandinavian jihad, the first four sections cover the early years, starting with the Algerian Civil War and ending with the US occupation of Iraq. This era from the early 1990s to 2011 has been associated with the rise of Al Qaeda. This was also the time when the first global jihadi networks started to emerge with the increasing ease of international travel, increasing availability of satellite-based news reporting, and improving communications technology available to potential jihadis. Before the spread of the internet and its pivotal role in disseminating jihadi propaganda, jihadis relied mostly on personal contacts to spread their ideas and to recruit new members. However, even during the Bosnian war in the early 1990s, a young recruit argued that the nature of jihad was changing as electronic communication was increasing the opportunities for networking:

> They don't know that we can telephone or fax anywhere in the world. They don't know that this is a nice holiday for us where you meet some of the best people you have ever met in your life. People from all over the world, people from Brazil, from Japan, from China, from the Middle East, from America, North, South, Canada, Australia, all over the world you meet people.[15]

The final section concentrates on the impact of the Syrian civil war and the ISIS effect, as the numbers of Scandinavian jihadi foreign fighters started to increase. The chapter argues that, while much of the Scandinavian jihad has been affected by global ideas and 'brands' such as Al Qaeda and ISIS, it has also been characterized by connections to local struggles, such as the Algerian and Somali civil wars. Moreover, despite clear connections to the centre of gravity of global jihad in Afghanistan, Iraq and Syria, in the form of inflowing ideas and exported manpower, local networks, events and grievances have also played a prominent role in defining the nature and dynamics of Scandinavian jihad.

From al-Gamaʿa al-Islamiyya to al-Shabaab

While some veterans of the Soviet–Afghan War in the 1980s eventually ended up in Scandinavia, the roots of the early Scandinavian jihad in the 1990s lie in al-Gamaʿa al-Islamiyya's struggle in Egypt. Between 1992 and 1998, the group was involved in an armed conflict with the Egyptian state with the aim of overthrowing the government and replacing it with an islamic state. Tala Fouad Qassim, the group's spokesman, was sentenced to prison for his alleged role in the 1982 assassination of Anwar al-Sadat, the president of Egypt. However, he escaped in 1989 and found his way to Pakistan, which had become the base for the Arab mujahedeen during the Soviet military presence in Afghanistan. As the Pakistani government eventually closed the jihadi safe houses after the Soviet withdrawal and started to crack down on the jihadi networks, Qassim fled and was granted asylum in Denmark.

In Copenhagen, he became a widely renowned Islamist speaker, giving sermons at a local mosque. He even hosted a TV programme on Saturdays and edited the periodical *al-Murabitoun* with Ayman al-Zawahiri, the current leader of Al Qaeda. Qassim also convened the first meeting of the Shura Council of the European Union in Denmark, at which he advocated the use of charitable organizations to finance jihad in North Africa. He had been sentenced to death in absentia in Egypt, and on his way to Bosnia in 1995 he was arrested in Croatia, ending up in the hands of Egyptian authorities. One Egyptian official ominously commented that 'European countries like Denmark, Sweden, Switzerland, England and others, which give sanctuary to these terrorists should now understand it will come back to haunt them where they live'.[16] In response to Qassim's arrest, the first suicide bombing in Europe was carried out by al-Gamaʿa al-Islamiyya in Croatia.[17] However, it was described as a retaliatory measure and the spectre of global jihad was not yet over Europe, as the aims of al-Gamaʿa al-Islamiyya's jihad in Egypt were very local.

In the 1990s, radical Islamism in Norway became most visible in the activism of the Kurdish Najmuddin Faraj Ahmad, also called Mullah Krekar. He had come to Norway as a refugee in 1991 and was later considered both a domestic and international threat. Spending considerable time in northern Iraq, he became the leader of Ansar al-Islam, a jihadi group formed in 2001 in the Kurdish-controlled area of northern Iraq and later fighting both the US occupation forces and the Iraqi government, though mainly in the Kurdish areas. The group had possible ties with Al Qaeda, as it had allegedly been responsible for training one of Ansar al-Islam's predecessor organizations, Jund al-Islam. Moreover, some members of Ansar al-Islam were veterans of the Soviet–Afghan War in the 1980s, as they had fought together with bin Laden in the mujahedeen.[18]

As the USA was preparing to invade Iraq in 2002, Ansar al-Islam was famously accused by the Bush administration of being a link between Saddam Hussein and Al Qaeda. The accusations were never proven, but in 2005 Mullah Krekar was nevertheless placed on the UN terrorist list. A lively public discussion developed in Norway, with many calling for his extradition to Iraq. However, these calls were deemed problematic because he risked facing the death penalty there. In 2013, Mullah Krekar was convicted of terrorism-related offences in Norway after having, for example, threatened the life of Erna Solberg, a Norwegian party leader, if he were to be extradited. At this time, he was estimated to have amassed 200–300 supporters in Norway.[19] In 2015 he was again arrested as the presumed leader of Rawti Shax, an offshoot of Ansar al-Islam, accused of recruiting mainly Kurdish fighters to ISIS and plotting attacks against, for example, Norwegian diplomats.[20] However, his global influence was in decline because of his long stay in Norway, prison time and the long distance from Iraq.[21]

While the early struggles of al-Gama'a al-Islamiyya were local, with Krekar's emergence the local jihadi movement became characterized by a mixture of ethnic and global inspirations and aspirations. He had deep roots in Kurdish Islamist movements and had apparently established a connection to Al Qaeda during the US occupation of Iraq. To what extent this was a strategic move as a result of the changing realities of the group in northern Iraq, or a matter of principle, is unclear. Despite this possible Al Qaeda connection, much of the Scandinavian jihad of the time was still quite ethnically bound, lacking the broader aims articulated by bin Laden in 1998 when he announced the World Islamic Front against the Jews and Crusaders.

Krekar was not Norway's only concern, as some Norwegian foreign fighters started to join the civil war in Somalia. Possibly as many as thirty Norwegian Somalis were recruited to al-Shabaab, the youth wing of Somalia's Islamic Courts Union (ICU), which became a significant player after the ICU was ousted in 2006. One Norwegian recruit even took part in the 2013 terrorist attack against the Westgate Mall in Nairobi. However, most recruitment activities took place in Sweden and Denmark. The total number of recruits from Scandinavia is unknown but could exceed eighty.[22] In 2009, Abid Rahman Mohamed became the first Danish suicide bomber, killing 24 people at a Mogadishu hotel during a graduation ceremony for local medical doctors.[23] However, most recruits belonged to local Somali communities, giving the phenomenon a distinct ethnic identity. Global ideology could not fully explain the mobilization of the Somali diaspora to participate in the civil war in Somalia, and al-Shabaab's aim was to establish a local Islamic order in Somalia. Its success in mobilizing ethnic Somalis has depended on its ability to frame itself as a nationalist group rather than on the idea of global jihad. According to Stig Jarle Hansen, a Norwegian expert on al-Shabaab, support and funding for the organization diminished as a result of its increasing use of terror tactics.[24]

Many Swedes of mainly Somali origin became involved in al-Shabaab, some even achieving high-ranking positions. Fuad Shangole came to Sweden in 1992 and was an imam at a mosque in Stockholm. In 2004, he left for Somalia and became a high-ranking leader of al-Shabaab.[25] Indeed, he emerged as a principal ideologue of the organization and has been described as 'probably the most prominent foreign fighter from Europe'.[26] However, as he came to Sweden from Somalia as an adult, it is unclear whether he should be defined as a foreign fighter. While in Stockholm, he preached the necessity of jihad, actively supporting militant Islamists in Somalia, and during the rule of the ICU, Shangole was the organization's minster of education.

However, even before the ICU, which was founded in 2000, another militant Islamist from Sweden came to play a prominent role in Somalia. In 1996, Gouled Hassan Dourad, who had come to Sweden from Somalia as a teenager, received jihadi training in Afghanistan and relocated to his old home country the same year. When the civil war started after the fall of the Siad Barre regime, Osama bin Laden took advantage of the disorder to support al-Itihaad al-Islamiyah, a militant Islamist group with the goal of creating an islamic state in the region. He also sent foreign jihadis to train and fight alongside the local fighters.[27] Dourad both took part in jihad and trained new recruits between 1997 and 2002. The following two years he reportedly supported Al Qaeda operatives, was tasked with arranging safe houses, weapons and explosives, and was also involved in money transfers.[28] However, the struggles of al-Shabaab had distinctly local goals and it was not until 2012 that official ties to Al Qaeda were created, as a result of some Al Qaeda fighters' presence in Somalia and the need for financing, training and logistical support. Even then, al-Shabaab remained predominantly focused on Somali issues and dynamics rather than on global ideology, which explains its refusal to support ISIS.[29]

The impact of local events

The interest of representatives of global jihad in targeting the Scandinavian countries was initially low. In 2004, bin Laden explicitly mentioned Sweden in one of his speeches, asking why Al Qaeda targets the USA and 'why we don't strike, for example, Sweden?' He explained that the reason is that the organization seeks only 'to punish the oppressors'.[30] However, this lack of interest in Scandinavia dramatically changed the following year. The crisis began after the Danish newspaper *Jyllands-Posten* published a dozen editorial cartoons on 30 September 2005, most of which depicted the Prophet Mohammed. Flemming Rose, the culture editor, wrote that he had 'commissioned the cartoons in response to several incidents of self-censorship in Europe caused by widening fears and feelings of intimidation in dealing with issues related to Islam'.[31]

Some Muslim groups in Denmark took up the issue, attracting public attention in both the West and the Middle East, triggering protests and even violent riots in some Muslim countries. One of the twelve cartoons, depicting Mohammed with a bomb in his turban, was drawn by Kurt Westergaard, who received much attention from radical circles, as several plots against him were uncovered after the publication. In 2008, the Danish police arrested two Tunisians and a Dane for having planned to murder Westergaard. In 2010, Muhudiin Muhammed Geele, who had come to Denmark from Somalia, attacked Westergaard with an axe at his home, and two years later two Danish-Somali brothers were arrested for plotting to murder him. According to the Danish security services, one brother had received training with al-Shabaab and had a prominent position in the organization in Somalia.[32]

The caricatures also mobilized some Norwegians to act. In 2010, three men plotted to attack *Jyllands-Posten* that had published the Mohammed caricatures. Mikael Davud, a Norwegian citizen of Uighur origin, was suspected of being the leader of a Norwegian Al Qaeda cell.[33] According to a Norwegian court, the men intended to attack the Danish *Jyllands-Posten*.[34] They were building a bomb in a basement laboratory in Oslo and Davud planned to carry out the attack by placing it outside *Jyllands-Posten*'s offices in Denmark. The plot was linked to the same Al Qaeda planners behind thwarted attacks against the New York subway system and a Manchester shopping mall in 2009. According to the court, Davud had 'planned the attack together with Al Qaeda'. The plot was revealed as emails from an Al Qaeda operative in Pakistan were intercepted by the authorities, who also secretly replaced a key bomb-making ingredient with a harmless liquid when it was ordered from a local pharmacy.[35] However, rather than taking up the connection to global jihad, Davud argued during the trial that his struggle was for the rights of the oppressed Uighur minority in China, and the bomb was meant to be detonated near the Chinese embassy in Oslo.[36]

Two years later, the incident of the Danish Mohammed caricatures was followed by a rather similar incident in Sweden. In 2007, *Nerikes Allehanda*, a Swedish newspaper, published three caricatures by Lars Vilks, depicting the Prophet Mohammed as a dog. According to the newspaper, the rationale was similar to that of the Danish publication, namely, to raise awareness of self-censorship regarding Islam and the need to protect free speech in a liberal society.[37] This further attracted the attention of the global jihadi movement, as not only Al Qaeda but also the leader of the islamic state of Iraq, Abu Bakr al-Baghdadi, called for reprisals in Sweden for the cartoons. In an audio message, al-Baghdadi also offered cash for killing the cartoonist.[38]

In 2010, three additional Swedish newspapers published the drawings in reaction to a plot discovered in Ireland to attack Vilks. On 11 May 2010, Vilks publicly showed a film featuring homosexuals wearing masks depicting Mohammed and Ali, the prophet's cousin, whereupon he was attacked by an audience member.[39] A few days later, two Swedish-Albanian brothers tried to burn down his house. Indicating the level of indignation created by the publication of the caricatures among many local Muslims and the motivational force it had created in the radical circles, during their trial, one of the brothers called Vilks 'Islam's worst enemy right now'.[40] On 28 December 2010, four men left Stockholm by car for Copenhagen, Denmark. Five men, three of them Swedish citizens, were later arrested in an apartment near Copenhagen for plotting to target *Jyllands-Posten*, the newspaper that had published the first Mohammed caricatures. A machine-gun with a silencer, a pistol and 108 bullets were among items found in the suspects' possession.[41]

As the issue had not only created indignation among local Muslims but also attracted the interest of the global jihadi movement, which hoped to use it as a means to mobilize locals, it was no wonder that the problem resurfaced in 2015 in Copenhagen, when Vilks attended a debate on art, blasphemy and freedom of speech. Two years earlier, three men armed with knives had forced a Danish

National Guard soldier to relinquish his assault rifle. The assailants belonged to a local gang with sympathies for radical Islamism, and the weapon later found its way into the hands of the Danish-Palestinian Omar Abdel Hamid El-Hussein, who had also been involved in gang criminality.[42] On 14 February 2015, he fired through the windows of the Culture Centre in Copenhagen, missing the likely target of the attack, Lars Vilks, but killing a Danish documentary filmmaker and wounding three police officers. The attack took place only a month after the *Charlie Hebdo* incident in Paris, suggesting that the local tensions and indignation against Vilks had converged with tactical learning from Paris, where firearms were used to wreak havoc against the satirical magazine that had published the Mohammad cartoons. The following night, El-Hussein approached a synagogue, acting drunk. As the security guard drew near, El-Hussein killed the guard with a pistol and wounded two police officers. In the morning, the perpetrator was located by the police and killed in a fire fight.[43]

The case seems to indicate a very local jihadi dynamic, as a Copenhagen gang was associated with the terrorist attack. To carry out successful attacks, terrorists need not only the intent but also adequate capacity. Increased capacity can be acquired by gaining access to weapons and explosives, and by learning how to use them. International connections have often been crucial to spreading knowledge of terror tactics and of how to build bombs from seemingly harmless ingredients available in stores. Such instructions could be obtained, for example, in Al Qaeda training camps and then disseminated online, as the use of the internet increased. However, as the Copenhagen incident showed, local criminal connections can also be important for successfully planning and executing a terrorist plot.

Fundraising for global and local jihad

Having access to adequate funds has been essential to jihadi organizations' ability to act. Fundraising was already taking place in Scandinavia in the 1990s, sometimes in the form of violent crimes. When an armoured car was robbed in Copenhagen in 1997, the police soon found out that the getaway car was registered to a Lebanese-Swedish man named Mustafa Ramadan. About USD 100,000 were discovered in apartments belonging to him and his brother, much of it sewn into the clothes of Ramadan's children. Moreover, the police found plane tickets for a flight departing for Jordan the following day. The money was suspected of being destined for radical Islamist groups in Lebanon. Ramadan was sentenced to three and a half years in prison. A few years after having served his prison sentence, in 2003 Ramadan was located in Iraq, working with the network of Abu Musab al-Zarqawi, eventually operating as one of his chief aides and holding the title of military emir. Before leaving for Iraq, Ramadan left in secret for Sweden, where he met Ali Berzengi, an imam in Stockholm.[44]

Ali Berzengi, who first lived in Norway but then moved to Stockholm after marrying a local woman, and Ferman Abdullah, who owned a falafel stand in Malmö in southern Sweden, claimed to be raising funds for Islamic charity. However, the funds were channelled through the informal *hawala* money transfer system to Iraq and Ansar al-Islam. In 2004, German and US authorities informed the Swedish police that Berzengi and Abdullah may have financed two suicide attacks, which had left 109 dead in the Kurdish city of Erbil. Berzengi and Abdullah were arrested and, in Abdullah's apartment, Swedish police discovered a letter indicating a connection to Abu Musab al-Zarqawi, the leader of Al Qaeda in Iraq. The following year, Abdullah and Berzengi were convicted of planning terrorist offences and public devastation. According to the Swedish court, they had transferred funds to Ansar al-Islam for the purpose of financing terrorist attacks, of which at least USD 70,000 were probably linked to the 2004 suicide bombings in Erbil.[45]

In 2001, armed robbery was used to fund a local jihadi connected to Front Islamique du Salut (FIS), an Islamist party in Algeria. The three robbers who targeted a bank in Copenhagen lived in France. However, the person responsible for planning the robbery, Athmane Mehiri, had come to Denmark from Algeria where he had been a member of FIS. He had procured the weapons and provided a hideout for the robbers. Despite plans to raise almost USD 1 million, the robbers got only about USD 12,000 from the cashier and all were soon apprehended by the police. One police officer was shot in the leg during the chase. The incident revealed a distinct European dimension of jihad in Scandinavia, as several similar robberies had taken place in France in the 1990s to fund the armed struggle in Algeria. Apparently, North African jihadi activity had spread to Denmark from France, as Scandinavian banks were seen as easy targets with less security.[46] Also, the newsletter of Groupe Islamique Armé (GIA), an Algerian terrorist organization, was published by members of a local mosque in Brandbergen, Stockholm, as Scandinavia had become a safe place for North African jihadis. This Algerian network later became more global through connections to jihadi training camps in Afghanistan, and even to the USA: Oussama Kassir left Sweden in 1999 to establish a training camp in Oregon.[47] Abu Omar, who was among the militant leaders in Brandbergen mosque, eventually also functioned as a connection between the older generation of jihadis and new recruits to ISIS.

Al Qaeda connections: Real and imaginary

While the early Scandinavian jihad was not always fully characterized by global aspirations, individuals at least partially inspired by global jihad started to appear in the 1990s with the establishment of Al Qaeda. Sometimes local events, such as the publication of the Mohammed caricatures, were ideologically framed by Al Qaeda as part of a clash of civilizations requiring mobilization for global jihad. In 2007, for example, one of the Swedish *Jyllands-Posten* plotters, Munir Awad, was arrested in Somalia on suspicion of terrorism, and two years later he was arrested in Pakistan because of his suspected links to Al Qaeda. In both cases, however, he was released.[48]

Some Scandinavian jihadis rose high in the ranks of Al Qaeda. Swedish-Moroccan Mohammed Moumou belonged to the older generation of jihadis who had received training at bin Laden's camps in Afghanistan in the 1990s, and in Sweden he worked to establish connections between Swedish jihadi circles and the global ambitions of Al Qaeda. In 2004, he was briefly arrested in Denmark on suspicion of having been involved in the Casablanca terrorist attacks that killed thirty-three people. According to US authorities, he may have functioned as Abu Mus'ab al-Zarqawi's representative in Europe. By 2008, when he was killed in Iraq, Moumou had risen to the position of second-in-command of ISIS in Iraq.[49]

Rather than fighting in the central battlefields of global jihad, some individuals have chosen to act in their home countries. Their motivations have usually mixed references to local events and a need to protect or avenge *Ummah* – the abstract global community of Muslims – for injustices committed by the West. On 11 December 2010, Sweden was shocked by its first suicide bomber, as Taimour Abdulwahab al-Abdaly first set his car on fire, which was followed by a series of explosions from gas canisters placed inside the vehicle, and then detonated his bomb belt next to a busy shopping street in Stockholm. The explosion killed only the perpetrator and wounded two passers-by. In 2001, al-Abdaly had moved from Sweden to Britain to study at the University of Luton, and had spent much of the decade in Luton, long known as a hotbed of radicalization.[50] Sources at the local Islamic Centre reported that his views were deemed so extreme that he was asked to leave after he began giving sermons. He returned to Sweden shortly before the attack and argued in an audio recording that the reasons for the attacks were Vilks and the presence of Swedish soldiers in Afghanistan:

> Thanks to Lars Vilks and his paintings of the Prophet Mohammad, peace be upon him, and your soldiers in Afghanistan and your silence on all this so shall your children, daughters, brothers and sisters die in the same way as our brothers and sisters and children die. Now the islamic states have fulfilled what they promised you. We are here in Europe and in Sweden, we are a reality, not an invention, I will not say more about this. Our actions will speak for themselves, as long as you do not end your war against Islam and humiliation of the prophet and your stupid support for the pig Vilks.[51]

Al-Abdaly also said that he had been in Iraq; this was confirmed by Iraqi authorities, who reported that he had received training at an Al Qaeda camp and had been in contact with a senior Al Qaeda commander when he was preparing for the attack.[52] However, not all Scandinavians suspected or convicted of terrorism-related charges have visited the battlefields of global jihad or had direct contact with Al Qaeda, despite claims of being part of the organization. Instead, some members of the younger generation have been inspired by the internet and local preachers, some having a history of foreign fighting.[53] In 2005, Mirsad Bektasevic, a seventeen-year-old Bosnian-Swede, had started chatting with a Danish youngster who shared his fascination with radical Islam. When Bektasevic later went to visit his new friend in Copenhagen, he was introduced to the Turkish-Danish Abdulkadir Cesur and two other young men.

Eventually they started planning a jihadi terrorist group and received advice on the matter from like-minded young radicals through online contacts, such as Younis Tsouli from Britain, who had administered a pro-Al Qaeda online forum. Their manifesto, published on 11 September 2005, was signed 'Al Qaeda's Committee in Northern Europe'[54] and made reference to standard jihadi rhetoric, that is, a need to sacrifice one's life in jihad to fight 'oppression' and 'injustice' and to defend the 'honour' of Muslims. However, Bektasevic's chat log with other members of the group reveals a youth struggling to establish a jihadi identity and credibility in the eyes of more reputable jihadis: 'First of all, are we a group? Are we Al Qaeda in Northern Europe? Do we have a council? Who is the head of the council? Do we have a plan? Do we have people and money?'[55] 'Maybe aqua [i.e. Al Qaeda] will get angry if we do not have their approval?'[56]

Despite these uncertainties about their identity and the use of the Al Qaeda brand, they stuck to the plan and in 2005 Bektasevic, and soon afterwards also Cesur, travelled by bus to Bosnia to start their jihadi careers. Bektasevic had rented an apartment and established local contacts that could provide them with weapons and explosives. However, the local police had received intelligence about a plot to establish a local training camp for jihadis. With the help of a picture of Bektasevic, the apartment was located and raided. The police found a bomb belt, 20 kg of explosives, a pistol and a video-recording featuring two masked men saying that they were planning attacks against Europe because of its military presence in Afghanistan and Iraq. Bektasevic and Cesur were later convicted by a Bosnian court of planning a terrorist attack.[57]

The ISIS effect

While much of the early Norwegian jihad centred around the Kurdish personality of Mullah Krekar and the Somalis supporting al-Shabaab's struggle to establish Islamic rule in Somalia, most of the Norwegian foreign fighters soon found themselves fighting for the most radical organizations with global ambitions, such as the Al Qaeda-associated Jabhat al-Nusra and ISIS.[58] Not only did the variety of Norwegian jihadis increase with the rise of the Syrian civil war, but their tactics also changed, with the first suicide bomber from Norway detonating his explosives in Iraq as part of the ISIS military campaign, in 2014.[59]

Many Norwegian foreign fighters who joined ISIS had a background in the Prophet's Ummah, an Islamist group, established in 2012, that succeeded in creating a multi-ethnic radical network in the Oslo region.[60] The group established contacts with experienced jihadis in other Scandinavian and European countries, and with limited legal obstacles to travelling to Syria to fight, the numbers of Norwegian foreign fighters increased dramatically.[61] According to the leader of the Prophet's Ummah, Ubaydullah Hussain, about a dozen had left Norway for Syria by 2012, not to join any jihadi organization with global aims but 'to defend the civilian population'.[62] Indeed, according to the Norwegian security service, most of the first Norwegian foreign fighters seemed not very ideologically motivated and therefore did not care about global jihad.[63] There was also a similar relative lack of ideological motivation and global aims among the first Swedes to go to Syria, as the need to help local Muslims was often cited as the main motivational factor.⁶⁴ Moreover, ISIS was not the only jihadi group in Syria. In Sweden, especially in the west and south of the country, the recruiters of the Al Qaeda-associated Jabhat al-Nusra were much more active, though ISIS recruitment eventually gained strength with reports of ISIS military achievements and increasing online activity.

With the increasing difficulty of reaching ISIS-controlled territory in 2016, there were fears that ISIS sympathizers would, instead, stage terrorist attacks in their home countries. On 7 April 2017, Akman Rakhmat Akilov, an asylum seeker from Uzbekistan, hijacked a lorry in Central Stockholm. At high speed, he ploughed the heavy vehicle through the crowds in a busy shopping street, killing five and injuring fourteen. After being caught, he said to the Swedish authorities that he had initially wanted to join ISIS in Syria but was then inspired by an ISIS call for attacks in Europe.⁶⁵ His tactic apparently copied similar attacks the previous year in Berlin, when a lorry driver killed twelve at a local Christmas market, and in Nice, where eighty-six people were killed on the seaside promenade under similar circumstances. Two days after the Stockholm attack, a 17-year-old Russian boy who had sought asylum in Norway was apprehended in Oslo with an explosive device. The Norwegian security services stated that there was a probable connection to the terrorist attack in Stockholm.⁶⁶

On 6 June 2017, Farid Ikken, a Swedish-Algerian researcher, attacked a French police officer in front of the Notre Dame Cathedral in Paris. The officer believed that he was a tourist asking for directions but, on approaching him, received a hammer blow to the head. Ikken had previously studied and worked as a journalist in Sweden, but was now a PhD student at the University of Paris II – Assas. He had earlier sworn allegiance to ISIS in a video-recording and shouted at the time of the attack that 'this is for Syria' and that he was a 'soldier of the Caliphate'.⁶⁷ He had no criminal record and, rather than having shown signs of radicalization, was considered an intellectual. Ikken told investigators that he had radicalized himself over a period of ten months. At his home, the police found a computer and USB key containing, in addition to the video message, the ISIS manual for lone-wolf terrorists, images of the London attack three days before and videos glorifying previous attacks in Paris and Brussels.⁶⁸ Scandinavian jihadis have therefore not only been motivated by the global ideology of ISIS but also been inspired by events in neighbouring European countries.

Abu Omar, who belonged to the older North African network centred on the Brandbergen mosque, owned two shops in Stockholm. He had been under investigation by the Swedish security services for about fifteen years, but was not convicted of any terrorism-related charges. Several Swedish ISIS fighters had lived in the same apartment with him and his shops functioned as a meeting place for radical Islamists, as he used his money and international contacts to support jihadism. Mohamed Belkaid had come to Sweden from Algeria in 2009 and worked as an intern in one of Abu Omar's shops. He had been a petty criminal and was not considered a radical.⁶⁹ However, after getting to know Abu Omar, he travelled to Syria to join ISIS in 2014. Upon joining the organization, he was among the few who directly wanted to join a suicide squad, but he was eventually selected for a special group preparing for attacks in Europe. When on 13 November 2015 Paris was hit by a barrage of attacks killing more than 130 people, Belkaid was found to be one of the masterminds of the plot, managing the attack by phone from Brussels. Four months later, when three coordinated explosions killed thirty-two people in Brussels, he was again suspected of planning the attacks. He was finally killed by the Belgian police on 15 March 2016 when they raided an apartment in Brussels housing several wanted terrorists.[70] Another Swede, Osama Krayem, had travelled with Belkaid from Syria to France and was involved in the Brussels attacks, although he did not detonate his bomb.[71]

Conclusion

During the early years of the Syrian civil war, the numbers of Scandinavian foreign fighters were modest. When the ISIS declared the birth of a caliphate with global aspirations in 2014, the Syrian civil war took on the more distinct characteristics of global jihad. More Swedish recruits poured in, mainly from Gothenburg, Malmö, Stockholm and Örebro. Danish foreign fighters hailed mainly from Copenhagen and Århus, while most of the Norwegians came from south-eastern Norway, around Oslo. Moreover, the number of women travelling to the newly declared caliphate increased.[72] By 2014, when many men had died in battle, about 40 per cent of the Swedes in the conflict zone were women.[73] However, by 2016, most of the Swedish travellers were joining Jabhat Fateh al-Sham (rebranded from Jabhat al-Nusra),[74] as ISIS was coming under military pressure and travelling to ISIS-controlled territory was becoming increasingly difficult.

In 2017, when the Norwegian security services concluded that the greatest terror threat to Norway was from people associated with Al Qaeda and ISIS, it was also clear that Norway was not a prioritized target. The security services expected that 'the number of new persons who are radicalized to extreme Islamism will continue to be low', compared with 2014 when activity in radical circles had peaked. This was expected to affect the number of both foreign fighters and those willing to act in Norway. The reason for the expected weakening of the jihadi community was that several members and potential recruiters of new members were now serving time in prison or had been killed in Syria.[75]

Although ISIS has today lost its territorial foothold in Syria, it still has numerous sympathizers and there are fears that the organization's online presence in the form of a virtual global caliphate will continue inspiring a new generation of jihadis who will carry out attacks in their home countries. However, the history of jihad teaches us that large-scale mobilization will now be difficult. Most of the foreign volunteers in Afghanistan were inspired by jihad only after the local mujahideen had already gained the upper hand after mid-1980s and controlled considerable territory.[76] In addition, Al Qaeda found that the idea of global jihad was inadequate to inspire the masses it had hoped to recruit after the 9/11 attacks, as it did not succeed in gaining control over considerable swathes of territory in Iraq. As Gerges has argued, the ideology of global jihad did not manage to put down deep roots among most jihadis.[77] Moreover, the history of Scandinavian jihad shows that mobilization increases most when global ideas are coupled with the local aspirations of the periphery, such as revenge for the Mohammed caricatures, ethnic connections to local struggles (e.g. in Algeria and Somalia) or disgruntled youth seeking an alternative life project in an already established territorial reality.

Notes

1. Marc Sageman, *Understanding Terror Networks* (Philadelphia: University of Pennsylvania Press, 2004), p. 137.
2. Faisal Devji, *Landscapes of Jihad: Militancy, Morality and Modernity* (London: Hurst Publishers, 2005), p. 63.
3. PST 2016, Temarapport: Hvilken bakgrunn har personer som frekventerer ekstreme islamistiske miljøer i Norge før de blir radikalisert?
4. *Foreign Fighters: An Updated Assessment of the Flow of Foreign Fighters into Syria and Iraq* (New York: The Soufan Group, 2015). Bo Elkjær and Natascha Ree Mikkelsen, 'GRAFIK: Her er de danske syrienkrigere', *DR*, 15 September 2016. Available at https://www.dr.dk/nyheder/indland/grafik-her-er-de-danske-syrienkrigere-0.
5. Petter Nesser, Anne Stenersen and Emilie Oftedal, 'Jihadi terrorism in Europe: The ISIS-effect', *Perspectives on Terrorism*, 10, no. 6 (2016): 8.
6. Ibid., p. 7.
7. Quintan Wiktorowicz, *Radical Islam Rising: Muslim Extremism in the West* (Oxford: Rowman & Littlefield Publishers, 2005).
8. Robert S. Leiken, *Europe's Angry Muslims* (Oxford: Oxford University Press, 2012), p. 157.
9. Ibid., p. 11.
10. Marco Nilsson, 'Hard and soft targets: The lethality of suicide terrorism', *Journal of International Relations and Development* (2015). Available at https://doi.org/10.1057/jird.2015.25.
11. Monica Kleja, 'Bombmannen fick tekniska problem', *Ny Teknik*, 16 December 2010. Available at https://www.nyteknik.se/digitalisering/bombmannen-fick-tekniska-problem-6423610.
12. Nesser, Stenersen and Oftedal, 'Jihadi Terrorism in Europe', p. 14.
13. Ibid., p. 18.
14. Michael Taarnby Jensen, *Jihad in Denmark: An Overview and Analysis of Jihadi Activity in Denmark 1990-2006*, DIIS Working Paper no 2006/35 (Copenhagen: Danish Institute for International Studies, 2006); Frank J. Cilluffo, Jeffrey B. Cozzens and Magnus Ranstorp, *Foreign Fighters: Trends, Trajectories & Conflict Zones* (The George Washington University, Homeland Security Policy Institute, 2010).
15. Frazer Egerton, *Jihad in the West: The Rise of Militant Salafism* (Cambridge: Cambridge University Press, 2011), p. 124.
16. Taarnby Jensen, *Jihad in Denmark*, p. 18.
17. Evan Kohlman, *Al-Qaida's Jihad in Europe* (Oxford: Berg Publishers, 2004).
18. Pam O'Toole, 'Mullah denies Iraq al-Qaeda link', *BBC News*, 31 January 2003. Available at http://news.bbc.co.uk/2/hi/middle_east/2713749.stm.
19. Lars Akerhaug, Rune Thomas Ege and Morten S. Hopperstad, 'Krekar dømt til fem år for terror- og drapstrusler', *VG*, 26 March 2012. Available at http://www.vg.no/nyheter/innenriks/mulla-krekar/krekar-doemt-til-fem-aar-for-terror-og-drapstrusler/a/10064736/.

20 Oda Leraan Skjetne, Sindre Granly Meldalen and Anders Holth Johansen. 'Slik styrte Krekar terrornettverket', *Dagbladet*, 12 November 2015. Available at https://www.dagbladet.no/nyheter/slik-styrte-krekar-terrornettverket/60594751.
21 Bjørn-Martin Nordby, 'Sakkyndig: Krekars rolle mer og mer marginal', *VG*, 13 October 2015. Available at http://www.vg.no/nyheter/innenriks/mulla-krekar/sakkyndig-krekars-rolle-mer-og-mer-marginal/a/23541475/.
22 Michael Taarnby and Lars Hallunbaek, *Al-Shabaab: The Internationalization of Militant Islamism in Somalia and the Implications for Radicalization Processes in Europe* (Copenhagen: Danish Ministry of Justice, 2010), p. 42.
23 Taarnby and Hallunbaek, *Al-Shabaab*, p. 45.
24 Norsk Telegrambyrå, 'Advarer mot norsk-somaliere i al-Shabaab', *VG*, 20 March 2014. Available at http://www.vg.no/nyheter/utenriks/somalia/advarer-mot-norsk-somaliere-i-al-shabaab/a/10146546/.
25 Richard Aschberg, 'Värvade på fritidsgård', *Aftonbladet*, 16 December 2010. Available at http://www.aftonbladet.se/nyheter/article12707887.ab.
26 Taarnby and Hallunbaek, *Al-Shabaab*, p. 43.
27 Joshua Hammer, 'The African front', *The New York Times*, 23 December 2007. Available at http://www.nytimes.com/2007/12/23/magazine/23kenya-t.html?ex=1356066000&en=c558476ab344449e&ei=5124&partner=permalink&exprod=permalink.
28 Taarnby and Hallunbaek, *Al-Shabaab*, p. 44.
29 Conor Gaffey, 'Why Al-Shabaab is not Joining ISIS', *Newsweek*, 22 January 2016. Available at http://www.newsweek.com/al-shabab-not-joining-isis-418656; Aislinn Laing, 'How al-Qaeda and Islamic State are competing for al-Shabaab in Somalia', *The Telegraph*, 12 January 2016. Available at http://www.telegraph.co.uk/news/worldnews/islamic-state/12015075/How-al-Qaeda-and-Islamic-State-are-fighting-for-al-Shabaab-affections-in-Somalia.html.
30 Al Jazeera, 'Full transcript of bin Laden's speech', 1 November 2004. Available at http://www.aljazeera.com/archive/2004/11/200849163336457223.html.
31 Flemming Rose, 'Why I published those cartoons', *Washington Post*, 19 February 2006. Available at http://www.washingtonpost.com/wp-dyn/content/article/2006/02/17/AR2006021702499.html.
32 Søren Astrup, 'Dansk-somaliere afhøres af PET efter terroranholdelser', *Politiken*, 29 May 2012. Available at http://politiken.dk/indland/art5388752/Dansk-somaliere-afh%C3%B8res-af-PET-efter-terroranholdelser; Lars Halskov, 'Kenya: Øksemand med i toppen af terrorgruppe', *Politiken*, 9 January 2010. Available at http://politiken.dk/indland/art4833544/Kenya-%C3%98ksemand-med-i-toppen-af-terrorgruppe.
33 Walter Gibbs and John Acher, 'Suspect in Norway admits plot against Danish paper', *Reuters*, 28 September 2010. Available at http://uk.reuters.com/article/idINIndia-51789820100928.
34 Jørgen Svarstad and Lene Li Dragland, 'Dømt i terrorsak fikk tre år for hvitvasking', *Aftenposten*, 24 November 2012. Available at https://www.aftenposten.no/norge/i/BRwjG/Domt-i-terrorsak-fikk-tre-ar-for-hvitvasking.
35 Associated Press, 'Norway convicts two men over al-Qaeda plot on Danish newspaper', *The Telegraph*, 30 January 2012. Available at http://www.telegraph.co.uk/news/worldnews/al-qaeda/9049416/Norway-convicts-two-men-over-al-Qaeda-plot-on-Danish-newspaper.html.
36 Hans O. Torgesen, 'Retten: Davud planla terror sammen med al-Qaida', *Aftenposten*, 30 January 2012. Available at https://www.aftenposten.no/norge/i/Wb5xd/Retten-Davud-planla-terror-sammen-med-al-Qaida.

37 Lars Ströman, 'Rätten att förlöjliga en religion', *Nerikes Allehanda*, 28 August 2008. Available at https://web.archive.org/web/20070906190721/http://www.na.se/artikel.asp?intId=1209627.
38 Ian Black, 'Stockholm bombing: Iraqi group linked to al-Qaida praises attack', *The Guardian*, 13 December 2010. Available at https://www.theguardian.com/world/2010/dec/13/stockholm-bomber-praised-islamist-website.
39 'Vilks överfallen under föreläsning', *Dagens Nyheter*, 11 May 2010. Available at http://www.dn.se/nyheter/sverige/vilks-overfallen-under-forelasning/.
40 Anna Mattsson, 'Fängelse för brandattentatet mot Lars Vilks', *Expressen*, 15 July 2010. Available at http://www.expressen.se/kvallsposten/fangelse-for-brandattentatet-mot-lars-vilks/.
41 'Four guilty of Danish plot over Muhammad cartoons', *BBC News*, 4 June 2012. Available at http://www.bbc.com/news/world-europe-18321160.
42 Niels Fastrup, Lars Munck Rasmussen and Louise Dalsgaard, 'Religiøse bandemedlemmer bag terrorvåben brugt mod Krudttønden', *DR*, 3 March 2015. Available at http://www.dr.dk/nyheder/indland/religioese-bandemedlemmer-bag-terrorvaaben-brugt-mod-krudttoenden.
43 Alexander Vickhoff, 'Terrorn i Köpenhamn: 14 timmar av skräck', *Expressen*, 13 February 2016. Available at http://www.expressen.se/kvallsposten/terrorn-i-kopenhamn-14-timmar-av-skrack/.
44 Taarnby Jensen, *Jihad in Denmark*, pp. 42–3.
45 Associated Press, 'Two Iraqis charged in Sweden with transferring money to al-Zarqawi', *USA Today*, 5 April 2005. Available at https://usatoday30.usatoday.com/news/world/2005-04-05-alzarqawi-money_x.htm; Olle Lönnaeus, Niklas Orrenius and Erik Magnusson, 'Kiosken var en terrorbank', *Sydsvenskan*, 15 Februari 2006. Available at https://web.archive.org/web/20060215223827/http://sydsvenskan.se/sverige/article141850.ece.
46 Michael Taarnby and Lars Hallunbaek, 'Jihad in Denmark: An overview and analysis of jihadi activity in Denmark 1990-2006', Danish Institute for International Studies, p. 27.
47 Magnus Sandelin, *Svenska ISIS krigare: Från Al-Qaida till jihadi cool* (Stockholm: Fri Tanke, 2016), p. 7.
48 Josefine Elfström, 'Munir Awad en av de häktade – tidigare misstänkt som terrorist', *Expressen*, 30 December 2010. Available at http://www.expressen.se/nyheter/munir-awad-en-av-de-haktade---tidigare-misstankt-som-terrorist/.
49 Kaare Sørensen, *The Mind of a Terrorist: David Headley, the Mumbai Massacre, and His European Revenge* (New York: Arcade Publishing, 2016); U.S. Department of the Treasury, 'Treasury Designations Target Terrorist Facilitators, HP-191', 7 December 2006. Available at https://www.treasury.gov/press-center/press-releases/Pages/hp191.aspx.
50 Daily Mail Reporter, '"I never knew my husband had become a terrorist": Wife of British-based suicide bomber tells of her "devastation" over Stockholm attack', *Daily Mail*, 12 December 2010. Available at http://www.dailymail.co.uk/news/article-1337930/Sweden-suicide-bombers-wife-I-knew-husband-terrorist.html#ixzz4ryieBoKg.
51 Ibid.
52 Petter Ljunggren, 'Gripen al-Qaidaledare påstås ha varit Taimours kontakt', *SVT Nyheter*, 30 September 2015. Available at https://www.svt.se/nyheter/inrikes/gripen-al-qaidaledare-pastas-ha-varit-taimours-kontakt-1.
53 Petter Nesser, *Islamist Terrorism in Europe: A History* (Oxford: Oxford University Press, 2015), pp. 203–4.

54 Magnus Sandelin, *Jihad: Svenskarna i de islamistiska terrornätverken* (Stockholm: Månpocket, 2013), p. 59.
55 Ibid., p. 61.
56 Ibid., p. 63.
57 Dragan Risojevis, 'Rapport från domstolen', *Göteborgs-Posten*, 10 January 2007. Available at http://www.gp.se/nyheter/g%C3%B6teborg/rapport-fr%C3%A5n-domstolen-1.1171582.
58 Brynjar Lia and Petter Nesser, 'Norske Muslimske Fremmedkrigere', *Nytt Norsk Tidsskrift*, 4, no. 31 (2014): 408.
59 Lars Akerhaug, 'Var en helt vanlig muslim i Oslo - ble selvmordsbomber for ISIL', *Dagen*, 4 August 2014. Available at http://www.dagen.no/Nyheter/04/08/2014/Var_en_helt_vanlig_muslim_i_Oslo_-_ble_selvmordsbomber_for_ISIL-98825.
60 Olga Stokke, Lene Li Dragland and Andreas Bakke Foss, 'Dette er Profetens Ummah i Norge', *Aftenposten*, 13 July 2014. Available at https://www.aftenposten.no/norge/i/43EV/Dette-er-Profetens-Ummah-i-Norge.
61 Lia and Nesser, 'Norske Muslimske Fremmedkrigere', p. 407.
62 Simon Solheim and Martin Herman Wiedswang Zondag, 'Et titall medlemmer av vår organisasjon i Syria', *NRK*, 17 October 2012. Available at https://www.nrk.no/norge/_-er-der-for-a-forsvare-sivlie-1.8362077.
63 Olga Stokke, 'PST: Ikke alle som reiser til Syria, er islamister', *Aftenposten*, 3 March 2014. Available at https://www.aftenposten.no/norge/i/5zVz/PST-Ikke-alle-som-re iser-til-Syria_-er-islamister.
64 Marco Nilsson, 'Foreign fighters and the radicalization of local jihad: Interview evidence from Swedish jihadists', *Studies in Conflict & Terrorism*, 38, no. 5 (2015): 343–58.
65 Antonia Backlund, 'Rakhmat Akilov i förhör: Fick order att agera från ISIS', *Nyheter 24*, 23 April 2017. Available at https://nyheter24.se/nyheter/inrikes/882738-rakhmat-akilov-forhor-order-agera-is.
66 TT Nyhetsbyrån, 'Sverigekoppling utreds efter Oslobomb', *Svenska Dagbladet*, 2 April 2017.
67 Lill Sjölund and Johan Tollgerdt, 'Farid Ikken, 40, misstänks för hammar-attacken', *Expressen*, 7 June 2017. Available at http://www.aftonbladet.se/nyheter/a/Lr831/man nen-som-skots-till-dods-i-paris-har-bott-i-sverige.
68 BBC News, 'Notre-Dame attack: Farid Ikken appears in Paris court', 11 June 2017. Available at http://www.bbc.com/news/world-europe-40236305.
69 Isabelle Nordström and Niklas Svahn, 'Terroristen bodde i Sverige – så var hans okända liv', *Aftonbladet*, 18 March 2016. Available at http://www.aftonbladet.se/nyhe ter/article22471894.ab.
70 Bo-Göran Bodin, 'Så blev småtjuven Belkaid en ökänd terrorist', *SVT nyheter*, 30 November 2016. Available at https://www.svt.se/nyheter/lokalt/stockholm/sa-ble v-smatjuven-belkaid-en-okand-terrorist.
71 Hannes Lundberg Andersson, 'ISIS-svenskens terrorcell dödade 162 personer', *Expressen*, 22 March 2017. Available at https://www.expressen.se/nyheter/is-svenskens-terrorcell-dodade-162-personer/.
72 European Union Terrorism Situation and Trend Report 2015, *Europol*, p. 6. Linus Gustafsson and Magnus Ranstorp, *Swedish Foreign Fighters in Syria and Iraq: An Analysis of Open-Source Intelligence and Statistical Data* (Stockholm: Center for Asymmetric Threat Studies, 2017), p. 77.
73 Gustafsson and Ranstorp, *Swedish Foreign Fighters in Syria and Iraq*, p. 77.

74 Ibid., p. 79.
75 PST, Trusselvurdering 2017. Available at http://www.pst.no/media/82648/pst_trusselvurd_2017_no_web.pdf.
76 Gilles Kepel, *Jihad: The Trail of Political Islam* (Cambridge: The Belknap Press, 2002), p. 140.
77 Fawaz Gerges, *The Far Enemy: Why Jihad Went Global*, 2nd edn (Cambridge: Cambridge University Press, 2009), p. 275.

THE EVOLUTION OF THE JIHAD IN GERMANY

Jan Raudszus

Germany has long been the source of volunteers for jihad and a logistical base. Since the 2000s it has also become a target of their threats. This chapter will examine the case of Germany to decipher the crucial question of how the relationship between centre and periphery works in the case of the jihad in Germany. What it will show is that the relationship is dynamic and changes over time. In the early stages of the international jihad movement, its ideas, conflicts and activities were mostly an import from the centre to the periphery. During the 2000s the jihadi scene in Germany developed its own dynamic, which in itself had influence on the conflicts in the centre. While it is possible to identify phases in the process, these are not deterministic and they overlap. More precisely, what emerges is a multiphasic process. What centre and periphery mean at any given time and how these two 'places' interact with each other is dependent on the point in time and the individual acting. While conflicts within the jihadi 'centre' remain crucial drivers for jihadist activities in Germany, increasingly we observe conflict dynamics that are domestically focused.

To provide such an assessment this chapter will sketch out the history of jihad in Germany from its early beginnings to the most recent examples of recruitment networks that have sent foreign fighters to Germany and were involved in domestic terrorist plots. This chapter cannot and will not provide, however, a complete narration of all phases of jihadism in Germany. This would be impossible within the scope of this chapter and also not necessarily expedient considering the overall question this anthology plans to answer. Rather, it will offer a sketch. It will provide appropriate examples that illustrate the larger trends in German jihad. Since we will rely mostly on secondary literature, this will necessary reveal some blind spots in the research so far. In particular, we find significant gaps in the early history of jihadism in Germany. There simply has not been much work utilizing primary source materials on this subject.

Early history of jihadism in Germany

The history of jihadism in Germany probably reaches back to the 1980s. During these days jihadism was far from being a threat in Germany itself, though. Rather, it was essentially part of the wider struggle of the Cold War. There is the possibility of a German link during the war in Afghanistan after the Soviet invasion. Soviet troops fought against Afghans, supported by Western governments, Saudi Arabia and foreign fighters from the Arab World. In particular, it is conceivable that the Islamic Centre Munich (IZM) played a role. The centre to this day is a centre of Muslim Brotherhood activities, according to an annual report by the domestic intelligence service in Bavaria.[1] However, this link is rather opaque. Since the Second World War, the centre had been a focal point of Muslim anti-Soviet activity, aided by Western intelligence agencies, according to journalist Ian Johnson.[2] Since fighters from all over the world took part[3] in the struggle, it is possible this also included Muslims that had previously been living in Germany. We have some anecdotal evidence that suggests such mobilization was happening in Europe, though these examples consider France[4] and Spain.[5] Nevertheless, to date this is mostly speculation and in any case the numbers are likely to have been rather low. More crucial is the presence of some veterans of the conflict in Germany that would later help facilitate the spread of jihadist ideology as well as terrorist cells – one of which was responsible for the 9/11 attacks.

Crucial for the trajectory of jihad in Europe and Germany was the fact that once the war in Afghanistan had ended not all of the 'Afghan Arabs' were able to return home. While most of those from the Gulf States and Jordan could, those from Egypt, Syria and Libya were prosecuted by their home country's governments. Many moved on to other battlefields including Tajikistan, Chechnya and Bosnia. Many also settled in Europe. While many others found a new home in London, others also moved to Germany.[6]

This development was significant because it meant that the wider jihadist movement to which these individuals belonged now made significant links with Europe. From the centre of jihadism in the Middle East, the ideas of Jihad were exported to Europe via the battlefield of Central Asia. The blossoming networks in Germany remained linked with the conflicts abroad (e.g., Bosnia). For now, Europe remained largely a periphery with a small self-supporting jihadist scene that was largely dependent for cues from the conflicts abroad. In the early 1990s this most important conflict for the jihadist milieu in Germany was the war in Bosnia.

The war in Bosnia – creating networks

We know a bit more about the role that jihadists from Germany played in the war in Bosnia during the 1990s. Between 1992 and 1995 the conflict in Bosnia received a lot of attention in the Islamic world and was perceived as a religious struggle between Christian Serbs and Muslim Bosnians.[7] Apart from the aid that the Bosnian cause received from Iran, there was widespread support from Sunni Muslims. In 1992 the Egyptian Muslim Brotherhood declared jihad against the Serbs with reference to the Afghan jihad. However, the Egyptian government attempted to suppress all mobilization of armed jihad. Both the Egyptian and the Saudi governments emphasized humanitarian aid instead, fearful of the movement being controlled by forces hostile to their government.[8] Meanwhile, for Islamists residing in the rest of Europe, including Germany, the plight of the Bosnians was the opportunity to link together diverse Muslim communities in different European states that until then had to a certain degree remained separated from each other. Supporting fellow Muslims in danger was a common cause.

According to Giles Kepel, the jihadist support for Bosnia began with the arrival of 4000 men mostly from Saudi Arabia in 1992.[9] This was after the mujahedeen had conquered Kabul in Afghanistan and many other jihadists were going home (including to Egypt and Algeria). The jihadists that arrived thought they had found a new battlefield in the global fight for Islam. However, they were confronted with very different circumstances from Afghanistan. Famous for their brutality in battles against the Serbs, Bosnian authorities tried to rein them in partially. Another crucial reason for this was that they tried pressing their Salafist-jihadist ideas of Islam upon the Bosnian population. Ultimately, after the signing of the Dayton Accord in 1995 the last foreign fighter brigade was disbanded and the participants asked to leave the country. Some of them who had received Bosnian citizenship remained though and while Kepel was optimistic in 2000 that little of their ideology had survived in Bosnian society,[10] there are currently Salafist centres in Bosnia that broadly follow such ideas and have caused issues for local society; but they were also an important vantage point for jihadist foreign fighters that emigrated to Syria and Iraq after 2012.[11]

Bosnia became the first international conflict including jihadi foreign fighters, which, notably, featured protagonists from Germany. The group that has become known more widely was based in the German city of Freiburg. We know more about this particular group because after the war in Bosnia its members remained active in the Salafist and jihadist scene in Germany. The group gathered around the preacher Yahia Yusuf. In Egypt, he had been a member of al-Jama'a al-Islamiyya – a group that had been involved in militant action before he arrived in Germany in 1988. His affiliation probably is not an accident – it has been noted that the organization was heavily involved in the conflict in Bosnia.[12] He settled in Freiburg and became the local scene's most prominent figure. The mosque he preached in was mostly frequented by Arabs searching for militant teachings. While he and his followers reportedly were in contact with Algerian groups, they became interested in the conflict in Bosnia. The group was mostly involved in the provision of humanitarian aid, but some individuals also took part in the fighting there, according to the ex-wife of one group member.[13] This is backed up by recent research.[14] Several of the group members continued to play a significant role in the German jihadist scene. Yusuf himself became involved in the Multi-Cultural House in the city of Neu-Ulm, where he was apparently central in propagating the jihad in Chechnya (some people subsequently left to fight there) and he was also linked to the radicalization process of members of the so-called Sauerland plot targeting American military installations. Another protagonist was Aleem Nasir who later acted as a recruiter for Laskar-e Tayyiba and Al Qaeda. Muhammad Ciftci became one of Germany's most prominent Salafist preachers. Finally, Reda Seyam would continue to play a role in the German jihadist scene for almost another decade. Implicated in the 2002 Bali bombing he went on to become an official of ISIS in Iraq.[15] According to his ex-wife, in 1992 Seyam linked up with an Algerian ('Ahmed') who had trained in Afghanistan. Seyam had lived a secular life as an immigrant in Germany until the first Gulf War. The war apparently was a crucial moment in his radicalization process.[16] The mixture of Arab migrants linking up with people who had contact with jihadist networks, such as Yusuf and 'Ahmed', appears to have been crucial in creating the jihadist networks in Germany that belong also to the wider European scene.

The 9/11 cell

Notoriously, central parts of what would become the 9/11 attack cells emerged in the German city of Hamburg. This development was also connected to former jihadist foreign fighters. While the direct links between the milieu in Hamburg and the men who would attack the World Trade Centre in New York and the Pentagon in Washington have remained surprisingly opaque, the presence of such individuals in their direct vicinity is notable. According to Peter Nesser, the al-Quds Mosque in Hamburg was Germany's main jihadist hub before 9/11. Here, the future 9/11 attackers were able to meet Mamoun Darkazanli, another Afghanistan veteran, who was acting as imam.[17] Authorities in Spain and the United States have alleged that Darkazanli was an Al Qaeda money manager. However, German courts have acquitted him of all terrorism-related charges.[18] Darkazanli is believed by some authors to have been a crucial player in the early Al Qaeda network in Europe. He was linked with Mahmud Mamduh Salim, a leading Al Qaeda member who was arrested in Germany in 1998 and extradited to the United States. He had met Darkazanli on several occasions. The latter at some point had command over a bank account of Salim. Darkazanli's contacts consisted mostly of Syrians from Aleppo who had fled their home country after the failed revolt against the Assad regime in the early 1980s. Another crucial person close to the 9/11 cell was Muhammad Haida Zammar, who was also Syrian, had fought in Bosnia and trained in Al Qaeda camps in Afghanistan.[19] These contacts might have been crucial for the 9/11 cells in their recruitment and preparations for the attack.[20] However, there is no solid evidence for this. Darkazanli and others like Seyam were always able to evade prosecution – if they were ever found guilty of anything.

The members of the 9/11 cell were made up of young Arab men that had come to Hamburg to study here. In Hamburg they met the conditions that radicalized them and crucially the right people to make the necessary links with the European jihadist network that facilitated their travels to Afghanistan, where they were recruited for the 9/11 attacks. The 2001 attacks on the United States concluded the early phase of jihadism in Germany. As we have seen, this early scene was characterized by a parallel process. Former Afghanistan fighters had settled in Europe, including Germany. They exported jihadist ideas and enmity from the Middle East (often via Central Asia) to Europe. Here they met members of the Arab expat community who after radicalizing in the context of their host country (away from home, searching for community in radical mosques)[21] were eager to use links to the global jihadi movement these veterans provided. Sternberg has noted that after the embassy attacks in Africa after 1998, the popularity of Al Qaeda grew. This attracted young men from the European diaspora and the Hamburg group was part of this new trend.[22]

German jihad goes global

The 9/11 attacks were a watershed moment for Germany. In particular, the fact that the cell whose responsibility it was to pilot the airplanes had formed in Hamburg came as a shock to many Germans. However, the attacks had, indeed, not been the first instance of Germany being affected by jihadist violence. In 2000 police in Frankfurt had arrested a group of men planning to bomb the Strasbourg Christmas market.[23] From the evidence it appeared that the group had used apartments in Frankfurt to prepare for the bombing. The group was part of the North African jihadi networks in Europe and several of its members confessed they had been trained in Al Qaeda camps in Afghanistan.[24] This highlights that until 2001 Germany had mostly been a place for logistics and recruitment but not itself a target of jihadist activity. It probably lacked the colonial history of France and Britain to attract the attention of jihadists. Significantly, in the years following the attacks on the World Trade Centre and the Pentagon all plots failed and there was no successful terrorist attack in Germany. These plots often targeted foreign dignitaries or American military installations.

Guido Steinberg has described the evolution of jihadism in Germany in three overlapping phases. The 'organized' jihadis dominated the scene in Germany until 2005. They were proper members of a larger jihadist organization such as Al Qaeda and Abu Musab al-Zarqawi's Tauhid, as well as the Iraqi group Ansar al-Islam. These groups were ethnically homogenous and external, featuring no 'home-grown' members. They were using Germany as a resting place and logistical base. From these groups emerged some cells that planned attacks in Germany itself. One of these groups was linked with al-Zarqawi's Tauhid. Initially, the cell, made up mostly of Palestinians, provided financial and logistical support for the activities of the group in Afghanistan and Iran. However, shortly before the 9/11 attacks, Tauhid ordered its German cell to attack Jewish or Israeli targets in Germany. But German authorities intervened before the attack could take place.[25]

After 2005 the dynamic changed. Several independent plots emerged of which some continued to be planned by Muslim expats while others were 'home-grown', planned by young Muslims born in Germany. However, as the result of a lack of training and resources all these plots failed. One of the most notorious was the case of the so-called suitcase-bombers. In July 2006 two young Lebanese men tried to bomb trains in the state of North-Rhine Westphalia. Only by luck the attack failed. The device did not go off, because of its faulty construction. The two men had not been living in Germany for long and their radicalization process had taken place completely off the radar of the security agencies. One of the men was possibly influenced by the death of his brother who had been a member of the Lebanese jihadi organization Fatah al-Islam and was killed fighting against Lebanese government forces. However, according to the investigation the trigger for the plot was the controversy over the Mohammed caricatures, which at the time had sparked plots all over Europe.[26]

There was only one successful attack by an apparent 'lone wolf' and it was lagging behind the larger trend. On 2 March 2011, Arid Uka, a young man of Kosovar descent, killed two American soldiers at Frankfurt am Main Airport. Apparently incited by online videos and contemporary nasheeds,[27] he attacked a group of Air Force members on their way to Afghanistan, with a handgun. He would have likely killed more had his weapon not jammed.[28] Though a latecomer, this attack was also a bridge to the jihad in the Syrian phase as one of the nasheed singers Uka was reportedly inspired by was Denis Cuspert (see later).

This phase of 'independent' Jihad held an important lesson for the jihadist successors of the failed terrorists. They would need more training and resources to be successful in their plans. Hence, the new phase began: the phase of the 'New Internationalists'. These men (and women) were linked with a self-sustaining German scene that emerged after 2006. For the first time this scene transcended ethnical boundaries. Its members were either born in Germany or had lived in the country for most of their lives. As the scene became more 'German', more and more individuals of Turkish and Kurdish descent (the two biggest Muslim communities in Germany) became involved, while previously Arab men had dominated the scene. In addition, the protagonists were more integrated into transnational jihadi networks than before. Members of these groups were more likely to travel abroad as foreign fighters or receive training in jihadist camps in Pakistan.[29] With the conflict over the Mohammed caricatures, for the first time an issue was introduced to the conflict dynamic that was not external to Europe. Nevertheless, the conflicts outside the continent continued to play a significant role. Afghanistan and the Iraq war and, more generally, the perceived global conflict between Muslims and the West (in particular the US), increasingly triggered radicalization processes and attack plots.

While the conflict context continued to evolve, Germany also saw the emergence of a domestic self-sustaining Salafist scene, which contributed to the dynamic of jihadism there. Before 2005, as with the jihadist current of Salafism, external actors, preachers who had received their training mostly outside Germany, spread Salafism. In 2005, began the 'German phase': young preachers born and raised in Germany began to massively target non-Muslims in their missionary work. New associations, mosques, publishing houses and websites emerged. One of the protagonists was Muhamed Ciftci, who had been involved in the support for the Bosnian jihad. The massive campaign and the fact that it was undertaken mostly in German, made the movement accessible to a wide audience and hence was much more successful in attracting new followers. Some of these activities were supported by money that originated in Saudi Arabia.[30] The Salafist imams preaching a de-cultured form of Islam had a competitive advantage in Germany where many traditional imams spoke no, or very little, German and where converts were often expected to adapt to the culture of a specific Muslim country.

For second- and third-generation German Muslims it was an opportunity to transcend ethnical, national and lingual boundaries of their original communities to join a community thought global.[31]

The years from 2005 to the beginning of the Syrian civil war were marked by three interlinked developments: the widespread rise of the foreign fighter phenomenon among German Islamists, linked with the emergence of German-speaking jihad propaganda – some of which was threatening Germany directly – and increasing terrorist plots targeting Germany itself (rather than targets in Germany that were significant for other reasons). The foreign fighter phenomenon was at its height between 2009 and 2010. At this point about two hundred young Muslims from Germany are reported to have been living with jihadist groups in Pakistan. This development would serve as an example for future foreign fighters joining the jihad in Syria and Iraq.[32]

One significant case that exemplifies all of these dynamics is the so-called Sauerland Cell (named after the German region, where police forces arrested the cell members). Its members were involved in a significant terrorist plot but also acted as recruiters for a jihadi organization in Pakistan.[33] Its four members were radicalized in the Multi-Cultural House in Neu-Ulm, which after 2001 became the new centre of the internationalist current of German jihad (indeed, the support network surrounding the group was much larger). The Multi-Cultural House was an Islamist centre that included a mosque and a library reportedly containing extremist literature.[34] The radicalizing activities of Yahya Yusuf here seem to have been centred on the war in Chechnya. In 2002 four young men from the MKH travelled to Chechnya. All four were killed or disappeared there including a young convert to Islam. In videos – some produced by protagonists of the Multi-Cultural House – the conflict between the Chechen and the Russian states was depicted as the most brutal war between Christians and Jews on one side and Islam on the other. The men killed in Chechnya were celebrated as martyrs at the MKH. The general excitement over the conflict in Chechnya also engulfed the men who would go on to form the Sauerland Cell.

However, because it had become increasingly difficult to reach that specific battlefield and some of the 'Sauerland Cell' members were mostly driven by hate against the United States, the group ultimately decided to go to Iraq instead. To that end they first travelled to Damascus. However, they were unable to contact groups that would have smuggled them into Iraq. Instead, they met a group of men from Azerbaijan who promised to organize passage for them to Chechnya. However, the group from Germany first needed to receive military training before they could fight in Chechnya. It was suggested to them that this training could be undergone in the training camps of militant groups in Pakistan. After travelling to Pakistan, the future 'Sauerland Cell' contacted the Uzbek organization Islamic Jihad Union (IJU).[35] Since the men had a hard time adjusting to the harsh conditions in Waziristan, however, the IJU turned them back to Germany with the mission of attacking US targets there – at the time the IJU was focusing on the fight against Western forces in Afghanistan. Fortunately, German security forces were ultimately able to foil the plot that its planners had imagined as a second 9/11 attack.[36]

Following the failed attack, the IJU began to release videos and pictures of more and more German jihadists including Germany's first suicide attacker Cüneyt Ciftci and, later on, Eric Breininger. Breininger became the German face of the IJU. He urged other Muslims living in Germany to join the fight in Afghanistan. The growing number of German jihadists in Pakistan was made possible because while plotting for their ultimately failed attack, the 'Sauerland Cell' had been actively and very successfully recruiting associates to join the IJU as well. One of them was Breininger. His propaganda seems to have worked and contributed to the increase in the numbers of young Muslims going to Pakistan – which increasingly also included women, since Breininger urged prospective recruits to bring their families.[37] The large number of German foreign fighters in Pakistan ultimately joined several different organizations: the IJU, the Islamic Movement of Uzbekistan (IMU) from which several moved on to Al Qaeda, or Al Qaeda directly. Some also joined the short-lived German jihadist organization German Taliban Mujahedeen (GTM) that had branched out from the IJU.[38] However, after its leading members were killed, the GTM went out without a whimper. The IMU took over as the most important receiving organization of German jihadists.[39] Said points out that by 2011 the number of emigrants in the name of jihad was declining.[40]

Nevertheless, because of its friendly relations with the Uzbek government, Germany continued to be a target for the IMU and was repeatedly threatened by its propaganda. Two brothers, Monir and Yassin Chouka, originally from Bonn, were vital in issuing these threats. They would appear in several videos and threatened Germany with terrorist attacks. A March 2012 video urged Muslims in Germany to follow the example of Arid Uka and launch lone-wolf-attacks. In a May 2012 video, Yassin Chouka called for attacks on members of the far-right party Pro NRW in North-Rhine Westphalia. One group in Germany responded to these calls with a plot in March 2013 to kill the party's chairman. The plot was foiled at the last minute by the police.[41] In the meantime, Al Qaeda had tried to send some of the German volunteers that were populating villages in Pakistan back home to launch attacks against Germany itself. Al Qaeda's goal was to force Germany to withdraw its military forces from Afghanistan. In April 2011 police arrested a cell in Düsseldorf and Bochum that had been planning a bombing attack against civilian targets. In addition, two men were arrested in Vienna who reportedly had been tasked by Al Qaeda to form a cell and launch attacks.[42]

Subsequently, the problem of returnees from Afghanistan plotting attacks in Germany largely disappeared. From the discussion above it becomes clear how closely linked the jihadist scene in Germany had been to conflicts abroad.[43] Now, the impact of the war in Syria became significant.

German jihad in the context of the Syrian Civil War

Starting in 2011 the Salafist scene in Germany became increasingly politicized. This coincided with the first measures by the state to rein in this movement. A controversial campaign to distribute the Qur'an in Germany's city centres and shopping streets ('Lies!' in German, which translates to 'Read!' in English) was run by the organization *Die Wahre Religion* ('The True Religion') whose principal organizer Ibrahim Abou-Nagie had propagated takfiri positions calling leaders in Muslim countries apostates. The group had made contact with protagonists of the banned 'Islam4UK' and was publishing content on the same website (Salafimedia.com).[44] The campaign appears to have had a massive impact by radicalizing young Muslims in Germany, mobilizing them for activism and exposing them to extremist ideas. According to media reports, about 140[45] former 'Lies!' activists later emigrated to Syria and Iraq. Nevertheless, the campaign was somewhat overshadowed by another even more overtly extremist and militant organization: Millatu Ibrahim (MI).

MI was founded by the Austrian Salafist-jihadist activist Mohamed Mahmoud and the now internationally notorious Denis Cuspert. This was the same Cuspert, whose nasheeds Arid Uka had listened to before he shot two American soldiers at Frankfurt am Main Airport (see above). Cuspert was a former rap musician who emerged on the jihadist scene in Germany in 2010. Initially, he was in contact with political Salafists but he quickly came under the influence of *Die Wahre Religion*.[46] As a speaker at Salafist *Islam seminars*, he urged young Muslims to reject hip-hop culture and conform to a Salafist code of behaviour instead. Cuspert also released nasheeds propagating jihad and expressing his support for Osama bin Laden. He spread his new-found religious views in speeches all over Germany and in lectures on Paltalk.[47] His career as a famous jihadi really took off when he and Mahmoud founded MI in October 2011. They took the name of Millatu Ibrahim from the seminal work of Abu Muhammad al-Maqdisi, probably the most important scholar of modern militant Islamism.[48]

Mahmoud (aka Abu Usama al-Gharib) had only recently been released from prison, after serving time for his leadership of the German-speaking branch of the 'Global Islamic Media Front' (GIMF). GIMF is an online platform spreading Al Qaeda propaganda. For MI he acted as a particularly aggressive preacher who stated that the time for talking was over, and that Muslims should rise up, instead. The organization in Germany was rather short-lived as a result of its aggressive and militant nature. The Federal Minster of the Interior proscribed MI in late May 2012 in response to violent riots organized by its leadership. The protests were directed against the far-right party Pro NRW, which was displaying Mohammed caricatures as part of the state election campaign. In the city of Solingen, Salafist activists attacked police officers protecting the party rally. A few days later, during new protests in Bonn, a participant injured an officer with a knife. The state's response was a massive crackdown. Salafist mosques were raided nationwide, an investigation into *Die Wahre Religion* was launched and MI was banned by the end of the month.[49] The MI mosque in Solingen was closed down.[50] MI had mobilized for its protests and Salafists from all over Germany had responded. The organization whose main protagonists were mostly living in North-Rhine Westphalia, Hesse and Berlin were clearly able to reach followers nationwide.

When MI was banned Mahmoud had already left Germany for Egypt. Cuspert initially stayed behind. Now, he called on Muslims in Germany to emigrate or wage Jihad against the state, before he also left for Egypt.[51] It appears that their initial goal was to travel to Mali where for a brief time an Islamist state project was developing and which had drawn the attention of jihadists in Germany between 2011 and 2012, before the proto-state there ended under the onslaught of a French military operation.[52] Indeed, at the time the jihad in Syria quickly replaced the conflict in Mali.

Subsequently, many former members and associates of MI and the 'Read!' campaign left for Syria. Several of the former leading members of MI would later appear in ISIS propaganda videos. This of course included Denis Cuspert and Mohamed Mahmoud as well as others, for example Silvio Koblitz. While the first pictures of Cuspert in Syria emerged in August 2013, Mahmoud spent some time in jail in Turkey before he could join his compatriots in Syria.[53] Meanwhile, Cuspert had become the most prominent figurehead for German jihadists in Syria and Iraq. In April 2014 he publicly swore fealty to ISIS. A video of the pledge was released soon after. The men and women who went to fight in Syria and Iraq would urge others who had stayed behind to follow their example – with success. The number began to rise quickly from mid-2013 onwards. After a peak in 2014, the tempo of emigrations slowed considerably in 2015 and it has since come to all but a standstill. As of September 2018 authorities estimate that a total of 1000 people left for Syria and Iraq. The number has not changed since April 2018. It appears that jihadi-motivated emigration to these countries has halted.[54] After all, there is not much of a caliphate left to emigrate to. Hence, ISIS also will have problems to present itself as the 'strongest horse' among all the jihadist groups.

While there is anecdotal evidence that the networks built by MI and the 'Read!' Campaign were crucial in mobilizing these foreign fighters, we also know more about the emigrants now. In a comprehensive study,[55] federal authorities have collected and analysed the available data on people who left for Syria. It provides some basic descriptive statistics:[56] 79 per cent were male and 21 per cent were female. The mean age was 25.8 years, while the majority of individuals were between 22 and 25 years old. Over half of them were married according to either German law or Islamic rites. The phenomenon was urban and concentrated in thirteen cities all over the country (a total of 394 came from these cities). Notably, 61 per cent were born in Germany. Of the remaining individuals, for 193, their age on arrival in Germany is known: 39 per cent emigrated to Germany before their fourteenth birthday. What is significant here is that even the majority of those who were not born in Germany were socialized within German society. Hence, it is reasonable to consider the foreign fighter phenomenon to have a strong domestic component. This is further underlined by the fact that 62 per cent had (additionally) German citizenship (96 per cent had German as their first citizenship). Not surprisingly, 19 per cent also had Turkish and 7 per cent Moroccan citizenship, followed by Russian (5 per cent), Syrian (5 per cent), Tunisian (5 per cent) and Afghan (4 per cent).[57] It is also interesting to observe the motivation of the individuals in the study: 54 per cent were motivated by their desire to take part in the fighting in Syria, another 27 per cent wanted to join ISIS, humanitarian intentions came in third with 18 per cent (note that multiple selections were possible).[58] Ultimately, most of those that went to Syria and Iraq joined ISIS (80 per cent of those for whom the destination is known), while a much smaller percentage joined other jihadist organizations.⁵⁹ What is also significant, however, is that when the power of ISIS's caliphate vanished under the military onslaught of its enemies, its appeal for jihadists in Germany also dwindled. The organization had lost its appeal particularly among women and the more socially sophisticated individuals with jobs and education. The ones that still went tended to be young, but they had also committed a higher number of crimes (if they had a record). This underlines the fact that the idea of living in the Caliphate had lost its appeal among older individuals.⁶⁰ Meanwhile, the number of returnees began to rise. This highlights what the study cited here notes brilliantly: the Caliphate had become similar to a failed state, experiencing less immigration and more emigration.⁶¹

Nevertheless, the Salafist and jihadist scene in Germany had transformed into a self-sustaining milieu. This is highlighted by a certain continuity of personnel. After MI was banned, the organization *DawaFFM* carried on with extreme Salafist propaganda. Meanwhile, leading MI member Hasan Keskin ('Abu Ibrahim') who had stayed behind in Germany founded the organization Tauhid, which essentially was a successor organization to MI.⁶² Both organizations were subsequently proscribed by authorities. Nevertheless, when the jihadist preacher Abu Walaa made his entrance on the stage of Salafist-jihadism in Germany (see later), this was someone who had been active among the *DawaFFM* preachers in the past. Once Abu Walaa was arrested for recruiting individuals to fight in Syria, his propaganda outlets were taken over by the preacher Abdellatif Rouali who used to lead *DawaFFM*.⁶³

The section underlines the point that the developments in the Middle East (the centre of jihad) have had a significant impact on the evolution of the jihad in Germany. We have seen that Germany gained a domestic Salafist-jihadist scene with its own self-sustaining dynamic. Still, this scene did interact with the developments in the Middle East as is exemplified by the fact that members of MI went on to join ISIS although initially they were fascinated by the war in Mali. Most of those that went to Syria were 'sociologically' German -- they had been born in Germany or at least were socialized here. The fact that German foreign fighters arrived in Syria and supported one side in the conflict there underlines the fact that the periphery can have an impact on the centre, however small it might be (the number of 1000 will probably not have the largest impact on the conflict dynamic in Syria and Iraq). Nevertheless, from a German perspective the most significant effect of ISIS was the terrorist threat to the West and Germany that emerged from it.

ISIS threatens Germany

Denis Cuspert had threatened Germany already while he was still in the country. As a member of ISIS he and others continued to menace Germany in videos. In the fourth edition of the propaganda magazine ISIS Dabiq, Germany was explicitly mentioned as a target country in which Muslims should launch attacks.⁶⁴ This was further underlined by a video by the al-Hayat Centre of ISIS, which released a video (An Euch Feinde Allahs/To You Enemies of Allah) in April 2015 that had a very high production value and set pictures of beheadings and simulated terrorist attacks against a nasheed by Cuspert.

In an ultimate escalation of the threats a few months later Muhammad Mahmoud featured in a video threatening Germany and swearing at Chancellor Angela Merkel before he and another German man proceeded to shoot two prisoners. Their act underlines their willingness to part with their home countries and their societies. Both men must have been aware that by committing murder while it was being recorded, they would be risking their chance of return and redemption, with long, if not lifelong, prison sentences waiting for them. In his statement Mahmoud mirrored calls by ISIS spokesperson Abu Muhammad al-Adnani to use every means available to kill or hurt people in the West. Mahmoud had and would continue to use Twitter during that time to reiterate his calls to Muslims in Germany to launch knife-attacks in the West. The explicit targeting of Germany continued in early 2016 when collages released via social media called for attacks on targets in Germany. A quarrel between jihadi and political Salafist preachers in Germany spilled over into *Dabiq* when an article called for attacks on apostate preachers, including famous German non-jihadi preacher Pierre Vogel.[65] Meanwhile, in yet another nasheed Cuspert called for the taking of hostages and for terrorism in the West, including attacks against police officers. The threat against Germany was clear and manifest.

These threats and calls to action raised the level of alarm among German security services and, indeed, had an impact on the threat level in Germany – though in several cases that involved refugees, planning by ISIS operatives or Arabic-speaking propaganda has most likely been more crucial. In February 2016, a number of alleged ISIS supporters who authorities suspected were planning a terrorist attack in Berlin were arrested in several German cities.[66] According to media reports at the time Algerian suspects had entered Germany pretending to be refugees.[67] Already in November 2015, a national football team game in Hannover had been cancelled after intelligence suggested an imminent attack on the event.[68] The threat became more manifest when in late February 2016 a teenage Salafist attacked a police officer in Hannover with a knife. The attack had been a mission given to her by supporters of ISIS via messenger services after she failed to join them in Syria – her mother had intercepted the message in Istanbul. Initially, she was supposed to use explosives for the attack.[69] In April, two other teenagers[70] bombed a Sikh temple in Essen, leaving two injured.[71] The wave of jihadist attacks continued over the summer: on 18 July 2016 a young refugee attacked passengers on a train in the vicinity of the city of Würzburg, with an axe and a knife, injuring five people. He was shot and killed by police. A day later ISIS released a video by the man claiming responsibility for the attack.[72] Only four days previously, another ISIS supporter had killed eighty-six people and injured over 400 by driving a truck through crowds in Nice, which highlighted the fact that the attacks that hit Germany were part of a larger trend, obviously motivated by calls of ISIS supporters to use easily available weapons such as cars and knives to launch attacks. At the end of the month Germany saw another attack: this time a Syrian refugee blew himself up (probably by accident) in the city of Ansbach, injuring 15 people. He would have killed and injured more had he gained access to a festival area he had tried to enter prior to the explosion.[73]

The wave of attacks and attack plans culminated in the attack on 10 December 2016 in Berlin when Anis Amri, a Tunisian man who had claimed asylum in Germany under several different identities, drove a truck though a Christmas market killing eleven people and injuring fifty-five more. This was the first jihadist attack in Germany that caused deaths. Days later the ISIS released a video by Amri pledging allegiance to the leader of ISIS, Abu Bakr al-Baghdadi.[74] At least the Sikh temple and the Berlin attacks were linked with an ISIS network that also recruited individuals to emigrate to Syria and Iraq to fight. This network gathered around the preacher Abu Walaa, who was active at a mosque in Hildesheim.

Abu Walaa – Germany's last jihadist preacher?

Abu Walaa (his real name was Ahmad Abdelaziz Abdullah Abdullah) arrived in Germany in 2004 as a refugee. He was born in al-Tamim, Iraq, and apparently was an ethnic Kurd with possible links to Ansar al-Islam (see earlier), which had been in close contact with Abu Musab al-Zarqawi. He had previously been active in the by now proscribed organization *DawaFFM* before he became the imam at the mosque of the *Deutschsprachige Islamkreis* (DIK) in Hildesheim, Lower Saxony. According to one of his former followers, Abu Walaa used to be the ISIS representative for Germany. While he was active there, Hildesheim became a hotspot of the Salafist scene in Germany. He preached, and allegedly recruited for, the jihad in Syria. Meanwhile, his associates in North-Rhine Westphalia Boban Simeonovic (Abu Abdurahman) and Hasan Celenk (Abu Yahya al-Turki) indoctrinated people in Dortmund and Duisburg. Authorities reportedly believed that Abu Walaa appointed Simeonovic and Celenk as regional leaders. According to the Federal Prosecutor the three acted together in a work-sharing arrangement in which Simeonovic and Celenk taught classes in Arabic and ideologically prepared recruits to join ISIS. Meanwhile, Abu Walaa was the final gatekeeper on the way to ISIS, providing recruits with the necessary legitimation. Allegedly, Abu Walaa continued to be in close contact with ISIS and visited Iraq several times. The network allegedly radicalized at least 21 people who subsequently left for Syria. According to the authorities, it was also involved in financing foreign fighters in Syria by collecting donations, and some of its members committed burglaries theologically justified by Abu Walaa. Allegedly, the network was also in contact with several well-known German jihadist figures in Syria, some of whom had been members of Millatu Ibrahim, including Mohammed Mahmoud. In addition to its recruitment of foreign fighters, the network was linked to domestic radicalization and to several terrorist plots including the Berlin and Essen attacks. Abu Walaa and several of his accomplices were arrested on 8 November 2016 and are still standing trial at the time of writing.[75]

The Abu Walaa network was the last iteration of a nationwide jihadist radicalization and recruitment network in Germany. Since then, no visible outlet of this branch of Salafism remains in the country. That does not mean that militant activity has completely subsided. For example, in June 2018 authorities arrested a man in Cologne who allegedly was planning an attack using the poison Ricin. According to media reports, the suspect, a Tunisian man, had entered Germany in 2015 after marrying a German national. Reportedly, he had already been active in Salafist circles in Tunisia. He is said to have tried and failed to travel to Syria in fall of 2017.[76]

Conclusion

This chapter has examined the evolution of jihad in Germany. We have seen that the movement turned from a mostly external force with little integration into German society until at least 9/11, into something more. After the war in Afghanistan 'Arab Afghan' veterans formed networks across Europe. For the first time, these networks became active in supporting the jihad in Bosnia. In Germany, these initial networks would continue to nurture the Salafist and jihadist scenes. Through the development of a self-sustaining, domestic, wider and differentiated Salafist scene that encompassed a significant jihadist current, the movement became part of the social landscape of Germany. It was not an entirely foreign concept anymore. When the war in Syria arose, the mobilization by ISIS and other jihadist organizations was able to draw on a repository of young men and women who were susceptible to its message of a caliphate that would protect the global community of Muslims (and, in particular, Muslims in Syria) from attacks.

With regard to the debate about the centre and periphery of jihad, Germany can be located at the periphery of jihadist thinking. However, this chapter has tried to show – successfully the author believes – that the relationship between the two is never stable and ever changing. As a target, Germany apparently never was as important as France or the UK, for example. Still, it came under threat as a participant in the war in Afghanistan and in the fight against ISIS. The internal dynamic of Islam since 1979 – with the diffusion of Salafist and jihadist ideas – has also had an influence on Muslims in Germany, though the number of Salafists remains relatively low. Hence, while squarely on the periphery of jihad, Germany has brought forth its own militant movement with movement entrepreneurs (militant preachers) and social movement organizations (extremist groups). After the end of the Abu Walaa network, the question remains, though, how lasting the impact of these protagonists and their institutions will be.

Notes

1 Bayerisches Staatsministerium des Innen und für Integration, *Verfassungsschutzbericht 2017* (Munich: Bayern die Zukunft, 2018), pp. 42–3.
2 Ian Johnson, *A Mosque in Munich: Nazis, The CIA, and the Muslim Brotherhood in the West* (Boston: Houghton Mifflin Harcourt, 2010).
3 Peter Nesser, *Islamist Terrorism in Europe: A History* (London: Hurst Publishers, 2015), p. 25.

4 Gilles Kepel, *Jihad: The Trail of Political Islam* (London: IB Tauris & Co Ltd, 2000), p. 148.
5 Bryan Lia, *Architect of Global Jihad: The Life of al-Qaida Strategist Abu Musʽab al-Suri* (London: Hurst Publishers, 2007), pp. 69–70.
6 Ibid., p. 106.
7 Kepel, *Jihad*, p. 238.
8 Ibid., pp. 247–8.
9 Ibid., p. 239.
10 Ibid., pp. 249–51.
11 Jelena Beslin and Marija Ignjatijevic, 'Balkan foreign fighters: From Syria to Ukraine', *Issue Brief* (2017), p. 2.
12 Mustafa Hamid and Leah Farrall, *The Arabs at War in Afghanistan* (London: C. Hurst & Co. Publishers, 2015), p. 180.
13 Doris Glück, *Mundtot: Ich war die Frau eines Gotteskriegers* (Berlin: Ullstein Taschenbuch, 2004).
14 Jasper Schwampe, *Muslim Foreign Fighters in Armed Conflicts* (Aarhus: Politica, 2018).
15 Guido Steinberg, *Al-Qaidas deutsche Kämpfer. Die Globalisierung des islamistischen Terrorismus* (Hamburg: Körber-Stiftung 2014), pp. 92–3.
16 Glück, *Mundtot*, pp. 39–56.
17 Nesser, *Islamist Terrorism in Europe*, p. 38.
18 Lia, *Architect of Global Jihad*, p. 150.
19 Behnam T. Said, *Geschichte al-Qaidas. Bin Laden, der 11. September und die tausend Fronten des Terrors heute* (München: C.H. Beck Verlag, 2018), pp. 73–4.
20 Steinberg, *Al-Qaidas deutsche Kämpfer*, pp. 58–65.
21 See, e.g., Terry McDermott, *Perfect Soldiers: The 9/11 Hijackers. Who They Were, Why They Did It* (New York: Harper, 2005).
22 Steinberg, *Al-Qaidas deutsche Kämpfer*, p. 64.
23 Staff and Agencies, 'Four convicted of Strasbourg bomb plot', *The Guardian*, 10 March 2003. Available at https://www.theguardian.com/world/2003/mar/10/germany.france (accessed 17 February 2019).
24 The Guardian, 'Four convicted of Strasbourg bomb plot', *The Guardian*, 10 March 2003. Available at https://www.theguardian.com/world/2003/mar/10/germany.france (accessed 1 October 2018).
25 Steinberg, *Al-Qaidas deutsche Kämpfer*, pp. 67–73.
26 Ibid., pp. 74–80.
27 A nasheed is a form of vocal music sung acappella by Muslim men. It might be accompanied by percussion instruments. Its content is usually Islamic, and it may have militant overtones.
28 Wolf Schmidt, 'Höchststrafe für US-Soldaten-Mord', *Taz*, 10 February 2012. Available at http://www.taz.de/!5100917/ (accessed 1 October 2018).
29 Steinberg, *Al-Qaidas deutsche Kämpfer*, pp. 80–1.
30 Nina Wiedl, 'Geschichte des Salafismus in Deutschland', in Behnam T. Said and Hazim Fouad (eds), *Salafismus. Auf der Suche nach dem wahren Islam* (Freiburg am Breisgau: Herder, 2014), pp. 417–20.
31 Ibid., pp. 423–4.
32 Said, *Geschichte al-Qaidas*, p. 199.
33 There were other recruiters active in Germany during these years. However, this chapter will use the 'Sauerland Complex' as an example.

34 Unknown, 'Beckstein schließt Islamisten-Treffpunkt in Neu-Ulm', *Frankfurter Allgemeine Zeitung*, 28 December 2005. Available at https://www.faz.net/aktuell/po litik/inland/innere-sicherheit-beckstein-schliesst-islamisten-treffpunkt-in-neu-ulm-1 280087.html (accessed 17 February 2019).
35 That the group ended up with the IJU seems to be mostly the result of chance, aided by the fact that members of the group were of Turkish heritage, which made it easier to communicate with the men from Azerbaijan.
36 Steinberg, *Al-Qaidas deutsche Kämpfer*, pp. 92–112.
37 Ibid., pp. 146–8, 210–16.
38 Ibid., p. 220.
39 Ibid., pp. 250–2.
40 Said, *Geschichte al-Qaidas*, p. 200.
41 Steinberg, *Al-Qaidas deutsche Kämpfer*, pp. 286–92.
42 Ibid., pp. 336–9.
43 Matenia Sirseloudi, 'Radikalisierung gewaltbereiter Dschihadisten in Europa und Konflikte in der islamischen Welt', in P. Zoche, S. Kaufmann and H. Arnold (eds), *Sichere Zeiten? Gesellschaftliche Dimensionen der Sicherheitsforschung* (Münster: Lit Verlag, 2015).
44 Wiedl, 'Geschichte', pp. 428; 431–2.
45 Danijel Majid, 'Rückschlag für die Missionierung', *Frankfurter Rundschau*, 15 March 2018. Available at http://www.fr.de/rhein-main/salafisten-rueckschlag-fuer-die-missi onierung-a-1468381 (accessed 1 October 2018).
46 Behnam T. Said, *Islamischer Staat: ISIS-Miliz, al-Qaida und die deutschen Brigaden* (München: C.H. Beck Verlag, 2014), p. 124.
47 Wolf Schmidt, *Jung, deutsch, Taliban* (Berlin: Ch. Links Verlag, 2012), pp. 123–31.
48 See: Joas Wagemakers, *A Quietist Jihadi: The Ideology and Influence of Abu Muhammad al-Maqdisi* (New York: Cambridge University Press, 2012).
49 Significantly, the proscription order appears not to have included a single covert source. It was entirely based on the content of public lectures and speeches given by its leading members.
50 Wiedl, 'Geschichte', pp. 433–4.
51 Ibid., pp. 434–5.
52 Said, *Geschichte al-Qaidas*, p. 200.
53 Said, *Islamischer Staat*, pp. 129–32.
54 see: Bundesamt für Verfassungsschutz, *Islamistisch motivierte Reisebewegung in Richtung Syrien/Irak*. Available at https://www.verfassungsschutz.de/de/arbeitsfelder/ af-islamismus-und-islamistischer-terrorismus/zahlen-und-fakten-islamismus/zuf-is -reisebewegungen-in-richtung-syrien-irak (accessed 1 October 2018).
55 The study was last updated in October 2016 and is based on the data of 784 cases.
56 For a more detailed discussion see: Daniel Heinke and Jan Raudszus, 'German foreign fighters in Syria and Iraq', *CTC Sentinel*, 8, no. 1 (2015): 18–22 and Daniel Heinke, 'German foreign fighters in Syria and Iraq: The updated data and its implications', *CTC Sentinel*, 10, no. 3 (2017): 17–22.
57 Federal Criminal Police, Federal Office for the Protection of the Constitution and the Hesse Information and Competence Centre against Extremism, *Analysis of the background and process of radicalisation among persons who left Germany to travel to Syria or Iraq based on Islamist motivation*. Available at https://www.bka.de/Shared Docs/Downloads/DE/Publikationen/Publikationsreihen/Forschungsergebnisse/201 7AnalysisOfTheBackgroundAndProcessOfRadicalization.html (accessed 1 October 2018), pp. 11–15.

58 Federal Criminal Police, Federal Office for the Protection of the Constitution and the Hesse Information and Competence Centre against Extremism, *Analysis*, pp. 24–5.
59 Ibid., pp. 28–9.
60 Ibid., pp. 31–4.
61 Ibid., p. 36.
62 Miguel Sanches, 'Verbot für Salafisten-Verein', *Der Westen*, 26 March 2015.
63 Michael Evers, 'Verfassungsschutz sieht Phase der Verunsicherung in Salafisten-Szene', *Die Welt*, 19 December 2017.
64 Unknown, 'Reflections on the Final Crusade', *Dabiq*, 4 (2015): 44.
65 Unknown, 'Kill the Imams of Kufr in the West', *Dabiq*, 14 (2016): 8–17.
66 We will discuss only a selection of the most prominent cases here. It is, however, necessary to point out that there were several other incidents, as well.
67 Unknown, 'Islamisten Planten Anschlag am Alexanderplatz in Berlin', *Berliner Zeitung*, 4 February 2016. Available at https://www.bz-berlin.de/berlin/hier-nimmt-die-polizei-einen-terror-verdaechtigen-in-berlin-fest (accessed 1 October 2018).
68 Peter Ahren, 'Mit Sicherheit richtig', *Spiegel*, 17 November 2015. Available at http://www.spiegel.de/sport/fussball/hannover-laenderspiel-absage-deutschland-niederlande-die-hintergruende-a-1063322.html (accessed 1 October 2018).
69 Der Bundesgerichtshof, Urteil v. 19 April 2018, Az. 3 StR 286/17, pp. 4–17.
70 They had allegedly been radicalized by the Abu Walaa network (see below).
71 Landgericht Essen, 'Strafsache wegen Anschlags auf Gebetshaus der Sikh-Gemeinde. Urteilsverkündung am 21 March 2017'; 'Angeklagte zu Jugendstrafe verurteilt'. Available at http://www.lg-essen.nrw.de/behoerde/presse/Presseerklaerungen/Archiv-2017/09_Anschlag-auf-Gebetshaus-der-Sikh-Gemeinde/index.php (accessed 1 October 2018).
72 Unknown, 'Hermann: Täter könnte sich selbst radikalisiert haben', *Frankfurter Allgemeine Zeitung*, 19 July 2016. Available at http://www.faz.net/aktuell/politik/inland/herrmann-keine-hinweise-auf-vernetzung-mit-terrormiliz-is-14347325.html (accessed 1 October 2018).
73 Unknown, '27-jähriger tötet sich in Menschenmenge mit Sprengsatz', *Spiegel*, 25 Juli 2016. Available at http://www.spiegel.de/panorama/bayern-explosion-in-ansbacher-innenstadt-ein-toter-a-1104496.html (accessed 1 October 2018).
74 Mohamed Amjahid, Daniel Müller, Yassin Musharbash, Holger Stark and Fritz Zimmermann, 'An attack is expected', *Die Zeit*, 7 April 2017. Available at https://www.zeit.de/politik/deutschland/2017-04/berlin-attack-christmas-market-breitscheidplatz-anis-amri (accessed 17 February 2019).
75 Georg Heil, 'The Berlin attack and the "Abu Walaa" Islamic state recruitment network', *CTC Sentinel*, 10, no. 2 (2017): 1–11.
76 Florian Flade, 'The June 2018 Cologne Ricin Plot: A new threshold in Jihadi Bio Terror', *CTC Sentinel*, 11, no. 7 (2018): 1–4.

AL-ANDALUS

THE CALIPHATE OF CORDOBA REIMAGINED

Maria do Céu Pinto Arena

Introduction

Al Qaeda and ISIS have tapped into the dissatisfaction of many Muslims and the failed integration of Muslim diasporas to build a narrative. In this narrative,[1] Islamist struggles are nested within a global confrontation that sets the Muslim world in the position of having to defend itself against both its own governments and the West-dominated global order. A series of interlocking narratives produced by those movements proves that it is the duty of all true believers to engage in jihad, in order to fight apostate Muslim governments and the Western onslaught on the Islamic world.[2] Jihadism has become 'a cloak patched from different sources of local discontent, real and perceived, stitched together by a puritanical and radical interpretation of Islam, and thriving on an enabling global momentum'.[3] Harnessing local causes to the broad and undefined aim of creating a Sharia-committed universal order, or caliphate, is the hallmark of a 'glocal' phenomenon, in which complex and often incoherent relationships are established between a global context and local circumstances.[4] As a 'glocal' phenomenon,[5] it absorbs flows of people, technology, money, information and political ideas, flows that Iberia has absorbed in its Muslim history.

This has resulted in a complex set of interwoven terrorist hubs across Spain, hinged on the bonding Al Qaeda narrative[6] of a terrorist assault of the West against the Muslim world. Since the 11 September 2001 terrorist attacks (9/11) and the Madrid 11 March 2004 attacks (3/11), police and prosecutors in Spain have uncovered dozens of plots and several interconnected, polymorphous networks of Muslim militants. The picture that emerges from the vast information collected so far on *terrorist networks* in Spain is, arguably, that jihadis have become a 'structural phenomenon'.[7] Spain is a natural meeting point for Islamic militants, mainly due to its proximity to the Maghreb, and its enclaves of Ceuta and Melilla, which have increasingly emerged as recruitment hubs. It has been a major recruiting ground for a host of jihads: from Bosnia, Chechnya and Afghanistan, in the 1990s, to the war in Syria in 2011. It is also a strategic area for logistical activities,[8] such as financing and recycling identities.[9]

The cells uncovered in Spain since 9/11, being intersected, have moved and re-formed constantly, overlapping in highly complex manners, either at the domestic level or with connected networks abroad. Global jihad cells centred in Spain exhibit a series of nested interactions, that is, they are embedded in other broader, encompassing networks. They build on the first Al Qaeda network created on Spanish territory, engaged in recruitment for the Afghan war and as a revolving door to other jihadi locations. Many of the earlier networks were dismantled, although the ones broken up in the wake of 9/11 were rebuilt on a previous infrastructure, at least partially. The incredible connectivity of these cells is confirmed, at different levels, in the 3/11 bombings: they involved different groups that had links to other plots in other countries, and members located in Spain, Italy, Morocco and Belgium.[10] By contrast, Portugal perceives the threat of terrorism as lower than in other European countries,[11] but around fourteen Portuguese nationals or residents left for Syria/Iraq after 2011. The majority were recent converts, and had long lived abroad.

This chapter will analyse the evolution of extremist networks in Spain, starting with the cells of the 1990s, continuing with the 3/11 network and including the more recent rings to recruit young people as Islamist militants to foreign jihads. This is followed by an analysis of the phenomenon of Portuguese foreign fighters.

In Spain, the Muslim share of the population is 2.3 per cent, that is, 1,021,000 people.[12] In terms of national origin, the main Muslim group are Moroccans. To that one must now add the growing Pakistani group (a majority in some cities, like Barcelona and Valencia). Moroccans, Algerians, Senegalese and Pakistanis together make up 86 per cent of the total. These groups show very different age and sex distribution, due to their different immigration histories. The Moroccan community, being the most long-standing immigrant community in Spain, has a strong family focus. The main sector of Muslim employment is services. The construction sector has traditionally been an important source of employment for immigrants, followed by industry and agriculture. Only a small minority are self-employed, mostly Pakistanis.[13] In general, the Muslim population work in jobs requiring less training and at the most basic levels of the labour market. It is a group with little formal education, in which the absence of studies and illiteracy (9%) is triple that of the level of the whole of Spanish society. Just over a third (36%) leave school before reaching ten years of age, and, among them, only 9 per cent have a university degree.[14] With regard to their geographical location, the Muslim settlements are higher in number in the south-eastern half of the country: Andalusia, Catalonia, Madrid, Valencia and Murcia.

In Portugal, the Muslim population of approximately sixty thousand people accounts for around 0.6 per cent of the total Portuguese population, representing the largest religious minority in the country.[15] Most are Sunni Muslims living in the Greater Lisbon area (Lisbon, Odivelas, Laranjeiro, Palmela and Barreiro) and in the south. Muslims in the country generally have their roots in the former African colonies – Mozambique and Guinea-Bissau – but newcomers include people from Bangladesh, Senegal, Morocco and Pakistan, among others. When they arrived at the metropolis, the initially small community of Portuguese Muslims belonged to a cultured middle class, and were mainly well-educated people, working in the services sector or in business.[16] The Muslim immigrants that have arrived in

Portugal since the 1990s have to cope with greater obstacles to their social and professional integration and even to obtaining legal status because they do not speak Portuguese and do not have any kind of ties with the host country. Some of them live in poverty – especially those coming from sub-Saharan Africa – and they work mainly as traders and street sellers and in the construction sector.

Spain: A plotter's terrain

From the 1990s, Spain was a focal point for key support networks upon which Al Qaeda depended, as well as for activities such as fundraising, recruiting and propaganda. Spain provided a staging post for Al Qaeda in preparation for the 9/11 attacks. It was a major focal point of the international investigation launched in its wake. From the investigation, it emerged that Spain was a natural meeting point for Islamic militants from all over the world, as well as a recruiting ground and a strategic point for support activities.[17] The 9/11 attacks, as well as the plots uncovered in their wake, offer an example of the scope and reach of the presence of an interlocking set of terrorist cells that spanned Europe across Spain, Italy, Germany, Britain, France, Belgium and the Netherlands, with supporters in numerous other countries. Since the 9/11 attacks, Spanish police and prosecutors have made hundreds of arrests[18] and uncovered a large, interconnected network of Muslim extremists with extensive links to other countries and continents.

The protagonists of an amazing web of plots, some of which are interconnected, have crossed through Spain or used its territory as a refuge or a safe ground from where to command and orchestrate terror acts. These terror plots include the planned attacks against the US embassy in Paris, the US embassy in Rome, the Strasbourg cathedral, and those actually carried out against the Djerba synagogue in Tunisia and the US embassies in East Africa, as well as the 2003 Casablanca bombings.[19]

The evidence produced by the police and intelligence work provided an inside look at groups operating at the edges of Islamic terrorism in Europe, inspired by Osama bin Laden.[20] Their large distance from the core Al Qaeda underscores what terrorism experts have described as one of Al Qaeda's central organizational principles: its strong decentralization. The 3/11 attacks in Madrid are a confirmation that some groups of Arab radicals in Europe gradually moved from their support and logistics role to active involvement in terror. Some of the main suspects behind the 3/11 attacks were third-tier figures on the fringes of a Madrid Al Qaeda cell that was dismantled in late 2001 for providing logistical support to the 9/11 hijackers. Some of those suspects' contacts were gleaned from numerous other European probes.[21]

Spain's proximity to North Africa has allowed a significant Muslim immigrant population, both legal and illegal, to take root. Heavy immigration – both legal and illegal – from North Africa (Morocco, Tunisia, and Algeria) and South Asia (Pakistan and Bangladesh) has turned Spain into a magnet for terrorist recruiters. The region of Catalonia not only has the highest Muslim population in Spain but also is where hard-line Islamist movements, such as Salafism, have a strong presence. Many towns in Catalonia have become centres for Salafi Islam.[22] Over 30 per cent of the individuals sentenced for jihadi-related terrorist criminal offences were arrested in Catalonia or were resident in that Autonomous Community.[23]

Al Qaeda's network in Spain

The first arrests of extremist elements were conducted in 1995 when Spanish authorities uncovered cells of the Algerian Groupe Islamique Armé (GIA). Many GIA members took part in the Afghanistan war and, upon their return home, hardened their stance against the military regime in Algiers. The group established a presence outside Algeria and launched terror attacks in France in late 1994. In Spain, the group infiltrated Algerian communities settled in the south and east of the country.[24] The group has evolved, as well as generated a splinter group, the Salafist Group for Preaching and Combat (GSPC – 'Groupe Salafiste per la Prédication et le Combat'), which announced its adherence to Al Qaeda in October 2003.[25]

In September and November 2001, Spanish police broke up two Al Qaeda-affiliated cells. The six men arrested, members of the GSPC, constituted a support unit for other cells linked to bin Laden across Europe, providing forged documents, passports and credit cards.[26] The group – believed to have been established between 1994 and 1995 – was also used as a base camp for Islamic fighters operating in Bosnia, Chechnya and Afghanistan.[27] The cell leader, Mohammed Boualem Khnouni, lived in the municipality of Valencia, in southern Spain. The police arrested him at the insistence of the Belgian investigating magistrate dealing with Nizar Trabelsi, the alleged would-be bomber of the US embassy in Paris. Trabelsi had travelled to Spain in July 2001 for meetings with the Salafists, with whom he was in regular contact.[28] A Tunisian ex-soccer player, Trabelsi was an accomplice of Algerian-born Frenchman, Djamal Beghal, the ringleader of an Al Qaeda-linked group caught in October 2001 by airport authorities, in the United Arab Emirates, while trying to travel to Europe on a fake French passport. Trabelsi and Beghal had known each other for a long time. Both men had lived in London in the late 1990s and had attended several London mosques, notably the one where Salafi cleric, Abu Qatada, preached. Through Qatada, a prominent leader of the Islamist fringe, both Beghal and Trabelsi went to two terrorist training camps in Afghanistan.[29]

Under interrogation, Beghal revealed having been recruited in Afghanistan by bin Laden's deputy, Abu Zubaydah, for a suicide mission against the US embassy in Paris.[30] In fact, Beghal was a key member of the multi-celled network. He provided investigators with details of terrorist cells operating in Paris, Spain, Belgium and Rotterdam. Trabelsi used the Takfir wal-Hijra Rotterdam cell as a logistics base for the planned attack on the Paris embassy and, possibly, for another attack on the Belgian air force base at Kleine Brogel, used by the US.[31] The Spanish cell had also been in contact with another potentially lethal bin Laden cell based in Frankfurt: the so-called Meliani cell led by Algerian Mohammed Bensakhria, the Al Qaeda's chief of operations in Europe. The Algerian was reportedly close to Mohammed Atta – the 9/11 ringleader – and a member of the Hamburg cell until Atta moved to the United States to enrol in flight schools.[32] The dismantling of the Frankfurt cell took place just in time: two plots were foiled after German police disrupted the cell in a series of raids in December 2000. In cooperation with members of the Al Qaeda network in Italy, Britain and France, the 'Meliani commando' was just about to launch terrorist attacks in Strasbourg, presumably against the Christmas market, using a chemical product, possibly Sarin nerve gas.[33] Bensakhria escaped to Spain where he was arrested in June 2001 in Alicante – he was living there disguised as a poor immigrant.[34]

Spanish police also found out that two members of the Spanish Salafist group met with Essid Sami ben Khemais, a Tunisian whom the police believes to have been sent from Afghanistan to supervise bin Laden's terrorist operations in Europe.[35] Ben Khemais and five other people were arrested in Italy in April 2001, in connection with an alleged plan to attack the US embassy in Rome. The range of the GSPC contacts, both in Spain (notably with other Syrian, Moroccan and Tunisian cells),[36] is a testimony to the already high degree of overlapping and cooperation between terrorist networks. This system of clustered networks would be found in the 3/11 attacks.

Many Salafist cells have been uncovered in Spain over the years. In 2006, one of them, self-entitled as 'Martyrs for Morocco', intended to bomb the National Audience (the Court that specializes in terrorism) in Madrid with a truck bomb. It appears that it also intended to carry out a second phase of attacks in other locations in the capital, targeting, among others, the Atocha train station, the Real Madrid football stadium and Madrid's tallest building, the Picasso Tower.[37] Another important extremist cluster in Spain was formed by a group of former Syrian Muslim Brotherhood members who had escaped that country in the wake of the repression conducted by the Hafez al-Assad regime, in particular, the February 1982 Hama massacre. In November 2001, Spanish police launched 'Operation Dátil', arresting eight alleged members of an Al Qaeda cell during a raid in Madrid and Granada. They were among eleven men from Tunisian, Algerian and Syrian backgrounds. Judge Garzón was quoted as saying the men 'were directly related to the preparation and development of the attacks perpetrated by the suicide pilots on September 11'.[38] It was the most direct connection to that date, in Europe, between the attacks and a terrorist cell.

Among the men who took shelter in Spain was Mustafa Setmarian, alias Abu Mus'ab al-Suri, a former member of the Syrian Fighting Vanguard, a Sunni Islamist guerrilla group, and a spin-off of the Muslim Brotherhood that was engaged in terrorist action against the Syrian regime since the late 1980s. He was a seasoned fighter of the Afghan war and a major ideologue: he contributed decisively to formulating Al Qaeda's global warfare strategy.[39] In late 2004 he published online The Global Islamic Resistance Call, a major piece of Al Qaeda's strategy, in which he appealed for jihad to be conducted on a decentralized basis, rather than in a hierarchical, organizational way.[40] Al-Suri settled in Spain for a few years, where he enlisted other former Muslim Brotherhood members to join the cause of global jihad. He moved to London in 1994,[41] becoming editor of the London-based GIA bulletin, Al Ansar, and subsequently went to Afghanistan to work with bin Laden after the Taliban's takeover.

A Palestinian radical, Anwar Adnan Mohamed Salah, also known as 'Chej Salah', also played a critical role in organizing exiles and recruits in Spain to support the international jihadi movement. Chej started the Madrid cell in 1994.[42] Eventually he moved to Peshawar, Pakistan, in 1995, to provide training to Arab militants. Upon their departure, the Syrian Imad Eddin Yarkas (Abu Dahdah) took charge of the organization. He lived with his Spanish wife, a Muslim convert, and their four children, in a middle-class neighbourhood in Madrid. He founded an organization, the 'Islamic Alliance', whose radical core later formed 'The Soldiers of Allah' centred on the Abu Bakr mosque.

In late 2001, Abu Dahdah, along with the other seven, was accused of belonging to a terrorist organization, of recruiting people to Al Qaeda terrorist training camps and of sending them to fight in Bosnia, Chechnya and Afghanistan. Abu Dahdah's cell was directly affiliated with Al Qaeda; according to Reinares, it was one of the most important cells in Western Europe.[43] The Spanish network offered logistical support, accommodation and false documents to activists travelling through Spain and other countries where Abu Dahdah had good contacts. They were also charged with providing false identification to recruits, along with document falsification, robbery and possession of weapons.[44] Abu Dahdah reportedly met with bin Laden twice and was in close contact with the Saudi-born fugitive's top deputy, Mohammed Atef, who orchestrated Al Qaeda-sponsored terrorist attacks, and with Abu Zubaydah, who was in charge of Al Qaeda's cells abroad.[45] Abu Dahdah and his co-conspirators were constantly on the move to send recruits and, when possible, to channel money for supporting Al Qaeda. He started his recruiting activities in the Madrid Tetuán neighbourhood, sending the candidates to Peshawar, from where they were directed to camps in Afghanistan.[46] In court papers, a detailed picture of Abu Dahdah shows him contacting militant Islamists in other parts of Europe: Britain (to which he made more than seventeen visits),[47] Belgium, Denmark, Sweden, as well as Turkey, Indonesia, Malaysia, Jordan and Yemen. His list of travels and contacts was too extensive for a modest used-car dealer. Abu Dahdah was a frequent visitor to Abu Qatada's house in London.[48]

There is substantial evidence linking Abu Dahdah and his associates to the 9/11 cell. German investigators searching the Hamburg apartment once occupied by Atta found Abu Dahdah's name and phone number there.[49] The court indictment charged Abu Dahdah's cell of collecting money for the Hamburg cell, where the 9/11 hijackers lived for several years, although the extent of their involvement is unclear.[50] These early terrorist cells had mostly a nationalist agenda linked to national causes, such as GIA and GSPC. What stands out clearly is that, with the arrival of the Afghan war veterans in Spain, the local extremist individuals and cells were harnessed into a more global agenda. Groups were flexibly intertwined into a more entangled web of terror, a fact that was already evidenced by Abu Dahdah's network: it 'moved into the general directives of the global Jihad but acted in an autonomous style, thanks to the initiative and personal contacts of the members of the first and second level', that is, committed members and sympathizers.[51]

Abu Dahdah created a transnational network, mostly from Moroccan, Algerian and Syrian elements. In the 1990s, the diffuse network included the GIA, the Tunisian Islamic Combatant Group (TICG) of the GSPC, and the Moroccan Islamic Combatant Group (MICG).[52] The jihadist network led by Abu Dahdah was a multi-task enterprise: it organized transactions among different nodes, as well as the supply of money, equipment, false documents, propaganda and other resources. It raised funds and channelled them to support similar groups in Europe, namely to support terrorist infrastructures in other continents, and to finance the trips of recruits to attend terrorist training camps abroad.[53] It recruited volunteers who were sent to training camps in Bosnia, and particularly in Afghanistan, as well as in Kashmir and Chechnya. The network also helped initiate a training camp in the Indonesian region of Poso.[54]

The breakup of that cell enabled investigators to track extremist operatives and disrupt support networks. A major operative was Al Qaeda financier Ahmed Brahim. His arrest was the fruit of several months of investigation, and of the collaboration of police from several countries, including the US, France and Germany. Investigators traced more than $650,000 in payments to Al Qaeda operatives in at least nine countries, including members of the Hamburg cell.[55] In March 2003, a Spanish businessman, Enrique Cerdá, and a Pakistani, Ahmed Ruksar, were jailed in Valencia and Logroño, respectively. They were involved in money laundering and transfers of money to a number of countries and organizations linked to Al Qaeda,[56] in particular to the group involved in the synagogue bombing on the Tunisian resort island of Djerba, in April 2002, in which more than twenty people were killed.[57]

Abu Dahdah's network supported Al Qaeda's representative in Europe, Tarek Maaroufi, a Tunisian with Belgian citizenship. Maaroufi was the leader of the Tunisian Combatant Group. The group was associated with Al Qaeda and other North African Islamic extremists in Europe, mainly implicated in anti-US terrorist plots there, and to cells in Italy and the UK.[58] Tunisians, associated with the TCG, are part of the support network of the international Salafist movement, and Maaroufi was the kingpin among them.[59] The arrest of Maaroufi, in late 2001, was part of an investigation into the stolen passports used by two suicide bombers who killed Afghan opposition leader, Ahmad Shah Massoud, just two days before 9/11.[60]

When the first extremist cells were detected in Spain in the 1990s, they were characterized by their national homogeneity: in GIA, and then GSPC, all members were Algerian.[61] With the dismantlement of the Abu Dahdah network in late 2001, some members were imprisoned and others, with a low militant profile, remained free because of lack of evidence to convict them. They later emerged in connection with the Madrid 2004 bombings.[62] The dismantling of older networks led to the emergence of reconstituted cells, whose defining characteristic was the interconnection between radicals of different nationalities, embracing the global political agenda of jihad. Thus, the Maghrebi networks involved in support activities for jihads in their home countries shifted their priorities to supporting globalized jihad.[63]

The 3/11 attacks

On 11 March, ten bombs ripped through four trains in Madrid, during the rush hour commute, killing 191 passengers and wounding more than 1,400. It is thought that the bombs, carried in sports bags or rucksacks, were detonated by mobile phones. Two days after the Madrid attacks, the police found a videotape in which a man claiming to speak on behalf of Al Qaeda said the group carried out the bombings in reprisal for Spain's collaboration with the United States and for 'crimes in Iraq and Afghanistan'.[64] In a video found in the rubble of a Madrid apartment, where seven suspects of the bombings blew themselves up three weeks after the attacks, three men claimed responsibility for the train bombings in the name of Al Qaeda inside Spain.

The evidence unearthed in the weeks following the attacks indicated that they were mostly organized locally, with the planning, bomb-building, funding and execution carried out mainly by Moroccans. Investigators have established the connections with Moroccan extremist groups, like the Salafia Jihadiya, a secretive, radical Islamic group accused by the Moroccan government of organizing five nearly simultaneous attacks in Casablanca, on 16 May 2003, using twelve suicide bombers. They targeted Jewish sites and a Spanish restaurant, killing thirty-three people. The investigators focused their investigations on the MICG: an Al Qaeda-linked group and a forerunner of Salafia Jihadiya.[65]

Many pieces of the investigation, however, indicated that the bombings were more centrally organized, and that there was some kind of link to Al Qaeda. The connection is not only ideological, but also operational. One of the suspected masterminds of the Madrid bombings, the Moroccan Amer el-Azizi, had connections to several major Al Qaeda plots, including in the organization of the July 2001 meeting in Tarragona, which preceded the 9/11 attacks.[66] He had received training in Al Qaeda camps in Afghanistan, and facilitated the recruitment of Spanish elements. He was close to Abu Dahdah, the leader of the Spanish cell.[67] He had fled from Spain in November 2000, just before the police dismantled that cell. Azizi is the first suspect directly linked to the September 11 attacks, and to the March 11 train bombings. He was the link between Al Qaeda's leadership approval and the organization of the plot, by engaging his trusted collaborators and former members of Abu Dahdah's cell.[68]

The operational head of the 3/11 plot was a Tunisian immigrant, Sarhane ben Abdelmajid Fakhet. Jamal Ahmidan, a Moroccan, former hashish trafficker turned fundamentalist, was Fakhet's lieutenant and chief fundraiser. He was a major drug dealer, moving hashish from Morocco to Spain, using the profits to buy guns and explosives.[69] A major operative of the cell and material author of the attacks, Jamal Zougam, was arrested and convicted in 2007, and subsequently sentenced to forty years in prison.[70] According to documents found in their apartment, the bombers had planned to attack a shopping centre in their residential area, and a Jewish community centre and a cemetery outside Madrid.[71] On 2 April, a partly assembled bomb was found on a busy high-speed rail line linking Madrid and Seville. The explosives matched the type used in the 11 March attacks.[72]

The investigation of the 3/11 attacks highlighted the ever-increasing global-networked nature of terrorist organizations. As regards the particular nature of the 3/11 network, some aspects are worth highlighting. The first is that Al Qaeda – such as ISIS – has become a network with a 'diffuse structure, indirect connections, and non-traditional modes of communication'.[73] This is in line with research on network analysis, which highlights the advantages of relational systems in shaping collective action, including underground organizations. Al Qaeda has evolved into a global, complex, decentralized network, with few hierarchical or organizational boundaries. It relies on loose, flexible forms of relations, such as isolated networks and terrorist home-grown cells.[74] Network connections enable terrorist cells to maintain operative ties with a broader network, from which they can draw material support and receive ideological inspiration, while the core network maintains its operational capacity and its ability to constantly relay its message. As highlighted by Rodriguez regarding the 3/11 network, this sort of network presents a number of additional advantages over hierarchical terrorist organizations: 'They give them stability in the face of arrests or mission failures, 2) they confer flexibility, so that last minute adaptations can be made, 3) and security, in that they remain largely invisible to police forces.'[75]

Spanish expert Javier Jordán contends that the 3/11 attack was an example of home-grown terrorism. He developed a model to explain when disparate individuals and groups can form what he terms grassroots jihadi networks (GJN), which, although not formally part of a hierarchical organization (Global Jihad Movement – GJMV), share the same ideals and concur with the strategic aims of global jihadism.[76] The 3/11 network was based on different levels of cooperation between different nuclei: starting with a core group composed of ringleaders and frontline operator, to ordinary delinquents who may not share the goals, but collaborate for profit.[77] In such a case, although not subordinated to a GJMV, there is functional subordination, as GJN members abide by the directives of the larger organization. These nebulous organizations may interact and cooperate with other GJNs or with more structured organizations. Flexibility allows for any number of factions to align and flow together in different forms. Eventually, as members of the nebula interact in organizing a plot, they may create a new GJN. In the case of the 3/11, it was the outcome of cooperation between small radical subgroups or localized factions, even individuals, who may have had no direct contact with the centre, but strove to associate themselves with the propounded vision and the trademark organization.[78]

GJN cells are of an informal nature, mostly relying on personal ties and a shared common ideology. There may be a central core of the network, with more contacts and more intense relationships, around which simpler substructures and less implicated actors revolve. Some members play an important role in intermediation, and in interconnecting the various parts of the network. There being no hierarchical subordination, the cement that binds the units together is 'personal links and a shared common ideology'.[79] The thesis of a grassroots jihadi network is held by Jordán, Mañas, and Horsburgh and Sageman,[80] but is confuted by Reinares and Lorenzo, who stand by the opinion that the plot was directed from Al Qaeda's core and its affiliates.[81] As the judicial investigation evolved, scholars were divided over the design and direction of the plot. Even after the National Court of Spain delivered the final verdicts – October 2017 there were conflicting accounts on the master plan behind the bombings. It is unclear whether the idea originated from a senior element of central Al Qaeda – through any of the main operatives – or if the idea originated from the local GJN.[82] In fact, according to Reinares, it was a collaborative endeavour, directed from Al Qaeda through its North African affiliates active in Europe, involving the remnants of a local Al Qaeda cell, and a support network, an assorted GJN.[83]

Reinares' thesis is that the 3/11 network, made up of twenty-seven individuals,[84] was formed out of three different clusters: the first one was the aforementioned network created by Abu Dahdah. Although the cell was dismantled in 2001, in the wake of 9/11 and the mounting evidence of connections with other European cells, some members managed to escape. Members of the Abu Dahdah cell were, actually, the 'most notorious members of the Madrid bombing network'.[85] Those involved were not only residents in Spain, but also from cells based in Italy and Belgium. A main member of the cell was Azizi, radicalized and recruited into Abu Dahdah's cell and, in fact, his lieutenant.[86] He received training in military camps in Afghanistan, managed by North Africans. After 2001, he fled to the Afghanistan–Pakistan area, becoming an adjunct to Al Qaeda's commander for external actions, the Egyptian Abu Hamza Rabia.[87] He became the main organizer of the plot. In late 2003, he travelled from Pakistan to Madrid to convey Al Qaeda's support for the plot, and help finalize the preparations for the attack.[88]

In March 2002, Azizi's friend, the Moroccan Mustafa Maymouni initiated the formation of the initial 3/11 cell, but was imprisoned in Morocco due to his involvement in the Casablanca attacks.[89] Eventually, the task fell on Fakhet, the 'Tunisian', who had been radicalized and recruited by Azizi into Al Qaeda's Spanish cell in the late 1990s. He became the ringleader of the attack.[90] A second strand of the 3/11 group were members of MICG, a group originally founded by Moroccan veterans in Afghanistan, in 1996. That was the case of two prominent members based in Belgium, Hassan el-Haski[91] and Youssef Belhadj,[92] and of the terrorists who launched suicide bombings in Casablanca.[93] The third cluster was composed of different individuals, sixteen of whom were convicted in Spain (12), Morocco (3) and Italy (1). Part of the group was initially composed of a criminal gang, led by Ahmidan, who ran a narcotics ring that sold hashish and Ecstasy throughout Western Europe, and stolen vehicles. The 3/11 group received no funding from outside extremists, as it relied on profits from Ahmidan's drug trade.[94] The 3/11 group capabilities were greatly amplified, as they were able to recruit criminals who had technical expertise and access to illicit material,[95] such as industrial dynamite and detonators.

As regards the network's connections, it was found that there were links between different groups: Allekama Lamari had been imprisoned in Spain in 1997 for his links to the GIA;[96] Rabei Osman, residing in Italy, was a former member of the Egyptian Islamic Jihad Group, which fused with Al Qaeda. According to Reinares, the plot was a truly transnational enterprise, as it involved North African Al Qaeda affiliates: the collaboration of operatives of the LIFG and the TCG, both based in Afghanistan and running military camps where recruits were trained and indoctrinated.[97] The real picture of the Madrid plot brings to light the simultaneous allegiance and membership in various networks, as, for instance, the overlap of 3/11 with Abu Dahdah's cell, GIA, MICG and the North African Al Qaeda affiliates.[98]

The 3/11 case also highlights the importance of social networks in the formation and activity of the group. All major Spanish experts concur that personal relationships and commitment to the jihad are more significant characteristics than loyalty to an abstract organization. The 3/11 group built upon knowledge and trust generated by prior relationships. In many cases, these social networks are based on long friendship ties, for example, the childhood friendship between Jamal Ahmidan and the Tétouan friends, and Zougam and the Tangiers friends.[99] Other ties were family-based, as between the two sets of brothers, Mohannad and Moutaz Almallah Dabas, and Mohammed and Rachid Oulad Akcha. Some were related through marriage (Fakhet with Maymouni's sister).[100] This is what Rodriguez entitled an 'interaction-based trust network', based on kinship, friendship and contact, co-habitation or repeated encounters.[101]

A recent study on patterns of the jihadi radicalization of 178 individuals detained in Spain between 2013 and 2016 also bears out the importance of prior social links, particularly the relevance of local networks built on interpersonal ties, in facilitating jihadi radicalization and recruitment. Jihadist radicalization, leading to involvement with terrorism, is closely associated with social interactions through which individuals learn and endorse ideas that justify terrorism. 'The importance of contact with one or more agents of radicalization underlines the relevance of ideology in the process through which attitudes and beliefs of a violent Salafism are acquired. The extent of previous social links indicates that affective ties within local networks facilitate the processes of radicalization and jihadi recruitment.'[102]

Mobilization for the war in Syria

Since 3/11, counterterrorism authorities have carried out 181 operations in Spain, more than two-thirds of which related to the war in Syria alone.[103] Spain remains an important centre for Islamist activity on the continent. In the aftermath of 3/11, the central core of Al Qaeda ceded to the regional nodes in Iraq and North Africa, contributing to the recruitment of fighters to Iraq or to wars in North Africa, through former GSPC and Al Qaeda networks in the Maghreb.[104] Most of the individuals arrested in Spain in the period between 2004 and 2013 had connections to groups and individuals outside of Spain.[105] In March 2014, Spanish authorities arrested Mustafá Maya in Melilla; he was a radical agitator who had turned the autonomous city into one of the main centres for global recruitment of terrorists. The six members of that cell managed to send twenty-six recruits living in Spain to conflict zones. They were part of an international network for recruiting and sending jihadis to terrorist organizations based in Mali and Libya, in particular, to Al Qaeda in the Islamic Maghreb, and to the Movement for Oneness and Jihad in West Africa.

Since the outbreak of the war in Syria, Spain became an important recruiting ground for mobilizing jihadis to fight in both Syria and Iraq: as many as 139 Spaniards or residents in Spain[106] may have travelled to those countries to join the ranks of the ISIS or Al Qaeda-affiliated groups. Between 2012 and 2015 alone, sixty-two anti-terrorist operations in Spain and seventeen abroad detained 139 individuals in Spain and fifty-eight abroad linked to jihadism, a total of 197.[107] Amaya recruited volunteers from nine different countries to fight for ISIS in Syria, and cooperated with other individuals based in Spain, Belgium, Luxembourg, Turkey, Tunisia, Libya, Mali, France and Morocco, who were involved in recruitment, funding and falsification of documents, as well as putting volunteers in contact with intermediaries in other states. The cell used 'Sharia4Spain', the social media platform created in 2010 to recruit jihadis to fight in the ranks of what would later become ISIS.[108] Spain has also become a major financing hub for jihadi terrorists in Syria and Iraq through an extensive network of phone shops, call centres, butcher shops and neighbourhood grocery stores, where money is transferred through the hawala system.[109]

The military pressure being exerted on ISIS in the war zone has led to a huge increase in the jihadi demand for new fighters, equipment, arms and other military supplies, tasks for which Spain has proven useful as a base or a throughway. Recruitment continued strenuously, despite increased vigilance and repression, even as ISIS was losing ground in Syria and Iraq. The police uncovered small cells engaged in *constant communication with ISIS fighters in Syria*: since 2015 – the year in which the Spanish government increased the terrorism threat level in the country from three to four – national security forces arrested a total of 186 jihadis.[110] Most recruits – about 150 – came from Madrid, Barcelona, Ceuta and Melilla alone.[111] Recruiters provided logistical support for terrorist activities, and recruited and indoctrinated women and young adults, as well as children.[112]

Spain is also important from a symbolic viewpoint: in the jihadis' imaginary, it is the ancient territory of Al-Andalus, a former part of the Muslim Ummah (for 780 years, between 711 and the fall of the Kingdom of Granada in 1492), before the Christian kings of Spain and Portugal retrieved it in the 'Reconquista' campaign. Calls for taking back Al-Andalus became more frequent and more strident. In 2016, ISIS and other jihadi groups engaged in an impressive media campaign[113] to announce their plans to liberate Al-Andalus from non-Muslims, warning that Spain will 'pay dearly' for the expulsion of Muslims.[114] Calls to reconquer Al-Andalus are becoming more frequent and more strident.[115] The threat materialized on 17 August 2017, when Younes Abouyaaqoub drove a van onto Barcelona's La Rambla boulevard, crashing into pedestrians and killing thirteen people of ten different nationalities. Nine hours after the Barcelona attack, Abouyaaqoub and four other men drove into pedestrians in nearby Cambrils, killing one woman and injuring six others. The terrorists intended to provoke an even worse massacre, as their original plan was to drive the van after loading it with explosives.[116] The group's plans were derailed when, inside an abandoned house in the Catalonian town of Alcanar, the explosive powder caused the mixture to detonate, killing two members of the cell and injuring another. Notwithstanding the apparently home-grown nature of the attack, it was a more sophisticated operation than previous jihadi vehicle attacks in Europe, as it was carried out by a cell of around a dozen people.[117]

Portuguese jihadists

In the years following 9/11, some data reported the presence in Portugal of Maghreb and Pakistani immigrants, who constituted small hubs of political and religious radicalism.[118] In point of fact, logistical support and funding networks were actually detected and disrupted, but no conditions were found – as in other countries – that facilitated the formation of radical groups. Nor was there any sustained evidence of terrorists planning activities on Portuguese soil. Its territory was a crossing point for elements suspected of membership in and association with European jihadi groups, and was used by Islamic extremists for logistic purposes, namely falsification of documents, fundraising, as a place of rest and hiding and, possibly, indoctrination.[119] With the start of the war in Syria, the situation has completely changed. At least twelve Portuguese citizens or people of Portuguese descent[120] have enlisted for the jihad.[121] Some of them are said to have risen in the ISIS hierarchy, and are now involved, at high levels, in recruitment and propaganda.

Profile of the Portuguese foreign fighters

The Portuguese were filled with astonishment and alarm when in 2014 the minister of Foreign Affairs disclosed that there were twelve to fifteen Portuguese jihadis fighting alongside ISIS.[122] Syria and Iraq became a magnet for Portuguese individuals to the Al Qaeda-fuelled jihad. The threat of Islamist terrorism evolved, especially as far as logistical support structures, radicalization and recruitment are concerned.[123] There are a few characteristics that bring together the Portuguese who have enlisted in the jihadi ranks. Indeed, their profile corroborates some of the stereotypes of Western converts, elicited so far from policy and academic research focused on terrorism. Apart from one individual, all jihadis were converts to Islam. Indeed, the most striking feature of the Portuguese case study is that almost all individuals are recent converts to Islam. They are part of a larger trend of European individuals converted to violent strains of Islam who were enticed to join the jihad in Syria and Iraq. This is part of a trend that has been identified as a distinctive feature of the Syrian war: a surging number of young people from non-Muslim backgrounds, flocking to the Middle East to wage jihad. Many are

European, new to war, and also new to Islam. The majority converted to Islam within a few years to months before travelling to the conflict zone. The Portuguese volunteers have no family, cultural or ethnic links to Syria/Iraq. Their age range is between twenty and the mid-thirties. They come from European suburban areas; have no previous record of involvement with extremism; and no significant record of criminal or other markedly anti-social behaviour.[124] They have a low or medium level of education, and originate from low or lower-middle-class socioeconomic backgrounds.

Most of the Portuguese recruits to jihad were brought up as Catholics. A group of them has family roots in former Portuguese African colonies, including Guinea-Bissau, Cape Verde and Angola. This group – the so-called Leyton or London group – is composed of six men who emigrated to London on different dates, starting from the early 2000s. They are descendants of families of immigrants, and originate from the Greater Lisbon region. They moved to London where they converted to Islam. The second group had lived in other European countries (France, Luxembourg and The Netherlands) for a longer time than they lived in Portugal, and many also held dual nationalities from other European countries. The London group of five young men moved from Portugal to East London over a period of several years, either to study or to find a job. They arrived one by one from the dormitory towns between Lisbon and the outlying area of Sintra, and gradually dropped out of circulation. Most of them converted to Islam and were subsequently radicalized, deciding to travel to Syria to join ISIS's and Al Qaeda's ranks. The men, who lived in Leyton and Walthamstow, London's north-eastern periphery, had long been under the radar of British intelligence officials.[125]

The radicalization process

As has been evidenced by the 3/11 network, radicalization involves circles of friends or relatives that radicalize as a group, and, in some cases, that decide to leave jointly for ISIS territories. The Leyton group was partly composed of childhood friends, who met and grew up in the Lisbon suburbs (Celso and Edgar, plus Sandro and Sadjo), and kin (brothers Celso and Edgar). In London, the group of six eventually came together. Sandro was the last of the Leyton cell members to leave Sintra for London, where he joined the brothers Costa, of whom he had been a schoolmate. He was also a friend of Sadjo. What Edgar, Celso and Sadjo shared in common was the fact that they had attended the same school in the Lisbon suburbs of Massamá, and had been part of a hip-hop band. The Leyton group rented joint apartments or lived in nearby areas. They were radicalized by a notorious 'hate preacher' who had inspired dozens of young people to turn to terrorism. They shared resources, attended the same mosque and practised sports together. They took care of one another under trying conditions, in a context of professional and personal hardship.

The Portuguese jihadis underwent a quick radicalization process, a trend that has been identified as a typical feature of this generation of jihadis.[126] As elicited by Roy, within the context of conversion and radicalization of new-born Muslims, almost all Portuguese jihadis share the pattern of a sudden conversion, immediately followed by political radicalization.[127] After arriving in London in 2011, Fábio converted to Islam within a two-year time span. That happened after he moved into an apartment in Leyton, where he met the other group of Portuguese immigrants. In March 2013, he was already radicalized, and, by October, he had left for Syria.[128] Radicalization took place over a very short time span, due to their involvement with Islamist militant milieus. It is believed that the Portuguese jihadis may have come under the influence of Anjem Choudary, a former leader of the extremist organization Islam4UK, and al-Muhajiroun.[129]

The slide towards violent extremism occurred within a radical environment: in the Forest Gate mosque, in the case of the Leyton group, or in the radical mosque of Esch-sur-Alzette for Steve Duarte, or at the Villiers-sur-Marne mosque for Mickaël dos Santos and Mikael Batista, radicalized by imam Mustapha Mraoui. Ângela Barreto was radicalized online. She spent quite a lot of time online in extremist websites, even managing a site of her own. She rejected her friends, and changed her dress and diet.[130] She was recruited by Fábio while browsing the internet, using extremist online sites and Facebook. The internet worked as a second, parallel, radicalization gateway, reinforcing bonds and group dynamics: after converting, the new Muslim devotees purposely sought out radical sites and forums. The Portuguese descendants also spent a lot of time online, watching radical videos, as is reportedly the case with the London group and Mickaël.[131]

Conclusion

Spain will likely remain a target for Islamist terrorists for ideological reasons, which bin Laden and ISIS leaders have repeatedly invoked. The recovery of Al-Andalus, and its incorporation into the House of Islam (dar al-Islam), especially because it was seized and occupied by infidels, is a duty and should eventually lead to the reinstatement of the historical territory of the Caliphate. Spanish sovereignty over the enclaves of Ceuta and Melilla, on the Moroccan coast, is also considered an offence to Muslim pride. Islamist plots against Spain have continued after 3/11 because of other reasons, namely, the presence of a large Muslim community, enabling the development of logistic and support activities by extremist networks, with a small portion being vulnerable to being recruited by jihadi groups; migrants from North Africa, Pakistan and Bangladesh who have turned the region into a breeding ground for extremists; and connections to the Spanish enclaves in North Africa creating hubs that link criminal organizations and mosques to various terror groups, providing resources to finance terror activities.

Strangely enough, in the case of Portugal, Syria and Iraq also became a magnet for Portuguese individuals to the Al Qaeda-fuelled jihad. Portuguese citizens and descendants, especially converts, became combatants, and then turned to actively recruiting and facilitating the transit of fighters into Syria and Iraq. For the most part, the Portuguese who enlisted in the jihadi ranks are recent converts to Islam.

They converted and were radicalized while living abroad in European metropolitan and suburban areas with a large concentration of Muslim populations.

Notes

1. See Richard Jackson, 'Religion, politics and terrorism: A critical analysis of narratives of "Islamic terrorism"', Centre for International Politics Working Paper Series No. 21, October 2006, p. 3; Olivier Roy, *Globalised Islam: The Search for a New Ummah* (London: Hurst and Company, 2004), p. 245; Bruce Hoffman and Fernando Reinares, 'Al Qaeda's continued core strategy and disquieting leader-led trajectory', ARI 37/2013, Real Instituto Elcano, 2013, p. 5.
2. V. J. Julie Rajan, *Al Qaeda's Global Crisis: The Islamic State, Takfir, and the Genocide of Muslims* (London and New York: Routledge, 2015), pp. 87, 89.
3. Rik Coolsaet, 'Between al-Andalus and a failing integration: Europe's Pursuit of a long-term counterterrorism strategy in the post al-Qaeda era'. Royal Institute for International Relations (IRRI-KIIB), Brussels, May, Egmont Papers 5 (2005), p. 4.
4. Roland Robertson, 'Glocalization: Time-space and homogeneity-heterogeneity', in M. Featherstone, S. Lash and R. Robertson (eds), *Global Modernities* (London: Sage, 1995).
5. Glocalization 'means the simultaneity – the co-presence – of both universalizing and particularizing tendencies': Roland Robertson, 'Comments on the "global triad" and "glocalization"', Institute for Japanese Culture and Classics, Kokugakuin University, 1997. Available at http://www2.kokugakuin.ac.jp/ijcc/wp/global/15robertson.html (accessed 7 November 2017).
6. Jeffrey Cozzens, 'Approaching Al-Qaida's warfare: Function, culture and grand strategy', in M. Ranstorp (ed.), *Mapping Terrorism Research: State of the Art, Gaps and Future Direction* (Abingdon: Routledge, 2007), p. 137, 162.
7. Javier Jordán, 'Anatomy of Spain's 28 disrupted Jihadist networks', *CTC Sentinel*, 1, issue 11 (October 2008): 10–11.
8. Rogerio Alonso, 'The Madrid attacks on March 11: An analysis of the jihadist threat in Spain and main counterterrorist measures', in J. J. F. Forest (ed.), *Countering Terrorism and Insurgency in the 21st Century – International Perspectives, Volume 3* (Westport: Praeger, 2007), p. 203.
9. Javier Valenzuela, *España en el punto de mira: La amenaza del integrismo islámico* (Madrid: Temas de Hoy, 2002).
10. See Fernando Reinares, 'The 2004 Madrid train bombings', in B. Hoffman and F. Reinares (eds), *The Evolution of the Global Terrorist Threat: Cases from 9/11 to Osama Bin Laden's Death* (New York: Cambridge University Press, 2014).
11. Liliana Borges, 'Reino Unido diz que Portugal não está imune à ameaça de atentados', *Público*, 25 March 2018. Available at https://www.publico.pt/2018/03/29/sociedade/noticia/portugal-nao-esta-livre-de-um-ataque-terrorista-alerta-governo-britanico-1808574 (accessed 29 July 2018).
12. 'Muslim populations by country: How big will each Muslim population be by 2030?', 2016. Available at https://www.theguardian.com/news/datablog/2011/jan/28/muslim-population-country-projection-2030#data (accessed 16 November 2018).
13. 'Islam in Spain: 800% population increase in a mere 13 years'. Available at https://muslimstatistics.wordpress.com/2014/04/11/islam-in-spain-800-population-increase-in-mere-13-years/ (accessed 9 July 2018).

14 'Gobierno de España et al., 'La Comunidad Musulmana de Origen Inmigrante en España', October 2007. Available at http://www.mitramiss.gob.es/oberaxe/ficheros/documentos/EstudioOpinion2007_ComunidadMusulmanaOrigenInmigrante.pdf.
15 'Muslim populations by country'.
16 'Muçulmanos em Portugal "sob suspeita"', O Jornal Económico, 3 January 2017. Available at http://www.jornaleconomico.sapo.pt/noticias/muculmanos-portugal-sob-suspeita-106388; 'Muslim populations by country'.
17 See Fernando Reinares, *Al-Qaeda's Revenge: The 2004 Madrid Train Bombings* (Washington DC: Woodrow Wilson Center Press; New York: Columbia University Press, 2017).
18 Fernando Reinares and Carola García-Calvo, '233 Jihadists were arrested in Spain over the period 2013-2017', ARI 82/2018, 27 June 2018. Available at http://www.realinstitutoelcano.org/wps/portal/rielcano_en/contenido?WCM_GLOBAL_CONTEXT=/elcano/elcano_in/zonas_in/ari82-2018-reinares-garciacalvo-moroccans-second-generation-among-jihadists-spain (accessed 15 November 2018).
19 See Bruce Hoffman and Fernando Reinares (eds), *The Evolving Global Terrorism Threat: Cases from 9/11 to Osama Bin Laden's Death* (New York: Columbia University Press, 2014); Angel Rabasa and Cheryl Benard, *EuroJihad: Patterns of Islamist Radicalization and Terrorism in Europe* (New York: Cambridge University Press, 2015).
20 'Spain's 11 September "Connection"', BBC, 22 April 2005. Available at http://news.bbc.co.uk/2/hi/europe/4472377.stm (accessed 19 September 2018).
21 Keith Johnson and David Crawford, 'Spain refocuses terrorism probe following arrests', *The Wall Street Journal*, 5 April 2004, p. 17.
22 Soeren Kern, 'The Islamic Republic of Catalonia', 12 October 2012. Available at https://www.gatestoneinstitute.org/3393/catalonia-islamic-republic (accessed 11 January 2018).
23 Fernando Reinares and Carola García-Calvo, 'Catalonia and the evolution of jihadist terrorism in Spain', Expert Comment 33/2015, 30 April 2015. Available at http://www.realinstitutoelcano.org/wps/portal/rielcano_en/contenido?WCM_GLOBAL_CONTEXT=/elcano/elcano_in/zonas_in/international+terrorism/commentary-reinares-garciacalvo-catalonia-and-the-evolution-of-jihadist-terrorism-in-spain (accessed 11 January 2018).
24 Javier Jordán and Nicola Horsburgh, 'Mapping jihadist terrorism in Spain', *Studies in Conflict & Terrorism*, xxviii, no. 3 (2005): 170–1.
25 It rebranded itself, on 11 September 2006, as al-Qaeda in the Islamic Maghreb (AQIM), also sometimes referred to as al-Qaeda in the Lands of the Islamic Maghreb (AQLIM) when Ayman al-Zawahiri, al-Qaeda's second-in-command, announced the union.
26 Martin Bright et al., 'The secret war, Part 2', *The Observer*. Available at http://www.observer.co.U.K./focus/story/0,6903,560658,00.html (accessed 27 June 2004).
27 Reinares, *Al-Qaeda's Revenge*.
28 Bright et al., 'The secret war, Part 2'.
29 Chris Hedges, 'A Glimpse behind the plot against the American Embassy in Paris', *New York Times*, 28 October 2001.
30 'Paris suspect denies Bin Laden link', BBC News, 2 October 2001. Available at http://news.bbc.co.uk/2/hi/europe/1574842.stm; 'Bin Laden "named" in Paris plot', BBC News, 2 October 2001. Available at http://news.bbc.co.uk/2/hi/south_asia/1575019.stm (accessed 12 January 2018); Marlise Simons, 'Ninth man held in suspected plot

against Paris embassy', *NYTimes.com*, 4 October 2001. Available at ww.nytimes.com/2001/10/04/international/ninth-man-held-in-suspected-plot-against-paris-embassy.html (accessed 12 January 2018).
31 Beatrice de Graaf, 'The Van Gogh murder and beyond', in B. Hoffman and F. Reinares (eds), *The Evolution of the Global Terrorist Threat: Cases from 9/11 to Osama Bin Laden's Death* (New York: Cambridge University Press, 2014), pp. 109–10: Andrew Osborn, 'Bin Laden disciple jailed for 10 years in Belgium', *The Guardian*, 1 October 2003. Available at https://www.theguardian.com/world/2003/oct/01/alqaida.terrorism (accessed 12 January 2018).
32 Lorenzo Vidino, *Al-Qaeda in Europe* (Amherst: Prometheus Books, 2006), pp. 164–5.
33 Rabasa and Benard, *EuroJihad*, p. 43; John Hooper, 'German police arrest Islamists with UK links', *Guardian.Unlimited*, 24 April 2002 (accessed 13 January 2018).
34 Al Goodman, Peter Humi and Kelli Arena, 'Bin Laden associate arrested in Spain', *CNN.com*, 22 June 2001. Available at http://edition.cnn.com/2001/WORLD/europe/06/22/spain.arrest/ (accessed 13 January 2018). The Frankfurt arrests led to further arrests in Britain, and confirmed the suspicions Italian police harboured against a cell in Milan. The Frankfurt, Milan and British cells were planning poison gas attacks in Europe. In October 2001, investigators found out a cell of Algerians based in London, working with their counterparts in Italy and Germany, and directly funded by bin Laden, were plotting to attack the European Parliament in Strasbourg. The attack was said to be scheduled to take place during the parliamentary sessions, and was to be the first in a series of assaults against prominent buildings across Europe: David Bamber, Chris Hastings and Rajeev Syal, 'Bin Laden British cell planned gas attack on European Parliament', *Electronic Telegraph*, 16 September 2001. Available at http://www.telegraph.co.uk/news/worldnews/asia/afghanistan/1340692/Bin-Laden-British-cell-planned-gas-attack-on-EU-Parliament.html (accessed 12 January 2018).
35 Jeff Israely, 'The second time around', *Time*, clix, no. 9 (4 March 2002): 2.
36 Rohan Gunaratna, *Inside Al Qaeda: Global Network of Terror* (New York: Columbia University Press, 2002), p. 129.
37 Reinares, 'The 2004 Madrid', p. 40; Jordán and Horsburgh, 'Mapping jihadist terrorism in Spain', p. 172; Al Goodman, '33 charged in failed Spain bombing', 31 March 2006. Available at http://edition.cnn.com/2006/WORLD/europe/03/21/spain.indictments/ CNN (accessed 15 January 2018).
38 Peter Finn and Pamela Rolfe, 'Spain holds 8 linked to Sept. 11 plot', *Washington Post*, 19 November 2001.
39 Lawrence Wright, 'The master plan: For the new theorists of jihad, Al Qaeda is just the beginning', *The New Yorker*, 11 September 2006. Available at https://www.newyorker.com/magazine/2006/09/11/the-master-plan (accessed 15 January 2018).
40 Raphael Lefevre, *Ashes of Hama: The Muslim Brotherhood in Syria* (London: Hurst, 2013), p. 145. Brynjar Lia, *Architect of Global Jihad: The Life of Al-Qaida Strategist Abu Mus'ab al-Suri* (London: C. Hurst & Co. Ltd., 2009).
41 Reinares, 'The 2004 Madrid', p. 54.
42 Rabasa and Benard, *EuroJihad*, p. 47.
43 Javier Jordán, 'Las redes yihadistas en España. Evolución desde el 3/11', *Athena Intelligence Journal*, ii, no. 3 (2007): 7; Carole García-Calvo and Fernando Reinares, 'Pautas de implicación entre condenados por actividades relacionadas con el terrorismo yihadista o muertos en acto de terrorismo suicida en España (1996-2013)', Documento de Trabajo 15/2014, Real Instituto Elcano, 17 November 2014, p. 6; Lefevre, *Ashes of Hama*, p. 145; Javier Jordán, Fernando M. Mañas and Nicola

Horsburgh, 'Strengths and weaknesses of grassroot jihadist networks: The Madrid bombings', *Studies in Conflict & Terrorism*, xxxi, no. 1 (2008): 25.

44 William Neuman and Post Wires, 'Spain's eight suspects aided 9/11 thugs: Judge', *New York Post*, 19 November 2001. Available at https://nypost.com/2001/11/19/spains-eight-suspects-aided-911-thugs-judge/ (accessed 27 December 2017).

45 Finn and Rolfe, 'Spain holds 8'. Juzgado Central de Instrucción No. 005, Madrid, Summary (Ordinary Proc.) 0000035/2001 E, 17 September 2003, pp. 63–4 and p. 93.

46 José Maria Irujo, 'Las piezas españolas de la trama Al Qaeda', *El País*, 8 September 2002. Available at https://elpais.com/diario/2002/09/08/domingo/1031457153_850215.html (accessed 27 December 2017).

47 Juzgado Central, 2003, p. 26 and pp. 91–103; Jordán and Horsburgh, 'Mapping jihadist terrorism', p. 176.

48 Irujo, 'Las piezas españolas'.

49 James Graff, 'Bust in Madrid', *Time*, clxviii, no. 22 (3 December 2001): 4. Juzgado Central, 2003, p. 90 and pp. 103–5. The Madrid cell had links to Mamoun Darkazanli, a Syrian-born businessman in Hamburg, described by Spanish authorities as 'belonging to the most intimate circle of Mohammed Atta'. Juzgado Central 2003, pp. 36–42 and p. 91. Darkazanli, a naturalized German citizen who moved to Hamburg from Syria in 1982, knew Atta, Marwan al-Shehhi and Ziad Jarrah, the three pilots of the September 11 plot: John Crewdson, 'CIA stalked al-Qaeda in Hamburg', *The Chicago Tribune*, 17 November 2002. Available at http://articles.chicagotribune.com/2002-11-17/news/0211170296_1_al-qaeda-mamoun-darkazanli-insular-muslim-community (accessed 2 November 2017). Atta visited Spain in January and July 2001, after he had moved from Hamburg to the US. It is now believed that he met with Ramzi Binalshibih on those trips and with some of the Spanish cell members. Investigators say he might have been in Spain to pass instructions to al-Qaeda members after the arrest of Mohammed Bensakhria in Alicante a few weeks earlier: 'Spain remands al-Qaeda suspects', *CNN.com*, 22 September 2003. Available at http://edition.cnn.com/2003/WORLD/europe/09/22/spain.alqaeda/index.html (accessed November 2 2017); Juzgado Central, 2003, p. 320 and 324; Reinares, 'The 2004 Madrid', p. 34; Vidino, *Al Qaeda*, p. 300.

50 Jordán and Horsburgh, 'Mapping jihadist terrorism', p. 178. In 2005, Abu Dahdah was convicted to a 27-year sentence, having been accused of leading a terrorist organization and conspiring to perpetrate the 9/11 attacks. In June 2006 the Spanish Supreme Court reduced the sentence to 12 years because, although acknowledging that he was a member of a terrorist organization, he did not take part in the 9/11 preparations.

51 Jordán and Horsburgh, 'Mapping jihadist terrorism', p. 184, 181.

52 Jórdan, 'Las redes yihadistas', p. 3.

53 Reinares, *Al-Qaeda's Revenge*, p. 17.

54 Jordán and Horsburgh, 'Mapping jihadist terrorism', p. 184. Reinares, *Al-Qaeda's Revenge*; Rabasa and Benard, *EuroJihad*, p. 47.

55 Douglas Frantz, 'A nation challenged: Terror network; Spain arrests Algerian man suspected as Qaeda Aide', *New York Times*, 15 April 2002. Available at http://www.nytimes.com/2002/04/15/world/nation-challenged-terror-network-spain-arrests-algerian-man-suspected-qaeda-aide.html (accessed 12 November 2017); Lorenzo Silva, 'Así cayó Brahim, el banquero', *El Mundo: Cronica*, no. 340, 21 April 2002. Available at http://www.el-mundo.es/cronica/2002/340/1019461035.html (accessed 19 January 2018); 'Spain arrests senior Al Qaeda suspect', *CNN.com*, 14 April 2002. Available at

http://edition.cnn.com/2002/WORLD/europe/04/14/inq.spain.arrest/index.html?related (accessed 12 November 2017). In 2006 he was convicted to ten years in prison for creating a website to spread al-Qaeda 'fatwas' – Islamic decrees – and to recruit Islamist terrorists: 'Condenado a 10 años de prisión un islamista por fomentar el terrorismo a través de Internet', *elmundoes*, 3 April 2006. Available at http://www.elmundo.es/elmundo/2006/04/03/espana/1144093975.html (accessed 15 November 2017).

56 Al Goodman, 'Spain holds al-Qaeda link suspects', 8 March 2003. Available at http://edition.cnn.com/2003/WORLD/europe/03/08/spain.arrests/index.html.

57 José Yoldi, 'Un empresario español, condenado a cinco años de prisión por financiar a Al Qaeda', *El País*, 11 May 2006. Available at https://elpais.com/diario/2006/05/11/espana/1147298432_850215.html (accessed 22 November 2017); José Maria Irujo, *El agujero: España invadida por la yihad* (Madrid: Aguilar, 2005).

58 United Nations Security Council, 'Tunisian Combatant Group'. Available at https://www.un.org/sc/suborg/en/sanctions/1267/aq_sanctions_list/summaries/entity/tunisian-combatant-group (accessed 12 November 2017).

59 Maria do Céu Pinto, *Islamist and Middle Eastern Terrorism: A Threat to Europe?* (Rome: Centro Militare di Studi Strategici – CeMISS/Rubbettino, 2004), p. 35.

60 Ibid., p. 52.

61 Javier Jordán and Robert Wesley, 'After 3/11: The evolution of jihadist networks in Spain', *Terrorism Monitor*, iv, no. 1 (2006). Available at https://jamestown.org/program/after-311-the-evolution-of-jihadist-networks-in-spain/ (accessed 2 January 2018).

62 Such as Sarhane ben Adelmajid Fakhet, Jamal Zougam and Said Berraj, as well as Allekema Lamari, Nouredine Abdoumalou and Abdelkrim Bensmail: Reinares, 'The 2004 Madrid', p. 35.

63 Jordán and Wesley, 'After 3/11'.

64 Giles Tremlet, 'We bombed Madrid, says al-Qaeda tape', *CBSNEWS.com*, 14 March 2004. Available at https://www.theguardian.com/world/2004/mar/14/spain.terrorism3 (accessed 31 October 2017).

65 Rabasa and Benard, *EuroJihad*, p. 46.

66 See Juzgado Central, 2003, pp. 267–72; Rabasa and Benard, *EuroJihad*, p. 48. AP, 'Spain indicts fugitive on 9/11 charges', 29 April 2004. Available at https://www.washingtontimes.com/news/2004/apr/29/20040429-122231-3092r/ (accessed 17 January 2018).

67 Juzgado Central, 2003, p. 268.

68 Reinares, 'The 2004 Madrid'; Keith Johnson and David Crawford, 'Madrid bombing suspect is key al-Qaeda liaison', *The Wall Street Journal*, 7 April 2004, p. A17; Elaine Sciolino, '3 more Moroccans arrested in Madrid train bombings', *NYTimes.com*, 13 April 2004. Available at http://www.nytimes.com/2004/04/13/world/3-more-moroccans-arrested-in-madrid-train-bombings.html (accessed 17 January 2018). Hasan al-Haski, a leader of the MICG, was extradited to Morocco from Spain, where he was already serving a 13-year jail term for his involvement in the Madrid bombings. In 2009, he was sentenced to 10 years in prison for his role in the 2003 Casablanca suicide bomb attacks. Youssef Belhadj was another Moroccan residing in Belgium who took part in the Madrid plot: Reinares, 'The 2004 Madrid', pp. 35–6.

69 Reinares, 'The 2004 Madrid', p. 37.

70 A Moroccan, he owned a mobile phone shop in the Lavapiés neighbourhood; he allegedly supplied cell phones used as detonators in the 10 backpack bombs that ripped through the trains. He had come under investigation in Spain due to his

connection to Abu Dahdah's al-Qaeda cell: Reinares, 'The 2004 Madrid', p. 55. Moroccan officials uncovered ties between him and several Islamist radicals, who were jailed for the Casablanca bombings. Despite the attention Zougam received from the three governments after the Casablanca bombings, and the discovery of his ties to several important al-Qaeda figures, Spanish officials were unable to develop enough evidence to charge him with any crime. Eventually, they eased off their scrutiny: 'Bombings in Madrid: The investigation; Madrid suspect under scrutiny in 3 countries', 17 March 2004. http://www.nytimes.com/2004/03/17/world/bombings-madrid-investigation-madrid-suspect-under-scrutiny-3-countries.htm l (accessed 17 January 2018). The Benyaich brothers (Abdelaziz and Salaheddin) had befriended Zougam in Tangiers, where all of them came from. Abdelaziz, who fought with jihad groups in Bosnia, Chechnya and Dagestan, Russia, apparently recruited Zougam in Tangiers. Abdelaziz emerged as a central figure in the Moroccan militant network aligned with al-Qaeda. He provided operational and financial support to the Casablanca attacks: Craig S. Smith, 'A long fuse links Tangier to bombings in Madrid', *NYTimes.com*, 28 March 2004. Available at http://www.nytimes.com/20 04/03/28/world/a-long-fuse-links-tangier-to-bombings-in-madrid.html (accessed 11 January 2018). Zougam was also close to Abdelaziz's brother, Salaheddin, an acolyte of Abu Dahdah and a militant who went to receive training in Afghanistan (Reinares, 'The 2004 Madrid', p. 56) and Bosnia, and lost an eye there: Rogelio Alonso and Fernando Reinares, 'Maghreb immigrants becoming suicide terrorists: A case study on religious radicalization processes in Spain', in Amy Pedahzur (ed.), *Root Causes of Suicide Terrorism: The Globalization of Martyrdom* (New York: Routledge, 2006), pp. 179–98. Thus, the two Tangiers-born brothers acted as connecting nodes between al-Qaeda operatives in Spain and the movement's acolytes in Morocco. Other Moroccans arrested for the Casablanca bombings were Driss Chebli, and Abdelatif Mourafik, a Moroccan operative of the Libyan Islamic Fighting Group (LIFG) based in Afghanistan, who conferred with Azizi in Karachi in December 2001 to have the 3/11 Spanish cell established: Reinares, 'The 2004 Madrid', p. 44; Reinares, *Al-Qaeda's Revenge*, pp. 102–3. Zougam also had ties to two brothers, charged in connection with the Casablanca bomb plot: Mohammed el-Hadi Chedadi, the brother of Said Chedadi (a member of Abu Dahdah's cell), an alleged al-Qaeda operative, who was arrested in 2001, believed to be a follower of Abu Dahdah.

71 Gile Tremlett, 'Madrid bombers planned more attacks', *Guardian.Unlimited*, 9 April 2004. Available at https://www.theguardian.com/world/2004/apr/09/spain.gilestre mlett1 (accessed 17 January 2018).
72 Reinares, 'The 2004 Madrid', p. 31.
73 Boaz Ganor, 'Terrorism networks: It takes a network to beat a network', in P. R. Kleindorfer and Y. Wind (eds), *The Network Challenge: Strategy, Profit, and Risk in an Interlinked World* (Upper Saddle River: Pearson Education, 2009), p. 454.
74 Ibid.
75 José A. Rodríguez, 'The March 11th terrorist network: In its weakness lies its strength', Working Paper WP EPP-LEA: 3, Power and Privilege Studies Group, Department of Sociology, University of Barcelona, December 2005, p. 1.
76 Jordan, Mañas and Horsburgh, 'Strengths and weaknesses', p. 17.
77 Most of those involved in supplying the explosives stolen from a mine in Asturias had no extremist beliefs, being little more than opportunistic petty criminals.
78 Audrey Kurth Cronin, *Ending Terrorism: Lessons for Defeating al-Qaeda* (London: IISS, Adelphi Paper 394, 2008), p. 170.

79 Rodríguez, 'The March 11th terrorist network'.
80 Jordán, Mañas and Horsburgh, 'Strengths and weaknesses'; Sageman, *Misunderstanding Terrorism* (Philadelphia: University of Pennsylvania Press, 2016), pp. 48–9.
81 Reinares, 'The 2004 Madrid'.
82 Jordán, Mañas and Horsburgh, 'Strengths and weaknesses', p. 25.
83 Jórdan, 'Las redes yihadistas', pp. 4–5; Jordan, Mañas and Horsburgh, 'Strengths and weaknesses', p. 19.
84 Reinares, 'The 2004 Madrid', p. 35.
85 Ibid., p. 39.
86 Ibid., p. 43, 59.
87 Ibid., p. 42.
88 Ibid., p. 46.
89 Other Moroccans arrested for the Casablanca bombings, such as Driss Chebli, Abdellatif Benayaich and Mourafik: Reinares, 'The 2004 Madrid', p. 44; Reinares, *Al-Qaeda's Revenge*, p. 80, 116.
90 Reinares, 'The 2004 Madrid', p. 46.
91 A leader of GICM, Reinares, *Al-Qaeda's Revenge*, p. 46, 51.
92 Reinares, 'The 2004 Madrid', pp. 35–6.
93 Reinares, 'The Madrid bombings and global jihadism', *Survival*, lii, no. 2 (2010): 89; Petter Nesser, 'Jihadism in Western Europe after the invasion of Iraq: Tracing motivational influences from the Iraq War on jihadist terrorism in Western Europe', *Studies in Conflict and Terrorism*, xxix, no. 4 (2006): 329.
94 Sageman, *Misunderstanding Terrorism*, p. 51.
95 John Rollins, Liana Sun Wyler and Seth Rosen, *International Terrorism and Transnational Crime: Security Threats, U.S. Policy, and Considerations for Congress*, Congressional Research Service 7-5700, 5 January 2010, p. 19.
96 Jordán and Horsburgh, 'Mapping jihadist terrorism', 21.
97 Reinares, 'The 2004 Madrid', pp. 44–5.
98 Jordan and Horsburgh, 'Mapping jihadist terrorism', 183.
99 Reinares, 'The 2004 Madrid', pp. 41–2.
100 Jordan, Mañas and Horsburgh, 'Strengths and weaknesses', pp. 33–4.
101 Rodríguez, 'The March 11th terrorist network', p. 18.
102 Fernando Reinares, Carole Garcia-Calvo and Álvaro Vicente, 'Dos factores que explican la radicalización yihadista en España', ARI 62/2017, Real Instituto Elcano, 8 August 2017. Available at http://www.realinstitutoelcano.org/wps/portal/rielcano_es/contenido?WCM_GLOBAL_CONTEXT=/elcano/elcano_es/zonas_es/ari62-2017-reinares-garciacalvo-vicente-dos-factores-explican-radicalizacion-yihadista-espana (accessed 2 December 2017), p. 1.
103 Patricia Ortega Dolz, 'Los yihadistas hablan castellano y "apuntan" a España', 30 November 2016. Available at http://politica.elpais.com/politica/2016/08/28/actualidad/1472377344_245080.html (accessed 12 December 2016).
104 Jórdan, 'Las redes yihadistas', p. 7.
105 Ibid., p. 9; García-Calvo and Reinares, 'Pautas de implicación', pp. 5, 19.
106 Bérénice Boutin et al., *The Foreign Fighters Phenomenon: Profiles, Threats & Policies*, International Centre for Counter-Terrorism, ICCT Research Paper, April 2016, p. 38. Garcia Calvo and Reinares put the estimate at 190, regarding those who, until the summer of 2016, departed from Spain to join the ranks of ISIS in Syria and Iraq: Carola García-Calvo and Fernando Reinares, 'Patterns of involvement among

individuals arrested for Islamic state-related terrorist activities in Spain, 2013-2016', *Perspectives on Terrorism*, x, no. 6 (2016): 109.
107 Dolz, 'Los yihadistas'.
108 Melchor Sáiz-Prado, 'El islam dominará España y la Constitución será reemplazada por la Sharia', 5 January 2015. Available at http://www.diariodeleon.es/noticias/espana/el-islam-dominara-espana-constitucion-sera-reemplazada_947061.html.
109 José Maria Irujo, 'Network of 250 Spanish butchers and phone shops funding jihadists in Syria', *El País*, 6 February 2015. Available at https://elpais.com/elpais/2015/02/02/inenglish/1422892172_955064.html (accessed 2 November 2017).
110 Europapress, 'España ha detenido a 186 yihadistas desde que se subió la alerta a 4 en junio de 2015', 17 August 2017. Available at http://www.europapress.es/nacional/noticia-espana-detenido-186-yihadistas-subio-alerta-junio-2015-20170817205158.html (accessed 20 January 2018).
111 José Maria Irujo, 'Jihadist terrorism: Could there be a new attack on Spanish soil?', *El País*, 5 June 2017. https://elpais.com/elpais/2017/06/05/inenglish/1496668582_639298.html.
112 Christopher Woody, 'Inside Spain's quiet fight on the frontline of Europe's war on terror', 5 June 2017. Available at http://uk.businessinsider.com/spain-anti-terrorism-campaign-border-security-2017-6 (accessed 23 January 2018).
113 Manuel Ricardo Torres-Soriano, 'Jihadist propaganda as a threat indicator: The case of Spain', *Terrorism and Political Violence* (2017): 1–17.
114 Flora Drury, 'ISIS threaten an attack on Britain so horrific it will "turn children's hair white" as latest video shows white jihadi warning of further outrages in Europe and shooting captives', *MailOnline*, 30 January 2016. Available at http://www.dailymail.co.uk/news/article-3424684/White-jihadi-s-chilling-threat-ISIS-warn-West-pay-dearly-terror-attacks-worse-9-11-crushing-Muslim-rule-Spain-500-years-ago.html (accessed 22 January 2018).
115 'El Estado Islámico apunta a Madrid: "Hay demasiados paganos"', *La Gaceta*, 8 September 2017. Available at https://gaceta.es/espana/estado-islamico-apunta-madrid-demasiados-paganos-20170908-1216/ (accessed 20 January 2018).
116 Rukmini Callimachi, 'Cell behind Barcelona attack may have had sights on Eiffel Tower', 24 January 2018. Available at https://www.nytimes.com/2018/01/24/world/europe/isis-barcelona-attack.html (accessed 19 July 2018).
117 'Strategic analysis of Barcelona terrorist attack', Fortuna's Corner, 1 September 2017. Available at https://fortunascorner.com/2017/09/01/strategic-analysis-of-barcelona-terrorist-attack/ (accessed 19 January 2018).
118 Catarina Carvalho and Valentina Marcelino, 'Radicais islâmicos em Portugal escolhem mesquitas clandestinas', *Expresso*, 20 November 2004.
119 See Maria do Céu Pinto, 'An evaluation of the jihadist threat in Portugal', *Journal of Policing, Intelligence and Counter Terrorism*, vii, no. 2 (2012): 115–33.
120 The number is not exact, as authorities do not provide updated information.
121 Five of whom have reportedly died: Boutin et al., *The Foreign Fighters Phenomenon*, p. 47; Nuno Ribeiro, 'Doze jihadistas de origem portuguesa combatem na Síria e no Iraque', *Público*, 2 September 2014. Available at https://www.publico.pt/politica/noticia/doze-jihadistas-de-origem-portuguesa-combatem-na-siria-e-no-iraque-1668361 (accessed 22 January 2018); Nuno Ribeiro, 'Jihadistas portugueses com mandados de captura', *Público*, 3 April 2015. Available at https://www.publico.pt/politica/noticia/jihadistas-portugueses-com-mandados-de-captura-1691190 (accessed 2 June 2017).

122 TVI24, 'Tensão entre ministros por causa de jihadistas portugueses', 24 October 2014. Available at http://www.tvi24.iol.pt/politica/miguel-macedo/mai-revelacoes-de-rui-machete-sobre-jihadistas-portugueses-sao-inaceitaveis (accessed 22 January 2018).
123 Sistema de Segurança Interna, *Relatório 2015*, p. 79.
124 It matches the typical profile of foreign fighters sketched by the Soufan Group: Richard Barrett, *Foreign Fighters in Syria* (New York, June 2014), p. 18.
125 Raquel Moleiro, Hugo Franco and Joana Beleza, 'Killing and dying for Allah – Five Portuguese members of Islamic state', *Expresso*, undated. Available at http://multimedia.expresso.pt/jihad/EN/killing-and-dying/ (accessed 22 January 2018).
126 A. Dalgaard-Nielsen, 'Violent radicalization in Europe: What we know and what we do not know', *Studies in Conflict & Terrorism*, xxxiii, no. 9 (2010): 799.
127 Olivier Roy, 'What is the driving force behind jihadist terrorism?', *Inside Story*, 18 December 2015. Available at http://insidestory.org.au/what-is-the-driving-force-behind-jihadist-terrorism (accessed 22 January 2018).
128 Hugo Franco and Raquel Moleiro, *Os jihadistas portugueses* (Alfragide: Lua de Papel, 2015), p. 36.
129 Hugo Franco and Raquel Moleiro, 'Jihad. Portugueses ligados a clérigo radical de Londres', *Expresso*, 15 February 2015. Available at http://expresso.sapo.pt/sociedade/jihad-portugueses-ligados-a-clerigo-radical-de-londres=f910970 (accessed 22 January 2018); D. Gadher and M. Hookham, 'Harrods sales assistant linked to Jihadi John', *The Sunday Times*, 15 February 2015. Available at http://www.thesundaytimes.co.uk/sto/news/uk_news/People/article1519396.ece 2015; Hugo Franco, 'Condenados os líderes religiosos radicais que recrutaram portugueses', *Expresso*, 12 March 2017. Available at http://expresso.sapo.pt/sociedade/2017-03-12-Condenados-os-lideres-religiosos-radicais-que-recrutaram-portugueses (accessed 22 January 2018); Moleiro, Franco and Beleza, 'Killing and dying for Allah'; Soeren Kern, 'Anjem Choudary, in his own words', Gatestone Institute, 2014. Available at http://www.gatestoneinstitute.org/4745/anjem-choudary (accessed 22 January 2018); Soeren Kern, 'Portugal's jihadists', Gatestone Institute, 2014. Available at http://www.gatestoneinstitute.org/4697/portugal-jihadists (accessed 22 January 2018).
130 Franco and Moleiro, *Os jihadistas*, p. 45.
131 Ibid., pp. 92, 71.

INDEX

Abdulmutallab, Umar Farouk 1, 151–2
Abu Salim Martyrs Brigade
    (ASMB) 126–9
Afghanistan 1, 9, 44, 47, 56, 59, 75, 98–9,
    115, 121–4, 126–7, 130–1, 140–5,
    150, 181, 187, 189–90, 192, 195–7,
    199, 205–12, 218, 223, 226–30,
    232–3
Al Mourabitoun 55, 58, 80–7
Al Qaeda 2, 4–5, 10
    in France 157
    in Germany 207–9, 212–13
    in Iberia 224–37
    in Kenya 38–41, 44–5, 47
    in Libya 113, 119, 121–5, 127–9
    in Low Countries 176, 178, 181–3
    in Mali 73–4, 77, 79, 85, 87–9
    in Nigeria 95, 99–101, 103–5
    in Sahel 56–60, 67
    in Scandinavia 188–99
    in Somalia 15, 27
    in UK 147, 149, 152
Al Qaeda in East Africa (AQEA) 40,
    43–5
Al Qaeda in Iraq (AQI) 74, 188, 195
Al Qaeda in the Islamic Maghreb
    (AQIM) 55–9, 61, 74–81, 83–6,
    88, 95, 99–101, 104, 124–5, 128, 131
Al Shabaab 13–29, 37–42, 45–9, 104–5,
    178, 190–2
Ansar al-Sharia 55, 126–8, 131
Ansar Dine 55, 57–8, 75–87, 100
Ansaru 55, 57, 101, 104
Arab Spring 29, 115–18, 124–6, 130
Armed Islamic Group (GIA) 99, 122–3,
    141, 195, 226, 228–9, 233
Atran, Scott 6
al-Awlaki, Anwar 1, 12, 46, 148, 176,
    181, 183
Azawad National Liberation Movement
    (MNLA) 55, 76–7, 79–83, 100,
    125

Azzam, Abdullah 141, 148

al-Baghdadi, Abu Bakr 66, 84, 107,
    127–9, 181–2, 193, 217
al-Barnawi, Abu Musab 66, 101, 104,
    107
Belmokhtar, Mokhtar 56, 58, 75, 80–1,
    83–6, 100–1, 128
bin Laden, Osama 4–5, 44, 99, 103, 121,
    123, 126, 140, 143, 146, 149, 153,
    190–2, 213, 225–8
Boko Haram 55–8, 62–6, 74, 80, 95–108

Choudary, Anjem 142, 147, 176, 237
clans 13, 15, 17–28, 73–4, 85, 88–9, 115,
    117–18, 121, 167
colonialism 9, 14, 21, 41–2, 73, 89, 95–8,
    153, 158, 160–9
crime 127, 129, 166–8, 170, 178, 194, 215

Devji, Faisal 2, 4, 6, 175, 184, 187

ethnicity 3–4, 46–7, 61, 63, 65–6, 77, 81–
    4, 88–9, 113, 116–19, 124, 126, 131,
    162, 182, 191, 197, 200, 217, 236

family 17, 19, 25, 47, 62–3, 75–7, 79,
    88, 116, 118, 175, 182–4, 212, 224,
    233, 236
financing 15, 19, 47, 56, 64, 98, 101, 104,
    121, 128, 147, 151, 190, 192, 195,
    209, 217, 223, 229, 234, 237
fundraising 38, 45, 141, 194–5, 225, 230,
    235

Gaddafi, Muammar 55, 102, 113–22,
    124–7, 129, 131
al-Gama'a al-Islamiyya 190–1
Gerges, Fawaz 6, 199
Godane, Axmed Cabdi 15, 23, 47

Halliday, Fred 4, 6

Hizb-ut-Tahrir 141–2

ISIS 2, 4–5, 10
  in Germany 208, 214–18
  in Iberia 234–6
  in Libya 125–6, 128–32
  in Low Countries 175–6, 181–2, 184
  in Mali 74, 84–5, 88–9
  in Nigeria 95, 102–3, 105–8
  in Sahel 55–6, 58–60, 66
  in Scandinavia 188–9, 192, 195–200
  in Somalia 21, 27
  in UK 139–40, 151
Israel 2, 40, 41, 45, 145, 150, 158, 187, 209

Jabhat al-Nusra 175, 178, 181–2, 197–9
Jund al-Khilafah 58

Koufa, Amadou 78, 84–5

language 15, 42, 44, 103, 118, 119, 124, 144, 161
Libyan Islamic Fighting Group (LIFG) 122–6, 233

Macina Liberation Front (MLF) 55, 57–8, 65–6, 83–4
Majlis Shura Shabab al-Islam (MSSI) 128–9
marriage 44, 75, 85, 98, 150, 180, 184
al-Masri, Abu Hamza 143–4, 146, 149–50
Mohammed, Omar Bakri 141–3, 147, 176–7
Movement for Oneness and Jihad in West Africa (MUJAO) 55, 75–84, 100–1, 234
al-Muhajiroun 139, 142–3, 237

orientalism 3, 157, 159–60, 166–7

Palestine 2, 5–6, 44, 47, 121, 130, 142, 145, 147, 149, 158, 176, 194, 209, 228
propaganda 2, 4–6, 16, 20–1, 25, 85, 106–7, 139–42, 147, 151, 184, 189, 211–16, 225, 229, 235

Qatada, Abu 141, 226
Qumu, Abu Sufyan Bin 126–8

radicalization 1, 14, 28–9, 40, 63, 67, 74–5, 108, 124, 131, 147, 163–6, 175, 180, 183–4, 187, 196, 198, 207–10, 217, 233, 235–7
recruitment 29, 40, 45–6, 63–5, 74, 103, 119, 131, 142, 147, 175–6, 179–83, 188, 191, 198, 205, 208–9, 217, 223–4, 230, 233–5
Roy, Olivier 2, 3–4, 39, 175, 183, 236

al-Sahraoui, Adnan Abu Walid 84–5, 88
Salafi 3, 17, 21, 62, 98, 115, 122, 126, 165, 168, 176, 180, 207, 212–13, 215–18, 226–7, 233
Salafist Group for Preaching and Combat (GSPC) 99–100, 124, 226–9, 233
Saudi Arabia 19, 60, 98, 104, 130, 141, 149, 206–7
Sharia 14, 21, 23, 25, 38, 40, 73, 84, 89, 98, 100, 115, 122, 129, 142, 223
Shekau, Abu 62, 66, 96, 98–9, 101–7
social media 16, 20, 103, 106, 129, 176, 180, 184, 216, 234
Soviet-Afghan war 44, 56, 115, 140, 190, 205

tribalism 16. 20. 75, 85, 113–21, 124, 126, 129, 131
Tuareg 55, 57, 63–4, 67, 73–7, 79–88, 100, 120, 125

Wahhabi 3, 14, 38, 46, 75
Walaa, Abu 215, 217–18

Yusuf, Muhammad 62, 96, 98–9, 101, 103
Yusuf, Yahia 207–8, 211

al-Zarqawi, Abu Musab 124, 126, 194–5, 217
al-Zawahiri, Ayman 58, 123, 126–7, 190
Zerkani, Khalid (and Zerkani network) 176, 178–9, 182, 184

Ingram Content Group UK Ltd.
Milton Keynes UK
UKHW020641070423
419799UK00006B/219